*Politics, Personality, and Social Science
in the Twentieth Century*

Politics, Personality, and Social Science in the Twentieth Century

ESSAYS IN HONOR OF HAROLD D. LASSWELL

Edited by ARNOLD A. ROGOW

THE UNIVERSITY OF CHICAGO PRESS

Chicago & London

Standard Book Number: 226–72399–2

Library of Congress Catalog Card Number: 76–75812

The University of Chicago Press, Chicago 60637

The University of Chicago Press, Ltd., London W.C. 1

© 1969 by The University of Chicago

Contents

v

Preface

ARNOLD A. ROGOW

INSOFAR as this volume can be said to have a spiritual beginning as opposed to the literary one, that beginning was almost twenty years ago when Harold D. Lasswell came to Princeton one evening to address the Politics Club, a gathering of political science graduate students. I no longer remember precisely what he said— as I no longer remember what other distinguished visitors said on similar occasions—but I do recall the excitement I shared with the rest of the audience. The occasion for it was a vision of the social sciences that was totally new to us in 1948, a vision that suggested there was more to political science than exegesis, whether legalistic, historical, or philosophical. I had read some of Lasswell's books before that occasion (by that time who hadn't read *Politics: Who Gets What, When, How*), but even so the vision was wholly invigorating. I was particularly impressed by the notion that psychology and psychiatry might have some connection with politics and that it was perfectly legitimate for political scientists to investigate this connection. Impressed and encouraged, I should say, because there were those on the Princeton faculty at that time who would have jumped from the roof of the Firestone Library rather than admit that Freud, that dirty old man, had made a contribution to political science. With one such professor I had gotten nowhere when I tried to enroll in a psychology course. "Who needs it?" he asked rhetorically, and instead I was signed up for seminars in public administration and political parties—but about these seminars the less said, the better.

The inspiration for this volume, then, goes back a score of years, although it was not until 1954 that I met Lasswell and

vii

began a dialogue with him that has continued, I am happy to say, to this day. At that time both of us were fellows at the Center for Advanced Study in the Behavioral Sciences, on the campus of Stanford University, and during the year we became involved, with other fellows, in a number of research and writing projects, most of which have been published by now. Again there was the exhilaration I had first experienced at Princeton in 1948, if anything intensified by the heady intellectual atmosphere of the Center, which was wholly given over to the ferment of ideas. There were few, if any, fellows in 1954 and 1955 who did not take away from the experience more than they brought to it; speaking for myself, I believe it was the most intellectually rewarding year of my life, not least because I was in almost daily contact not just with Lasswell—that would have been reward enough—but also with Christian Bay, Eugene Burdick, Clyde Kluckhohn, Else Frenkel-Brunswik, Paul F. Lazarsfeld, Richard Christie, Charles E. Lindblom, Kenneth Boulding, R. Duncan Luce, Herbert Kelman, Sanford Dornbusch, Louis Schneider, and many others among the thirty-six or so fellows. When the recent history of American social science is written, I will be very surprised if the Center is not given a very large measure of credit for the leadership position of the United States in the behavioral and social sciences.

Since that year at the Center I have spent a fair amount of time in Lasswell's company, but I would not want any reader to think that this time has been completely devoted to cerebration or mental gymnastics. If man does not live by bread alone, neither does he live entirely by brain, and while there are those who think of Lasswell as composed exclusively of gray cells, his friends know better. In addition to his other merits, he is *good company,* whether the scene is a cocktail lounge, a dinner party, the Central Park Zoo, one of several clubs in New York and Washington, the National Gallery in London or the Museum of Modern Art in New York, a New Haven restaurant, one of England's "stately homes," or his own apartment. Like Leo Rosten, I have never heard him tell a joke, but his stories and anecdotes, always witty and frequently hilarious, are far superior to most jokes one hears in academic circles. Moreover, his gaiety and charm are contagious; I have seen more than one dull gathering or morose individual completely transformed by a Lasswell reminiscence of the University of Chicago in the days of Merriam, or by an account of certain escapades in and around Shanghai as it was in the 1930s. Lasswell can endow a lecture visit to some hinterland university with the kind of humor, fantasy, and nightmare reality that would have resulted had Lewis Carroll, Marcel Proust, and Dostoevsky collaborated on *Alice in Wonderland.*

In an age when there is no clear distinction between person and persona, when the picture tube is no more than a clear glass window between the exhibitionists in the studio and the voyeurs in the living room, Lasswell is that rare individual, an intensely private person, by which I mean someone for whom privacy is a supreme value in life and not merely a fortuitous by-product of time and place. Valuing my own privacy, I have no wish to invade his, but I do not think I intrude when I say something about a side of him that most of his academic colleagues know little about. He is, to begin with, a connoisseur of the good life, an epicure and a gourmet. He knows much about architecture, oriental culture, poetry, Renaissance furniture and painting (of which he owns several superb examples), science fiction, and the history of the cinema. His comments on modern art are apt to be pithy and to the point. He is also fully possessed of a creative imagination or inventive flair that is productive of ideas no matter what the subject. If, for example, you were to mention in his presence that your fireplace was not working properly, he would come up with five or six possible explanations and another five or six suggestions of what to do about it, although he knows nothing whatever about fireplaces and much less about their idiosyncrasies and ailments. I have heard him discuss with children topics of interest to *them,* and discuss these topics, moreover, in their own language, a faculty that most parents (and Lasswell is not a parent) lack. He also seems to be able to communicate with cats and other animals, or at any rate they behave as if there were no language barriers between Lasswell and them, although, again, he does not own a cat or any other pet.

I could go on in this vein, but it is Lasswell the scholar, after all, that this book is about. Of course, he does not need a volume of this type. He is without question America's most distinguished political scientist as well as one of our best known and most respected behavioral scientists. His books and articles have been translated and published in many parts of the world, and it is these writings that speak definitively for and about Lasswell, not the essays that follow this preface. Still, it may be useful to make these initial commentaries and evaluations available as a means of arriving at a preliminary estimate of his achievements. Whether or not Lasswell, like Stendhal, has deliberately pursued "a policy of immortality," his works will be read as long as there are men who care about the issues and problems associated not just with the social and behavioral sciences but with the worldwide achievement of human dignity.

September 1968

1

Harold Lasswell: A Memoir

Leo Rosten

YOU must not expect me to write about him coolly. Nor will I try to mislead you by adopting that austerity of language behind which Harold Lasswell has always concealed his romanticism about "detachment." I begin this memoir with a confession: I respect, I admire, and I *like* him.

I met him two hundred years ago, in 1927, in a classroom at the University of Chicago. I was a grubby sophomore and he was the callow instructor of a course in political science—one of the earliest, I think, he ever gave.

I thought him a bit of a freak: pedantic, verbose, and quite ill at ease. He wore his hair in a short, stiff, Prussian cut, and his knowledge in a high, stiff, abrasive manner. He was only twenty-five, and he lectured us desperately, with a glazed stare into space, conspicuously unaware of whether we understood him and visibly unconcerned with what we might be thinking.

He talked so fast, so frantically, tumbling idea upon idea in a torrent of excitation, that his nonstop monologues became a polysyllabic blur from which only startling phrases emerged to penetrate my dumbfoundedness: "context . . . frame of reference . . . thanks to . . . anxiety . . . systematic . . . rigorous . . . quantify . . . symbols . . . expectations . . . explicit . . . insecurity . . . participant-observer . . . symbols . . . thanks to . . . world revolution of our times."

He baffled—nay, flabbergasted—me. He did not lecture so much as smother. He seemed unable to leave a moment of time

A shorter version of this memoir was published in the *Saturday Review*, April 15, 1967.

unoccupied by language. I even wondered if he did not suffer from some strange speech impediment which he was trying to drown in a flood, or throttle in a glut, of words. I was not helped, of course, by the fact that he blithely scrambled together technical terms from a dozen unhomogenized disciplines: philosophy, sociology, political science, psychology, economics, anthropology, psychiatry, statistics, pediatrics, psychoanalysis, physiology, physics (oh, yes).

The play of his nostrils, as he monologized, intrigued me. Please do not scoff. His globular cheeks puffed out like those of a chipmunk with a nut in each pouch, and from those two round protubererances sailed forth a surprisingly thin nose—with most mobile and expressive nostrils. They flared and narrowed and quivered in tune with his meaning, signaling a disdain here, an esteem there, not expressed by his words—since he was in the grip, then as now, of a compulsion to be entirely objective. The goal was inhuman, to say nothing of inhumane.

I shall never forget my first tête-à-tête with him. I was considerably miffed because, apart from not understanding what this antiseptic pastor was talking about, I was groaning under the burdens of a bizarre assignment he had given me: to subscribe to two Arizona newspapers and to measure each story in them in column inches, classifying the figures in categories that ranged from city hall shenanigans to astrological advice. After three weeks of this carpentry, which had not yet been elevated to the elegance of "content analysis," I mobilized my indignation (and my courage) and marched to Dr. Lasswell's office. It was the first time I had ever been alone with an instructor.

I gulped out my heartfelt complaints like a burgher at Calais. He listened steely-eyed and silent. Thrown off-base by his clinical stare, which made me feel like a case study, I even quavered that I often did not understand what on earth he was talking about.

To these anguished protestations Lasswell at last sniffed icily: "Communication is, after all, but the fortuitous parallelism of biophysic variables." I staggered out . . . I could not repress reluctant admiration over the beauty and precision of that ad lib. Save for "fortuitous," I still know no better definition of communication, that hypnotic rubric to which at least five thousand earnest researchers are today indentured. It took me years to discover why this phenomenally intelligent, prodigiously articulate man resorts to such outlandish lingo: He is entirely at home with it. It is, indeed, his natural patois. When launched on a spree of euphoric cerebration, he does not choose words; he goes into an intellectual trance in which words choose—or, better, possess—him. Only after prolonged prayer did it dawn on me that whereas most men use language clumsily, in an effort to express their banal ideas and conceal their complex feelings, Lasswell uses words brilliantly to conceal simple feelings and express complex ideas. I think he has a passion to be comprehended, and marmoreal defenses against being understood.

In those days, he always said "we"—never, never "I." He also shunned small talk, gossip, or the conventional exchange of nonideas. He would proceed directly from an obligatory "Greetings!" (he eschewed all clichés, including "Hello") to his latest lucubrations on Ibn Khaldun. Emphatically egalitarian, he was likely to enlighten dazed coeds about both Pareto and penis envy. His totem was ideas; his taboo, boredom. I once heard a harmless hostess ask him, "Isn't it wonderful weather we're having?" Only after Lasswell recovered sufficiently to analyze her motivations did he answer, "Yes." I was surprised that he did not diagnose the meterological determinants of the weather we were having.

Lasswell mystifies the uninitiated by his massive verbiage. What the Philistines do not see is that he thinks by listening to what he says, then mines it to separate gold from dross. To him, talking is a form of testing, of dropping plumb lines into the gigantic reservoir of his knowledge. He talks the way other men daydream. His monologues are symposiums with invisible peers. Who has not heard him verbalize for hours without the faintest idea of what he was getting at, or even around, flitting from Peter the Great to projective mechanisms, from "equilibrium analysis" to "time-space manifolds," until—bingo!—he hit upon some attractive hunch or slant or self-illumination which he then seized with relief and extrapolated feverishly?

Lasswell is a system builder, a thwarted cosmologist, an exuberant virtuoso of fanciful ad hoc correlations, in which he revels. He finds connections between the Gothic arch and, say, feudal ambivalence about copulation, between German philanthropy and Oedipal guilt, between bureaucracy and breast-feeding. Sometimes he sounds like a cross between Machiavelli and Freud, as recorded by Veblen.

I remember emerging from one class stunned by a parenthetical comment he had tossed off which ran something like this: "If one postulates that the conventional wisdom, encapsulated in the equilibrium (as opposed to configurational) analysis that underlies capitalistic mythology, is a makeshift evasion of those unconscious drives that account for persistent irrationality, and if one regards contemporary institutions as but functional arrangements designed to accommodate those contradictory symbols that emasculate ego-threatening impulses, then to support the League of Nations may be interpreted as a cynical concession to human perversity."

In lunches or dinners with him, which I came to prize, I was struck by the ballet of his hands. They are library hands, very pale, soft, unsullied by physical exertion. When Harold talks, over drinks or food, his hands make small gyrations, in the same ritual of gestures. The left hand is motionless, its thumb and forefinger forming an "O"; the right hand hovers over and dances around that "O." If, say, he is trying to illustrate Planck's constant or the dynamics of introjection, the right hand pulls an invisible thread through an invisible needle on a path horizontal to and away from the inert circle of the left hand "O." It is astounding how Harold hemstitches theoretical points into imaginary petit point.

I was also fascinated by his glasses—which were always spotless, as if perpetually cleaned by invisible wipers. Only twice in almost four decades have I seen him remove his glasses to polish them. His eyes look no different.

Lasswell is essentially self-oriented, and exceptionally self-sufficient. He is the Compleat Intellectual—egocentric, not egotistic; he has not, I think, a shred of vanity. In language he might find more congenial, he is, *au fond*, narcissistic. I believe he is by all odds the most interesting man he has ever known. The callithump* of his ideas never stops, never flags, never pauses for rest or recuperation or revival. I have dined with him hundreds of times, and, leaving for a moment to make a phone call, returned to find him scribbling notes as though he had just solved the last theorem of Fermat. I'm sure they were his words, not mine, that he was preserving in amber.

Our hero's erudition is, of course, inordinate. It is coupled to the one lifelong passion that consumes him: the passion for omniscience. His mountainous knowledge may, in my opinion, inhibit a very high capacity for original thinking and sometimes sterilizes his most fecund insights. Some childhood overvaluation of Teutonic scholarship (which carries with it inescapable anal values, I hear), or some residues of an early need to impress his elders in the academic dodge, has led H.D.L. to overload his works with references, footnotes, bibliography, and learned (if irrelevant) digressions. I yield to no man in my respect for reading, but I cannot help feeling that Harold uses his bibliography the way Ethel Merman delivers a "sock" number. He may not so intend it (I hesitate to probe beneath the surface of his self-revelation), but his compulsive use of citations serves not simply to fortify an argument but to clobber the reader. I wish that loyal friends would join with me in helping to emancipate him from the stultifying standards of academe, perhaps by giving him a plaque that proclaims him our ambulatory Library of Congress.

Harold luxuriates in company, but seems to need it less than anyone I ever knew. Not that he does not have friends. They come in legions, literally, and continental subdivisions. He has met, charmed, offended, or mesmerized more people than anyone I have ever met. Strangers, uncued by any comment from me,

---

* It pleases me to think he may have to look this up.

have brought up his name in places as far removed as Sebastopol and Council Bluffs. He is a proficient socializer but seems capable of spending unlimited days alone, happily reading, writing, ruminating. He is a triumph of autogeny.

Harold abhors anything that borders on sentiment or suggests dependence. No one is a warmer or more generous friend— but he is, essentially and quite oddly, *shy*. No one of my acquaintance has ever been so parsimonious in the revelation of personal data. Ask him a truly personal question and he will hem and haw and evade, and his face will swarm with as many hues of red as could be found in the American labor movement from 1932 to 1941. He is embarrassed not so much by affection as by the *display* thereof—on your part, surely, and more surely on his. He is like a Calvinist who has learned how to laugh.

He gives unstintingly of his time, encouragement, expertise, but he is embarrassed by intimacy—at least as others define it. I have never seen the knob on the door of any quarters he ever occupied.

He was raised in Decatur, Illinois, and spent summers in Indiana with an uncle who was an M.D. This uncle, baffled by his inability to relieve a patient of a paralysis of the arm that had no physical cause, heard of the work of a certain doctor in Vienna who was curing cases of "hysterical paralysis." The Indiana medic wrote to Europe and ordered some German books by one Sigmund Freud. Young Harold, then fourteen or fifteen, read them. They seemed rather sensible. "It was not until I was a junior at the University of Chicago," Harold once told me, "that I discovered that Freud was controversial."

At one point in Chicago, Harold's reputation spread beyond the small, fervent circle of his apostles (Gabriel Almond, Philleo Nash, Edith Rosenfels, Dorothy Blumenstock, William T. R. Fox, and certain awed, though not baptized, followers, including an M.A. from Tennessee who mumbled to himself and spent all his time changing the Dictaphone cylinders Lasswell used while psychoanalyzing volunteer students and refugees from the Loop). At the beginning of one spring term I entered the classroom with our professor to discover almost thirty expectant students waiting. I had never known more than ten or twelve at a time to brave the hurricane of Lasswell's pedagogy. Harold looked as though he had stumbled into a Holy Roller festival, sniffed, and *sotto voce* said, "We shall reduce the number forthwith."

The forthwith Harold used, out of shame at finding so many poltroons afflicted with *hubris*, was to expatiate on certain cases he had recently observed in a mental hospital. To make sure that the bourgeoisie he faced would not turn up again in his classroom, Doctor Lasswell, fluttering those nostrils, quoted one psychotic inmate as having confided that he (the patient) was both a considerable genius and a titanic fornicator. A chair in the last row, tilted back against the wall by the student on it, promptly and explosively slammed down to the floor. Harold stared balefully at the flaming child who was picking up his notebooks and protective talismans, flared his nostrils outward, and icily continued his excursion into psychopathology. After the class, when the students were well out of earshot, Harold exploded with laughter—and how many men do you know who explode with such percussive resonance?

Lasswell is perennially youthful. His prevailing mood is ebullience. I have seen him distracted, but never, I think, depressed. And I have never known him to be frustrated. Even at sixty-five he seems precocious.

Harold is sometimes exhausting, but always inexhaustible. This I attribute to his phenomenal and endearing capacity for enthusiasm. He has a ravenous, a ferocious, an insatiable appetite for every conceivable aspect of living. He is surely the most indefatigable talker, drinker, eater, traveler, conferee, collaborator, lecturer, bibliophile, and notetaker in the world.

As my houseguest in California, he once delivered a three-hour monologue before cocktails and topped it off at dinner with verbalizing that went on until 2:30 A.M. It remains one of the most extraordinary exhibitions of brilliance and nonalcoholic inebriation I have ever heard. It started with China (Harold had just returned from a teaching stint in Peking), and from there made leaping gambadoes to British club mores in Shanghai, phallic artifacts in Cambodia, the paralysis of Marxist ideology, the latent homosexuality of geisha-loving Japanese, Jung on the persona, Freud on Jung, Lasswell on Jung and Freud and Adler (sniff), the journalism of Karl Radek, the delusions of French foreign policy in the Far East, the puerility of Thomas Wolfe, Los Angeles as an architectural projection of masturbatory fantasies, the partial insights of Melanie Klein, Georg Lukacz as a literary critic, the vectors of L. L. Thurstone, the illuminations of Sherrington and L. J. Henderson and Anton Carlson on brain and blood, the Bhagavad Gita, Lao Tse, the symbolism in Zuni dances, Sapir's illuminations of linguistics, R. H. Tawney and Max Weber, Oriental "face" as an exercise in stylized hostility, Heisenberg and Schrodinger on indeterminacy, Rousseau's muddle-headedness and Catlin's pragmatism, leg fetishism in American high schools, Charles Merriam's beatification of credenda, miranda, and charisma, Malaparte's variations on the coup d'état—plus assorted comments, appraisals, footnotes, and gibes at Sorel, Dicey, Sombart, Keynes, Bryce, Whitehead, Lenin, Eddington, C. I. Lewis, Boas, Roberto Michels, and Spengler, to say nothing of the Dolly Sisters and the Comte de Guiche. This too-brief résumé must, I regret, omit those parenthetical flourishes with which Harold customarily garnishes one of his hypomanic seizures. I have seen strangers, during one of these roaring improvisations, act as if they had fallen into an automatic washer with Immanuel Kant.

Of his many and original contributions to the sociosexual sciences, others will sing in this *Festschrift*. I want merely to say that I consider H.D.L. the most fertile catalyst and theorist of his generation. After the surface forays of Graham Wallas and Walter Lippmann, Lasswell—armed with a mastery of psychoanalytic theory, fieldwork among its practitioners in Vienna, Berlin, Boston, and Washington, and acquaintanceship with Einstein's revolution—carried the corpus of political behavior theory to the couch, there to be infused and invigorated by his insights and imagination. His analyses of psychoanalysis are, to me, unsurpassed among the keepers of the flame. His pioneering contributions to propaganda analysis, "the pyramid of power," content analysis, political symbols, and political psychology are indisputable and historic.

He is, of course, neither omniscient nor flawless. Because he operates best with high abstractions and adores the game of multivariable ping-pong, Lasswell will move heaven and earth to find the picayune meaningful. His unreserved interest in *everything* long ago drove him to seek some all-inclusive frame or scheme, which is understandable; but just as some men have no eye for color, Harold has an imperfect gauge for proportion. He may devote as many words to chiropody, should it happen to get on the roller coaster of his speculations, as to bank deposits. His work has remarkable range, pyrotechnic effects, profundity, brilliance, suggestibility, and insights galore—but haphazard proportion and uneven focus. This has always puzzled me, perhaps because I am a simple man who gets the bends when the rise and fall of Papuan hemlines pops up in the middle of a dissection of the class origins of post office employees in Kenosha, Wisconsin.

Lasswell shelters not the faintest prejudice against serendipity, which is, in fact, the closest thing to religion he observes. He is easily seduced by an idea—any idea. He is often excited by what interests no one else. His infatuation with objectivity drives him to adopt the stance of a surgeon and the style of an engineer; most conversation strikes him as "the production of propitiating noises," and a speech by a ward heeler at a wake becomes "symbol manipulation." Much of this is meant to illuminate via irony, and is both elegant and witty, but sometimes it uses cannons to kill flies.

Yet Harold can be as simple and clear as Jello. (Children, for instance, get along fine with him.) Under duress, and given rigid word limits, he produces analytic gems: for example, his articles in the *Encyclopedia of the Social Sciences* (Bribery, Chauvinism, Feuds, Morale); his 1933 article on the rise of Hitler; his classic *Politics: Who Gets What, When, How;* parts of *World Politics and Personal Insecurity;* truly original, trenchant pieces on public opinion, symbols, power, Marxist fallacies, international relations, the psychology of revolution, *et*, as they say, *cetera.*

Lasswell longed to be a "participant-observer" in every culture, society, revolution, and laboratory experiment of his time. This led him, years ago, into "world surveys" that were to be scooped up in regional dragnets labeled "focus of attention" studies. *Manibus pedibusque*, and hot as a pistol, he proceeded to correspond with brainwashed accomplices from Australia to Zagreb who poured dubious nuggets of data into his inventory of critical factors in those political convulsions he was the first, I think, to dub the "world revolution of our time." ("Rising expectations" and "garrison state" are also his striking coinages.) Lasswell was often electrifying in his political predictions, but they bore little relation to the ragout of erratic guesses and peculiar *obiter dicta* he was receiving from excitable Serbs, Afrikaners, and Cretans whom he had conned into transcendental illusions. He is a most starry-eyed sophisticate.

I think it was God's manifest will that in 1938 a moving van bound for New York, which contained Harold's voluminous reports from the paranoid zones of the world between 1928 and 1938, burned to a crisp. The fire freed him from the prison of his files.

Shortly thereafter, unable to get a university post (believe it or not), Harold proceeded to write a series of programs for radio, dramatizing traumatic moments in the life of Caesar, Mohammed, Napoleon, and others. The series remains one of the most sparkling applications of knowledge to public enlightenment that has yet appeared in the mass media. It also remains a striking example of Harold's capacity to be dazzlingly lucid.

My friend and mentor has a delicious sense of satire, but he is rarely malicious and never petty. He is, as a matter of fact, a very kind man, exceptionally generous in his professional judgments. Except where the evidence is overwhelming, he eschews derogation. (He once wrote the following book review: "Rhetoric." End of review.) He can be sardonic but not really cynical. And all this is so, I think, because he has always identified himself with the long, high line of theorists—past and future—and spurned the ad hominem squabbles of his critics.

Harold has never displayed noticeable anxiety about his health or possible demise. His equanimity vis-à-vis the Grim Reaper has a certain bounce to it. I once heard him console an embarrassed companion, who had imbibed too much, with these gentle words: "One must, at times, defer to the banal demands of the soma." I have heard him mourn the death of a colleague kindly, sadly, yet somehow in the way a commuter might regret having missed the 6:10 to New Haven. Not that he is callous—far from it; he is just better at analyzing emotions than expressing them. He feels, I think, very deeply—when no one is watching. Neutrality is his shield.

I have never heard him tell a joke, but no one is a better audience for the risible. His laughter is Falstaffian. He adores anecdotes, but I have never heard him tell a story. He venerates the analytic rather than the discursive. His desired image of himself is cerebral—100 percent pure scientist who tries to maintain rigorous detachment in what he insists on calling "interpersonal relations." His humanness is ample enough but hides behind transparent curtains. It is not surprising that people who do not know him consider him a mortician of ideas. They confuse their confusion with (allegedly) his.

Lasswell is a phenomenal generator of ideas but an ineffective editor—of either his writings or the work of others. This long puzzled me because he is a most acute critic. The trouble is, I suspect, his fear of confessing that something just may not be "relevant." Since *he* is always learning, arranging, recording, storing, what possible facts or speculations *might* not—someday, somewhere, somehow—be useful? Think of what Sigmund Freud discovered, after all. It was Freud who opened Lasswell's eyes to how important the "trivial" may be, and how common the bizarre.

One cannot give a true picture of this truly unique man without mentioning, however reluctantly, the vocal hopscotch to

which he is prone. ("The—uh—possible extrapolations—mmh
—of these—mmh—implicit categories may—er—be designed to
—uh—expedite analytic clarity if—mm—one conjectures that—
well—the intellectuals of *mittel Europa* were—oh—say—characterized—uh—by—er—preoccupation with literary, as distinct
from systematic, formulations—er—mmh—thanks to—the overvaluation of—mmh—solipsistic dexterity.") I think Harold
falls into such faltering because he blames himself for not automatically producing instant, definitive formulas in answer to any
question on any occasion. This is why one never hears him say, "I
don't know," or "I haven't the faintest idea." I have heard him
say, "*We* know little about this," but that meant that man's accumulated knowledge had not yet reached the point where an
answer was possible; if it had, Harold would, clearly, have
known it.

How do I rate him as a teacher? For 90 percent of the un-
shaven who dipped their toes in his raging waters, Harold was
not a teacher but a torrent, to be resisted, resented, endured, and
survived. They could no more understand him then they could
understand the *Principia Mathematica* in Urdu. Easily bored in
and by a classroom, the master often retreated into highfalutin'
ambiguity—or reveries too arcane to convey meaning to anyone
but a psychiatric symbolist. He was impatient with mediocrity
and could become testy, clipping the wings of fledgling theorists
with sardonic rejoinders.

For another 5 percent of his students Lasswell was a galvan-
izing, unnerving, seditious comet who had roared in from some
alien planet of the intellect (surely alien to the narcotic drone and
tranquilizing platitudes of most college pedagogy). He required
in students brain, discipline, fearful bibliography, and a determination to crack the stainless-steel cover in which the superego
is enclosed.

And to the final 5 percent Harold was an eye-opener, a mind-
liberator, a horizon-widener unlike anyone they would ever run
into again, in this world or the next. He was original, disruptive,
challenging, derisive. He hurdled the barriers that block the ef-

forts most of us make to communicate: differences in age, culture, temperament, style, metabolism, repression, orality. He proceeded on the sanguine assumption that he *could* be understood, and he was grateful to anyone who was interested in what he had to say. He was also fascinated by anyone who was fascinated by him. I was, unashamedly, in the latter group.

I learned, or was encouraged and jolted and inspired to learn, more from him than from anyone I ever met. One can not easily measure, or hope to repay, such indebtedness.

2

The Maddening Methods of Harold D. Lasswell: Some Philosophical Underpinnings

HEINZ EULAU

LASSWELL'S methods are maddening, of course, only to those who do not want to understand them in the first place. This is as true today as it was thirty years ago when I first encountered the opening chapter of his *World Politics and Personal Insecurity*, entitled "The Configurative Analysis of the World Value Pyramids." At that time I was a student of something called "international relations," a rather dissonant potpourri of diplomatic history, international law, and current events. His book was quite a shocker—an encounter, as I said. I sought to get some guidance from my teachers, but they shrugged him off as eccentric and inconsequential. (Needless to say, this was at U. C., Berkeley, not U. C., Chicago.)

To this day I am not sure whether it was what Lasswell said or how he said it that offended the sensibilities of political scientists. In conversations about him I sensed a good deal of respect for an intellectual effort that was not understood, but there was always some comment that he was slightly mad, and that what he wrote should not be taken too seriously. There was, of course, the overt resistance to the psychoanalytic vocabulary and to his neologisms, but I felt that this was not the real source of scholarly discomfort. More relevant, I think, was the dim realization that Lasswell was a more consistent and threatening advocate than others of the "behavioral revolution" in political science that smoldered at the University of Chicago in the late twenties and

A version of this essay was published in the *Journal of Politics*, 30 (February 1968):3–24.

thirties. He seemed to be the most uncompromising member of a movement which conventional political science could not easily co-opt precisely because its incorporation would mean the end of the ancestral order. But as long as the behavioral revolution was only a one-campus revolt, the prevailing attitude was one of condescension toward Lasswell and the happy few who appreciated him.

All this changed in the late forties and early fifties. The seeds planted at Chicago had spread across the prairies of academe and grown into plants. Chicagoans turned out to be the most innovative of American political scientists. Herbert Simon published his attack on conventional public administration in 1947;[1] V. O. Key breathed new life into American studies in 1949;[2] Gabriel Almond tackled the ticklish relationship between public opinion and foreign policy in 1950;[3] David Truman established contact with the group notions of the neglected pioneer Arthur Bentley in 1951;[4] and Lasswell himself, with the help of Abraham Kaplan, codified much of his thinking in 1950.[5] The ferment of the early fifties brought with it a change in attitude toward Lasswell among political scientists. Criticism became more relevant and appropriate. No longer was it possible to shrug his work off as peripheral or inconsequential to the mainstream of political science.

There are few ideas in contemporary political science that cannot be found in Lasswell's early work. Too much emphasis, I think, is often put on his psychoanalytically influenced interest in political personality. It is, of course, an important part of his total work, but it is only one component. Many other current enthusiasms can be found in his early writings. In a volume in which different specialists deal with his work, there is no need for me to exhaust the catalog of items that constitutes Harold Lasswell as a "manifold of events." He anticipated the current interest in system theory, in functional analysis, in the study of roles, in the diagnosis of symbolic behavior, in the science of public policy, and in many methodological topics such as content analysis, participant observation, objectifying interviews, and experimental design. Careful reading of his work shows that these things are all there, even if, at times, the nomenclature is different. I am not saying this because I want to make Lasswell a fountainhead of contemporary virtues. A propagandist for his points of view he was and is, but a savior he was not and is not. Yet many political scientists could have saved themselves a lot of travail if they had paid more attention to his messages. Then as now they have had to discover and rediscover Lasswell. This is, perhaps, all to the good. It has made for the eclecticism of the behavioral movement and, through this eclecticism, for its pervasiveness. Moreover, not being chained to an entourage of disciples, though often aided by able collaborators, Lasswell was able to continue as the spearhead of the movement. Where he would go next always fascinated even those who knew him best.

Although contemporary political science bears the mark of his influence, Lasswell remains an enigma to many of his professional colleagues. Despite all the words he has written, there seems to be something inscrutable and elusive about his ideas. It is my feeling that there has been a failure to understand and appreciate the philosophical underpinnings of his theoretical, methodological, and substantive writings. For this reason, going back to Lasswell's early work may prove to be especially fruitful, for, unlike most of us, he was profoundly concerned with philosophical matters that were the current coin of the realm in his formative years.

Some of the major premises of his approach to politics are either well enough known or will undoubtedly be treated in other essays in this book. His adaptation for the study of political behavior of Freudian propositions about the powerful working of unconscious and often irrational motivations is common knowledge. The sources of his interest in values and public policy, on the other hand, are less clearly understood. One must go back to the chapter in his *Psychopathology* entitled "The Politics of Prevention" to appreciate Lasswell's strong and lasting commitment to political science as a therapeutic enterprise.[6] But these are only the more obvious premises that fertilized his work. Others are more difficult to identify, for Lasswell's simultaneously curt

style and discursive form of presentation do not easily lend themselves to textual exegesis. Moreover, because Lasswell made these
philosophical underpinnings his *working* assumptions, he evidently felt compelled to explicate them only occasionally and
then in the barest manner. Much of the failure of political scientists to understand what Lasswell is all about has been due to
their failure to concern themselves with any but the most obvious
philosophical assumptions of his work. And I think that even today few appreciate the philosophical complexity of his thought.

II

THERE are some overt clues that are suggestive. In what is still
the most significant methodological essay he ever published,
"General Framework: Person, Personality, Group, Culture,"
Lasswell explicitly states that his terminology "owes something
to the Cambridge Logical School, and especially to A. N. Whitehead. The debt is evident in the use of such expressions as 'event'
and 'event manifold.' "[7] What interests me is Lasswell's use of
the notion of "manifold of events" and the methodological implications of this use for some of the problems of political science
as a behavioral science.

As far as I know, Lasswell never discussed Whitehead's cos-
mology in detail. Useful as he apparently found the British phi-
losopher-scientist's concepts, he did not subscribe to his intricate
metaphysics. One can only do violence to Whitehead's thought
by seeking to summarize it in a few lines. I shall do so at the risk
of enormous simplification, but I hope that this summary will
pinpoint Lasswell's indebtedness to Whitehead.

For Whitehead the world is the product of a "creative advance
of nature"—a process that pervades the whole of nature and
produces "events" that never existed before. The world is always
incomplete, but it moves toward novelty and further completeness through the workings of something that Whitehead called
the "Principle of Concretion." As nature is a purposive process

moving toward achievement, indeterminate actualities are trans-
muted into determinate ones. Actualities and potentialities are
the two poles of nature that the process of emergence seeks to link
and unify.

It is easy to see why this philosophy of emergence should be
attractive to Lasswell. Throughout his work he was preoccupied
with actualities and potentialities. But unlike Whitehead, Lasswell did not consider the potentialities teleological properties inherent in nature. Rather, they resided in man as an action-
oriented, purposive animal.

In using the concept of "event manifold," Lasswell confronted a central and critical problem of political analysis that
still confronts us today. "Implications," he wrote in the last chapter of *Psychopathology and Politics* ("The State as a Manifold
of Events"), "have continually been drawn in the foregoing
pages about the bearing of the intensive study of *individual* personalities upon the *meaning* of the political process as a *whole*."[8]
I am taking the liberty of italicizing three key words in the sentence because they bring out the problem. How can one make
meaningful, empirically reliable statements about wholes—that
is, human collectivities—on the basis of knowledge about individual behavior? For, Lasswell continues, "since the psychopathological approach to the individual is the most elaborate procedure yet devised for the study of human personality, it would
appear to raise in the most acute form the thorny problem of the
relation between research on the individual and research upon
society."[9]

Why did Lasswell see a problem where most other political
scientists saw none? The simplest answer is that political scientists saw no problem because they had no problem. They largely
ignored individual behavior and concerned themselves only with
large-scale institutions and processes. But once the strange fruit
of individual behavior had been tasted, the joy was soured by the
"thorny problem." Lasswell set out to cut the Gordian knot of
the familiar dualism between individual and society:

It may be asserted at the outset that our thinking is vitiated unless we dispose of the fictitious cleavage which is sometimes supposed to separate the study of the "individual" from the study of "society." There is no cleavage; there is but a gradual gradation of reference points. Some events have their locus in but a single individual, and are unsuitable for comparative investigation. Some events are widely distributed among individuals, like breathing, but have no special importance for interpersonal relations.* Our starting-point as social scientists is the statement of a distinctive event which is widely spread among human beings who occupy a particular time-space manifold.[10]

But denying the dualism of individual and society by mere assertion is not enough. Lasswell's denial involved a search for philosophical underpinnings. To follow his search one must appreciate the fact that philosophy, and notably the philosophy of science, is a search for answers to certain recurring questions. Often these questions are put in dualistic form. Perhaps the best-known example is the dualism of "soul" and "body" inherited from primitive thought and Greek philosophy, a dualism that still persists, if in diluted form, in the distinction between psychological processes and the processes of the nervous system. In biology the dualism between "organic" and "inorganic," and in physics the old dualism between "force" and "matter," are other instances from the history of scientific thought. The dualism of individual and society is of the same generic class.

Often a dualism is of such long standing that it becomes part of the cultural heritage, hardened and resistant to resolution precisely because its reality is taken for granted. A dualism, then, assumes the existence of two kinds of entities or processes which are seen as interacting, but the interaction is yet to be explained. Once a dualism "exists," it serves as a powerful stimulus to thought, but it represents a "problem" because the interaction of the two poles of the dualism proves elusive. Moreover, the prob-

---

* I don't think Lasswell would give this example of a widely distributed individual event today. Air pollution is a major physical problem of collective survival, but the interpersonal importance of breathing is evident.

lem involved may be a pseudoproblem if the dualism is merely a figment of the intellectual imagination. In that case, the problem has only subjective significance and is not a soluble scientific problem. If, on the other hand, the dualism has been empirically discovered, as for instance the dualism between consciousness and unconsciousness, the problem is genuinely scientific because, though two kinds of reality may be involved, their relationship is presumably connected in some causal manner that can be investigated and explained.

But a dualism may be the result of both intellectual imagination and empirical inquiry. In this case it is extremely difficult to disentangle its speculative and empirical components. As it is in the nature of a dualism to make for increasing polarization and hardening of the lines between its end terms, the dualism is likely to give rise to antagonistic "schools of thought" that stress the primacy of one pole over the other. Not surprisingly, the history of political and social theory has often been written as a history of conflict between the individual and society.

Decomposing the speculative and empirical components of a dualism has been the achievement of logical positivism in that it distinguished between *statements* that are subject to falsification and those that are not. The specific problem of resolving the question of whether the dualism of individual and society is an empirically viable phenomenon or a pseudophenomenon was facilitated by the scientific theory of "emergent evolution" or the philosophical idea of "emergence" that became prominent in the 1920s and had its most distinguished philosophical exponent in A. N. Whitehead. Though Lasswell never explicitly and directly discussed emergence as a philosophical assumption, his frequent use of the terms "event manifold" and "emergent" indicates his acceptance, it not of the doctrine of emergent evolution, at least of the philosophical notion of emergence. For instance: "If the significant political changes of the past were signalized by revolutionary patterns which rose and spread until they were blocked or superseded by new revolutionary innovations, the future may well follow the same course of development. Hence our 'present' would be transition between the latest and the impending world revolutionary emergent."[11]

Lasswell's consistent emphasis on the need for developmental analysis of political processes, from his earliest major writings to his latest, supports this contention.[12] Moreover, the topography of his "General Framework" is predicated on a necessary corollary of the assumption of emergence—the conception of discrete levels of organization and analysis.

Because in attacking the problem of the individual-society dualism Lasswell also called for a new form of thinking about social phenomena, it may be useful to review, if only superficially, earlier attempts to cope with the dualism problem in cognition. Materialism—from Thomas Hobbes to the behavioristic psychology of John Watson—eliminated the dualism of mind and matter by reducing everything to a single basic reality, material substance. For Hobbes, thinking was but the motion of some unidentified substance in the head; for Watson thinking was simply "subvocal speech." On the other hand, idealists from Bishop Berkeley on sought to abolish the dualism of the physical and the psychical by reducing everything to some fundamental spiritual reality. As a result of these formulations, the dualism was aggravated rather than resolved by the arguments and counterarguments of the materialist and idealist warriors. Escape from the materialist-idealist cul-de-sac could be had only if it was possible to occupy a new observational standpoint. Such a new standpoint was also sought by the theory of "emergent evolution."

This aspect of the new philosophsy of emergent evolution must have been attractive to Lasswell in his attempt to overcome the dualism of logical and free-associational modes of thinking. The "new position" he came to occupy, and for which he became famous in his own right, was of course his insight that Freudian psychology could serve not only as an instrument of mental therapy but also as a powerful instrument of thought. In the third chapter of the *Psychopathology*, "A New Technique of Thinking," Lasswell attacked the prevailing emphasis on logic as the sole mode of thinking about politics:

A totally different technique of thinking is needed to get on with the task of ridding the mind of the distorting results of unseen compulsions. . . . Logical thinking is but one of the special methods of using the mind, and cannot itself achieve an adequate inspection of reality because it is unable to achieve self-knowledge without the aid of other forms of thinking.[13]

. . . The mind is a fit instrument of reality testing when both blades are sharpened—those of logic and free-fantasy.[14]

III

"EMERGENT evolution" was a philosophical doctrine that was bred by crossing Darwin and Hegel. It implied, therefore, two conceptions—one of *existential* emergence and one of *functional* emergence. These conceptions are by no means opposed to each other. Existential emergence means that in the course of development certain qualities, objects, or events come into existence which did not previously exist, and that knowledge about such novel types of existents—that is, emergents—cannot be derived from knowledge of what existed previously. Functional emergence means that the functioning of different types of existents is irreducible, so that no single theory can explain the characteristic functions of all types. These functional discontinuities are due to the existence of "levels of organization," regardless of whether these levels are novel or were always present. If novelty is stressed, the notion of functional emergence, like that of existential emergence, holds that the emergents cannot be explained by propositions that could explain previously existing phenomena; if levels of organization are emphasized, the doctrine holds that explanations of lower-level phenomena cannot be applied to the functioning of higher-level phenomena. But regardless of where the accent is put, the notion of emergence assumes an ultimate pluralism in the propositions that are needed to describe and explain the functioning of different types of phenomena. Both existential and functional emergence assert the nondeducibility of the phenomena with which they are concerned. In the case of existential emergence, this nondeducibility can be called "unpredictability." In the case of functional emergence, it can be called "irreducibility."

I do not know whether Lasswell, had he been explicit, would have preferred the notion of existential emergence or the idea of functional emergence. It does not matter in any case because for Lasswell ideas are never rigid formulas whose internal logic is to be respected, but rather suggestive starting points for innovative thinking. In other words, it is not clear whether he viewed emergence as descriptive of an actual process of progressive development in the cosmos whereby the present variety of physical, biological, and social phenomena emerged from a primitive stage characterized by undifferentiated and isolated elements, while the future contains unpredictable novelties; or whether he accepted emergence as a conception of an irreducible hierarchical organization of phenomena or processes and of the existence of properties at "higher" levels of organization that cannot be deduced or predicted from properties characteristic of "lower" levels.[15] My inclination is to believe that he toyed with both conceptions but did not adopt either in its pristine purity.

The notion of emergence has aided in overcoming many old dualisms. Just as such "nothing but" ways of thinking—pluralism versus monism, determinism versus free will, or materialism versus idealism—could be abandoned by philosophy, so Lasswell could dispose of the logic versus free-fantasy dualism and suggest a compromise. In this new mode of thought it was unnecessary to make a choice between extreme views. What appears to be antithetical is reconciled on a new plane. It represents a position which Lasswell has repeated time and again in his various writings when he enjoins us to occupy as many observational standpoints as possible in the analysis of individual, social, and cultural phenomena.

But what of the "thorny problem" of research on individual and society that bothered Lasswell? We can see now that it was linked in his mind to the problem of utilizing appropriate ways of thinking about the phenomena involved. In the *Psychopathology* he had probed deeply into the microbehavior of individuals, but there remained the problem of how such knowledge could be made relevant to an explanation of the behavior of social entities. Lasswell did not assume, as is sometimes assumed by less sophisticated students of individual behavior, that societal phenomena can be explained solely by means of a theory concerning their microstructures. Insight into societal behavior at the level of the individual may be a necessary condition for explanation of social phenomena, but it is not a sufficient condition. Lasswell came to identify classes of events in society and culture which could not be explained by theoretical propositions about the behavior of individuals in terms of personality. His concern, clearly, was a theory of classes of events that were unexplained. Similar concerns were at the root of the doctrine of emergence.

IV

EMERGENCE, we have seen, refers to the process by which *new* effects (or processes or events) arise from the operation of antecedent causes (or processes or events). As a result of emergence new *wholes* (or configurations) appear which include or show *novel* properties that are qualitatively different from the sum of the properties of their constituent parts. This is not to say that aggregation of individual properties is not a legitimate operation to describe new wholes. For instance, if we speak of the median age of a group, the property "age" is stated in the form of a summation. But when we speak of a group's cohesion or integration, we do not refer to some arithmetic value, but to something new— an emergent property that cannot be reduced to some characteristic of its individual members. The new phenomenon is a "whole" that cannot be dissected or taken apart and then reassembled like an automobile. We can see better now, I think, what Lasswell meant when he characterized the state as a manifold of events. What he meant was that state behavior cannot be analyzed by disassembling it into parts. In this connection, we must not make too much of Lasswell's use of the term "state," which, at the time, was still the prevailing theoretical concept in political science for what we would call today "political system." A political system can be any political whole whose boundaries are identifiable—the historical "state" as much as a "legislature" or a "party" or a "party system." The important point to keep in mind is that in leading to a conception of the whole, the idea of emergence called attention to the manifold of events that constitutes the whole. Lasswell articulated the relationship between thinking in terms of emergence and wholes as follows:

> Sound political analysis is nothing less than correct orientation in the continuum which embraces the past, present, and future. Unless the salient features of the all-inclusive whole are discerned, details will be incorrectly located. . . .[16]
>
> . . . The gradual creation of a sense of wholeness, and of assurance in the discovery of interdetail connections within the all-encompassing totality, also requires new methods of formal exposition.[17]

Lasswell's words and concepts, as I suggested earlier, sounded strange to his contemporaries in political science (but not to behavioral scientists in other disciplines, who recognized his stature earlier, I think, than political scientists did). It is by now abundantly clear that Lasswell was not playing with neologisms for effect, as some of his critics alleged. As his later research and the research of those whom he influenced have amply demonstrated, these were not empty or meaningless words. Yet Lasswell felt compelled to defend himself when he wrote that "our function is not to introduce a new cult but to give a sounder general analysis than has been possible heretofore."[18] His approach to politics was not a cult because he knew, as his critics did not know, that in utilizing the ideas of emergence and wholeness he was anticipating the course of social scientific inquiry in the next few decades, with its emphasis on *gestalt* thinking, interdisciplinary frames of reference, development, functional categories and procedures, and, last but not least, the distinction between levels of analysis.

To understand the levels of analysis "problem," we must keep in mind a distinction between resultant effects and emergent effects. Resultant effects—as in the parallelogram of forces model of mechanics—are analyzable in terms of the independent forces or vectors whose confluence can be expressed algebraically or geometrically. In the case of emergent effects, on the other hand, the component "events" interact to produce a new whole in such a way that they are no longer independent of each other. Emergent wholes like "personality," "society," or "culture" are units that are something more than the sum of the items, elements, or traits that constitute them individually. An emergent whole differs, for instance, from the collection and arrangement of pieces of furniture in a room where individual pieces may be introduced or removed without disturbing the basic arrangement. Of course, a configuration is an emergent whole made up of parts, but statements about its "shape" or "pattern" can neither be deduced from knowledge of the properties of its individual parts nor reduced to the properties of the constituent parts.

If it is correct, then, that in the course of interaction of individual parts new properties appear or emerge that characterize the whole, the behavior of parts and whole must be analyzed on different levels—a macroscopic and microscopic level. And as behavior on the macrolevel is new and emergent, it requires new descriptive concepts and possibly new empirical propositions that are independent of the concepts and propositions relevant to the microlevel. Confusion of levels has disastrous consequences for scientific explanation and interpretation. If macrolevel explanations are simply extrapolated from observations of behavior on the microlevel, as for instance in the older "national character" studies, the behavior of the whole is likely to be misunderstood and misinterpreted. On the other hand, if the behavior of the whole, say a society, is used to explain the behavior of its component individuals, violence is done to the explanation of the constituent parts. For instance, if it is proper to characterize German society as "authoritarian," in the political-structural sense on the macrolevel of analysis, it does not follow that the behavior of all Germans or even most Germans is "authoritarian" in some psychological sense on the microlevel of analysis.

The notion that human behavior in its totality can and must be analyzed from the perspective of different analytical levels does not imply empirical discontinuity from one level to the next. On the contrary, as the new macrolevel configuration emerges out of the behavior of the constituent parts that is also observable on the old or microlevel, empirical continuity is implicitly assumed. Macrolevel phenomena, then, are not mere epiphenomena or in any sense less "real" than microlevel phenomena. The behavior involved, whatever the level of analysis, is the same. A group, for instance, is a unit of interacting individuals whose behavior is the same regardless of whether the analyst occupies a microlevel or macrolevel standpoint of observation. But if the behavior of the individuals is observed from the group or macrolevel perspective, it is possible to identify qualities which are new because they do not exist if any one constituent individual is observed as a single unit. For instance, on the microlevel of the individual, no analytic operation whatsoever enables the analyst to describe a group's "cohesion" or "solidarity." (In other words, an individual's *feeling* of solidarity is a property of the individual, not of the group; "group solidarity" is an analytically distinct property of the whole group.) It is for just this reason that the conception of levels of analysis and the notion of emergence are complementary. Emergence entails the appearance of new levels of organization; the recognition of new levels entails a developmental perspective and the need to distinguish between levels of analysis.

Although Lasswell did not deal directly with considerations of this kind, they are clearly implicit in his "General Framework." The key concepts that constitute the framework—person, personality, group, culture—refer to different levels of behavioral organization and to different levels of analysis. The "thorny problem" that he had identified in "The State as a Manifold of Events"—the relation between research on the individual and on society—was the problem of how one can move empirically from one level to another. The answers he gave differ in degree of strength and scope. Minimally, there is the issue of frequency: many new patterns that emerge out of individual behavior at the group level of analysis can be analyzed as statistical regularities. Lasswell's early commitment to quantitative analysis did not stem from some compulsion to "count" for the sake of counting. Rather:

> What is known as the "quantitative method" provides a valuable discipline for the student of culture because it directs his attention toward the discovery of events which are often enough repeated to raise a strong presumption that a particular sequence does actually exist. These events must be so defined that similar events can be identified by other workers. This necessitates an operational definition of the concept, which is to say, terms must be used to specify the position of the observer in relation to the configuration which it is proposed to describe.[19]

Lasswell was, above all, sensitive to the deficiency of macro-level explanations. He complained about "the impatience among students of culture with the slow-footed quantitative approach" which "is partly due to the diffuse, implicit nature of the experiences upon which is based the judgment about a subjective event outside one's self, and the resulting bias of the student of culture against exaggerating the significance of items in the pattern."[20] This theme is continued in "General Framework" and linked to the theme of configurative analysis: "Although we have defined culture trait and personality trait, we have not defined culture or personality. These terms refer to wholes, and as wholes they include *not only* the traits of which they are composed, but the interrelationships of these traits" (italics added).[21]

Lasswell's emphasis on quantification led, as is well known, to his pioneering studies of political elites and symbols. The purpose of these studies was to reveal the emergence and shape of the world configuration of values.[22] But his acceptance of the notion of emergent levels as real, empirically continuous phenomena also implied the further analysis of the causal conditions under which the new phenomena occur and of the immanent conditions that maintain them independent of the component events. Hence his attention turned to the analysis of wholes as developmental as well as equilibriated phenomena. And just as he had encountered opposition to the "slow-footed" method of quantification, so he noted opposition to "systematic" analysis: "To some extent, there has been resistance against this mode of conceiving the task of students of personality and culture."[23] Not that this resistance was due to a lack of knowledge of the calculus of variations on the part of social scientists. Psychologists, for instance,

> have operated with variables, but they have not undertaken to se-
> lect a list in terms of which they could describe the fluctuations
> of the whole personality in relation to its environment. The essen-
> tial point about the "systemic" pattern of analysis is not that it
> uses variables, but that it chooses a list whose interrelations are
> studied with regard to fluctuations in the environment.[24]

In part, then, the problem was to develop specific categories and modes of observation for systematic analyses of such configurative wholes as personality or culture. Yet, Lasswell pointed out, "science seemed to be growing by the discovery and exploration of new standpoints, and by the discovery of interpart relations independent of explicit modes of describing 'wholeness.' "[25] Organic metaphors and analogies were suspect on political grounds. Here Lasswell once more acknowledges the suggestiveness of the doctrine of emergence: "It is not one of the least distinctive achievements of Whitehead that he lifted the conception of the organic from the battle-scarred phraseology of preceding centuries."[26]

V

MY task here is not to review Lasswell's particular substantive formulations. The significant point is that, in "General Framework," he clearly distinguished between levels of organization and raised the issue of the relationship between levels. The methodological issue is, essentially, that of reduction and nonreduction, or of continuity and discontinuity of levels. I don't think that the issue has been in any way resolved. The reductionist standpoint envisages a unified science of human behavior in which all the sciences are integrated in terms of a microlevel theory of behavior. This theory, it is argued, is the only guarantee of scientific knowledge of any phenomenon, on whatever level it is observed, for it alone gives insight into the "inner workings," so to speak, of phenomena. But if levels are seen as discontinuous, analysis on each level presumes the generation of empirical propositions appropriate to that level and not applicable to another. Hence the continued autonomy of the three basic behavioral sciences, each primarily concerned with the study of human behavior from a particular level-relevant perspective—psychology with behavior at the level of the individual person, sociology with behavior at the level of the group (society), and anthropology with behavior at the level of culture. Nevertheless, as behavior on different levels gives rise to independent empirical phenomena, the study of the interstices between levels makes for the development of intermediate disciplines, such as social psychology, political sociology, or culture and personality, that are in search of principles which can connect macro- and microcharacteristics of behavior as parts of total analysis.

If I understand it correctly, the "General Framework" was Lasswell's attempt to come to grips with the problem of interlevel relations. What motivated him to deal with the problem was, I suspect, his desire to avoid the reductionist trap into which his preoccupation with individual psychological mechanisms might have led him, as is indeed the case with many psychologists interested in societal phenomena. He was too much of a social and political scientist not to sense that behavior at the level of group or culture followed laws that were quite independent of propositions about microscopic behavior items. Yet, though he resisted reduction, or perhaps because he resisted it, Lasswell recognized problems of interlevel or translevel relationships that must necessarily arise if reduction is not feasible. The amazing thing is, I think, that his essay is as suggestive today as it was almost thirty years ago, for we have made little progress in the solution of the problem. Although the essay was reprinted in a volume devoted to political behavior, its original appearance in *Psychiatry* as well as its unfamiliar vocabulary seems to have deterred political scientists from following up on his suggestions; and this despite the fact that political science occupies an eminently interstitial position between the three basic behavioral sciences. I am confident that in the future, as political scientists must come to terms with the interstitial position of their discipline and hence with the problem of emergent properties in the macrostructures and processes that interest them, they will have to turn to the "General Framework" for guidance and enlightenment.

Careful reading of the essay will also show, I think, that Lasswell was concerned with another problem—namely, whether and how, after the emergence of higher-level phenomena, the behavior of the lower-level units might be changed so that the behavior of these units follows empirical laws not discoverable when there is no "intervention" of the emergent phenomenon. Lasswell must have had this problem in mind when he referred to an observer who

> uses the expression "trait of a specified culture" to refer to an act which is expected to appear and which does occur with at least a specified minimum frequency in a given field of observation. Our observer may use the word "conduct" to refer to an act which conforms to a culture trait and the word "behavior" to refer to an act which does not conform. We may note that an act which is behavior in one community may be conduct in another community, but it is also possible that an act may conform to no pattern anywhere.[27]

In another example a person's "career line" rather than culture is the emergent. The observer "is also interested in placing the act in proper relationship to another dimension of this manifold of events. The act is one of the acts which compose the career line of the actor. Some of the acts are representative of the person under specified conditions."[28]

In other words, because the behavior of individuals takes place in what Lasswell called the "personality-culture manifold," the behavior should be expected to follow empirical laws which are not operative if it takes place independently of such higher-level phenomena as personality or culture. In simpler language, we would say that the cultural content of behavior permeates otherwise nonpatterned acts of behavior. Culture is, of course, the most pervasive emergent in human relations. But on the social level too the impact of an emergent phenomenon on its constituent parts can be observed. Recent studies of "structural effects" or "compositional effects" seek to measure the impact of emerging group properties on the behavior of the individuals who constitute the group.[29]

In Lasswell's terminology, the possibility of analyzing behavior on several and diverse levels brings into play what he has sometimes called the "contextual principle," sometimes the "principle of interdetermination." Precisely because certain phenomena, say "value systems" or the "language of politics," can have considerable internal independence so as to constitute distinct levels of organization in society or culture, they may be analyzed on their own level. But they may also be analyzed in terms of development from presumably prior or lower levels to present levels. The traditional procedure of nineteenth-century social science had been to search for single-factor explanations. In rejecting single-factor approaches, Lasswell did not simply substitute a multifactor design. Let us listen carefully:

> This standpoint [i.e., of interdetermination, as against overdetermination] is sometimes formulated as a principle of "multiple causation." *But more is involved than multiple causes;* there are multiple effects as well, and more important, there are patterns of interaction in which it is impossible to distinguish between cause and effect [italics added].[30]

Or he may speak of a "principle of situational reference":

> Empirical significance requires that the propositions of social science, rather than affirming unqualifiedly universal invariances,

state relations between variables assuming different magnitude *in different social contexts* [italics added].[31]

Contextual analysis and developmental analysis may go hand in hand. Individuals, Lasswell stated early in "Configurative Analysis,"

> may be investigated by special methods to disclose the genetic sequence of personality development and to place the individual career line in relation to the career line of others living in the same epoch. *It is a question solely of expediency and not of principle* whether the total configuration is approached extensively or intensively by the individual observer, since either starting point draws the investigator toward the opposite [italics added].[32]

Here, once more, we encounter the impact of thinking of emergence in modern terms with an emphasis on avoiding the mistakes and simplifications of nineteenth-century evolutionary thought. Rather, whatever phenomena are to be observed on whatever level of analysis—political institutions, social structures, cultural patterns, norms of conduct, symbolic systems, and so on—they are to be observed in relation to the total context in a given stage of human development. Just as developmental analysis is predicated on the existence of stages in terms of which the developmental process can be ascertained, so contextual analysis is predicated on the existence of levels in terms of which behavior is given meaning. For meaning changes from level to level.

It is for all of these reasons that the behavioral scientist must at all times be cognizant of the level of analysis that defines for him the frame of reference or observational standpoint from which he generalizes about the phenomena at his focus of attention. What on one level, say that of culture, may appear as a generic value may also, on the social level, appear as a norm of interpersonal conduct; and it may appear, at the level of personality, as a rationalization of hidden motives. The behavior that is observed is the same; what is different is the emergent level—be it culture, society, or personality—that defines the appropriate mode of analysis and guides interpretation. Confusion of levels is to be avoided. A system of values as a cultural phenomenon cannot be analyzed as a set of mechanisms of defense that may be appropriate on the level of personality. Similarly, a group's "interest" is something different from the private agendas that are rooted at the level of personality. Mobilizing all levels of analysis in behalf of understanding or explaining the manifold of events that constitutes any one particular phenomenon, like Lasswell's "state," is a strategy of research, not a confusion of levels of analysis.

VI

THE conception of emergence has certain implications for the problem of scientific prediction in human affairs. If emergent properties at a higher level of organization cannot be deduced with logical rigor from statements about the constituent parts of a whole, prediction is not always possible. But this does not foreclose the making of anticipatory statements that are sometimes more than fortunate guesses. In other words, emergents as altogether novel phenomena are unpredictable only in a strictly logical sense. But this does not necessarily mean that an emergent phenomenon, *on its own level of analysis,* cannot be predicted from determinate conditions for the occurrence of all events, whatever the level. Put differently, emergence is not incompatible with assumptions about causation. It does not involve some acceptance of either indeterminism or teleological principle. An emergent property is not some ontological, immanent aspect of a phenomenon. Rather, one can assume that the probability of its being observed is relative to the state of theoretical knowledge at a given time. An emergent property may lose its emergent status as level-relevant theoretical propositions become available, so that the phenomenon can be explained or predicted on its own level. For instance, a group's cohesion may vary with varying threats to the group's survival. In other words, an emergent phenomenon is always contingent on the total configuration in which the emergent event occurs. The difficulty is that the configuration may be unique and for this reason make prediction hazardous. Note Lasswell's early statement of the predicament:

Now the whole world of "causation" is implicated in any event, and the whole number of significant mechanisms which may be discerned in the "mind at the moment" is infinite. So our hypothetical volume might conclude by accepting the assumption that some events can be brought about by more than chance frequency, subject to the reservation that experimental confirmation is never reliable as to the future. *The critical configurations may never "reappear."* We commonly say that the probability of an event's future repetition is greater if it has been oft repeated in the past. *But there is no means of demonstrating that the future contains analogous configurations to the elapsed.* The probability of the future repetition of an event is "no probability." If events appear to be predictable, this is so because our knowledge of contingencies is limited, and our sequences of similar configurations may still be treated as special instances of "no sequence." The stable is a special case of the unstable, to put the ultimate paradox [italics added].[33]

The problem of prediction, then, is not just a matter of logical deduction but of multilevel empirical investigation into the manifold of events that constitutes the context of emergence. Lasswell stated this problem in "Configurative Analysis" as follows:

Now it is impossible to abolish uncertainty by the refinement of restrospective observations, by the accumulation of historical detail, by the application of precision methods to elapsed events; the crucial test of adequate analysis is nothing less than the future verification of the insight into the nature of the master configuration against which details are constructed. Each specific interpretation is subject to redefinition as the structural potentialities of the future become actualized in the past and present of participant observers. The analyst moves between the contemplation of detail and of configuration, knowing that the soundness of the result is an act of creative orientation rather than of automatic projection. The search for precision in the routines of the past must be constantly chastened and given relevance and direction by reference to the task of self-orientation which is the goal of analysis.[34]

In this quotation Lasswell's indebtedness to A. N. Whitehead is most evident. The problem of relating actualities to potentialities is a problem of the creative orientation of the observer. The evidence is overwhelming that Lasswell was fascinated by this problem and that it was this problem, perhaps more than any other, that led him to his deep interest in what, in later writings, he called the "problem-solving approach." In a magisterial statement addressed to his colleagues in *The Future of Political Science*, he stated his position succinctly:

> Any problem-solving approach to human affairs poses five intellectual tasks, which we designate by five terms familiar to political scientists—goal, trend, conditions, projection, and alternative. The first question, relating to goal, raises the traditional problem of clarifying the legitimate aims of a body politic. After goals are provisionally clarified, the historical question arises. In the broadest context, the principal issue is whether the trend of events in America or throughout the world community has been toward or away from the realization of preferred events. The next question goes beyond the simple inventories of change and asks which factors condition one another and determine history. When trend and factor knowledge is at hand, it is possible to project the course of future developments on the preliminary assumption that we do not ourselves influence the future. Finally, what policy alternatives promise to bring all preferred goals to optimal fulfillment?[35]

In its cool simplicity this statement conceals the intellectual labor that had gone into it over a professional career of forty years. There are still those who accuse Lasswell of braggadocio and empty phrase-making. What they miss is Lasswell's profound and lifelong concern with the most subtle philosophical underpinnings of a science of politics and social science in general. While he may have had an image of the complex problems involved early in his career and envisaged in a broad perspective possible solutions, his incessant quest led him to touch all bases rather than only one or two. In Lasswell's master orientation—I cannot think of a better expression to describe his intellectual style and stance—there is little room for exclusiveness. But there is ample room for a great variety of approaches to knowledge. Because, perhaps more than any other contemporary behavioral scientist, he disdained intellectual simplicity in a world of great practical complexity, he was not satisfied with occupying just one or two observational standpoints—a task which, for most of us, is a lifetime effort. He could not afford to be a "pure" theoretician, and he could not afford to be satisfied with doing empirical work alone; he could not afford being a student only of the past or the present, but always had to occupy himself with the future; he could not limit himself merely to the analysis of values, but had to recommend their application in the crucible of public policy-making; he could not sacrifice causal for functional analysis just as he could not surrender an interest in details to an interest in wholes. The intellectual edifice he erected resembles a Gothic cathedral with its turrets and spires and arches and niches which, on close inspection, may evince flaws of one kind or another. But, like a Gothic cathedral, the edifice is built on firm foundations and it is wondrous to behold in its total complexity and splendor.

REFERENCES

1. Herbert A. Simon, *Administrative Behavior* (New York: Macmillan, 1947).

2. V. O. Key, Jr., *Southern Politics in State and Nation* (New York: Knopf, 1949).

3. Gabriel A. Almond, *The American People and Foreign Policy* (Princeton, N.J.: Princeton University Press, 1950).

4. David B. Truman, *The Governmental Process* (New York: Knopf, 1951).

5. Harold D. Lasswell and Abraham Kaplan, *Power and Society* (New Haven, Conn.: Yale University Press, 1950).

6. Professor Easton is wrong, I think, in dating Lasswell's commitment to democratic values from the beginning of World War II. See David Easton, "Harold Lasswell; Policy Scientist for a Democratic Society," *Journal of Politics*, 12 (1950):450–77.

7. Harold D. Lasswell, "General Framework: Person, Person-

ality, Group, Culture," *The Analysis of Political Behavior* (New York: Oxford University Press, 1948), p. 195. This essay first appeared in *Psychiatry*, 2 (1939):533–61.

8. Harold D. Lasswell, *Psychopathology and Politics* (Chicago: University of Chicago Press, 1930), p. 240.

9. *Ibid.*

10. *Ibid.*

11. Harold D. Lasswell, *World Politics and Personal Insecurity* (New York: McGraw-Hill, 1935), p. 4.

12. See Heinz Eulau, "H. D. Lasswell's Developmental Analysis," *Western Political Quarterly*, 11 (1958):229–42.

13. *Psychopathology*, pp. 31–32.

14. *Ibid.*, p. 37.

15. For a discussion of the distinction between emergence as part of an evolutionary cosmogony and as a thesis about hierarchical organization, see Ernest Nagel, *The Structure of Science* (New York: Harcourt, Brace & World, 1961), pp. 366–80. Nagel argues that the evolutionary version of the emergence doctrine is not entailed by the conception of emergence as irreducible hierarchical organization.

16. *World Politics*, p. 4.

17. *Ibid.*, p. 16.

18. *Ibid.*, p. 17.

19. *Psychopathology*, p. 251.

20. *Ibid.*

21. *Analysis of Political Behavior*, p. 202.

22. See Harold D. Lasswell, Nathan Leites, *et al.*, *Language of Politics* (New York: Stewart, 1949), and Harold D. Lasswell, *The World Revolution of Our Time* (Stanford, Calif.: Stanford University Press, 1951).

23. *Analysis of Political Behavior*, p. 208.

24. *Ibid.*, p. 210.

25. *Ibid.*, p. 211.

26. *Ibid.*

27. *Ibid.*, p. 200.

28. *Ibid.*

29. See Peter M. Blau, "Structural Effects," *American Sociological Review*, 25 (1960):178–93; James A. Davis, "Problem and Method: Compositional Effects and the Survival of Small Social Systems," in *Great Books and Small Groups* (New York: Free Press, 1961), pp. 1–25.

30. *Power and Society*, p. xvii.

31. *Ibid.*, p. xxi.

32. *World Politics*, p. 24.

33. *Psychopathology*, p. 260.

34. *World Politics*, p. 17.

35. Harold D. Lasswell, *The Future of Political Science* (New York: Atherton, 1963), pp. 1–2.

3

The Mystifying Intellectual History of Harold D. Lasswell

Bruce Lannes Smith

In Harold D. Lasswell we have a mystifying man: a lively bon vivant with a somewhat puritanical social conscience; a surprisingly modest narcissist; a prolific writer on "elites" who is publicly committed to the widespread sharing of such currently ill-distributed values as income, health, deference, and education; a scintillating intellectual giant who tolerates the typical social scientist suavely; an extremely lucid thinker who sometimes verbigerates (intermittently, though) with hypersesquipedalian anfractuosity; a topflight builder of pure theories and towering theoretical frameworks who advocates alternating "hours of high abstraction and days of patient contact with humble detail"—and actually follows his own advice; a tireless quantifier who also reads tirelessly in unquantified history and philosophy; a man who combines with many a warm friendship a detachment often described as "icy." We have here, in fact, a kind of Leonardo da Vinci of the behavioral sciences: author of some forty volumes of substantial works in such assorted areas as anthropology, international relations, political philosophy, empirical political science, economic policy, labor relations, psychiatry, quantitative semantics, and even such far-out fields as the law (if any) of outer space.

Obviously the redoubtable Mr. Lasswell is bound to spread confusion among future biographers and cultural historians. One can even imagine that some of them will "resolve" this confusion by inventing a Shakespeare-and-Bacon myth to the effect that several men named Lasswell existed: one who wrote political science, one who was a law-school professor, and one who is probably the author of the surviving fragments originally attributed to such writers as Daniel Lerner and the later Charles Edward Merriam. Or perhaps experts will agree that this torrent of scholarship was turned out by a large, computerized law firm in New Haven called Lasswell, Lasswell, Lasswell, Yale, and McDougal.

Adding to the mystery surrounding the historical reconstruction will be the discrepancy between the obscurity of Lasswell's social origins and the levels of intellectual and social prominence that he achieved. It is well established—by Lasswell's own "elite studies," among others—that academic performance and social awareness are far more probable among children of those who are highly educated, and who are well established in the upper middle classes of the big coastal cities, than among children born, as Lasswell was, to a fairly humble Presbyterian clergyman and his unassuming schoolteacher wife in an unprominent town like Donnellson, Illinois (population, even in 1960: 292). Further, the town was in a highly improbable region on the cultural map: the very heartland of the Midwest, which even today is culturally a semideveloped area, despite its having produced, at rare intervals, such people as Abraham Lincoln and the Adlai Stevenson family.

Admittedly, the minister and the schoolteacher stand near the summit or "elite level" of the socioeconomic pyramid of a town like Donnellson. Moreover, Lasswell's parents were "symbol specialists," as he was later to put it: both made their livings by thinking, talking, and giving advice. Both had a high regard for education and saw in it the means of arriving at social and ethical prescriptions that were both authoritative and legitimate. They gave enlightenment and received respect. The self-assurance that may come from early savoring of a community's deference toward one's parents may help to explain the young Lasswell's drive and sensitivity with respect to the "pyramids of enlightenment and of deference," as well as toward those other pyramids—the pyramids of income and of physical welfare—of which Midwestern Americans are typically so much more conscious.

His budding sensitivities must have been heightened by the contrast between his culturally and financially modest early surroundings and the world he discovered when he entered the ultra-intellectual and highly cosmopolitan University of Chicago on a scholarship, at the age of sixteen. But obviously some further explanations are needed; many another young man from near the top of a small, local pyramid has gone to a major university and found a far larger world, and yet has not become a Lasswell.

Perhaps, one lovely day, some psychoanalytically-oriented information or communication theorist, employing possibly the sort of cybernetic model that Karl Deutsch has presented in *The Nerves of Government*,[1] will be able to chart the contents and rates of the information-inputs that led to the distinctive Lasswellian personality syndrome, with its persistent and almost aggressive allocation of energies to information gathering, information retention, and information sorting, combined with an immense facility in relevant information suppression, information retrieval, further information recombination, and almost continuous information publication.

Or, conceivably, a theorist using some macrovariety of general systems theory (of which the elaborate-looking Deutschian cybernetic analysis is of course but a simplified special case) can some day specify the complex of "man-machine-information processes" by which a highly inconspicuous sub-sub-sub-sub-system of the world's social system (such as a small boy in a rather humble family in a microscopic Midwestern town) can be transformed, in a matter of thirty or forty years, into an internationally respected scientific authority and a valued consultant at the levels of national and even world policy-making.

But in the present state of things we cannot easily surmise—much less describe in the soul-satisfying jargon of behavioral science—just what syndrome led to this mystifying transformation. So possibly there is some justification for this present essay by one who happens to have known Lasswell for some thirty-nine years as one of his students and one of his friends. One can at least submit for the record a few facts and a few conjectures that might be of some use to more rigorous analysts in the future.

THE BOY AND THE TEEN-AGE PRODIGY

SHEER physical vigor apparently has been important in Lasswell's make-up from the start. Although he is rather disdainful of athletics and even of exercise, he is a large and robust man who always seems to have enjoyed a long and exacting working day and yet to have been ready to dine and drink well and to carry on work and conversation far into the night. He does all this with an awe-inspiring mixture of gusto, high-proof alcohol, and socio-psychoanalytic verbalisms. "Harold, you are a psychosomatic monster," moaned his close friend, the celebrated but easily wearied psychiatrist Harry Stack Sullivan (rather enviously) at about five o'clock one morning, after Lasswell had just given a characteristically comprehensive (and highly respectful) nonstop commentary on some of Sullivan's concepts that were to appear, years later, in Sullivan's famous book, *The Interpersonal Theory of Psychiatry*.[2] The commentary had begun as cocktail conversation at about four o'clock the afternoon before.

But what undoubtedly is far more important than this high level of physical energy is the extraordinary combination of symbols, as Lasswell would say (or "information," as present-day behavioral theory might put it), that must have been imprinted upon him at some very early age and must have been restimulated and reinforced by many other intellectuality-inducing inflows in later years. We have no firm data about this, but whatever the combination was, we can see in retrospect that it must have generated, both in his early and in his later years, what he probably would call, in Freudian lingo, a "polymorphous oral" optimism about the high payoff (the high "indulgence-to-deprivation" or "I/D" ratio, to use another of Lasswell's characteristic terms) to be expected from keeping oneself open and alert to symbols of practically every sort: religious, civic, scientific, historical, philo-sophical, medico-psychiatric, legal, or what you will.

In very close relation to this "omnivore" imprint there must have been another imprint that gave him a predisposition to com-prehensiveness, to holism, to blocking out the entirety of what-ever subject he took up. Whenever a topic interests him, he seems to push the study of it to its outer limits—galloping across the boundaries of existing disciplines and bodies of knowledge until he has what he calls a "totalistic formulation." In short, he has a predisposition to "grand theory" and macrothought, as against that easy or resigned acceptance of "partial" and "middle-level" theory and that microscopic reexamination of tidbits and frag-ments of thought which is the typical preoccupation of most academics.

His optimism about this particular kind of omnivorousness must also have been related to some sort of personality-structuring that fostered a great capacity to metabolize these massive infor-mation inputs so as to avoid being choked or drowned by them; for Lasswell's intellectual history has been notable not only for his immense appetites but also for a striking continuity, coher-ence, and orderliness. As Karl Deutsch might put it, his facilities for selecting, digesting, abstracting, classifying, and filing infor-mation-inputs have always been highly efficient, and his internal servo-mechanisms are intricate yet rugged.

He is also capable of enormous and continuous symbol *out-puts*. One wonders whether this may not in part represent an attempt to save himself from the "indigestion effects" of the sheer quantities of information which he pours into himself. Un-doubtedly, almost every man of science—especially of social science and of its new neighbors such as nuclear physics and global military strategy—is likely to suffer acutely from "infor-mation overload" in this epoch of explosions of knowledge, of populations, and of bombs. In the face of these assorted explo-sions, can mental self-preservation and psychological security be sought best through continuous high-speed information publication, which involves not only self-clarification but also the prompt and frequent testing of one's own formulations and reformulations against those made by others?

However that may be, "self-clarification," "self-orientation," "self-enlightenment," "insight about the self" are among the "key values" most frequently alluded to by Lasswell. And as Lasswell has matured (and has perhaps become more secure himself, or at least better able to endure the uncertainties of an anxious epoch), he has referred more and more often to the "*sharing* of enlightenment" (to "*mutual* clarification" and "*mutual* orientation," as we might put it) as being a key value also, especially for those who have what he calls "democratic character."

Possibly one of the experiences that led to an early seriousness and an acute need for self-orientation was the loss of his only sibling, a slightly older brother who died in childhood, when Lasswell was five years old. This left the young Lasswell in the role of a "psychological only child." He was to become something of a brooding "loner" for the rest of his life. In his thirties he was to quote, with qualified approval, an eloquent introspective statement by Albert Einstein:

> "I am a horse for single harness, not cut out for tandem or team-work. I have never belonged wholeheartedly to country or state, to my circle of friends, or even to my own family. These ties have always been accompanied by a vague aloofness, and the wish to withdraw into myself increases with the years. . . . My passionate interest in social justice and social responsibility has always stood in curious contrast to a marked lack of desire for direct association with men and women."[3]

Those who know Lasswell may feel that something of the sort could equally be said of him.

Yet, although Lasswell has never married, there must always have been, alongside his sometimes wistful aloofness, a persistent desire for companionship. For over forty-five years he has been engaged almost continuously in one collaboration after another.

His very first book—*Labor Attitudes and Problems*[4]—was written with the economist Willard E. Atkins. Since then he has written on an astounding diversity of topics with an astonishing variety of other coauthors, among them:

Hayward R. Alker, Jr.
(political scientist)
Gabriel Almond
(political scientist)
Richard Arens (lawyer)
Janet Besse (political scientist)
Dorothy Blumenstock
(political scientist)
Ralph D. Casey
(professor of journalism)
Richard C. Donnelly (lawyer)
George H. Dession (lawyer)
Karl W. Deutsch
(political scientist)
Abraham Geller (psychologist)
Joseph M. Goldsen
(political scientist)
Alan Grey (psychologist)
Allan Holmberg (anthropologist)
Irving L. Janis (psychologist)
Abraham Kaplan
(professor of philosophy)
David Kaplan (psychologist)
John L. Kennedy (psychologist)

Nathan C. Leites
(political scientist)
Daniel Lerner
(political sociologist)
Myres S. McDougal (lawyer)
Charles E. Merriam
(political scientist)
Royal E. Montgomery
(economist)
Ithiel de Sola Pool
(political scientist)
Arnold A. Rogow
(political scientist)
C. Easton Rothwell (historian)
Robert Rubenstein (psychiatrist)
Bruce M. Russett
(political scientist)
Renzo Sereno (political scientist)
Bruce L. Smith
(political scientist)
Ivan A. Vlasic (lawyer)
Douglas Waples
(professor of library science)
Sergius Yakobson (historian)

Possibly a few significant coauthors of his researches in Europe, India, Peru, Hong Kong, or elsewhere have been inadvertently omitted from this list: it is no small job to keep track of the far-flung Lasswellian publications. At all events, many people who have been his collaborators or assistants have testified to his eagerness to cooperate, his patience and considerateness, his cheerful frankness in accepting criticism, his tact and humor in giving it, and the generosity with which he praises and encourages the efforts of others. (If there is, in the praise he bestows, a trace, at times, of the smiling and skilful psychiatrist's indulgence toward the pathetically confused patient, at least it seems apt to be more therapeutic than destructive. It flows from obvious kindness, or at least from courtesy and uncontentiousness, as well as from self-satisfaction.)

Whatever the childrearing habits, the early schooling, and the other interpersonal experiences that generated his almost incredible information-processing facilities, he seems to have been a prodigy in the Decatur, Illinois, high school. He was not only a high-grade student but a debater. He was an editor of the school paper, and valedictorian, and the winner of a competitive examination on modern history held by the University of Chicago (for which the prize was a scholarship at that university).

Among the strongest influences in his turning toward the social sciences were two of his high school teachers. One was Mrs. Lucy H. Nelson, a teacher of English, whom he has described as "living in a cosmopolitan world." She introduced him to such writers as Havelock Ellis and Karl Marx. The other was a teacher of civics, William Cornell Casey. The sensitive and effervescent Casey was intensely skeptical about easy solutions to public issues. He also had a sophisticate's interest in history, politics, psychology, the economy, and the field that was later to become known as semantics. In conversation he was a Socratic gadfly of the first order. In later years he studied at the London School of Economics and became a professor of social sciences at Millikin University, then at the University of Chicago, and finally at Columbia University. Unquestionably he stimulated both the depth and the range of Lasswell's curiosities and skepticism in many ways. In 1934 Lasswell wrote, in the preface to *World Politics and Personal Insecurity,* in rather typical wording, an acknowledgment of "my obligation to an inimitable friend of the last twenty years, William Cornell Casey, now of Columbia University, whose great acumen and tempered sensitivity are liberating and fructifying respites from an epoch heavy-laden with rancorous sterility."

THE COLLEGE YEARS

ENTERING the University of Chicago in 1918, the sixteen-year-old Lasswell, who had always felt a bit lonely because "I was usually younger than my schoolmates," was to encounter a number of other immensely capable parent-substitutes who added greatly to the indulgences (and diminished the deprivations) that he experienced in his omnivorous pursuit of more and more information.

The broad, multidisciplinary approach that is so characteristic of everything Lasswell has done was greatly strengthened by his exposure, as undergraduate and graduate student and as a young teacher, to the extraordinary department of sociology that evolved between about 1900 and the 1940s at the University of Chicago. Under the leadership of men like Albion W. Small and Charles Henderson, the "Chicago school" had developed a far more pronounced emphasis on social reform policy and on direct observation and quantitative research than was customary elsewhere. Especially after the recruitment in 1895 of William I. Thomas, who wrote, with Florian Znaniecki, the now classical study *The Polish Peasant in Europe and America*,[5] the department was largely inspired by, and recruited and trained to gratify, the enormously energetic fact-gathering and theory-building proclivities of Thomas and of Robert E. Park, whom Thomas had in turn recruited.

This highly empiricist department accentuated its own preoccupations and methods by a high degree of inbreeding. "With the exception of William F. Ogburn," writes Morris Janowitz,

> the new members of the Department of Sociology were trained at the University of Chicago. Ernest Burgess studied directly under both Thomas and Park. Ellsworth Faris, Louis Wirth, Robert Redfield and Everett Hughes were trained by Park after Thomas left the campus [in 1918, the year of Lasswell's arrival], but they all knew Thomas personally and were strongly influenced by his writings. . . . Subsequently, Samuel Stouffer and Herbert Blumer,

after they had been exposed to the same influences, joined the Department. . . . Stouffer's interest in attitude research was stimulated by Thomas and supported by the prior work of [L. L.] Thurstone, who had also been exposed to Thomas. . . . A host of graduate students from the period of Thomas and Park produced the empirical monographs about the city of Chicago which characterized the Chicago school.[6]

As is well known, Thomas laid great emphasis on voluminous interviews intended to produce "life-history documents" describing exhaustively the total careers and social mobility patterns of individuals, and also the lifelong patterns of their subjective experiences. He was also committed to the importance of participant-observation—actually sharing the lives of many of the people he studied. He was highly skeptical of the value of viewing them from a distance through the telescopes of the abstract sociological theories that were fashionable in his day. Yet the selection of individuals for study was to be guided in part by theory: they were to be chosen for their presumed representativeness for certain social groups or theoretical problems. But, for the most part, they and the groups and the problems for study were to be chosen on the basis of the sheer curiosity and informed hunches of the investigator; for Thomas was very much the pragmatist, ever open to the discovery of unexpected relationships, and convinced that the science of society was in its very infancy. Robert E. Park, in Lasswell's day, carried on and enriched this tradition, combining with it the theory-building techniques of such German sociologists as Georg Simmel and Max Weber (for Park had done his own doctorate in Germany).

The Chicago sociologists' emphasis on the life-history document may have laid groundwork for Lasswell's later preoccupation with the psychiatric case history as a means of gaining insight into social and political relations. One can surmise too that the unfettered pragmatism of the Chicago school may have dovetailed with the as yet unstructured scientific curiosities of a small-town undergraduate, newly arrived in that sprawling, brawling, multicultural metropolis. At least, it dovetailed *for a while*, until his more rigorous mind became impatient of local fact-gathering undisciplined by systematic macropolitical and macroeconomic theory.

That Lasswell was strongly drawn to the sociologists is attested by the fact that he read endlessly in the field and that a large part of his output in the opening years of his career consisted of articles and book reviews contributed to sociological journals. Thus, in 1925, he had no less than seven book reviews and one article in the *American Journal of Sociology*, and one article in the *Journal of Social Forces*. In 1926 he had five more reviews in the former, and in 1927, thirteen. (Naturally, all this was in addition to a book and two articles in the political science media.)

He also worked vigorously in economics. Although he does not appear to have emphasized it as much as political sociology, one of his first two articles, published in 1923, shortly after he received his bachelor's degree, was entitled "Political Policies and the International Investment Market."[7] Also, as mentioned above, his first published book, *Labor Attitudes and Problems* (with the economist Willard E. Atkins) appeared the following year. It was among the earliest and sprightliest texts in the field of labor economics. Thus, by the time he was well into graduate school, Lasswell was publishing across the board in the social sciences.

He also had interests in general philosophy. These were to flower into lifelong friendships and a number of collaborative inquiries with the philosophers T. V. Smith and Charles W. Morris, and were to lead him to undertake in the 1940s, with another philosopher, Abraham Kaplan, a formal and systematic statement (not unreminiscent of Aquinas' *Summa Theologica*) on the entire propositional structure of political science (*Power and Society: A Framework for Political Inquiry*).[8]

There is little doubt that Lasswell was predisposed to his later investigation of Freudian thought by his familiarity as an undergraduate and graduate student with John Dewey's pragmatism and with the "social interactionist" psychology of the philosopher

George Herbert Mead. This wholly naturalistic, empirically oriented view of the evolution of man in society had been developed during Mead's thirty years of teaching (1900–1930) at the University of Chicago, especially in a highly influential course called "Social Psychology." As Charles W. Morris has written, "Year after year students with psychological, sociological, linguistic, educational, philanthropic, and philosophical interests attended the course, frequently for a number of years; and book after book has borne testimony to the impact of Mead's ideas on his numerous students."[9] One of these students was Lasswell, who had both course work and numerous conversations with Dewey and Mead and their associates.

Thus, a rational, secular, holistic conception of personality in society and culture entered early into his education, under the influence of Dewey and Mead as well as of Thomas and Thomas' successors. Mead saw the "mind," the "self," the "I," the "me" as entirely the product of a human organism's having been born into his particular family and other social groups and having unconsciously incorporated the norms of these "significant others" and rationalized them into systems of self-identification and of ethical and social beliefs.

A similar influence was exerted upon Lasswell, he has said, by the parallel and equally naturalistic work of the logical positivist philosophers of the Cambridge school, especially Alfred North Whitehead, whose *Enquiry concerning the Principles of Natural Knowledge*[10] appeared in 1919 and was followed by his *The Concept of Nature* (1920)[11] and by *Symbolism: Its Meaning and Effect* (1928).[12] These books appealed greatly to Lasswell. Nor could any alert young man in the 1920s have failed to be impressed by both the philosophical and the reformist activities of Whitehead's great associate, Bertrand Russell, or by the positivist formulation of the science of semantics by C. K. Ogden and I. A. Richards in *The Meaning of Meaning* (1925).[13]

Nevertheless, in terms of personal solicitude, professional guidance, and all-around helpfulness, the most important influence upon Lasswell in his student years was probably Charles Edward Merriam (1874–1953), who was head of the Political Science Department in Lasswell's time. A large and genial man, Merriam was also a scholar of breadth and of some profundity. As an undergraduate at Lenox College (in Iowa) he had majored in classics and mathematics; in graduate school at Columbia University, in economics and politics. He felt considerably frustrated by what he took to be the narrowness of the conventional "Constitution-worshiping" political science of the day and its irrelevance to the realistic promotion of the good life. While Lasswell was still an undergraduate, Merriam apparently recognized this precocious youngster's potential and saw in him a means of advancing Merriam's own interests in what Merriam called "new aspects of politics"—especially the psychological aspects and the substitution of interviews, direct observation, voting statistics, attitude scales, and other quantifiable data for legalistic studies and armchair speculation about political developments.[14]

Charles Edward Merriam was well able to give a young scholar not only paternal encouragement and intellectual guidance but also much practical assistance. The son of a self-made small-town Iowa banker, he was interested both in immediate high returns and in risk-taking: the prudent investment and the decidedly hypothetical. Like Lasswell, he had Presbyterian antecedents and a mother who was a schoolteacher. After taking his doctorate at Columbia, he taught at Chicago all the rest of his life. He was very reflective although not highly verbal, and wrote a considerable shelf of books. They ranged from such unexceptionable topics as *The History of the Theory of Sovereignty since Rousseau* (1900; his doctoral dissertation)[15] and a conventionally phrased *History of American Political Theories* (1903)[16] to a variety of books on American political parties and political behavior, including *Chicago: A More Intimate View of Urban Politics* (1929), an empirical glimpse of the seamy side of life that somewhat upset the city fathers.[17] His life's ambition appears to have been to write a "great book" testing classical political theory against empirical political research, and he nearly achieved it in *Systematic Politics* (1945), which appeared shortly before his death.[18]

He was also an active civic reformer. From 1915 onward, he frequently campaigned for (and sometimes won) a seat on the Chicago Board of Aldermen. He cultivated a wealth of contacts among practical politicians of both the reform and the counter-reform elements. Many of these contacts he put at the disposal of his better students. Reflecting one of Merriam's interests, Lasswell's first published article was a participant-observer analysis of machine politics: "Chicago's Old First Ward: A Case Study in Political Behavior."[19]

As time went on and the Great Depression approached, Merriam's concerns embraced the national level as well. In 1929 he became a vice-president of President Herbert Hoover's Commission on Recent Social Trends, and from 1933 to 1943 he was a member of President Franklin Roosevelt's National Planning Board and its successors, and later of the Presidential Committees on Administrative Management and on Public Service Personnel.

Just as much to the point, for empirical research is always expensive, Professor Merriam developed extensive contacts among the well-to-do. He became an officer of such philanthropies as the Rosenwald Fund, the Laura Spelman Rockefeller Memorial Fund, and the Walgreen Foundation. From 1923 to 1927 he was president of the Social Science Research Council. Thus, financing was often available for the University of Chicago's projects in social science; and Lasswell was able to learn at an early age, and from a master, the delicate skills involved in raising money for expensive researches.

Not only Lasswell but also several other young empiricists were given generous encouragement and facilities by Merriam. One of these men was Harold F. Gosnell, a Spelman Fund grantee who became famous as an early quantifier of data on voting behavior and as the author of first-hand studies of Negro politicians,[20] of Chicago's machine politics,[21] and of the political tactics of Franklin D. Roosevelt,[22] to name just a few of his many writings. Another was Frederick L. Schuman, who became a celebrated professor and prolific writer in the field of international relations. Yet another was Quincy Wright, also one of the major figures in the empirical as well as the legal analysis of international relations, whom Merriam brought to Chicago from the University of Minnesota as a full professor at the age of thirty-three. Another productive member of the department was Leonard D. White, in public administration. In addition to Merriam himself and his colleagues Wright and White, five of Merriam's students eventually became presidents of the American Political Science Association: Gabriel A. Almond, V. O. Key, Lasswell, C. Herman Pritchett, and David B. Truman.

Professor Merriam's active interests ran the gamut from the minor politicians and the machine-ridden voters and administrators in Chicago's grimier wards to the major questions of world affairs. His interest in the latter had been stimulated when he was still a graduate student: he had spent the academic year 1899–1900 in the study of political thought at the Universities of Paris and Berlin and had returned with uneasy feelings. His fears were borne out by his first-hand observations of the frightfulness of World War I. He spent 1917 and 1918 in Italy as a captain in the Signal Corps and as a propagandist for the United States Government's Committee on Public Information, the first officially organized incarnation of the present-day United States Information Agency. He wrote of some of his experiences in "American Publicity in Italy,"[23] and from 1919 onward he went frequently to Europe to see how things were going.

A devotee of skepticism and of what he called "political prudence," Merriam found it hard to stomach either the military and propagandistic excesses of the war or the uncritical acceptance of bright-eyed Wilsonian idealism. It was a period when the League of Nations appeared to some to hold great promise, but it also seemed to writers like John Maynard Keynes that the dragon's seed had already been sown by the Treaty of Versailles, the Congressional defeat of Wilsonianism, and the American nation's regression into Babbittry and "business as usual" under such presidents as Harding and Coolidge. Merriam increasingly felt a need for a thorough empirical study of the psychology, sociology, and politics of nationalism. His feelings about this were to have great implications for Lasswell (and also for Schuman and Quincy Wright and many of their students).

In 1922, at the age of twenty, Lasswell, who by now had quite a reputation as a scholar and as a frequent collegiate debater, received his bachelor's degree at Chicago. Merriam immediately employed him as a teaching assistant and facilitated his going, for fifteen months during 1923 and 1924 and again in the summer of 1925, to study at the Universities of London, Geneva, Paris, and Berlin. In 1925 Lasswell published two articles. Both were on topics very close to Merriam's own experiences and concerns.

One was "Prussian Schoolbooks and International Amity."[24] Its aim was to disclose any content that "might be regarded as dangerous for international reconciliation . . . to uncover anything which presents any foreign nation or all foreign nations as an enemy; which puts foreigners in an unfavorable light; which exalts war by glorifying military heroes and military successes; which tends to feed national vanity by direct or strongly implied assertions of superiority." An attempt was made, he says, "in every case to indicate by some quantitative measurement the importance of the item to which reference is made." The methods used were rather simple, but it was one of the earliest examples of the technique that was to become known as "content analysis" or "quantitative semantics," and that, in far more elaborated forms, was to make Lasswell famous in later years.

The other article he did in 1925, in a neighboring field, was "The Status of Research on International Propaganda and Opinion."[25] In 1926 he wrote, and in 1927 Alfred A. Knopf published, his dissertation, *Propaganda Technique in the World War*.[26] This not only reflected many of Merriam's interests but embodied much of Lasswell's analytic skill. It was an important step in the initiation of Lasswell's career as perhaps the world's foremost specialist, and the originator of many unexpected tech-

niques, in the scientific analysis of propaganda and later of communication processes in general.

The dissertation was timely in topic and was (for that day)
somewhat sensational in tone. Unreservedly objective with respect
to each of the governments concerned, it pulled no punches in
describing the duplicity and irrationality to which elites resort
in wartime. It also pointed the way to more profound study of
the reasons why the masses so often believe, or at least *do*, what
they are told. Thus it laid a part of the groundwork for a nine-
volume series of studies by several authors, which Merriam was
to initiate and coedit, entitled "Studies in the Making of Citizens." In these volumes, comparative analyses were undertaken
of the "civic training" (through textbooks, youth organizations,
religious experience, political parties, and other media) received
by young people in several countries, including the USSR, the
USA, Nazi Germany, and Mussolini's Italy. It was a start toward
the study of what we refer to today as "political socialization."[27]

The rapidly spreading fame of Lasswell's book at home and
abroad enabled him to receive, for 1928–29, a Social Science
Research Council fellowship for further study in Europe. This
led to a major turning point in his own career and in the development of the entire "Chicago school" of political science: it was on
this trip, apparently, that Lasswell first became fully alert to the
political implications of both psychoanalysis and Marxism.

THE MEETING OF FREUD AND MARX

WHILE in Berlin he undertook, out of both personal and scientific curiosity, to be psychoanalyzed. The analyst was Theodor
Reik, a well-known writer on psychanalytic theory and a first-
generation disciple of Freud. As noted above, it is probable that
Lasswell was already in some ways predisposed to accept the
major propositions of Freudian theory by his study of Havelock
Ellis and of W. I. Thomas' conceptions of "social personality,"
as well as by his knowledge of the "symbolic interactionism" of
Alfred North Whitehead and George Herbert Mead. In the mid-

dle 1920s, too, the psychological views of Graham Wallas, expressed in his *The Great Society*[28] and in *Human Nature in Politics*,[29] were in the air, as were the laboratory discoveries of Ivan Pavlov and John B. Watson on conditioned reflexes. It seemed as if the psychologists were about to revolutionize everyone's thought about the nature of man and society.

But Thomas, Mead, Wallas, Whitehead, and the Pavlovians were far from being Freudian. For one thing, Mead and Whitehead, and even the reflexologists, although persuasive intellectually, held forth on a very high plane of generality. To be sure, Thomas was highly conscious of the role of sexuality; and Mead, like Freud, had stressed the cross-pressures among components of the personality: within Mead's "self," the "I" and the "me" watched and at times opposed each other, very much like the "ego" and the "superego" in Freud. These other writers, however, did not have Freud's clinical experience, nor had they his knowledge and boldness concerning exciting particulars and extreme pathological cases. For a perceptive young man of twenty-six brought up in the Thomas and Merriam traditions of direct empiricism and participant observation, Mead and Whitehead and Pavlov and Watson opened the door to highly generalized naturalistic thinking about personality in society, but it was observation in the mental hospital and participant observation on the psychoanalytic couch that produced the "real data." Freud was trying to discover *all* the facts, however depressing or repulsive or contrary to received doctrine. Moreover, Freud, like Lasswell, was given to holistic theorizing about the total sets of forces *behind* the immediately observed phenomena. All this was in refreshing contrast to the tendency of many American thinkers of that day to settle for euphemism and for partial or "middle-level" theory.

Also, Lasswell, with his grounding in philosophies and social sciences, was quick to see that Freud's insights, although drawn from the specific life-histories and mechanisms of particular patients at a particular point in history and geographic space, could profitably be generalized, at least provisionally, to far broader realms of thought. Since prominent politicians and other leaders, as well as the social underdogs, so often presented a clinical picture involving symptoms well known to psychiatry, Lasswell conjectured that it might be possible to reduce social disorder by some form of preventive or curative mental hygiene. To test this view, however, it would first be necessary to secure dependable records of the admittedly ill and then to generalize valid inferences from them to those whom society regarded as "normal" and to those who had only *some* of the symptoms that lead a desparate human being to the psychoanalytic couch.

In 1929 Lasswell produced two articles on the problems of securing adequate personality records and on the study of the ill as a method of research on political personalities.[30] In 1930 he published his celebrated *Psychopathology and Politics*.[31] It was a book that somewhat irreverently removed the fig leaf from many a statuesque politician, administrator, and jurist, and it caused more than one political theorist to cover his *id* in sudden embarrassment. As if at a shotgun wedding, traditional political science —the political science of such austere and inhibited figures as Frank J. Goodnow, Woodrow Wilson, John W. Burgess, and William Archibald Dunning—was invited to embrace neo-Freudianism.

Unabashedly the book proclaimed that "our problem is to be ruled by the truth about the conditions of harmonious human relations, and the discovery of the truth is an object of specialized research" (p. 197). And the truth, as Lasswell saw it, is that human motives (including political and economic motives) are generated very largely in the nursery, in the bedroom, in childhood sexual and excretory experiences and reveries, and in a whole network of interpersonal contacts generally thought of as "private." The whole of political science, he declared, may be conceived most realistically as the study of the extremely intricate ways in which "private motives," arising in private lives and elaborated frequently into wholly unrealistic fantasies and reveries, become more or less unconsciously and irrationally displaced onto "public causes" and political and military crusades, and then adorned (after the fact) with sanctifying and moralistic rationalizations—in the name of patriotism, justice, religion, the class struggle, racial superiority, the rights of man, or whatever symbols are psychologically and socially acceptable at the moment. The idea is familiar and well accepted now; thirty-nine years ago, when it appeared, it was a bit of a shocker.

It follows, he said, that the traditional theorists have all been barking up the wrong trees.

> Generalizing broadly, political methods have historically been of three kinds: the methods of violence, of exhortation, and of discussion. . . . The contribution of politics has been thought to be in the elaboration of methods by which conflicts are resolved. . . . In some vague way, . . . this is at once assumed to depend upon the modification of the mechanisms of government. Democratic theorists in particular have hastily assumed that social harmony depends upon discussion, and that discussion depends upon the formal consultation of all those affected by social policies. The time has come to abandon the assumption. . . . Discussion frequently complicates social difficulties, for the discussion by far-flung interests arouses a psychology of conflict which produces obstructive, fictitious and irrelevant values. The problem of politics is less to solve conflicts than to prevent them; less to serve as a safety valve for social protest than to apply social energy to the abolition of the recurrent sources of strain in society. This redefinition of the problem of politics may be called the idea of preventive politics. The politics of prevention draws attention squarely to the central problem of reducing the level of strain and maladaptation in society. . . . In some measure it will proceed by improving the machinery of settling disputes, but this will be subordinated to a comprehensive program [*Psychopathology and Politics*, pp. 196–97].

The "comprehensive program" is in many respects analogous to the modern practice of preventive medicine, which emphasizes immunization and hygiene as better than the treatment of an epidemic of cholera or yellow fever after it occurs. In effect, Lasswell "draws attention squarely" to the advisability of considering "society as a patient" (to borrow a term coined, apparently, by

Lawrence K. Frank) and of training the "social doctors"—political scientists, sociologists, economists, teachers, judges, attorneys, and all others in positions of authoritative decision-making—in preventive mental hygiene.

Here, then, is no naïve Rousseauian or early Marxian faith in the vast good sense of the uninstructed electorate, and no naïve Madisonian faith in a political and economic pluralism whose invisible hand, like that of the classical economists, balances "interest groups" and "regional groups" against each other and in the long run produces a magical cure-all for the ills of society. On the other hand, it is not a justification of any kind of dictatorship, whether individual or collective:

> The recognition that people [at the present low levels of mass and elite education] are poor judges of their own interest is often supposed to lead to the conclusion that a dictator is essential. But no student of individual psychology can fail to share the conviction of Kempf that "Society is not safe . . . when it is forced to follow the dictations of one individual, or of one autonomic apparatus, no matter how splendidly and altruistically it may be conditioned" [*ibid.*, 197].

In fact, the Lasswellian belief, as here set forth, is close to Jefferson's faith in the possible ultimate educability of elites and masses, through the study of natural and social sciences. But Lasswell would add to Jeffersonian general education the study of psychiatry to a level at which people can practice mental hygiene and preventive politics for themselves by general consensus, much as they already have begun to accept and practice preventive measures of public health, such as vaccination and the fluoridation of water.

The whole idea, including a number of the major Freudian postulates that underlie it, may be considered to be generally accepted by the university-educated today—at least in principle or tentatively. But in 1930 it aroused a certain amount of resistance, as it continues to do in some quarters even now.

One reason for the resistance is that parts of *Psychopathology and Politics* were hastily, even incoherently, drafted. Even though the opening pages declare that the enterprise is "highly provisional," the reader is often left wondering whether the upshot of the book has been, as proclaimed in the opening pages, the production of proof as to "what developmental experiences are significant for the political traits and interests of the mature" and to "deepen our understanding of the whole social and political order," or whether the result has simply been to suggest a number of rather provocative hypotheses for possible future research. Perhaps Lasswell would grant today that the chains of reasoning and the adduction of evidence in *Psychopathology and Politics* are decidedly inconclusive. And perhaps this hastiness of draftsmanship is one of the reasons why behavioral scientists in the ensuing thirty-seven years have published very few political biographies that attempt to put Lasswell's categories to use. Additional reasons would include, of course, the extreme difficulty of getting such intimate data and especially of publishing the data while the subject, his relatives, his physician(s), his psychiatrist(s), his attorney(s), and his immediate heirs are still alive. It may well be that the most fruitful use of the psychiatric life-history, at least for the study of *high-level* political and economic processes, will be found in the analysis of persons who have been dead for two or three generations or longer but whose careers are sufficiently parallel to those of the living to furnish highly suggestive insights. Two valuable illustrations of what is meant here are the psychoanalytic biographies of Woodrow Wilson by Alexander L. George and Juliette L. George,[32] and of Defense Secretary James V. Forrestal by Arnold A. Rogow.[33] These writers acknowledge indebtedness to Lasswell, whose writings on power and personality, they say, have provided some of the central ideas.

There is the further fact that the time that would be needed for the adequate psychiatric training of future social scientists, jurists, and so on, during their college years, has tended to be crowded out of the curriculum by the "knowledge-explosion" of recent years concerning such investigative techniques as survey research, attitude-scaling, and efforts to design empirically testable "systems models." It is generally far easier for a graduate student in the present generation to see why he should spend, say, two years acquiring sophistication and statistical techniques with respect to these matters instead of two years or more undergoing a clinical training course and reading psychiatry. And it is very time-consuming and expensive to do both. (We leave aside such questions as whether foundations and governments are sufficiently willing to support the relevant psychiatric training, and whether optimal teaching materials have been written.)

In any event, what insufficiency in draftsmanship there was in *Psychopathology and Politics* was largely made up by Lasswell in a rigorous essay published in 1954, entitled "The Selective Effect of Personality on Political Participation."[34] In this essay he stated in very orderly fashion not only the personality variables that interplay in various types of political personalties, but also the types of social opportunities and social constraints that determine whether people actually get a chance to act out their impulses upon the public stage.

His trips to Europe in connection with his psychoanalysis and his subsequent researches in psychopathology brought him entrée into the company of a great many of the most distinguished European psychiatrists and psychoanalysts—people like Alfred Adler, Franz Alexander, Paul Federn, Sandor Ferenczi, Erich Fromm, Karen Horney, and their eminent colleagues in America and elsewhere such as Harry Stack Sullivan, Clara Thompson, and Sullivan's great teacher, William Alanson White. He also gained entrée to broader European circles that were outstanding in history and the social sciences.

He was impressed, he has said, with the general superiority of intellectual life in Europe in the 1920s and 1930s to that in the United States. Europeans were more likely to enjoy, like Lasswell, the sustained reading of history as well as of scientific materials. Nor did they shy away, like so many Americans, from the very mention of the "pure theory" and "philosophy" that might be derived from these things. To the impudent young Lasswell, it even seemed that there were some American university professors who were historically and theoretically shallow. They were, as he saw them, imbued with an amorphous frontiersman-like pragmatism and given to the unreflective collection of ill-assorted data. They were no match at all for the better Europeans, especially in the fields of social and political theory.

As a matter of fact, Europe probably *did* have, in the 1920s and early 1930s, the commanding intellectual lead that Lasswell attributed to it, even though the United States has very probably surpassed Europe in a number of respects since then—thanks in part to its importation and imitation of major European theorists, ranging from natural scientists like Einstein, Enrico Fermi, Leo Szilard, and Edward Teller to social theorists like Karl W. Deutsch, Carl Friedrich, Erich Fromm, Friedrich von Hayek, Hans Kelsen, Henry Kissinger, Paul F. Lazarsfeld, Hans Morgenthau, Franz Neumann, Louis B. Sohn, and Hans Speier, to mention only a very few.

At any rate, the young man was impressed—and especially impressed by the fact that his training in the United States did not seem to have included sufficient mention of a number of Europeans who turned out, on inspection of their work, to have been really major social thinkers. Among these, for example, were Karl Mannheim, Roberto Michels, Gaetano Mosca, and Vilfredo Pareto, who had done great jobs of data collection as well as of theorizing on political symbolisms and on the sociology and psychology of the "ruling" or "political" classes; Max Weber, whose massive and meticulous historical and theoretical works Lasswell read appreciatively, he has said, as they appeared in the *Archiv für Sozialwissenschaft*, although these were almost unknown in the United States until after World War II, even among the sociologists, for whom Weber became a great god when he was finally discovered; Werner Sombart, whose impressive historical works are still not widely known in America; and, above all, Karl Marx, who was scarcely alluded to in the political science schools in this country in the 1920s, even by such free and adventurous spirits as Charles Edward Merriam. The silence about Marx was caused in part by the fact that America was protected by geographic distance and its own affluence and provincialism from a realization of the significance of the class struggles in Europe, and in part by the "red scares" of the early 1920s, which apparently intimidated a considerable portion of the intelligentsia.

But Marxism was on the lips of all manner of people in Europe. The inherent ambiguity of the Marxist doctrine made possible the rationalization of a great range of political and social movements, from the most militant Leninism to the gentlest parliamentary reformism, in the name of "Marxian socialism." And it appeared to many that one or another of the Marxist or other "socialist" movements was almost certain to come to power eventually in Western Europe, as it already had done in the Soviet Union and seemed likely to do in China. After all, Mussolini had only recently spoken the language of socialism, and even the right-wing ethnocentric elements in Germany were organizing under the label of a National *Socialist* German *Workers'* Party. In general, the First World War could plausibly be explained in Marxian terms, and the Great Depression that ravaged Asia and Europe throughout the 1920s and the United States after 1929 appeared to many to conform to the Marxian image of a "crisis of capitalism" that could lead only through revolution (or drastic reform) to a further "victory of socialism."

Besides, the main political leaders of the Marxist movements, both Communist and Revisionist, were intellectuals of considerable stature (especially as compared with such leaders as Warren Harding and Calvin Coolidge). These leaders declared proudly that they were equipped with a comprehensive theory of universal history and of social, political, and economic change, and that the essence of Marxism (again, whether militant or revisionist) was "the unity of theory and practice." To an omnivorous theorist like the twenty-eight-year-old Lasswell it must have seemed obvious that the least one could do would be to undertake a thorough analysis of the theoretical structures and the behavioral patterns of the Marxist movements and their principal rivals. But of course it would be naïve to do so without taking fully into account as well the immensely important insights of Freud (and of the symbolic interactionist school in general) concerning the structures and intensities of the unconscious impulses—the "private motives"—of which the political movements were but the rationalized "displacements onto public causes."

It took even the fast-moving Lasswell about four years to do his reading on this and to draft his formulation. From 1931 through 1934 he published very little: only about fifteen articles (nearly all of them rather popularized restatements of points he had made in *Psychopathology and Politics*, but some of them important portions of his new endeavor), plus about twenty-five book reviews (mostly of books on psychiatry, but a number on politics) and about ten articles for the forthcoming *Encyclopedia of the Social Sciences*. With this light publishing schedule, and only a normal load of teaching and lecturing, he was able to get Marx and the Marxists psychoanalyzed (to his own satisfaction, though possibly not to theirs) by 1933. The diagnosis came out first in a brilliant and eloquent article entitled "The Strategy of Revolutionary and War Propaganda" in *Public Opinion and World Politics*, edited by Quincy Wright.[35]

> That the masses may be lured to action by millennial hopes is one of the oldest experiences of our society. Marx and Engels were not entirely candid in their failure to stress the utopian nature of their own symbol structure . . . but no one combined impressive documentation and propagandistic resonance as did Marx. . . . The great service of Marx had been to provide Western society with a singularly comprehensive theory of its destiny, enabling us to locate ourselves as transitional formations in the process by which the "classless" society of the future may emerge. That we may be led, even by the use of the dialectical method (as critically expounded by [Georg] Lukács), to dissent from the formulations of Marx is less important than that we shall be stimulated to sustained efforts at orientation.

Thus, Marx is a major thinker, even if "not entirely candid," but in the light of psychoanalytic theory we are obliged to note that the egocentricity of politics is somewhat obscured by the necessity which each individual senses for associating himself with some symbol of collective aspiration. He is too weak to say, "I want perfect safety, all the goods and services I can imagine, all the homage I can dream of." He must obtain his safety, income and deference somewhat surreptitiously by attaching himself to a collective symbol, like "patriot" or "proletarian." . . . [The full] lingual process does not unroll itself as a consecutive conscious process in the person; but the psychoanalytic method, when applied to representative persons, gradually reveals this structure by permitting the full waking elaboration of all the intervening steps.

Thus Marx and Engels, "by the sheer massing of detail in the architectonic of *Das Kapital* and the supporting publications . . . simply utilized the apparatus which, according to the [communication] styles of the nineteenth century, was most efficient in extracting deference." Thus "apparatus" was able to arouse a partially rational but partially irrational hostility to the existing social order. But other political movements, of course, have sought to do this. "The superiority of Marxism to many of its competitors" arises not only from its generally more impressive historical scholarship and rationality but also from the rather extreme *ir*rationality of its treatment of the future.

Marx left the socialist state ambiguous, speaking of the classless society as an utterly novel social formation which is incomprehensible by analogies from our experience with classbound societies. This left the future open for the gratifying fantasies most agreeable to the individual. . . . The symbol of the "classless society" frees the omnipotence cravings of the individual to transform [i.e., to imagine] the world in ways most gratifying to his yearnings for power. The person is free to project his potency fantasies into the future, and to identify himself with this remodeled symbol. . . . The words which are used to refer to the past and the future are not handled as tentative conjectures but as overwhelming compulsions of the world historical process. . . . Dialectical materialism is the reading of private preferences into universal history, the elevating of personal aspirations into cosmic necessities, the remolding of the universe in the pattern of desire, the completion of the crippled self by incorporating the symbol of the triumphant whole. No competing proletarian symbolism rose to such heights of compulsive construction; no rival was able to offer self-determination in utopia in the guise of overwhelming external coercion.

Much more is said in this essay, especially about the organization of revolutions and the recruitment and activities of their "symbol-carriers," but perhaps these excerpts will suffice to indicate that the meeting of Freud and Marx in the mind of Lasswell had produced a rather novel conception of world politics and of future scientific procedure. We can learn a great deal from Marxian (and other) world-historic scholarship, he felt, but we must learn from Freud how not to kid ourselves about the utopian elements that have consciously or unconsciously been imbedded in it. Specifically, if theory is to guide us to understanding of reality, we must demand tentative specifications of the future—provisional extrapolations of known trend lines from the past to specified points in the future—not mere timeless utopian visions concerning some state of affairs that has never existed before.

Here, then, is the beginning of Lasswell's years of preoccupation with the deliberate, self-conscious use of alternative "developmental constructs"—a preoccupation that he was to carry forward after World War II in very large projects of trend-line research at Stanford University's Hoover Institution and later in connection with the Yale Political Data Program begun about 1962 and currently in progress. One impressive result of this work is the set of projections to 1975 in *World Handbook of Political and Social Indicators*, edited in 1967 by Bruce M. Russett, Hayward Alker, Jr., and others, in collaboration with Lasswell and Karl W. Deutsch.[36] (Analogous efforts are being made by those who currently term themselves "futurists," exemplified in *The Year 2000: A Framework for Speculation on the Next Thirty-three Years*, by Herman Kahn and Anthony J. Wiener.)[37]

With Marx, Engels, and their followers thus psychoanalyzed, and with the proper lessons drawn from both Marx and Freud as to our future methodological if not political conduct, it remained to compare the Marxian social movements with their forerunners and principal current competitors, and thus to arrive at a provisional, all-encompassing diagnosis of our times. This Lasswell published in *World Politics and Personal Insecurity*.[38]

WORLD POLITICS AND PERSONAL INSECURITY

World Politics and Personal Insecurity is a large and difficult book that future critics may well consider its author's masterpiece. In a sense, almost all of his multifarious activities for the ensuing thirty-odd years might be thought of as elaborations, revisions, clarifications, and testings of many of the main ideas in this one volume. No attempt can be made here to summarize or paraphrase its line of argument, but a characterization of it can be offered in the hope of shedding some light on Lasswell's later activities and further intellectual growth.

Perhaps it can be described most aptly as a systematic, multidisciplinary study in the general historical sociology, or the sociological history, of the entire world in recent centuries. In this respect it closely resembles, in conception if not in particulars, the type of universalist historical sociology that has recently been called for by Raymond Aron at the University of Paris and by Stanley Hoffmann at Harvard in Part III of Hoffman's *Contemporary Theory in International Relations*.[39] While fulfilling the general criteria specified by these writers, it adds a dimension that they did not (and might not) recommend: a neo-Freudian brand of social interactionism.

Probably it is this neo-Freudian dimension that makes the book difficult to read, and even impossible to comprehend, for a considerable number of people who might otherwise enjoy it. A full understanding of it calls for a familiarity with the literature and practices of psychiatry and psychoanalysis that few political scientists or historians have ever found time for. At the time the book was written, it must have seemed plausible to its author—

and certainly it seemed plausible to a number of the graduate students at Chicago—that in the ensuing generation a thorough study of personality theory and of the essentials of psychiatry would become a standard part of almost every political scientist's training. A large proportion of all graduate students, it seemed, would undertake clinical studies, and possibly undergo "didactic" or "training" psychoanalysis, as part of acquiring the regular kit of professional tools. The kit also would include, of course, the old familiar tools like the history of social thought and the comparative description and analysis of local, provincial, national and international political, economic, administrative, and judicial systems.

If such a course of study were followed, it would be reasonably easy for the student to peruse a book like *World Politics and Personal Insecurity* and to enrich the literature himself by executing some of the prolonged and sophisticated research the volume called for. If this were done, and if the influence of this way of thinking diffused to wider and wider circles at home and abroad, we might see the slow evolution of that discriminating "Psychiatry of Peoples" which Harry Stack Sullivan called for in chapter 22 of his *The Interpersonal Theory of Psychiatry*.[40] Eventually, through teaching and publication, the sociopsychiatric pattern of thought and action might spread throughout society (as thought and action concerning preventive medicine, for example, are already doing). Our descendants, then, might see the gradual dawning of the "free man's commonwealth," the rational, humanistic, worldwide Great Society, cheerfully adopting the right childtraining habits, the right sex practices, the norms of humane "preventive politics," the more abundant economy, and the cooperative sharing of all the values that can be shared.

Just possibly this vision, however firmly held in check by scientific tentativeness, was about as utopian as that of Marx and Engels. But in this case at least it was plainly labeled a "developmental construct" and the mind was kept open to the collection of trend-line evidence and the possible building of other constructs. Just possibly, however, there might be enough reasonableness, self-discipline, and love in the human community at large (as there clearly was in some quarters of the psychiatric and social-scientific communities) to give the construct some validity —even though Father Freud, in *Civilization and Its Discontents,*[41] was pessimistic about this. (But after all, it was plain enough that Freud had never *really* studied the social sciences, and also that his relation to his father had been none too good.)

On publication, *World Politics and Personal Insecurity* was met with a kind of pop-eyed disbelief and dismay in many quarters. It received one of the most hostile reviews ever printed, in the *American Political Science Review* for June, 1935. (Indeed, it was not for another twenty years that Lasswell was elected president of the American Political Science Association.) On the other hand, George E. G. Catlin, the British political theorist, whose reactions were rather more typical of the European view, declared in the *Saturday Review of Literature* (April 20, 1935), that the book was

> a testimony of work in progress from that Chicago group, including Professors Merriam and T. V. Smith, that is beyond question making the most interesting and potentially important contribution to political theory in our generation. . . . If the Chicago school is successful in its attempt, . . . all earlier political theory will retain only that value which appertains to the writings of any intelligent layman. It alone takes the phrase "political science" seriously. It alone insists that politics is a quantitative study. Professor Lasswell is at each point prepared to test his psychological hypotheses by quantitive surveys. . . . Further, no intermediary study between this and Marx is of the same theoretical importance. That is a big claim. It will be for the future work of Professor Lasswell, rather than for the present small volume, to sustain this claim. . . . It is a striking attempt to bring in the new world of psychology to redress the old balance of economics. It will be recognized as an epoch-making book by those who are acquainted with the literature of the subject, and who are not committed to what Mr. Lasswell maliciously calls the "warfare of the universities on truth."

Here was a challenge to serious thought and research. But as things turned out, it was only shortly after the publication of

World Politics and Personal Insecurity that the Nazi horde descended upon Europe. Preoccupation with World War II and with its aftermaths—the Cold War, the dread tensions of the atomic age, the decolonialization and redevelopment of the new states—diverted the attention of many people in the behavioral science communities from what might have been the multidisciplinary discussion of the psychological and social roots of all these insecurities. Many of those who might have become the analysts of "preventive politics" have become, in effect, atomic air-raid wardens and economic first-aid administrators. (For a vigorous recent protest against the failure to take more significant preventive measures on the psychological level, see Hadley Cantril, *The Human Dimension: Adventures in Policy Research*.) [42] As already indicated, a further diversion of attention from these matters has been caused by the proliferation of new statistical and research methodologies and naïve "simulations" and "computerizations" that do not seem to those concerned to require a knowledge of psychological fundamentals, or even of social history.

For all this, it seems clear that the general line of thinking presented in *World Politics and Personal Insecurity*, although shorn of many of its specifically neo-Freudian features, has made considerable headway in the behavioral-scientific and even the policymaking communities. This can be traced in part to the more or less independent discovery of similar perspectives and data by a host of other investigators and in part to the industrious research and promotional activities of Lasswell himself, to which we now turn.

LASSWELL'S INTELLECTUAL ACTIVITY SINCE *WORLD POLITICS AND PERSONAL INSECURITY*

It was not to be expected that such matters as the excesses of the Stalin and Chiang Kai-shek eras, the Spanish Civil War, the Second World War, the Chinese Communist Revolution, the Cold War, or the prospect of the Last World War—the thermonuclear one—would give much pause to the perennially energetic Mr. Lasswell. "The best thing to do is to take these things in stride and proceed with our clarifications," he once said, with a rather taut expression, to a discouraged research assistant. In the space available here, we cannot begin to give a detailed idea of his efforts, over the past three decades, to harness some of the energies of each of these successive tides of history and to put them to use both in the testing and in the promotion of the ideas of "preventive politics," "social psychiatry," and the "free man's commonwealth." A look at his bibliography at the end of the present book will give some idea of the range of his enterprises, as will some of the other essays herein. At present we shall only try to characterize, very briefly, seven major intellectual contributions that he has made since *World Politics and Personal Insecurity* in the course of an intellectual odyssey that some day could be the subject of a fascinating book, or several. The seven are interrelated, of course—they are parts of a large, coherent pattern—but will be considered separately here for convenience. We can list them thus, and take up each in turn:

1. Organization of the academic field now known as "propaganda, communication, and public opinion"
2. Inventing procedures for the quantitative as well as the qualitative analysis of the contents of reverie and of communication in general
3. Development of alternative theoretical constructs concerning the worldwide evolution of elites and social systems
4. Specification of a theory of values
5. Establishment of linkages between classical political thought and empirical political science
6. Studies in legal theory, and specification of a theory of legal education
7. Collection of world-level trend-line data

1. *Organization of the Academic Field Now Known as "Propaganda, Communication, Public Opinion"*

In 1927, when *Propaganda Technique in the World War* was published, there was already a considerable literature on the connections between public opinion and propaganda and the other forms of communication. Walter Lippmann's influential *Public Opinion,* for example, had come out in 1922, and his *The Phantom Public* in 1925.[43] Ferdinand Toennies' *Kritik der öffentlichen Meinung*[44] and Freud's *Group Psychology and the Analysis of the Ego* also had appeared in 1922.[45] And a number of other highly suggestive writings were in circulation, especially among sociologists and in the budding field of social psychology.

But most of these writings were predominantly speculative, and few people knew just what or where, or of what value, the major and minor writings were. In 1925 Lasswell put down some views on one aspect of this in his article "The Status of Research on International Propaganda and Opinion."[46] This and related writings by Lasswell and others called attention to the desirability of very much fuller study, and contributed to the establishment in 1931 (apparently largely under the inspiration of Merriam and Lasswell) of the Social Science Research Council's Committee on Pressure Groups and Propaganda. Others on the Committee were Professors Ralph D. Casey (director of the University of Minnesota's School of Journalism), Merle Curti (historian), Harold F. Gosnell, E. Pendleton Herring, Peter Odegard, and Schuyler Wallace (political scientists), and Kimball Young (social psychologist).

The committee's interest (and its funds) gave stimulus to a worldwide search for relevant books, articles, and government publications. It was conducted under the general guidance of Lasswell, and the first results appeared in 1935 in a volume entitled *Propaganda and Promotional Activities: An Annotated Bibliography* by Lasswell, Ralph D. Casey, and Bruce Lannes Smith.[47] It described some 4,500 titles, from all countries, times, and languages, and sought to cross-classify them in ways that would reveal the current state and future requirements of research. The significance of all this was discussed in an introductory essay by Lasswell, "The Study and Practice of Propaganda." To some extent this effort brought order into an area that previously had been researched in a very desultory way, if at all, and that in the next three decades was to become a major field of social-scientific activity.

The work was continued in a more elaborately annotated volume, published in 1946, with much fuller introductory essays by three writers (Bruce Lannes Smith, Harold D. Lasswell, and Ralph D. Casey, *Propaganda, Communication, and Public Opinion: A Comprehensive Reference Guide*).[48] International aspects of the field were further surveyed and described in a third volume published in 1956: Bruce Lannes Smith and Chitra M. Smith, *International Communication and Political Opinion*.[49] Comparison of these three guides to the literature can hardly fail to show a marked increase in the sophistication, the empiricism, and the abundance of research—much of it inspired directly by Lasswell or by his guiding ideals, some of it by his numerous students.

Another strong contributing force was the establishment in 1937 of the *Public Opinion Quarterly*, a journal published at Princeton University and devoted to the promotion and analysis of research in this general area. Lasswell was an editor at the start and for some years. Another contributing force, in which Lasswell has had less direct involvement but in which he has been a frequent consultant, has been the development of the art and science of public opinion polling and survey research, dating from the pioneering efforts of such men as George Gallup and Elmo Roper in the early 1930s.

2. *Quantitative and Qualitative Content Analysis*

One of the first and most obvious reactions of critics of *Psychopathology and Politics* and of *World Politics and Personal Insecurity* was that it was "impossible" to quantify data about flows of communication or reverie or the elements of dreams as reported to psychiatrists. "The contents of the human mind cannot be measured," it was claimed. Therefore, psychoanalytic research, it was alleged, would be forever useless to the social sciences. So Lasswell has spent many months, over the years, designing means of recording and coding in theoretically relevant categories the contents of all forms of communication, from symbolic references during waking reveries and nighttime dreams ("communications from one part of the self to another") to the ideological and propaganda slogans used in the world's principal political movements. These procedures were put to practical use on a fairly large scale, and were further developed, during World War II, when Lasswell was director of the War Communications Research Division, established by the United States Government in the Library of Congress.[50] (See especially *Language of Politics: Studies in Quantitative Semantics*, by Lasswell, Nathan C. Leites, *et al.*)

Work of a similar type was carried still further, on sixty-year trend lines (1890–1950), in the Hoover Institution Symbol Series, produced after World War II when Lasswell was codirector of the Hoover Institution Studies at Stanford University.[51] Innumerable other researchers in the now well-established field of communication analysis have followed or adapted Lasswell's procedures of content analysis. However, the expense of securing a staff capable of applying the procedures meticulously on a sufficiently large scale has thus far precluded production of the "world weather maps of public opinion" that Lasswell has long advocated.[52]

3. *Alternative Developmental Constructs on World Elites and Social Orders*

As already indicated, one of Lasswell's principal criticisms of Marx and Engels was that they assumed that there could be only one possible outcome—namely, world proletarian revolution—after the age of capitalism had reached its zenith. Lasswell, on the basis of a review of almost a century of historical experience since the days of Marx, and also on the basis of psychological theory, considered this prediction to be not a foregone conclusion but a hypothesis to be researched along with hypotheses about alternative outcomes.

Especially by the mid-1930s, after the left-wing revolutions of the 1920s had failed in many countries, and in view of developments in the USSR under Stalinism and of the unmistakable successes of Hitlerism in defeating the German left wing and the German trade unions and in mobilizing the German upper and middle classes for class war and foreign aggression in the name of nationalism and racism, it seemed obvious that a number of outcomes were possible besides the one foretold by Marx. Two major alternatives presented themselves in Lasswell's mind: the main social group ascending to top-level power (the "rising elite") in the contemporary world might not be the proletarians after all, but rather those elements of the middle social strata who had enough higher and specialized education and relevant experience to manipulate successfully the intricacies of modern high technology and the complexities of modern social organization, national and international. He labeled these contenders "the middle income skill groups."[53] The relatively humane and enlightened social order they might (with a little bit of luck) set up, he called a "skill commonwealth."[54] It is plain from his writing that this is an outcome he would like to see.

Alternatively, the contradictions within the capitalist and the communist camps, and the clashes between the two, might grow so great over such a long period that the only elements capable of maintaining minimum social order might be the military and the police—who might well take advantage of the new technologies of surveillance and repression to keep the world in their grip more or less permanently. These contenders he called "the specialists on violence." The social order they might establish he termed the "garrison state." This outcome he personally found uncongenial, but he found it sufficiently probable to require analysis.

> The picture of the garrison state that is offered here is no dogmatic forecast. Rather it is a picture of the probable. It is not inevitable. It may not even have the same probability as some other descriptions of the future course of development. What, then, is the function of this picture for scientists? It is to stimulate the individual specialist to clarify for himself his expectations about the future, as a guide to the timing of scientific work. Side by side

with this "construct" of a garrison state there may be other constructs; the rational person will assign exponents of probability to every alternative picture.[55]

We cannot here go into the rationale of these constructs or the evidence that may confirm or disconfirm them. Our point at the moment is simply that in posing them for analysis, and in leading the way in the collection of data concerning them by a considerable number of other students, he has focused attention upon concepts that appear to be of high value in orienting ourselves to modern times.[56]

4. *Specification of a Theory of Values*

Lasswell has also shed much light on how the problem of "values" is to be handled in social analysis. This clearly has been a thorny issue ever since a strong preoccupation with high levels of rationalism and empiricism has become prominent in philosophy and the human sciences. Can we hold, in effect, that the term "values" should never be mentioned in behavioral science? Should the social scientist confine himself to simply inventing "value-free measures of behavior" such as fighting, money-making, vote-casting, nonvoting, and so forth, without raising questions as to any teleological elements in human nature or social history or any generalized individual want-patterns or social orders whose realization such behavior assists? Some say yes. Others declare that human action must, "in the nature of things," be oriented toward long-term goals of individual and collective actors, and these, too, can be objects of study. But such commentators often flounder when asked to specify the goals.

Indeed, on the surface at least, what different people and peoples want appears to vary so widely from culture to culture, country to country, social level to social level, and epoch to epoch, as to defy classification. Is it possible to devise a set of terms for values that is appropriate for cross-cultural, cross-national, cross-class, and transhistorical analysis, and that can be used to specify the aims, if any, that all men everywhere have in common? If not, it seems likely that the correct world view is a kaleidoscopic cultural relativism whose political implication would be a sort of general intergroup anarchy, or at its worst a dog-eat-dog variety of social Darwinism. On the other hand, if the similarities among men's goals outweigh the differences, and if these similarities can be emphasized in spite of local variations, a universalist world culture becomes thinkable and a coherent world social order may be considered possible.

Lasswell's consistent position from the start has been that "key" values common to all men do exist and can be stated, though stated at first only on a high plane of abstraction. He considers it possible to do research on the specifications that are given the general value-terms by particular actors. And research, he feels, can show whether there is sufficient compatibility of particulars to establish a given social order—for example, to "make the world safe for diversity"—or even for unity.

In his early writings, he classified the "key values" pursued by individual and collective actors under three general categories that have become so widely current among social scientists that they resemble a nursery rhyme: "income, deference, and safety." Discovering that there may be certain misleadingly hedonistic, egocentric, and ethnocentric overtones in the repeated use of these terms, he later expanded the list of "key value" terms to eight. These also now appear to be in process of becoming a part of the common vocabulary of social science.

For about the past twenty years, Lasswell seems to have found his eight-term list of key values satisfactory. He has left it unchanged, and indeed has used it (often with a great deal of ad hoc specification) in all of his writings, as a characterization, in a conveniently generalized form, of the total human motivational system. Evidently he considers it short enough for ready memorization and the practical purposes of research, politics, and administration, yet long enough and well-worded enough to have a desirable degree of specificity and to lead investigators' minds to additional specifications without undue semantic confusion. He postulates that all men seek these eight "key values":

Power (an effective share in group decision-making at every level
of organization, from the family system to the world system)
Wealth (income)
Enlightenment (education, information, insight)
Well-being (safety, health, welfare, recreation)
Respect (deference, approval, prestige, recognition)
Skill (excellence in arts, occupations, professions)
Affection (love, friendship)
Rectitude (an inner feeling, and the attribution by others, of righ-
teousness; "good conscience")

In principle, the combinations and specifications of these
values that are preferred, and the actual distributions of individuals' and groups' receipts of these values, are measurable with
respect to any social system in the world. As research progresses,
it becomes increasingly possible to say to what extent the value
patterns preferred, and the values actually received, by given
groups are sufficiently compatible to furnish a basis for cultural,
economic, and political agreements—even for a worldwide political, cultural, and economic community.

Moreover, "democracy" can be explicitly defined in his terms.
It would be a social system in which receipts of every one of the
specified values are very widely shared among all individual actors
in the system. Its opposite, "despotism," is defined as a social
system in which the distribution of receipts of any one or more
values is decidedly inequitable. Perhaps no other social scientist
has done so much to bring the discussion of such emotive and
ambiguous terms as "democracy" and "despotism" out of the
clouds of meaningless controversy and into the light of intelligible discussion and measurement as Lasswell, through his indefatigable application of these measurements to social systems of
many types. For example, he has applied them (with Richard
Arens) to an analysis of the social consequences of the entire system of American law—national, state, and local;[57] to the question of how to preserve a maximum of individual freedom in
case the garrison state emerges in the United States;[58] to analysis
of the consequences of the emergence of various kinds of elites

in various parts of the world;[59] and to a variety of studies in world public order, with Myres S. McDougal and others.[60] With each new testing-out, the degree of their scientific and social relevance becomes apparent.

5. *Establishment of Linkages between Classical Political Thought and Empirical Political Science*

Lasswell has also come to grips with the intensely committed empiricists who have often considered the study of the classical political writers—especially of the more openly normative ones, such as Plato, Aquinas, or Kant—to be a waste of time. Likewise, he has confronted the wrath of intensely committed classicists who take the opposite view.

In his own broadly universalistic perspective, it is probable that all theorists, like all other men, are pursuing the same broad categories of values, albeit in somewhat different combinations and often with specifications that are conspicuously different, though not necessarily incompatible. Moreover, the works of classicists often include empirical data or ideas for gathering them. In addition, the works of empiricists invariably rest on sets of normative presumptions, even if these are unavowed. It follows that, with exposure to semantic and other scientific insights, some realization of the ultimate potential compatibility of seemingly very different value-constellations, and of differing "empirical" reports of the "same" facts, may dawn upon the actors. The problem is largely one of enabling thinkers to realize the extent to which, and the reasons why, they are viewing the same sets of events from different observational and evaluational standpoints. This view is abundantly confirmed, of course, by records of psychoanalytic therapy of families and other small groups, where murderous hostilities have often been found to be based on difficulties that are "merely verbal" though rooted deeply and truculently in unconscious assumptions that are unassailably rationalized until examined under analysis. Analogous sets of events can be seen in the cases of formerly "rival" philosophers and theologians—in ecumenical movements, for example—who have discovered that they were "talking about the same things all the time," although in strikingly different words.

In efforts to serve as a marriage counselor with respect to the possibly over-hasty divorce plans of aggrieved classicists and extreme empiricists, and also with the express aim of clarifying his own scheme of thought, Lasswell teamed up in the 1940s with Abraham Kaplan, a student of the philosophy of science. Kaplan had specialized in the theory of language, signs, and semantics as developed by such writers as Rudolf Carnap, Charles Morris, Hans Reichenbach, and Bertrand Russell, and had also been a productive member of the War Communications Research Division of the Library of Congress. Both men were keenly aware of the problems of putting the theory of research into practice. The object of their teamwork was "to elaborate a conceptual framework within which inquiry into the political process may fruitfully proceed," by reviewing the major propositions of classical theory and also the major propositions that appear to emerge from the "extraordinarily rapid expansion of empirical research, which had experienced an epoch of unparalleled richness in inventing and applying new methods of observing and processing data." In a word, what seemed to be empirically valid or promising from both the classicists and the empiricists was to be brought into a unified frame of reference possessing the utmost logical rigor.

The outcome was Lasswell and Kaplan's *Power and Society: A Framework for Political Inquiry*.[61] Some critics have seen it as a major contribution to the reorganization of political science in the light of the recent "empirical revolution." Others call it a sterile exercise in definition-writing and empty formalism. At any rate, in numbered paragraphs and with a deliberate formalism that might well have been the envy of Thomas Aquinas, it proceeds from the introduction of explicitly undefined terms to the construction from these of definitions. By means of these definitions it articulates a set of propositions concerning the functions, the structures, and the processes of politics—all this with much reference to writings by both classicists and empiricists. No justice can be done the substance of the argument in this brief space. Further, even between the time of writing and the time of publication, the ever-galloping Lasswell writes, there were "many changes, both in the state of research in the field and in our own thinking. . . . Practical considerations have made it seem preferable to offer the material in its present form rather than attempt once more to reformulate it in accord with our continuing changes of viewpoint on this or that detail" (p. vi). Suffice it to say that what was brought forth was an integration, in characteristically Lasswellian terminology, of a vast amount of philosophical and empirical political thought, in a form that may be broadly described as systematic structural-functional analysis.

It remains to be seen, of course, whether this ambitious effort at nondirective counseling will in fact stay the divorce proceedings between injured philosophy and presumptuous science. Also, debate continues on whether the orientation the book recommends for political research will turn out to have been fruitful or frightful. In any case, there is little question that it repays a reading, if only to alert the reader to the definitional and propositional complexities of what Catlin called "taking the phrase 'political science' seriously."

A far less definitional and far more substantive effort to join political philosophy with the new political science is found in a book entitled *Power, Corruption, and Rectitude,* written by Lasswell and Arnold A. Rogow, a political scientist with a broad range of interests in both classical thought and behavioral science. Its authors, intrigued by Lord Acton's celebrated dictum that "power tends to corrupt and absolute power corrupts absolutely," examine the views of a number of other classical writers on this question and then set out to establish that Acton's rule is by no means an iron law of politics. On the contrary, they find, the extent to which power and rectitude are incompatible depends entirely on the context; that is, whether opportunities, capabilities, and perspectives favorable to corruption exist among the actors concerned. Once more the remedy is "preventive politics": if values are appropriately shared, the actors' perspectives will not strongly favor corruption, nor will they have so many opportunities and capabilities for getting away with it. The authors even conclude that the trends of the time, in the United States at least, give reason to believe that "many antidemocratic tendencies built into the effective constitutions of federal, state, and local governments will dissolve and the many situations conducive to corruption will be no more."[62]

6. Studies in Legal Theory, and Specification of a Theory of Legal Education

William Cornell Casey, Lasswell's mentor in high school, was fond of saying, in later years when Casey was a professor at the University of Chicago, that "the education of one top-level lawyer is more important to society than the education of fifty social scientists." He meant, of course, that the reflective scientist may have ideas on what things *might* be done, but the practical, extroverted attorney is far more likely to see that things *do* get done. Especially in the United States, with its strong respect for written constitutions, its complicated network of state and federal jurisdictions, and its plethora of business contracts which dispose of most of the nation's resources, a tradition of litigiousness is all-pervasive. It is attorneys, not scientists or professors, who constitute the majorities in legislatures and judiciaries and who offer the most influential advice at top levels in the executive branches of government and big business. Hence Casey paid particular attention to prelaw students in his undergraduate teaching, and often urged the more promising of his non-prelaw students to consider going to law school.

Perhaps it was some such reasoning as this that caused Lasswell to leave the University of Chicago as soon as his career was well launched and to accept a position in 1938 in the Yale University Law School, where he has been ever since. Clearly this position has not inhibited his ability to engage in the massive projects of group and statistical research to which he has always been committed and on which he was already well started. It has, in addition, given him prestigious entrée to the corridors of influence, both in official Washington and in the big business community. And it has offered him opportunities to share in the education of a number of members of the next generation's elite.

In these endeavors he has enjoyed a particularly fortunate collaboration with Myres S. McDougal, a Mississippi-born attorney with some years of Federal Government experience who has been a member of the Yale Law School faculty since 1934. Educated first at the University of Mississippi and then as a Rhodes Scholar at Oxford (where he took a B.A. Juris.), he received his doctorate in jurisprudence at Yale and has specialized for the most part in international law (and recently has been pioneering in space law).

Perhaps in part because of common perspectives due to mid-American origins and European as well as American educations, McDougal and Lasswell have engaged in highly productive teamwork for over twenty-five years. Almost from the time of their first contact, they have sought jointly to give a policy-oriented, humanistic direction to legal education. In March, 1943, they first published a highly articulate and well-rounded account of their views on legal education and public policy, advocating "professional training in the public interest."[63] Their view:

> A recurrent problem for all who are interested in implementing policy, the reform of legal education must become ever more urgent in a revolutionary world of cumulative crises and increasing violence . . . and despite much recent ferment and agitation among . . . teachers, little has actually been achieved in refashioning ancient educational practices to serve insistent contemporary needs. . . . What they think they have done to legal instruction may be recapitalized as a transition from lectures, to the analysis of appellate opinions, to confusion. . . .
>
> The major contours of our contemporary confusion have long been plainly visible. Heroic, but random, efforts to integrate "law" and "the other social sciences" fail through lack of clarity about what is being integrated, and how, and for what purposes.

Lip-service is paid to the proposition that legal concepts, institutions and practices are instrumental only; but the main organizing foci for determining both "fields" and "courses" are still timeworn, overlapping legal concepts of highest-level abstraction. Any relation between the factual problems that incidentally creep into particular fields or courses, in a curriculum so "organized," and the important problems of contemporary society, is purely coincidental; and all attempts to relate such fields or courses to each other are frustrated by lack of clear social goals and inadequate criteria of importance. The relevance of "non-legal" materials to effective "law" teaching is recognized, but efficient techniques for the investigation, collection and presentation of such materials are not devised. . . . Great emphasis is put upon historical studies, but too often these studies degenerate into an aimless, literary eclecticism that fails to come to grips with causes or conditions. Despite all the talk of "teleological jurisprudence" and of the necessity of evaluating legal structures, doctrines and procedures in terms of basic policy, there is little conscious, systematic effort to relate them clearly to the major problems of a society struggling to achieve democratic values. . . .

A first indispensable step toward the effective reform of legal education is to clarify ultimate aims. We submit this basic proposition: if legal education in the contemporary world is to serve the needs of a free and productive commonwealth, it must be conscious, efficient and systematic *training for policy-making*. The proper function of our law schools is, in short, to contribute to the training of policy-makers for the ever more complete achievement of the democratic values that constitute the professed ends of American policy. . . .

It should need no emphasis that the lawyer is today, even when not himself a "maker" of policy, the one indispensable adviser of every responsible policymaker of our society—whether we speak of the head of a government department or agency, of the executive of a corporation or labor union, of the secretary of a trade or other private association, or even of the humble independent enterpriser or professional man. As such an adviser the lawyer, when informing his policy-maker of what he can or cannot legally do, is in an unassailably strategic position to influence, if not create, policy.

After these fighting words and calls to responsibility, the article systematically examines the functions and activities of lawyers and law schools, with a view to specifying the perspectives and training required. What are, in fact, the policy goals of democracy? "How can incipient lawyers be trained in the clarification of values?" In social-scientific trend-line thinking? In the techniques of "planned observation" that may be required to produce, for example, a "Brandeis brief"? In the skills of management? In the skills of making advice acceptable? In the assessment of "pressure politics" affecting a case or a policy? How, specifically, can legal curricula be retooled so that these things will in fact be taught?

It may be that not all of the recommendations that McDougal and Lasswell set forth have been implemented in any one law school, even now, more than twenty-five years later. Indeed, the article itself declared that "years of transition" would be required to create a "policy-training law school." But it can be noted at least that some of the leading law schools have in fact been moving in the indicated direction, whether as a result of the type of thinking exemplified here or because of broader social pressures.

Some idea of Lasswell's application of his theories to substantive as well as pedagogical problems in the legal field may be gained from study of contributions to a massive volume entitled *Studies in World Public Order* by McDougal and others (1960)[64] and another massive volume entitled *Law and Public Order in Space* produced in 1963 by McDougal, Lasswell, and Ivan A. Vlasic.[65] In another collaborative book Lasswell, with Richard Arens, has also reviewed in some detail the American system of law as a whole, evaluating it in terms of its conformity to the Lasswellian scheme of "democratic values."[66] Regrettably, limitations of space preclude comment here on these studies.

7. *Collection of World-Level Trend-line Data*

Undoubtedly, Lasswell's alertness to the importance of charting our way across the tides of history by means of trend-line data was heightened by Charles Edward Merriam's activities on the directorate of President Hoover's research committee, which in 1933 produced a tremendous book of data entitled *Recent Social Trends in the United States*.[67] Reflecting to some extent the "raw empiricism" of the day, it included quantifications of almost every American phenomenon on which data could possibly be collected, and presented not only statistics but also interpretive articles by specialists. Much of the work on this was done at the University of Chicago under the general direction of the sociologist William F. Ogburn. The enterprise furnished much food for thought to junior social scientists of that day, such as Lasswell. He was also impressed, as he has said repeatedly, by the monumental quantifications that were being published by the National Bureau of Economic Research under such economists as Wesley C. Mitchell and Simon Kuznets. From an early time he became an energetic advocate of the production of comparable trend-line data on politics and social change in general.

Thus, as mentioned above, he has long advocated a "World Attention Survey" that would chart the flows of socially significant symbols that come to the attention of elites, middle strata, and lower strata of countries around the world, and would interpret the probable reactions to these symbols by means of psychoanalytically sophisticated content analysis, with a view to testing hypotheses concerning the coming social upheavals and perhaps to heading them off by measures of "preventive politics."[68] The probable expense has made widespread adoption of this program appear unfeasible thus far; and in any case some of the same general purposes can perhaps be served through the slow growth of worldwide opinion polling and information polling, as signalized, for example, in the recently established magazine *Polls* (Amsterdam: International Opinion Research Documents, 1966—).

We have also mentioned Lasswell's work at the Hoover Institution in the 1940s on trend-line data concerning elites, symbols, and institutions from 1890 to 1950.

In the article just described on "Legal Education and Public Policy," Lasswell and McDougal proposed, among the many teaching aids to be developed by the law schools, the production of a "trend book" that would open the eyes of the budding attorney to solid data concerning developments all over the world. Something approaching this "trend book" has begun to take shape at Yale since the establishment in 1962 of the Yale Political Data Program, financed largely by grants from the National Science Foundation, with additional support from the International Social Science Council and the United Nations Educational, Scientific and Cultural Organization. This vast project of worldwide, long-term data collection and computer analysis was formulated largely by Lasswell and Karl W. Deutsch, another political scientist then at Yale (later at Harvard). Much of the supervisory and interpretive work on it has been done by their students. A first issue of the *World Handbook of Political and Social Indicators* appeared in 1964 under the editorship of Bruce M. Russett, with the collaboration of Hayward R. Alker, Jr., and of Deutsch and Lasswell, and with the assistance of a number of others.[69] From Lasswell's point of view it must have been a high point in a lifetime of effort to "take the phrase 'political science' seriously." Yet much remains to be done: massive as it is, the *World Handbook* does not yet include the "symbol data," "attention data," "attitude data," and so forth, that Lasswell's theory holds to be indispensable; nor does it include indicators of the actual distributions in world society of the eight "key values." In terms of the psychological data required for prediction, its data under such headings as "Communication" and "Education" constitute at best a very good beginning.

LASSWELL'S PROMOTION OF THE "PREVENTIVE POLITICS" OF DEMOCRACY

We can hardly close even so cursory a review as this of Lasswell's many-sided intellectual history without a comment on his strenuous efforts to promote as well as to analyze the "preventive politics" of democracy. From the start of his career, he has been at least as consistent a devotee as any Marxist of the "unity of theory and practice." A vigorous champion of the view that the political scientist can never be a totally value-free, emotionless, irresponsible being entitled to live continuously in an ivory tower, he has been heard to comment almost intolerantly on colleagues who are "attempting to develop the perspectives of a mole." In his view, the alert scientist is inevitably a *participant* observer. While practicing the utmost detachment in his role as professional analyst, the man of science, he feels, has a co-role as a responsible political and economic man. The client of any professional, he has said repeatedly, is the general public, not any special interest. And Lasswell's commitment in that co-role, from the first days of his career, has been to the advancement of democracy, in the sense of the very wide sharing of the "key values." Thus, in the preface to his book in 1924 with Willard Atkins, we find these words:

> In place of a vague and abstract entity, the worker stands out as a citizen, the father of a family, a human being sensitive to a real and concrete environment. It is seen how he reacts to the six-hour day in the mines, to the twelve-hour day in the steel mills; how he is affected by prolonged fatigue, imperfectly-protected machinery, poor sanitary conditions—and their opposites. . . . In [considering] the intricate problems of what to change and what to conserve in our present system, it should never be forgotten that the factory exists for man and not man for the factory.[70]

These are clichés, no doubt—but a commitment. Consider also the following, from a section entitled "How to Integrate Science, Morals and Politics," in his book *The Analysis of Political Behavior:*

> In common with any branch of social and political science, psychology bears an instrumental relationship to morals and politics. Our moral values are *acquired* from the interplay of original nature with the culture into which we are born; our values are *derived* from that part of culture that includes the basic postulates of metaphysics and theology; our values are *implemented* by the part of culture called science and practice (including psychology and politics).

But social faith without behavioral-scientific knowledge is not enough:

> The developing science of democracy is an arsenal of implements for the achievement of democratic ideals. We know enough to know that democracies do not know how to live; they perish through ignorance—ignorance of how to sustain the will to live and of how to discover the means of life. Without knowledge, democracy will surely fall. With knowledge, democracy may succeed.[71]

In the same vein, in several recent volumes dealing mainly with legal norms and written in collaboration with such legal theorists as Richard Arens, Myres McDougal, and Ivan A. Vlasic, he explicitly postulates "the dignity of man as the overriding goal of public order in this commonwealth," and holds that "in American society this includes the demand to defend and fulfill the requirements of a collective way of life in which values are widely rather than narrowly held." He repeatedly insists on the placing of "a prime value on the individual—any individual, be he citizen or alien, useful or harmful, sane or mad."[72]

That he really *means* "sane or mad" is suggested by his coauthorship with the psychoanalyst Robert Rubenstein, codirector of the Yale Psychiatric Institute, of a substantial volume entitled *The Sharing of Power in a Psychiatric Hospital*.[73] The book reports efforts to establish a more therapeutic and democratic community by inviting patients to participate with staff members in decision-making and thereby to build up their defeated self-confidence and enable them to experience the habits of value-sharing in general.

In view of this lifelong commitment to the unity of theory and democratic practice, it is not surprising that a review of his record shows impressive efforts to make scientific findings more shareable as well as more valid. We have seen how he has attempted at the Yale Law School and in official Washington and elsewhere to publicize at the elite level his conception of democratic goals and preventive politics. In this connection, we can mention two more of his studies. These were directed primarily to audiences at the elite level in the big-business community. Under the auspices of the Committee for Economic Development, a policy-planning group of influential businessmen, Lasswell wrote two volumes on the problems of combining, under current conditions, high levels of employment and economic production with national security and with individual freedom.

The first, *World Politics Faces Economics*, focused on policy implications of future relations of the United States and the USSR. In very plain language, it forecast a period of rising Soviet-American tensions and undertook to specify practical means of easing them. It concluded:

> Certainly it is a mistake to assume that war for global mastery between the United States and Russia is inevitable. The future depends upon factors over which we can exercise much control. . . . By stabilizing our economy at home and strengthening balanced rather than predatory economies abroad, we can defer, and perhaps avoid, a final clash. America and Russia can work together for their own good and the good of humanity.[74]

He adopted an equally normative, prescriptive tone in the other volume he wrote for the CED: *National Security and Individual Freedom*.[75] By this time the Cold War had reached an intensity approaching crisis. Stalin was still in control in the USSR, and, although prudent, appeared menacing and possibly paranoidal. Communists had assumed control in China. The Communist camp gave an appearance of "monolithic unity" from East Germany to the China Sea and from the Arctic to the frontiers of Turkey, Persia, and India. These facts lent credibility to the classical Marxist prediction of the "historical inevitability" of its further spread.

In the United States, excited publicists and "preventive war" generals and paranoidal members of Congress were more inclined to blame "disloyal" Americans and hapless members of the State Department for this state of affairs than to seek its true causes in the economic and political miseries and the intellectual shortcomings of the Old World. There was reason to feel that the United States, in panic about its national defenses, might become —within a few years, if not immediately—a garrison state having some of the features of Stalin's Russia itself, or of Nazi Germany and the Chiang Kai-shek regime in China. There was much in the American tradition of "red scares" and anti-Communist propaganda to suggest that the country might be prepared to sacrifice both individual freedom and economic welfare to the overriding symbolic goal of "fighting Communism." If so, the country might end up unwittingly in the grip of the specialists on violence and police surveillance—for a very long time.

Thus Lasswell, encouraged and sponsored by thoughtful members of the Committee for Economic Development, felt called upon to write a book whose central problem, as he put it, was "how to maintain a proper balance between national security and individual freedom in a continuing crisis of national defense. The aim is more restricted . . . than considering how to bring the crisis to an end. The task is the more modest and less gratifying one of thinking how to endure the crisis with the least loss of fundamental freedoms" (p. 1).

In this practical guide to action in an hour of major international crisis, there are none of the provocative flights of imagination or high-level theorizing or amusing, hyperproliferated verbalism that one finds in most of his writings. As he had pointed out earlier, in an essay on "The Relation of Ideological Intelligence to Public Policy," "difficulty arises from the task of selecting and presenting certain kinds of information in a form deemed useful by policy-makers. Policy-makers are usually poised toward action. They want to choose between clear-cut courses of action. Hence intelligence material must be processed in a form that commends it to decision-makers."[76]

This book, then, was written deliberately in such a form. It is an outstanding example of the cool, factual communication of practical policy ideas to an elite audience and to other sophisticated members of the informed public. It is in very plain language. It has carefully worded chapter headings, and section catchlines that are themselves programmatic. A listing of the chapter headings will indicate the range of issues it covered:

I. The Continuing Crisis of National Defense
II. The Threat Inherent in the Garrison-Police State
III. The Meaning of National Security Policy
IV. Action by the President and the Executive
V. What the Congress Can Do
VI. What the Courts Can Do
VII. What the Public Can Do

Each chapter presents a reasoned inventory of specific steps that might feasibly be taken with a view to maintaining, as long and as fully as possible under garrison-state conditions, four principles of national policy: civilian supremacy, freedom of information, civil liberties, and a free economy. Realistic measures are suggested for preventing hysteria, preventing complacency, evoking a sense of individual responsibility, preventing excessive and spurious police surveillance, safeguarding the due process of law, maximizing public information. On the whole it is an outstanding illustration of preventive politics. Fortunately, the crisis in question receded with the death of Stalin and with the Soviet acquisition of an intercontinental thermo-nuclear capability that must give pause to even the most incautious advocates of war. The book remains—a major contribution to defenders of democratic traditions, in America and elsewhere, in future crises of the same type.

Finally, a word is in order about Lasswell's efforts to make the philosophy of preventive politics accessible in meaningful form to the broader public. In this area he has published less, and has perhaps been less successful, than in his "scientist-to-elite" communications. In part this is due to his conviction that it is above all necessary to get the conceptions of preventive politics across to the educated and the influential; if that is done, they will reach the masses eventually, through popularizations, authorized educational materials, and informational and entertainment media. Nonetheless, he has made a number of efforts of his own at direct "scientist to-public" communication.

Perhaps the most successful of these was the translation of much of the message of *World Politics and Personal Insecurity* into plain language in the book entitled *Politics: Who Gets What, When, How.*[77]

World Politics and Personal Insecurity had been criticized widely for "obscurity" and for "excessive use of jargon." Actually, much of its wording was hardly jargon at all, but rather the juxtaposition of standard terms from the specialized vocabularies of several sciences (especially from the psychiatric and symbolic interactionist literature). Yet even had the critics possessed these vocabularies, it would have been a difficult book. Hence, the year after *World Politics* appeared, Lasswell undertook a popularization (with some little aid from the present writer, who, as the reader will have noticed, almost never uses a word of more than one or two syllables). This shorter, clearer book made Lasswell's thinking available to a far wider audience, especially among undergraduates and professors. It is still to be recommended as a bridge between everyday talk about public affairs and the specialized lingos of the behavioral sciences. Perhaps every beginning student of Lasswell should read *Politics: Who Gets What, When, How* to get a clue to his main ideas before plunging into the deep waters of *World Politics and Personal Insecurity.*

In addition, Lasswell has made two other substantial ventures into popularization. One was his plain-language analysis, mainly for the benefit of citizens' discussion groups, of the means of maintaining and further developing enlightened public opinion in a democracy: *Democracy through Public Opinion.*[78] The other was an essay, "Democratic Character," in plain and simple words, on classical, Freudian, and neo-Freudian conceptions of personality, and on the relations of these to the requirements of political democracy.[79]

At times, also, he has coproduced radio shows on political psychology (for example, the "Human Nature in Action" series on NBC in the late 1930s), and has helped in making some of the *Encyclopaedia Britannica's* series of educational films, on such topics as "Democracy and Despotism." On the whole, however, he has not done nearly as much through the popular media as through the media for the highly informed and the policymakers. With his torrentially creative mind and immense vocabularies, he can be expected to be more at home among those who are highly sophisticated, skilled, and articulate.

This personal trait does not, however, imply either snobbery or cynicism in his relations with those who are less gifted. No words could better summarize the unity of scientific theory and democratic practice in the long, rich intellectual career of the mystifying Mr. Lasswell than the following words from his "Legal Education and Public Policy":

> One of the basic manifestations of deference to human beings is to give full weight to the fact that they have minds. People need to be equipped with knowledge of how democratic doctrines can be justified. They cannot be expected to remain loyal to democratic ideals through all the disappointments and disillusionments of life without a deep and enduring factual knowledge of the potentialities of human beings for congenial and productive human relations. As a means of maintaining a clear and realistic appraisal of human nature, there must be deeply based recognition . . . [that] the laborious work of modern science has provided a nonsentimental foundation for the intuitive confidence with which the poets and prophets of human brotherhood have regarded mankind. Buttressing the aspirations of these sensitive spirits stands the modern arsenal of facts about the benevolent potentialities of human nature, and a secure knowledge of the methods by which distorted personality growth can be prevented or cured.
>
> Through the further application of methods that have already achieved partial success, we can provide instruments capable of putting into practice admonitions of the moralists and visions of the dreamers. Without this knowledge, the intuitions of genius are helpless; armed with this knowledge, including knowledge of the means of further knowledge, moral intention becomes steadily capable of fulfilling itself in reality. There is no rational room for pessimism about the possibility of putting morals into practice on the basis of what we know, and know we can know, about the development of human personality.

THE FUTURE?

UNDOUBTEDLY, Lasswell would hold that no study of any phenomenon is complete unless it includes a projection of established
trends and a probability estimate of the future. But what can we
say about the future of so improbable a phenomenon as Lasswell
himself? Perhaps we can gather some clues from his own developmental constructs concerning the science of politics, in his book
entitled *The Future of Political Science*.[80] At the suggestion of a
number of other leading members of this problematic profession,
he set down in this volume his views on the most promising lines
of inquiry and also on the means of maximizing the creativity of
teachers, researchers, and students and of organizing them to
function effectively as a team.

As a lifelong exponent of multidisciplinary group research, he
considers himself a team player (though hardly an "organization
man"). Not unexpectedly, therefore, he renewed his long-
standing argument for a worldwide division of labor for trend-
line research ("basic data surveys"—"comprehensive, selective,
reliable"). To this end he outlined "a possible line of development in which the American Political Science Association and
other professional organizations in the United States and elsewhere can play a leading role." The Association would initiate
and coordinate (but not try to dominate) the basic data surveys.
"This has never been done, and the resulting loss of opportunity
has weakened every function of the profession." Work on the
surveys would sharpen the thinking and skills of established professionals. It would also offer important training opportunities to
junior professionals, from doctoral candidates to students in high
school. "It is not difficult to show [a high school student] that
participation in a Basic Data Survey would be worthwhile. Such a
survey is part of the adult world of social responsibility." It
would yield data that would in some ways resemble those of the
Yale Political Data Program plus those of such survey research
agencies as the Roper Center for Public Opinion Research and

the Inter-University Consortium that includes the University of Michigan's Survey Research Center. But it would go beyond these into a wider range of data, which Lasswell specifies.

In addition, the American Political Science Association would serve (as in part it already does, through the *American Political Science Review*) as a coordinator of other researches involving controlled experiments, gaming, and simulations. It also would foster prototyping ("innovation, typically small-scale, made in political practice primarily for scientific purposes"), such as the project on induced social change conducted in Vicos, Peru, under the direction of the late Allan R. Holmberg of Cornell (on which Lasswell was a consultant), and the project reported in *The Sharing of Power in a Psychiatric Hospital*.

To improve the discipline, the profession at large would systematically introduce the use of such media as "decision seminars" and "prelegislatures" (essentially, multidisciplinary and sometimes multinational conferences on major social issues, with very carefully planned agenda and exhibits—similar to the American Assembly at Arden House). It also would develop multidisciplinary "centers for advanced political science," again international. These would resemble the Center for Advanced Study in the Behavioral Sciences at Stanford University.

To popularize the discipline, certain political scientists would establish socioeconomic museums to help focus the attention of specialists, semispecialists, and policymakers on "the image of the entire social process." There would also be "social planetaria," along similar lines, for the general public ("Suppose that several buildings were available as part of the National Museum establishment in Washington, D.C."). The profession at large would build up banks of educational motion pictures and television tapes to furnish trend-line background and authoritative interpretation, to be put on the air in conjunction with broadcasts of the day's spot news.

Steps toward "the cultivation of creativity" would be taken by young and old in the profession. The graduate curriculum (especially the core courses on "scope and methods") would be restructured. Teachers would be chosen for capability in both teaching and research (not just one or the other), and for multidisciplinary (not unidisciplinary) competence. Students would be alerted to the problems of ethics, the moral dilemmas, and the intrapsychic and interpersonal strains that confront the professional.

Creativity would be maximized by opportunities for a continuous flow of collaborations with allied professionals—not only in other behavioral sciences, but also in journalism, the law, practical politics, business and trade union leadership, and public administration. The "intelligence functions" and the "policy-advising functions" of the political scientist require him to have easy intercourse with all these types, and others. Above all, in present times, it is important for the political scientist to keep productive contact with the physical and biological scientists—and vice versa. "It is only too obvious that mankind is drastically unprepared to cope with the grave new world into which we are being catapulted by science and technology." (This had also been the theme of Lasswell's presidential address to the American Political Science Association: "The Political Science of Science: An Inquiry into the Possible Reconciliation of Mastery and Freedom.")[81] It is also obvious, he reminds us, that our sights must be raised not only to new, high multidisciplinary levels, but also to new, high, bewildering multinational levels. "The need for a worldwide system of public order—a comprehensive plan of cooperation—is fearfully urgent." By 1968 he was an active member of the worldwide Committee on a World University, with the aim of putting these ideas and others into effect on a global scale.

In the light of these words and activities, we can have little doubt about the probabilities in our developmental construct concerning Mr. Lasswell. The best bookies in the profession are offering about a hundred to one that he will continue, in a thousand ingenious ways, his prodigious efforts to clarify our thinking; to chart our conscious and unconscious achievements, crimes, and follies on a worldwide trend-line basis; and to promote uni-

versal preventive politics and the free man's worldwide commonwealth—even as mankind goes plummeting, heels over head and
atom bombs in hand, into the grave new world.

REFERENCES

1. Karl W. Deutsch, *The Nerves of Government* (London and
New York: Free Press of Glencoe, 1963).

2. Harry Stack Sullivan, *The Interpersonal Theory of Psychiatry*,
ed. Helen Swick Perry (New York: W. W. Norton, 1953).

3. Quoted in Harold D. Lasswell, *World Politics and Personal
Insecurity* (New York: McGraw-Hill, 1935), p. 284.

4. Willard E. Atkins and Harold D. Lasswell, *Labor Attitudes
and Problems* (New York: Prentice-Hall, 1924).

5. William I. Thomas and Florian Znaniecki, *The Polish Peasant
in Europe and America*, 2d ed. (New York: Alfred A. Knopf, 1927).

6. William I. Thomas, *On Social Organization and Social Personality: Selected Papers*, ed. Morris Janowitz (Chicago: University of
Chicago Press, 1966), pp. liv–lv.

7. Harold D. Lasswell, "Political Policies and the International
Investment Market," *Journal of Political Economy*, 31 (1923):380–
400.

8. Harold D. Lasswell and Abraham Kaplan, *Power and Society:
A Framework for Political Inquiry* (New Haven: Yale University
Press, 1950).

9. George Herbert Mead, *Mind, Self, and Society*, introduction
by Charles W. Morris (Chicago: University of Chicago Press, 1934),
p. ix.

10. Alfred North Whitehead, *An Enquiry concerning the Principles of Natural Knowledge* (Cambridge: Cambridge University Press,
1919).

11. Alfred North Whitehead, *The Concept of Nature* (Cambridge: Cambridge University Press, 1920).

12. Alfred North Whitehead, *Symbolism: Its Meaning and Effect*
(New York: Macmillan, 1927).

13. Charles Kay Ogden and I. A. Richards, *The Meaning of
Meaning: A Study of the Influence of Language upon Thought and
of the Science of Symbolism* (New York: Harcourt, Brace; London:
Kegan Paul, Trench, and Trubner, 1925).

14. Charles Edward Merriam, *New Aspects of Politics* (Chicago:
University of Chicago Press, 1925).

15. Charles Edward Merriam, *The History of the Theory of Sovereignty since Rousseau* (New York: Columbia University Press, 1900).

16. Charles Edward Merriam, *A History of American Political Theories* (New York: Macmillan, 1903).

17. Charles Edward Merriam, *Chicago: A More Intimate View of Urban Politics* (New York: Macmillan, 1929).

18. Charles Edward Merriam, *Systematic Politics* (Chicago: University of Chicago Press, 1945).

19. Harold D. Lasswell, "Chicago's Old First Ward: A Case Study in Political Behavior," *National Municipal Review*, 12 (1923): 127–31.

20. Harold Foote Gosnell, *Negro Politicians: The Rise of Negro Politics in Chicago* (Chicago: University of Chicago Press, 1935).

21. Harold Foote Gosnell, *Machine Politics: Chicago Model* (Chicago: University of Chicago Press, 1937).

22. Harold Foote Gosnell, *Champion Campaigner: Franklin D. Roosevelt* (New York: Macmillan, 1952).

23. Charles Edward Merriam, "American Publicity in Italy," *American Political Science Review*, 13 (1919):541–55.

24. Harold D. Lasswell, "Prussian Schoolbooks and International Amity," *Journal of Social Forces*, 4 (1925):718–22.

25. Harold D. Lasswell, "The Status of Research on International Propaganda and Opinion," *American Journal of Sociology*, 32 (1925):198–209.

26. Harold D. Lasswell, *Propaganda Technique in the World War* (New York: Alfred A. Knopf, 1927).

27. See Charles E. Merriam, *The Making of Citizens: A Comparative Study of Methods of Civic Training* (Chicago: University of Chicago Press, 1931).

28. Graham Wallas, *The Great Society: A Psychological Analysis* (New York: Macmillan, 1914).

29. Graham, Wallas, *Human Nature in Politics,* 3d ed. (New York: Alfred A. Knopf, 1921).

30. Harold D. Lasswell, "The Problem of Adequate Personality Records: A Proposal," *American Journal of Psychiatry*, 8 (1929): 1057–66; and "The Study of the Ill as a Method of Research on Political Personalities," *American Political Science Review*, 23 (1929): 996–1001.

31. Harold D. Lasswell, *Psychopathology and Politics* (Chicago: University of Chicago Press, 1930).

32. Alexander L. George and Juliette L. George, *Woodrow Wil-

son and Colonel House: A Personality Study (New York: John Day, 1956).

33. Arnold A. Rogow, *James Forrestal: A Study of Personality, Politics and Policy* (New York: Macmillan, 1963).

34. Harold D. Lasswell, "The Selective Effect of Personality on Political Participation," in *Studies in the Scope and Method of "The Authoritarian Personality,"* ed. Richard Christie and Marie Jahoda (Glencoe, Ill.: Free Press, 1954), pp. 197–225.

35. Harold D. Lasswell, "The Strategy of Revolutionary and War Propaganda," in *Public Opinion and World Politics,* ed. Quincy Wright (Chicago: University of Chicago Press, 1933), pp. 187–221.

36. Bruce M. Russett, Hayward Alker, Jr., *et al.*, *World Handbook of Political and Social Indicators* (New Haven: Yale University Press, 1964).

37. Herman Kahn and Anthony J. Wiener, *The Year 2000: A Framework for Speculation on the Next Thirty-three Years* (New York: Macmillan, 1967).

38. Harold D. Lasswell, *World Politics and Personal Insecurity* (New York: McGraw-Hill, 1935; reprinted as a paperback, with a new introduction, New York: Free Press; and London: Collier-Macmillan, 1965).

39. Stanley Hoffmann, *Contemporary Theory in International Relations* (Englewood Cliffs, N.J.: Prentice-Hall, 1960).

40. Harry Stack Sullivan, *The Interpersonal Theory of Psychiatry* (see n. 2); the chapter in question appeared at greater length in *Psychiatry*, 11 (1948):105–16, and was reprinted in Hadley Cantril, ed., *Tensions that Cause Wars* (Urbana: University of Illinois Press, 1950).

41. Sigmund Freud, *Civilization and Its Discontents*, authorized transl. by Joan Rivière (London: Hogarth Press, 1930).

42. Hadley Cantril, *The Human Dimension: Adventures in Policy Research* (New Brunswick, N.J.: Rutgers University Press, 1967).

43. Walter Lippmann, *Public Opinion* (New York: Harcourt, Brace, 1922) and *The Phantom Public* (New York: Harcourt, Brace, 1925).

44. Ferdinand Toennies, *Kritik der öffentlichen Meinung* (Berlin: Springer, 1922).

45. Sigmund Freud, *Group Psychology and the Analysis of the Ego*, authorized transl. by James Strachey (New York: Boni and Liveright, 1922).

46. Harold D. Lasswell, "The Status of Research on International Propaganda and Opinion," *American Journal of Sociology*, 32 (1925):198–209.

47. Harold D. Lasswell, Ralph D. Casey, and Bruce Lannes Smith, *Propaganda and Promotional Activities: An Annotated Bibliography* (Minneapolis: University of Minnesota Press, 1935).

48. Bruce Lannes Smith, Harold D. Lasswell, and Ralph D. Casey, *Propaganda, Communication, and Public Opinion: A Comprehensive Reference Guide* (Princeton, N.J.: Princeton University Press, 1946).

49. Bruce Lannes Smith and Chitra M. Smith, *International Communication and Political Opinion: A Guide to the Literature* (Princeton, N.J.: Princeton University Press, 1956).

50. Harold D. Lasswell, Nathan C. Leites, *et al.*, *Language of Politics: Studies in Quantitative Semantics* (New York: George W. Stewart, 1949).

51. See, for example, Ithiel de Sola Pool *et al.*, *Symbols of Internationalism* (Stanford, Calif.: Stanford University Press, 1951).

52. See Harold D. Lasswell, "The World Attention Survey," *Public Opinion Quarterly*, 5 (1941):456–62; also, the essays on content analysis by Morris Janowitz and Ithiel de Sola Pool in the present volume.

53. See Harold D. Lasswell, "The Moral Vocation of the Middle Income Skill Groups," *International Journal of Ethics*, 45 (1935): 127–37; "The Relation of Skill Politics to Class Politics and National Politics," *Chinese Social and Political Science Review*, 21 (1937): 298–313; and *Politics: Who Gets What, When, How* (New York: McGraw-Hill, 1936), chap. 6.

54. Harold D. Lasswell, "Toward a Skill Commonwealth: A Workable Goal of World Politics," in Lyman Bryson, ed., *Approaches to Group Understanding* (New York: Harper, 1947), pp. 290–302.

55. Harold D. Lasswell, "The Garrison State and the Specialists on Violence," *American Journal of Sociology*, 46 (1941):455–68. Lasswell's more recent views on this will be found in his essay, "The Garrison State Hypothesis Today," in Samuel P. Huntington, ed., *Changing Patterns of Military Politics* (Glencoe, Ill.: Free Press, 1962).

56. See further, *inter alia*, Harold D. Lasswell, "World Organization and Society," *Yale Law Journal*, 55 (1946):889–909, reprinted in Harold D. Lasswell and Daniel Lerner, eds., *The Policy Sciences* (Stanford, Calif.: Stanford University Press, 1951), pp. 102–17; also Harold D. Lasswell and Daniel Lerner, eds., *World Revolutionary Elites: Studies in Coercive Ideological Movements* (Cambridge, Mass.: Massachusetts Institute of Technology Press, 1966).

57. Harold D. Lasswell and Richard Arens, *In Defense of Public Order: The Emerging Field of Sanction Law* (New York: Columbia University Press, 1961).

58. Harold D. Lasswell, *National Security and Individual Freedom* (New York: McGraw-Hill, 1950).

59. Harold D. Lasswell and Daniel Lerner, eds., *World Revolutionary Elites* (see n. 56, above).

60. Myres S. McDougal *et al.*, *Studies in World Public Order* (New Haven: Yale University Press, 1960).

61. Harold D. Lasswell and Abraham Kaplan, *Power and Society* (see n. 8, above).

62. Harold D. Lasswell and Arnold A. Rogow, *Power, Corruption and Rectitude* (Englewood Cliffs, N.J.: Prentice-Hall, 1963), p. 92.

63. Harold D. Lasswell and Myres S. McDougal, "Legal Education and Public Policy: Professional Training in the Public Interest," *Yale Law Journal*, 52 (1943):203–95; reprinted in Harold D. Lasswell, *The Analysis of Political Behavior* (New York and London: Oxford University Press, 1949), pp. 21–119; reprinted again in Myres S. McDougal *et al.*, *Studies in World Public Order* (see n. 60, above), pp. 42–154. See also McDougal's essay in the present volume.

64. See n. 60, above.

65. Myres S. McDougal, Harold D. Lasswell, and Ivan A. Vlasic, *Law and Public Order in Space* (New Haven and London: Yale University Press, 1963).

66. See n. 57, above.

67. *Recent Social Trends in the United States: Report of the President's Research Committee* (New York and London: McGraw-Hill, 1933).

68. See n. 52, above.

69. See n. 36, above.

70. *Labor Attitudes and Problems* (see n. 4, above), pp. iv, vi.

71. Harold D. Lasswell, *The Analysis of Political Behavior* (New York and London: Oxford University Press, 1947), pp. 13, 1.

72. Lasswell and Arens, *In Defense of Public Order* (see n. 57, above), pp. 7, 13, 23.

73. Robert Rubenstein and Harold D. Lasswell, *The Sharing of Power in a Psychiatric Hospital* (New Haven: Yale University Press, 1966).

74. Harold D. Lasswell, *World Politics Faces Economics* (New York and London: McGraw-Hill, 1945).

75. See n. 58, above.

76. Harold D. Lasswell, "The Relation of Ideological Intelligence to Public Policy," *Ethics*, 53 (1942):25–34; reprinted in Lasswell, *The Analysis of Political Behavior* (see n. 71, above).

77. Harold D. Lasswell, *Politics: Who Gets What, When, How*

(New York: McGraw-Hill, 1936); reprinted in 1951 by the Free Press of Glencoe, along with *Psychopathology and Politics* (see n. 31, above) and with Lasswell's essay "Democratic Character," in *Political Writings of Harold D. Lasswell;* reprinted again in 1958 as a Meridian Books paperback.

78. Harold D. Lasswell, *Democracy through Public Opinion* (Menasha, Wis.: George Banta Publishing Co., 1941).

79. Harold D. Lasswell, "Democratic Character," pp. 465–525 in *Political Writings of Harold D. Lasswell* (Glencoe, Ill.: Free Press, 1951). A similar work is his book, *Power and Personality* (New York: W. W. Norton, 1948).

80. Harold D. Lasswell, *The Future of Political Science* (New York: Atherton Press, 1963).

81. Harold D. Lasswell, "The Political Science of Science: An Inquiry into the Possible Reconciliation of Mastery and Freedom," *American Political Science Review*, 50 (1956):961–79; reprinted in *Scientific Monthly*, 84 (1957):34–44.

4

Psychoanalysis and the Study of Autonomic Behavior

Roy R. Grinker, Sr.

The new University of Chicago Medical School and its attached Billings Hospital opened their doors in 1927. The first very young full-time faculty, of which I was a member, immediately experienced the meaning of a hostile world. The faculty of its predecessor Rush Medical School resisted dissolution, the Chicago Medical Society protested the full-time faculty system and threatened to expel us, and the economic depression beginning in 1929 forced us to serve private patients who could afford fees so that our own salaries could be paid.

To top all this, in 1930 the psychoanalyst Dr. Franz Alexander arrived at the university as visiting professor of psychiatry in the department of medicine. He had been invited by a member of the department of social sciences who had undergone a personal analysis by him in Berlin. Because Alexander was a physician with academic ambitions, he insisted on working and teaching in the medical school. His seminar on psychoanalysis was attended by the medical, biological, and psychological faculty. Hardly had he spoken a few sentences at the first session when critical questions and violent arguments erupted, necessitating a communication from the dean commanding that discussion await the end of each presentation. Needless to say, Alexander left the University of Chicago at the end of the academic year. He returned to the city a year later, however, to found the Chicago Psychoanalytic Institute in 1932, independent of any academic affiliation.

Peace was not yet achieved because another eruption occurred when a professor discovered that a medical student was working afternoons and weekends to pay for his analytic fees at the new Institute. Finally, a last episode horrified the new faculty of Institute analysts more than those at the medical school when Harold D. Lasswell started analyzing volunteers while simultaneously measuring concomitant physiological changes!

It is almost incredible in view of the widespread acceptance, indeed uncritical acceptance, of psychoanalytic concepts today to remember the violent resistance the University of Chicago incident demonstrated in 1930. Shortly after the first Lasswell publication, the New York Psychoanalytic Institute forbade its members to record the contents of psychoanalytic interviews. Despite my own repeated attempts over the years, no member of the Chicago Psychoanalytic Institute would permit me to record physiological or biochemical processes in patients under psychoanalysis during or after emotional turbulence. Coincidentally it was Alexander, in the last years of his life in Los Angeles, who subjected patients and himself to observations from behind a one-way mirror, taped their verbalizations, and recorded physiological variables.

Let us now examine what Lasswell did and what he found in his researches published in 1935 and 1936, which no one remembers or quotes. To begin: Lasswell apparently psychoanalyzed patients and later volunteers. Certainly he had undergone no formal training in the field and his writing gives no clue to the technique he employed. Indeed, he writes about "psychoanalytic interviews," not about psychoanalysis. In my view this is unimportant because he observed and recorded phenomena which transpired in a dyadic relationship and for his research it makes little difference what formal label is placed on the procedure. Lasswell states that psychoanalysis is a process of repeated systematic observations which needs a consistent type of reporting.[1] Comparisons between sessions and between different patients are difficult because of variations in reporting practices. Neither behavior nor individual movements are usually described.

It should be kept in mind that Lasswell's investigations were done before the advent of "ego psychology" and the analysis of resistance. It was the era when the task was to make unconscious affects and conflicts conscious—to bring id processes within the scope of the ego. Accordingly, he was careful to keep what he termed "unconscious tension" within bearable limits lest it erupt into "conscious affect."

Lasswell's later subjects were volunteers who were not or were only slightly neurotic.[2] They lay on a couch at a regular time in the same place and for the same duration. A microphone transmitted and recorded the spoken words on wax cylinders. A blood-pressure cuff was attached to a leg and readings were obtained by the experimenter before, during, and after the interview. A pneumograph recorded respiratory rates. The bodily movements were recorded by the observer. Observed affects were correlated with physiological measurements. Reliability was tested by repetitive observations (!) and by rereading the records after a lapse of time.

Lasswell attempted to define stages in the development of insight: (1) initial reference to the problem, conflict, or affect with subsequent verbal and physical excitement; (2) rejection of the formulation; (3) repeated emergence of the unconscious "material"; (4) acceptance of the formulation with certainty; (5) reaffirmation despite countersuggestion and despite the passage of time; (6) reaffirmation with diminished excitement. He stated that affects were expressed in the "transference" relationship more fully than when the subject was alluding to persons in past time or space, or to self. Slow speech and motor inhibition indicated more tension than when the rate of speech and movement increased.

Physiological measurements included those of pulse rate and skin resistance. Pulse rate increased with outer affect (conscious) and skin conductivity increased with inner tension (unconscious). Using only these two measurements four pairs of permutations were possible.

Using indices of skin conduction, pulse rate, word frequency, and body movements, Lasswell divided his few subjects into four types. When a trend in these indices was absent there seemed to be little energy free for psychological work and a long drawn-out analysis with little insight could be predicted. A trend toward inactivity was associated with overdependence. Lower skin resistance and disturbance in motor activity spoke for much inner tension, and if retained in treatment these subjects worked hard. Increased skin resistance, increased motor activity, increased pulse rate, and slow speech were associated with responsiveness to treatment and progressive insight. This sketchy outline represents one of the first attempts to link autonomic and behavioral variables with personality as defined by therapeutic outcome and was a forerunner of much subsequent research in this field.

As Lasswell moved deeper into his chosen field of political science he still maintained his psychological interests. In 1938 he wrote that various roles in political life are connected with fundamental forms of personality which can be studied by psychiatrists but that there is no one-to-one relationship.[3]

He understood the use of symbols for political action. Finally, in 1939, Lasswell wrote with astounding prescience what is just now penetrating psychiatry through general systems theory.

Many more examples of Lasswell's psychological approach to political science can be found in his many papers dealing with social actions, propaganda, power, morals, etc. In almost all of his writings the psychoanalytic influence is apparent, but I leave to others the task of commenting on them.[4] I shall restrict my remarks to the psychosomatic field in an attempt to compare the contemporary theoretical and methodological approaches with those of Lasswell's pioneering days. In so doing, I am reporting no new information but am only culling data from work done by myself and colleagues which has previously been reported in psychiatric publications.

It is no surprise that the psychosomatic field, which involves both health and disease, has been dominated by psychoanalytic theory through its concepts of psychic energy. These concepts postulate that such energy which cannot be externally expressed in verbal or motoric behavior spends its force internally (Lasswell's "tensions"), producing disturbances in organs innervated by the autonomic nervous system and resulting eventually in tissue changes. Since Freud dismissed the age-old mind-body relationship by his famous phrase "the mysterious leap from psyche to soma," modern theorists have attempted to find explanations for mechanisms of relationships as they, at the same time, speak of mind-body unity. The psychosomatic field has been dominated by conceptual theories creating clinical stereotypes based on historical reconstructions, single causes, two variable correlations, and many assumptions and inferences but few operations with predictive value.[5]

The psychoanalytic method, utilizable in its purest form in therapy and jealously guarded at this time against the intrusion of measurements, can only relate psychological events in the transference process to subjective reportable complaints of the subject. There are several limitations inherent in this method: first, these inferences are not verifiable; second, the psychic and somatic events are separated in time; third, subjective complaints are not indices of a localization of dysfunction. Finally, when neither psychic processes nor organ functions are observable, but only inferred, correlations stand on weak ground indeed.

There are, however, aspects of psychoanalytic theory which are helpful for psychosomatic research. Among them I would include those that are concerned with genetic or developmental processes leading to proneness or susceptibility to various stimuli, personality structures, defense systems, and the dynamic concepts of anxiety. Some psychoanalysts and psychiatrists are beginning to recognize the help obtainable from constitutional or hereditary processes. Others have at least looked at sociological theory.[6] Yet, the "mysterious leap from psyche to soma" is not furthered by a knowledge of psychodynamics.[7] Despite Alexander's first exciting results of research on specific psychosomatic diseases based on psychoanalytic theory, psychodynamics alone are not sufficient for investigators in the field. Scientific investigations have proven that they are neither conceptually nor empirically sufficient.[8]

Psychoanalytic theory and the principles of psychodynamics

place too great a limiting restriction on the tremendous scope of psychosomatic problems. Psychogenesis, although currently blown up to extraordinary proportions, excludes a wide variety of hitherto neglected processes. To encompass all these, we are forced to apply the concepts of "field theory," which is simply another way of stating that all the know significant factors involved in human behavior, from genes to symbols, from heredity to culture, must be included.[9] As field theory is formulated, it not only encompasses a wide variety of variables in time and space, but it also facilitates the definition of specific and testable hypotheses. In other words, it combines the advantages of a cognitive map and at the same time has operational directions. Finally, it facilitates and permits the utilization of many kinds of observations and experiments, thereby furthering openness and flexibility.

Because field theory encompasses time, it includes genic (constitutional) and genetic experiences and precipitating events. It includes structural and functional aspects of psyche and soma. But more specifically, it requires consideration and study of multiple systems in transaction as foci in a total field, each one of which has some significance, although analysis of transactions of only part of the field with a few others at one time is possible. I shall not here delve into transactional concepts or their operations in research or therapy except to indicate that field theory depend on understanding the reciprocal reverberating effect of at least two systems in communication with each other (or two persons) with a third observer.

The human organism at birth comprises a relatively undifferentiated functional system from which are differentiated many smaller systems which still remain under the potential dominance of the whole in gradients but which are linked to each other in a circular process of transaction or communication just as the total organism is related to its environment.[10] The intrapersonal functions may be classified into many discrete parts, but the living boundaries between each are ill-defined, incomplete and variable, and dependent upon the transactions occurring in any particular time and place. The integration within and between each system, and the defenses against disintegration, constitute the forces that tend to maintain a steady state. Health and sickness are only variations in degree of the same process.

Activity in one system is communicated and stimulates within many others processes which are often of such small quantity and such short duration that they are not measurable by our existing methods. If a stimulus which impinges on an appropriate system is of such quantity or duration that it constitutes a strain, responses will set into action which tend to return that system to a relatively steady state, but other systems will also be involved in this process. When a given system is strained in handling a particular stress, the minor, perhaps unmeasurable preparatory changes in another system become intensified and apparent as another response to the initial stimulus. The integration within a single system is dependent upon its capacity to act alone without strain before a new order of action is set off within other systems with which it is in transaction.[11]

In either case, from a single system which may functionally disintegrate because of strain to all systems and eventually to a total response, activity progressively increases to facilitate the maintenance of an internal steady state. The result is a multiplicity of circular and corrective processes between systems which are oriented toward stabilizing the organism and maintaining its integration. A breakdown between boundaries only occurs when the stress becomes too severe and behavior resumes its primitive total pattern—that is, when the several systems which have been fractionated out of the total are no longer able to handle the stress.

Attempts to ascertain psychophysiological relations during the so-called resting or idling phases of life have not been very successful. As in all of medicine, integrated equilibrium is silent and symptom free. Can we find physiological or biochemical differences in various personality types or predict stress responses from functions at the idling level?

These are important questions which have great significance

for the understanding of the longitudinal course of illness and the prediction of future disease. There is some evidence that personalities characterized by extreme variability of ego functions are associated with wider and more intense synchronous biological stress-responses.[12] It is unfortunate that as yet we have developed only a few simple, easily applied tests that discriminate the structured components of personality from the transient psychological stress-responses and that we can use to make adequate physiological correlations. These are usually motoric in nature rather than cognitive or affective.[13]

During their resting levels, schizophrenics show few deviations in quality and quantity of biological responses but more variability under the same or dissimilar conditions. From the reverse point of view, the kind and degree of autonomic stability or instability, or even symptoms, do not have predictive value in determining the locus or intensity of individual stress-responses. In fact, idling variability in particular systems, such as the cardiovascular, does not portend somatic specificity of reaction to acute or chronic strains.[14]

Despite corrective efforts, the semantics of operations in psychosomatic research is still confused. We cannot utilize preconceptions regarding the expected effects of stimuli in evoking stress-responses. To be sure, there are catastrophes and holocausts in nature which are stressful to anyone. Ordinarily, stimuli are stressful (not stresses) only operationally if they evoke psychological or biological responses, or defenses against them, which indicate a disturbance in equilibrium—a measurable, significant change in one or more variables in any direction.

A stress response to *physical* stimuli is relatively easy to correlate with the strength of the stimulus; in fact, in experimental pharmacology the development of dose-response curves is a standard procedure. Psychological stimuli themselves have no standard responses, and our attempts to apply graded stimuli to evoke graded responses and to determine specific thresholds have been futile.

For a stimulus to have stress-evoking qualities, it must have personal meaning to the subject or constitute a universally appropriate threat. The latter is demonstrated by the fact that the strangeness of the experimental room and apparatus, even on a preexperimental day, is stressful for most subjects since it violates the human need for rapid cognitive orientation accompanying change.[15] Under these conditions, subjects with low anxiety respond to specific elements in the environment with considerable intensity. Those with high anxiety, however, respond less to specific stimuli and instead experience a gradual decrement of anxiety over time.[16]

We cannot predict with any certainty which personal stimuli will be meaningful to a given subject. For example, during a simple experiment with personnel moving in and out of the experimental chamber on appropriate occasions, it cannot be determined which subjects will respond with anxiety from being alone or from being with people. A knowledge of the personality of the experimental subject and his sensitive conflict areas affords clues to his vulnerability or proneness to specific probing stimuli. Fairly successful predictions can be made of the nature of the general stress response, that is, anxiety, anger, or depression. Although quality may be known, the necessary quantity of stimulus necessary to evoke a response is determined only by trial and error.[17]

Most successful in the production of stress-responses are nonspecific stimuli which impugn the subject's perceptual accuracy, threaten psychological disintegration, or impede or block communication.[18] These are much more effective than defense-removing, unconscious-conflict-probing specific stimuli, although lately motion pictures with a known central plot are being used for this purpose. This technique requires very careful control, especially of prior experiences and adaptations, and interpretations of the many possible meanings of the plot. For example, a group of healthy college students did not respond with anxiety on viewing a movie showing a bloody ocular operation because they had, unknown to us, witnessed many gory pictures of lung extirpations shown by a dean who hoped to discourage smoking.

Implicit attitudes are also a handicap in that patients in hospitals or clinics who are undergoing stress experiments do not readily accept threatening predictions that placebo capsules will make them sick or that physician-experimenters will in any way harm them.

Research in the stress field is handicapped by the fact that technical difficulties are present under all conditions: in studying stress-responses in life situations, in special field conditions such as war or training in dangerous skills, or in experimental and contrived situations. Efforts at teasing out the relative significance of general laws (nomothetic) and the special reactions or events (ideographic) require much greater control over the stimuli employed than heretofore applied. Specificity of stimuli is not a simple matter. Scientific studies require controls which are difficult to achieve with human beings because of their wide range of perceptions, experiences, and sensitivities. Yet it is necessary to determine comparable responses or their absence when a stressor is not applied.

Meaningful *psychological* stimuli evoke a variety of defensive psychological responses which are patterned in the individual as well as the stereotyped emotional and endocrine disturbances common to all stimuli. In fact, such a severe nonspecific stressor as epinephrine, which almost universally stimulates anxiety, is accompanied by physiological and subjective responses characteristic of the subject's stress-evoking experiences in his past life.[19]

Since our research designs prohibit action, the emotional responses of anxiety, anger, and depression, or combinations of them, become apparent. These may be observed as behavioral manifestations in gestures, movements, facial expressions, etc. They are also reportable by the subjects during the experience or are captured by interviews immediately after the experiment. There is a high reliability between observers' ratings and self-ratings in both quality and degree of emotional arousal. It is clear that to minimize inferences we cannot work with so-called unconscious affects. Using only verbally or behaviorally reportable emotions may narrow the field of content, but these alone are reliable and do achieve validity.

There is another serious problem in psychosomatic research which arises when physiological and psychological responses are disparate. This is the problem of defenses. How does a person adapt to or cope with the psychological stress, and to what degree and how do these defenses influence the homeostatic processes?

Here we have entered a field which requires special methods of observation, interviewing, reporting, and rating. Defenses or protective devices against stress-responses may be defined from several points of view because there are at least three categories of defenses. In the first the cues may not be consciously recognized by denial of perception or distortion of reality, so that the significance of the stimulus is not perceived—the "I won't look" technique.

The second group of psychological defenses is directed toward the affect itself, which is difficult for man to endure. For example, anxiety maintains alertness, interferes with sleep,[20] and is usually experienced as physical and mental "unpleasure." Man ascribes it to external causes, calls it fear, and moves away from the projected situation or person. Or he sets into operation numerous psychological defenses which become, as rituals, phobias, withdrawals, and regressions, the symptoms of some psychiatric syndromes. Social unrest is also dealt with by devices of repression.

The third category of defenses is direct against the effects of anxiety. Ego functions become strained to decrease the difficulties arising from lengthened perception-decision times, inaccuracy, decrease in confidence, and inability to learn. The source of danger becomes generalized, objectless, and discriminatory functions are lost. There is usually an accompanying feeling of disintegration, and this last-ditch defense may actually be a psychotic regressive break.

The highly acclaimed "breakthrough" into the understanding of the course of a variety of degenerative diseases, by ascribing a specific emotional etiology to each, has been disappointing. Psychosomatic research focusing on specific syndromes has been superseded by psychophysiological investigations utilizing modern instrumentation, into the phenomena of relationships between mind and body, concentrating mainly on emotions for the mental and on autonomic and endocrine functions for the somatic.

Unfortunately, these relationships cannot be reduced to the desired simplicity by considering somatic processes to be in the service of internal regulation and maintenance of homeostatic boundaries, and by considering the mental to be concerned with total behavior or outer adaptation to events, things, and other living objects. There are several reasons for this major difficulty: the inner-outer dichotomy breaks down operationally, the temporal characteristics of and within each system are widely different, and the mental is not examinable as a form of energy. Let me be more explicit.

1. Inner regulations do not consist only of reactions to outer stimuli, but also of responses to inner pressures leading to goal-seeking behavior. In addition, tension states are restlessly *sought* and facilitate *goal-changing behavior* which in turn requires a shift in internal regulation. In and out are inseparable as are man and his environment at every level of interaction from genes to behavior.

2. The temporal characteristics of mental operations are as rapid as neural conduction while other somatic processes, such as the endocrine secretions and peripheral sympathetic activities, are far slower and depend on chains or summations of effects involving autonomic, metabolic, and chemical processes.

Correspondingly, some of these processes occur later than those on which their sequence depends. Obviously, many somatic events may become evident long after the mental stimulus has apparently been dissipated, making correlations difficult if not impossible.

3. Mentation is a function which transcends space-time characteristics of bodily processes even though it is dependent on them. Although energy concepts cannot bridge the chasm between physiology and psychology, the history of American psy-

chology has nevertheless been replete with attempts to use the neural models of reflex activity relating stimulus and response, which ultimately minimizes the mental.

The multiplicity of variables requiring simultaneous observations demands the use of multidisciplinary research teams, which we were one of the first to develop in psychiatry. Our methodological general innovations—without specifying details—consisted of:

1. Simultaneous (as close as possible) measurement of variables studied
2. The development of reliable rating estimates of aroused anger, anxiety, and depression as well as defenses
3. The use of a transactional probing interview to stir up emotional responses through meaningful stimuli communicated to prone individuals
4. Measurements of hormonal changes, autonomic responses (heart rate and amplitude, respiratory rate, blood pressure, etc.), somatic voluntary muscle tension, affective responses, and total behavior

The general results indicate that many responses accompany any affective arousal and are not specific. For the economy of the organism these hormones may have significance for adaptation to physical stress by potentiating the activity of the sympathetic nervous system revealed in part by elevation of heart rate and blood pressure.[21] Yet their utility in psychological stress seems minimal. We have found that the neuromuscular system exhibits individual response-specificity as does the autonomic nervous system. It is expected that these will be related to personality traits—not diagnostic entities. Nor is it likely that any physiological response (as Lasswell reported) can be related to therapeutic outcome.

We have taken a simple theoretical concept of a specific emotional reaction to a specific physiological response and helped make it a highly complicated and puzzling field in which there is a complex transactional pattern of stressors, stress-responses, defenses, and personality involving, in various combinations, multiple chains of events from the central nervous system to its various peripheral outflows. Depending on the drives and needs of the organism and the changing environment, stimuli constantly entering the central nervous system, derived from meaningful environmental cues, set off responses in appropriately sensitive individuals. Depending upon the somatic and psychological sensitivity of the individual, the nature and intensity of the stimulus, the quality of the protective devices, and the defenses psychologically available, greater quantities of disturbance lasting for long periods of time (sometimes shorter as in bereavement) may end in so-called diseases. The ultimate application of this research is to determine the pathways to this end point of illness.

When a new field of investigation is explored, the initial results obtained are limited by current theory and by the available methods. The history of science reveals that pioneers usually open a Pandora's box of complexities, however well organized by man's proclivity for order and continuity. Lasswell started direct psychophysiological observations on humans during a stress situation. His available methods were crude according to current standards. He had no strain gauges, transducers, tape recorders, or electronic polygraphs. He worked with few subjects and no controls. There were no objective observers not involved in the dyadic transaction. In sum, his physiological and behavioral measures were primitive. Lasswell's psychological variables were indefinable and not referable to suitable criteria, and his personality variable was an unreliable outcome of therapy.

Yet, although untrained as an psychoanalyst, he ventured to record, at least in part, verbalizations, pulse rate, skin resistance, and body movements in a stressful interview. It was twenty-five years before scientists repeated this with better equipment and improved methods. His concept of personality as process and as a system in equilibrium is still imperfectly understood, and investigators even today do not understand the necessity of defining their positions as observers, of clarifying their level of discourse, and of clearing their semantic confusions.

REFERENCES

1. H. D. Lasswell, "Verbal References and Physiological Changes during the Psychoanalytic Interview," *Psychoanalytic Review*, 22 (1935):10–24.

2. H. D. Lasswell, "Certain Prognostic Changes during Trial (Psychoanalytic) Interviews," *Psychoanalytic Review*, 23 (1936): 241–47.

3. H. D. Lasswell, "What Psychiatrists and Political Scientists Can Learn from One Another," *Psychiatry*, 1 (1938):33–39.

4. H. D. Lasswell, "Person, Personality, Group, Culture," *Psychiatry*, 2 (1939):533–61.

5. R. R. Grinker, *Psychosomatic Research* (New York: W. W. Norton, 1953; rev. ed., New York: Grove Press, 1961).

6. J. L. Halliday, *Psychosocial Medicine: A Study of the Sick Society* (New York: W. W. Norton, 1948); T. Parsons, "Illness and the Role of the Physician: A Sociological Perspective," *American Journal of Orthopsychiatry*, 21 (1951):452; L. E. Hinkle and H. Wolff, "The Nature of Man's Adaptation to His Total Environment and the Relation of This to Illness," *Archives of Internal Medicine*, 99 (1957):442; J. Ruesch, "Psychosomatic Medicine and the Behavioral Sciences," *Psychosomatic Medicine*, 23 (1961):277.

7. F. Deutsch, ed., *On the Mysterious Leap from the Mind to the Body* (New York: International Universities Press, 1959).

8. F. Alexander, *Psychosomatic Medicine* (New York: W. W. Norton, 1950).

9. R. R. Grinker, ed., *Toward a Unified Theory of Human Behavior* (New York: Basic Books, 1956).

10. J. B. Richmond and E. Lipton, "Some Aspects of the Neurophysiology of the New-Born and Their Implications for Child Development," in *Dynamic Psychopathology in Childhood*, ed. L. Jessner and E. Pavenstedt (New York: Grune & Stratton, 1959); H. J. Grossman and N. H. Greenberg, "Psychosomatic Differentiation in Infancy," *Psychosomatic Medicine*, 19 (1957):293; N. Greenberg and J. Loesch, "A Longitudinal Evaluation of Some Relations between Behavior and Autonomic Activity in the First Three Months of Life" (in press); C. M. Child, *Patterns and Problems of Development* (Chicago: University of Chicago Press, 1941).

11. R. R. Grinker, S. Korchin, H. Basowitz, D. Hamburg, M. Sabshin, H. Persky, J. Chevalier, and F. Board, "A Theoretical and

122 / ROY R. GRINKER, SR.

Experimental Approach to Problems of Anxiety," *Archives of Neurology and Psychiatry,* 76 (1956):420.

12. H. Basowitz, H. Persky, S. J. Korchin, and R. R. Grinker, *Anxiety and Stress: An Interdisciplinary Study of a Life Situation* (New York, McGraw-Hill, 1955).

13. J. I. Lacey, "The Evaluation of Autonomic Responses: Toward a General Solution," *Annals of the New York Academy of Science,* 67 (1956):123.

14. D. Oken, R. R. Grinker, H. A. Heath, M. Herz, M. Sabshin, and N. B. Schwartz, "The Relation of Physiological Response to Affective Expression," *Archives of General Psychiatry,* 5 (1962): 336.

15. M. Sabshin, D. A. Hamburg, R. R. Grinker, H. Persky, H. Basowitz, S. Korchin, and J. Chevalier, "Significance of Preexperimental Studies in the Psychosomatic Laboratory," *Archives of Neurology and Psychiatry,* 78 (1957): 207.

16. M. Glickstein, J. Chevalier, S. Korchin, H. Basowitz, M. Sabshin, D. Hamburg, and R. R. Grinker, "Temporal Heart-Rate Patterns in Anxious Patients," *Archives of Neurology and Psychiatry,* 78 (1957):101.

17. D. A. Hamburg, M. Sabshin, F. Board, R. R. Grinker, S. Korchin, H. Basowitz, H. Heath, and H. Persky, "Classification and Rating of Emotional Experiences," *Archives of Neurology and Psychiatry,* 79 (1958):415.

18. S. Korchin, H. Basowitz, R. R. Grinker, D. A. Hamburg, H. Persky, M. Sabshin, H. Heath, and F. Board: "Experience of Perceptual Distortion as a Source of Anxiety," *Archives of Neurology and Psychiatry,* 80 (1958):98.

19. H. Basowitz, S. Korchin, D. Oken, M. Goldstein, and H. Gussack, "Anxiety and Performance Changes with a Minimal Dose of Epinephrine," *Archives of Neurology and Psychiatry,* 76 (1956): 98.

20. R. Jeans, and J. E. P. Toman, "Anxiety and Cerebral Excitability," *Archives of Neurology and Psychiatry,* 75 (1956):534.

21. B. T. Engel, "Stimulus-Response and Individual-Response Specificity," *A.M.A. Archives of General Psychiatry,* 2 (1960):305; J. I. Lacey, D. E. Bateman, and R. Van Lehn, "Autonomic Response Specificity: An Experimental Study," *Psychosomatic Medicine,* 15 (1953):8; M. A. Wenger, T. L. Clemens, D. R. Coleman, T. D. Cullen, and B. T. Engel, "Autonomic Response Specificity," *Psychosomatic Medicine,* 23 (1961):185.

5

Toward a Psychiatry of Politics

ARNOLD A. ROGOW

WHEN and if psychiatry and political science join forces against the multitude of social ills that afflict the world, the merger will be a culmination, in a sense, of Harold D. Lasswell's efforts over a period of more than forty years to demonstrate that certain types of psychopathology are both cause and effect in relationship to politics. While Lasswell was not the first to argue that unconscious as well as conscious mental states influence and are influenced by political behavior, he was and remains the most impressive exponent of the view that psychiatry, especially psychoanalysis, has much to offer political science.

Until recently it was possible to regard this view as a distinctly minority position shared by no more than a handful of his colleagues, and perhaps a brief review of some of the reasons for Lasswell's earlier isolation would not be out of order. To begin with, the political science fraternity, trained to think of political behavior as essentially the outcome of conscious mental processes (and hence susceptible to direct observation, measurement, and, more recently, rigorous quantification), has always preferred Calvin, Coke, and the contract theorists to the ideologues of the couch. It is also possible that the great majority of political scientists, unable or unwilling to master Lasswell's special vocabulary, has never understood what he was writing about. Thus, when Lasswell's *World Politics and Personal Insecurity* appeared in 1935, it was reviewed in the *American Political Science Review* by one of the Princeton brethren in the following terms:

I am greatly indebted to Thomas Kappner for research assistance above and beyond the call of graduate-student duty.

In this excellently printed, tempestuous, and obstreperous volume, Dr. Lasswell leaps about the cosmos of sociological-psycho-biological-obstetrical-psychiatric political science with the abandon of a flock of sparrows at a horse-show. The title may seem to include everything from here to there, but the book actually does so, and with a rattling fusillade of partially related footnotes. . . . Western Europe has known [about the dangers of insecurity] since Aristotle at best, and the Chinese sages since time immemorial. What this book contributes is the author's modernist-cubist anfractuosities of dialectical metaphysic. It is hard to see how our universities can help our laboring, lumbering democracy by telling people what they know in language they will not understand. . . .

But the review was not entirely uncomplimentary. In addition to praising the printing, Professor Walter Lincoln Whittlesey had a kind word for the "adequate index."

Another important factor is that Lasswell, most of whose teaching career has been at the Yale Law School, has not been a dominant figure in any political science department and he has never taught any large number of graduate students, much less created a "school" of disciples. A third difficulty is the problem of applying psychoanalytic and psychiatric findings to the group and institutional context of politics. While the relevance of such findings to *individual* behavior was widely accepted, most political scientists did not see themselves as biographers or even as catalogers of political types. Those interested in exploring psychiatry and psychoanalysis found it difficult and expensive to acquire the necessary training, and the intrepid few who underwent analysis or who were accepted as research candidates for training by the various psychoanalytic institutes often found the results somewhat disappointing in terms of both personal and professional rewards. For these and other reasons, political scientists have never built an expressway to Lasswell's door in accordance with the better mousetrap principle; indeed, most would have denied that any better mousetrap was involved.

By now, however, there is much evidence of a renewed interest in possible relationships between psychiatry and political science. No doubt this interest is partly due to an increasing suspicion that mental states and personal factors are often important in determining whether there is to be war or peace, alienation or participation, genocide or racial coexistence, violence or safety in the streets, lives that are mean and desperate or lives that are productive and worthwhile. More and more there is talk of a merger between preventive psychiatry, one of whose expressions is the growing community mental health program, and preventive politics, which may be defined as the politics that seeks to avoid war, gross poverty and inequality, prejudice, and vast increases in the number of those mentally ill.

All such programs, and many more, have been implicitly if not explicitly called for by Lasswell's work in psychiatry and politics, and what he has on occasion labeled *political psychiatry* and *integrative politics* is a key aspect of his insistence that political science is or should be a *policy science.* This emphasis appears to be congenial to the younger generation of practitioners who are impatient with some of the newer "objective," or "value-free" orientations and quantitative methodologies. Quite apart from his interest in psychodynamic areas, Lasswell has always been a macropolitical scientist, and in an age of continuing and seemingly endless crisis the desire to be relevant to the great issues holds more appeal for some younger political scientists than the desire to occupy a chair in micropolitics or comparative functionalism.

Lasswell's own concern with the implications for politics of psychiatry and psychoanalysis was encouraged by Charles E. Merriam, for many years chairman of the department of political science at the University of Chicago. Merriam, whose own interest in personality studies was reflected in a number of publications, created a permissive environment for Lasswell and other students who preferred psychological inquiry to the customary emphasis in political science on legalistic, historical, and philosophical exegesis. In accordance with this interest, Lasswell sought training in psychiatric hospitals and clinics, underwent a personal psychoanalysis, and embarked upon a study program that included conducting under supervision the psychoanalyses of others. Among his teachers were William Alanson White, Harry Stack Sullivan, and Nolan D. C. Lewis of Washington; Gregory Zilboorg in New York; Alfred Adler, Paul Federn, and Edward Hitschmann in Vienna; Sandor Ferenczi in Budapest; and Theodor Reik, Karen Horney, and Franz Alexander in Berlin.

On the basis of free-associative interviews and his study of the psychotherapeutic records of politicians who had been hospitalized, Lasswell published in 1930 what is probably his best-known book in the general area of political psychodynamics, *Psychopathology and Politics*.[1] In an effort to delineate the psychological profiles of certain political actors, notably administrators and agitators, Lasswell produced a behavioral inventory of political types and developed a good deal of insight into the psychology of political convictions. Almost four decades later, *Psychopathology and Politics* has still not been superseded by other works emanating from psychologically-minded political behaviorists; indeed, the book has achieved the status of a classic not just in the field of political psychodynamics but in the entire corpus of twentieth-century political science literature.

Psychopathology and Politics, however, was not Lasswell's first effort to develop a psychiatry of politics. As the bibliography demonstrates, Lasswell wrote a number of articles during the 1920s in the general area of personality and on the psychological aspects of national character, propaganda, and international order. The 1930s saw the publication of another enormously influential book in addition to the already mentioned *World Politics and Personal Insecurity*, Lasswell's *Politics: Who Gets What, When, How*.[2] He also wrote a vast number of monographs and articles on subjects ranging from propaganda analysis to the behavior of persons on relief. During the 1940s there appeared, among other books, *Personality and Politics*[3] (first presented as the Thomas William Salmon Memorial Lectures of the New York Academy of Medicine), and, again, a considerable number of shorter publications covering almost the whole spectrum of the social and behavioral sciences. With the exception of certain collaborative ventures, Lasswell's books since *Personality and Politics* have not been principally focused on politically psychodynamics, although there has been a continuing output of monographs and articles in that field.[4]

Any survey of such a rich, diverse, and comprehensive *oeuvre* faces a problem similar to that confronting the art critic who attempts to deal with the thousands of creations in every possible medium that are associated with Picasso; as one of them commented not long ago (on the occasion of Picasso's eighty-fifth birthday retrospective show in Paris), future generations would never believe that Picasso was one man—they would think he was an entire academy of artists. It is probable that Lasswell has written more than any other political scientist in history, living or dead, and the task of assessing this formidable contribution becomes only slightly easier by confining it to a single category of work, such as psychiatry and politics. My intention, therefore, is to deal selectively with Lasswell's writings concerned with political psychodynamics rather than to attempt to say something about each book, monograph, article, and book review. In particular, I am more interested in themes than in details and more concerned to explicate his general approach than to treat every facet of what Lasswell conceives of as the psychiatry of politics.

In broad terms, his writings in this area are distributed over three branches of the subject. The first is the study of personality as such, and includes a number of articles dealing with political types, problems of biography and personality data gathering, and certain relationships between personality systems and political behavior. Much of this writing, although by no means all, dates back to the latter half of the 1920s and reflects the influence upon Lasswell of George Herbert Mead, William I. Thomas, and Merriam, among others. These writings reflect an interest in psychoanalytic theory, but the emphasis is less psychoanalytic than psychological in the sense that the personality theory utilized by Lasswell derives from a variety of psychologists and sociologists.

The second category of his writings is concerned with aspects of psychiatry and psychoanalysis, and their implications for the study of politics. Here the influence of Freud, Adler, and Sullivan is apparent. The essential argument is that political behavior as such cannot be understood without the psychoanalysis of leaders and followers, revolutionaries and conformists, the sick and the well. This set of writings also includes several articles concerned with interviewing techniques, at least two of which are of a clinical nature in that they are designed to facilitate the perceptions and observations of psychoanalysts with reference to patients. It is worth noting that while much of this writing was or should have been relevant to the interests of political behaviorists, most of it did not appear in political science journals and was therefore, presumably, unread by most members of the American Political Science Association.

The third subfield of Lasswelliana might be termed applied psychoanalysis, that is, writings that attempt to psychoanalyze specific phenomena, events, or problems drawn from the political arena and the world scene. In this category can be grouped books and articles dealing with peace and international harmony, Hitlerism and fascism, communism, socialism, elites, symbols, communications and propaganda, myths, and values. The interaction of values, institutions, and personality in a democratic society has been a special concern within this category, and, indeed, few of Lasswell's writings in any field since 1940 have not been concerned with the shaping and sharing of values in a setting of respect for human dignity.

Inasmuch as his books in the area of political psychodynamics are well known and readily available—almost all of them have been published in paperback editions—the remainder of this essay will explore the articles, monographs, and reviews that have been appearing more or less regularly since 1925, many of which are unknown to poltical scientists including those who share Lasswell's interest in political psychiatry.

The first such article, apparently, was a review of two early books, both of them psychological inquiries into the nature of nationalism and patriotism. Appearing in the *American Political Science Review* in 1925, "Two Forgotten Studies in Political Psychology" dealt with J. G. Zimmerman's *Essay on National Pride* (Zurich, 1758) and Gottfried Duden's *Concerning the Essential Differences of States and the Motives of Human Nature* (Cologne, 1822).[5] Lasswell, characteristically it turned out, did not just "disinter" these two studies or review their contents. He endeavored to discover the possible motivations of the authors for their interest in psychological inquiry. This motivation, in Zimmerman's case, "was determined by a pathologically sensitive nature. He is said to have inherited from his mother those recurring fits of depression which often drove him from the society of men and finally developed into the derangement which appeared in the last few months of his life (1795)." About Duden Lasswell was able to discover nothing that might possibly explain his approach.

Following an outline of Zimmerman's thesis about the origins of natural pride and the role of pride in the relations between nations, Lasswell contrasts Zimmerman's approach with that of "modern" students of nationalism, and in so doing anticipates much of his own work in the area. Today's student of nationalism, wrote Lasswell, "would demand from the outset a more behavioristic idea of national pride than Zimmerman gives him. He would give more attention to the press as a means of controlling patriotism. . . . He would explore the possibility of using personality studies in an effort to explain super-patriots, sub-patriots, and other individualized types who appear in the national group."

One may infer that Lasswell in 1925 found Duden rather more provocative than Zimmerman, and, again, there is a tip to what Lasswell himself was later to investigate, especially in his 1936 book *Politics: Who Gets What, When, How*. Duden's importance, he observed, "lies in [his] attempt to conceive of political power as a psychological complex of many elements. He is rigidly objective and tries to explain the forces at work, rather than to justify the forces he prefers to work."[6] The significance of Duden's book, he continued, "lies in his analysis of the motives upon which power is based," in the course of which he "cut through the metaphysical abstractions of his time, ignored theological dogma, passed by the fiction of contract, and discarded the unitary theory of force. His hypotheses are psychological and take account of multiple elements." Lamenting the failure to follow up Duden's lead, Lasswell comments that Duden's analysis, "fragmentary though it was, consisting more of insights than of demonstrations, was pointed squarely in the direction of the most productive line of subsequent political thought."

In a 1929 essay, "Types of Political Personality,"[7] Lasswell pursued further lines of inquiry that had been drawn in some earlier writings, including the review of books by Zimmerman and Duden, and that were to receive fuller amplification in his *Psychopathology and Politics* of 1930. Political institutions, he began his essay, "have a twofold function: they favor the accession of men of particular attributes to positions of effective influence, and they continue to operate upon the personalities of the influential." Thus, "bourgeois democracy," "autocracy," and other political systems have their characteristic personality types, as do bureaucracy, diplomacy, reform and revolutionary movements, "responsible leadership," and bossism. "Aggressive innovative personalities," he also noted, "are favored in moments of social crisis (Lloyd George, Clemenceau); conciliatory, undramatic persons rise to prominence in the aftermath of crisis (Harding)." Lasswell's major emphasis, however, is the personality attributes of the agitator, the "responsible leader" or statesman, and the boss, and his delineations of these personality types are incisive and sharply drawn.

A later article of 1929, "Personality Types,"[8] is given over to a recurring interest, which is intellectual history with special reference to clinical and social psychologists, psychiatrists, and psychologically minded sociologists and political scientists. "Personality Types" deals perceptively with the contributions of G. H. Mead, W. I. Thomas, and, to a lesser extent, F. M. Thrasher,

L. Wirth, L. D. White, E. C. Hughes, E. W. Burgess, and others. About his former mentor Charles E. Merriam, Lasswell wrote that in the latter's 1922 publication, *The American Party System*, there had appeared a provisional list of traits characterizing political leaders and that Merriam had called for further studies of leaders focusing on investigations of heredity, environment, and techniques of power utilization. Some of this material, Lasswell commented, had been developed in graduate seminars led by Merriam, and had been productive of a number of master's theses, but much remained to be done. His essay concluded with a plea —since repeated many times—for a systematic collection of records about individuals who have been intensively studied "by almost every known method," including psychoanalysis.

Individuals to be intensively studied, Lasswell wrote in another article aimed at psychiatrists and published about the same time, should include "normal" people or those with only minor difficulties to facilitate determination of the degree to which material emanating from ordinary or "normal" persons differs from material obtained from pathological types. In an instance cited by Lasswell, a committee of physicians and other trained personnel, to whom a small number of intimate life histories were read, was unable to distinguish between the records of those who were institutionalized and those who were not (clinical information for the former had been eliminated). Urging the importance of comprehensive data-gathering with reference to persons, Lasswell suggested that the desired records should include:

autobiography (before beginning analysis)
verbatim account of the psychoanalysis (perhaps by tape recorder)
psychoanalyst's notes on the interview
subject's notes on the interview
mechanical record of couch movements
specimens of the subject's handwriting
biography of the subject
physical and psychometrical examination records
analyst's interpretation of the total development of the subject's
    personality

consultation record
records of experiments and their interpretations
subsequent history of the subject[9]

Other writings in 1929 and 1930, including an article that appeared in the *American Political Science Review*, continued to emphasize the importance for political-behavior study of life-history records more comprehensive than those usually available. In the article referred to, Lasswell recommended that "especially prominent figures" should be studied as well as ordinary people and those in institutions, arguing that the differences between the sick and the healthy are not as sharp as conventional public opinion is inclined to believe. "Neurotic symptoms and traits," he reminded his readers, "are never entirely absent from any life history." Moreover, the study of the ill would alert political and business administrators to possible personality problems in their own organizations, and in that fashion increase their skill in dealing with subordinates.[10]

An early version of what later became the *developmental construct* appeared for the first time in a 1930 article devoted to somatic expressions of the personality system, and here Lasswell's emphasis was explicitly psychoanalytic. Noting that psychiatrists were accustomed to view the personality system as a complex of "somatic reactions, autistic reveries, adjustive thinking, and object orientations," he argued that comparisons between personality systems could be made on the basis of their "substitutive reactions" when faced with similar conditions. By choosing his examples from the political world, Lasswell was demonstrating, in effect, that political behavior is itself a component part of the personality system, closely involved with other components, and not an action form independent of the personality system. Thus, "Mr. A.," a city councilman for whom political activity was a substitute for neurosis, developed autistic reveries and had to be confined to a sanitarium following defeat for reelection; "Mr. B.," for whom politics was a substitute for hysteria, became hypochondriacal and finally developed a host of gastrointestinal disturbances when he lost his campaign for the legislature; "Mr.

C.," dismissed from his administrative position, substituted a sexual-object orientation for the former political-object orientation by taking mistresses and consorting with prostitutes; "Mr. D.," on the other hand, practiced law following a defeat for Congress, "showing that his object orientation in politics was no more than one alternative orientation among many nonspecifically sexual objects."

Again there was emphasis on the utility for personality study of the "prolonged interview," so highly developed by Freud, as a way of facilitating "developmental" and "reactive" predictions regarding the individual's behavior. The "developmental sequence," Lasswell wrote, "would, schematically speaking, take some form such as this: Individuals who meet crisis A with pattern A^1 are likely to meet crisis B with pattern B^1. . . ." The crises referred to were those that accompany physical and psychological growth to maturity, such as weaning and toliet training; the context was development and prediction in personality terms rather than in terms of broad historical and sociological trends. But the interest in forecasting, predicting, and influencing events that later led Lasswell to advocate the *developmental construct* as a powerful tool of social science analysis and policy is apparent.[11]

In a 1932 article, the title of which expressed Lasswell's flair for dramatic and terse expression, he attempted to work out some political and sociological equivalents of Freud's division of the personality into id, ego, and superego components. "The Triple-Appeal Principle" argued that the personality divisions "function in special ways in person-to-person relationships, in the role and meaning of institutions, and in person-to-occasion relationships. . . . The tripartite principle may also be extended to analysis of policies and practices, doctrines, and myths and legends. It is particularly promising when applied to the problem of social dynamics." The article's essential point was that institutions, relationships, and behaviors of all sorts relate to id, ego, or superego demands, and to a very large degree derive their strength and survival capacity from their ability to gratify such demands. In customary fashion, "The Triple-Appeal Principle" was profusely illustrated with examples taken from worlds as far apart as business and art.[12]

The relationship between psychoanalysis, culture, and personality was the theme of a 1933 *Imago* article published in Vienna (it would be fascinating to know whether the article was read by Freud, founder of *Imago* and one of its editors in 1933). Stressing the interrelatedness of intensive (psychoanalytic) and extensive (sociological) methods of studying culture, Lasswell insisted that the meaning and implications of material elicited from patients by psychoanalysts cannot be properly evaluated unless the analyst is familiar with the cultural context of the material. In addition to urging that psychoanalytic methods be subjected to cross-cultural observations, he suggested that psychoanalysis could make, indeed was already making, an important contribution to the understanding of social change, knowledge of symbols, and the processes by which the "externalization of fantasy" undergoes change. In other words, the dialogue within culture and personality between the inner world of subjective events and the outer world of external reality could only be comprehended through the techniques and insights of psychoanalysis.[13]

One of the earliest and most perceptive analyses of Naziism, as well as a powerful demonstration of the relevance of psychiatry to an understanding of politics, appeared in July of 1933, not long after Hitler came to power. In "The Psychology of Hitlerism" there is a wealth of insight into the psychodynamics of the Nazi movement that, far from having been dated by the research undertaken since, receives fresh support from almost every new study of the subject. Perhaps it is even true that "The Psychology of Hitlerism" is the best short psychological treatment of Naziism that has ever been published.

Lasswell began by noting that any political order is endangered if it "fails to coincide with an era of international prestige and domestic prosperity," but it was necessary to look deeper than this for an explanation of Hitler's success. In fact, he continued, it was not necessary to assume, because Hitlerism was in part a "desperation reaction of the lower middle classes that had been developing since the close of the 19th century," that the lower middle classes were worse off at the end of that century than they were at the beginning. More significant from a psychological viewpoint was the overshadowing of the lower middle class by the workers and upper bourgeoisie "whose unions, cartels and parties took the center of the stage." The resulting "psychological impoverishment" set the stage for various mass movements of which Naziism was one type. As Lasswell put it, "rebuffed by a world which accorded them diminished deference, limited in the opportunities afforded by economic reality, the [lower middle class] needed new objects of devotion and new targets of aggression."

Nationalism, as one such object, substituted for the "fading appeal of institutionalized religion." Anti-Semitism fulfilled a variety of needs: guilt feelings "arising from lack of personal piety" could be expiated by persecuting Jews; Jewish profiteering instead of capitalism as such could be attacked, thus providing opportunities for the discharge of animosities toward rich capitalists without necessitating the embrace of socialism (in this respect anti-Semitism appealed also to the landed aristocracy); feelings of inferiority, especially on the part of non-Jewish intellectuals, could be appeased by focusing discontent on Jewish intellectuals, doctors, lawyers, writers, actors, and journalists.

A particularly astute portion of the article concerned the relationship between the achievements of certain Jewish intellectuals and the ascetic side of Naziism and Hitler's public personality. Observing that the German middle class had been scandalized even as it was fascinated by psychoanalysis, the invention of a Jewish physician, and by plays and other art forms emanating from Jews which were iconoclastic and sensationalist in nature, Lasswell pointed out that for many Germans Hitlerism became the embodiment of sexual abstinence, thrift, work, and piety—in short, the embodiment of all the solid but disappearing middle-class virtues. Hitler himself also played "a maternal role" in that he discoursed on all manner of pedagogical problems and was constantly preoccupied with "purity." Finally, Hitler was able to deflect aggressive impulses from those aspects of national character Germans did not like in themselves, aspects regarded as weak and immoral, to the Jews, who supposedly personified all that was base and evil in German life: "Since the Germans hate most in themselves, as a collective unit, cultural diversity and intellectual virtuosity (qualities which they simultaneously admire), it is scarcely surprising to discover that they have turned upon the Jew as the most typical exponent of their own limitations."[14]

The article on Hitlerism was followed by a study of the behavior exhibited by persons on relief toward relief administrators,[15] and two articles, referred to earlier, dealing with changes that occur in the course of the psychoanalytic interview.[16] In 1937, four years after the analysis of Hitlerism, Lasswell, in collaboration with Renzo Sereno, turned his attention to Fascist Italy, but the focus of attention was "class, skill, personality, and attitude characteristics of officials," rather than psychodynamics. Part of the article was given over to a classification of Italian public-law agencies in terms of their increasing or decreasing importance, and the remainder, anticipating the later elite or RADIR Project studies,[17] dealt with the social origins, skills, and other attributes of the personnel of these agencies.[18]

Lasswell's conceptions of political psychiatry and integrative politics began to take explicit form in a 1938 article that appeared in the first issue of *Psychiatry*, journal of the William Alanson White Psychiatric Foundation.[19] Observing that the psychiatrist speaks less and less of "human personality as the hazy corona which surrounds the syndrome . . . ," Lasswell argued that both psychiatry and political science must inevitably deal with the functioning and adjustment of the personality within a given environment. Noting that psychiatrists and political scientists are concerned with causal relationships, the former with reference to mental illness and the latter with regard to political relationships, Lasswell went on to note that the psychiatrist too has an interest in the conditions that promote harmonious as well as inharmonious political relations and nonviolent as well as violent change.

Psychiatry, he indicated, is indispensable for the study of symbols because the psychiatrist, trained in methods of intensive observation of individuals for prolonged periods of time, "can examine in great detail the degree to which a given set of political symbols is integrated with the other features of the total personality."

Lasswell also insisted on the relevance to psychiatry of certain subject matters customarily studied by political scientists, such as the political order and social structure, problems of personnel recruitment in the public service, and the organization of political action. Psychiatrists, he observed in this 1938 article, do not relate their patients to the social structure or pay much attention to the political roles that are played, but it is to be hoped "as psychiatrists become aware of the significance of their data for these problems that they will voluntarily modify their procedures accordingly."[20] Thirty years later, despite the rise of social and community psychiatry and the increasing interest of psychiatrists in the social sciences, this hope remains to be realized.

On the eve of World War II Lasswell dealt at length with some of the themes articulated in earlier articles concerned with relationships between psychiatry and politics, but, unfortunately, none of these pieces appeared in any political science journal. As the bibliography reveals, from 1937 to 1950 Lasswell did not publish a single article (as distinguished from book reviews) in the *American Political Science Review* or any other political science journal, although his writings appeared with some frequency in the *American Journal of Sociology, Public Opinion Quarterly*, and in many of the psychiatric journals. Since these journals were not and still are not usually perused by political scientists, it is extremely doubtful that much of this work was read, much less appreciated, by Lasswell's disciplinary confreres, and perhaps this is one more reason for the relative indifference of political scientists, as noted earlier, to the possible contributions of psychiatry.

In a 1939 essay bearing the title "Political Psychiatry: The Study and Practice of Integrative Politics," Lasswell again stressed that "one of the specialties of great aid to psychiatry is political science." As psychiatry moves from the study of the organism to the study of interpersonal relations and the whole pattern of culture, it will discover that political science, focusing on the social distributions of safety, income, and deference, is also interested in interpersonal relations and broad cultural patterns.

The fusion of these shared interests of psychiatry and political science Lasswell labeled "political psychiatry," the central question of which was: "is it possible to learn how to cope with the destructive tendencies of man so that social development may proceed at the lowest human cost?" In answering such a question, political psychiatrists necessarily become involved in the study and practice of "integrative politics," which is the politics of understanding, treating, and curing "the sick features of the total situation." Sources of insecurity must be identified and, if possible, the insecurities relieved by techniques of catharsis ranging from education to "situational therapy." The main problem of integrative politics "is to guide acquiescence toward the acts of leaders whose policies do, in point of fact, diminish the signficant sources of insecurity." While he did not identify these sources except in a general way, he left no doubt that "whatever destroys effective interpersonal relationships in the community as a whole is disease" and, hence, a condition requiring treatment by students and practitioners of integrative politics.[21]

In 1941, roughly two years after the concepts of political psychiatry and integrative politics had made their appearance, Lasswell made it clear that a key purpose of both psychiatry and politics in a democratic society is to promote self-respect and reduce those impulses which are destructive to the self and others. Calling for the establishment of a "commonwealth of mutual deference," Lasswell emphasized the importance in a democracy of a general sharing of power, respect, and insight. To share in power, he insisted, "is to be consulted on important decisions. . . . Closely associated with the democratization of power is the democratization of respect; respect is another part of deference. To be respected is to be appreciated. . . ." And, he noted, "our own civilization has been conspicuously deficient in the practice of mutual respect." Finally, there is the "democratization of insight," defining insight as "a sense of common purpose—an understanding of common methods—throughout the community. There is insight when men and women are equipped with the skill of observation that enables them to discover and to regulate their own destructive impulses. . . ." In the United States of 1969 it seems hardly necessary to call attention to the continuing lack of mutual respect, insight, and sense of common purpose, not to mention the threat posed to the democratic polity by destructive impulses of all degrees and varieties.[22]

During the 1940s a number of Lasswell's publications were concerned with the conditions—political, economic, social, and psychological—of peace and world harmony, and with substantive and methodological problems in communications. There were relatively few writings with an explicitly psychiatric orientation until the late 1950s, and then, in articles that began to appear in 1959, Lasswell returned to his old interest in the relations between personality and politics. In a 1959 article titled "Political Constitution and Character," which began with a discussion of Plato, especially the extent to which Plato had anticipated Freud in certain respects, Lasswell underlined the point that *"the stability of the constitution depends upon the moulding of the appropriate form of character (or personality)."* After commenting on certain aspects of anxiety and its role in society, and observing that no one in modern society is totally free from anxiety, Lasswell, with characteristic insight, went on to comment: "The young people who were adolescent during a period of slackness . . . probably experience the greatest inner conflict. It is from them that we would expect to find recruited the most striking examples of conformity to exaggerated ideals. And some will probably endure the tension necessary to reject the reinstated ideal, to seek new models." Once again, the freshness and relevance of this observation to the current scene needs hardly to be remarked. The remainder of the article was given over to some nineteen propositions that, in Lasswell's view, merited further discussion and investigation and that are no less deserving of thought and research today than they were in 1959.[23] Unfortunately, neither this article nor others in the same general area appeared in political science literature.

This brief sketch of Lasswell's seminal contributions in the field of psychiatry and politics cannot pretend to be a complete summary of an achievement that stretches over more than forty years of sustained creative thought, but perhaps it can serve as a basis for the question: what can be said about this vast outpouring of theories, ideas, hypotheses, propositions, developmental constructs, and equations that collectively constitute the still-infant science of political psychiatry? There is no disputing one statement: very little of this considerable output is dated either in terms of world events or research advances. As regards the former, much of the predictive side of Lasswell's writings has been confirmed in the course of on-going history: the developmental construct of the "garrison state," for example, is essentially a more refined and sophisticated—one is tempted to say more intelligent—version of President Eisenhower's "industrial-military complex" which Eisenhower himself, apparently without being aware of it, did so much to create between 1953 and 1961.

Research in the field of psychiatry and politics, far from undermining Lasswell's insights, has tended to support them, but it is more important to note that most of these insights remain untested. While Lasswell has repeatedly declared that there is a vital connection between institutions and democratic character, we still cannot say with any precision what these connections are, or, specifically, what institutional changes are required to preserve or promote democratic personality types. As Lasswell put it in the 1959 article previously referred to (in the form of "proposition 19"), "the optimum requirements of free government and free enterprise in a dynamic society (in so far as they concern character, education and recruitment) are imperfectly understood, and require study now." Perhaps the "now" should have been in italics, and no doubt it will be by 1984, when it may be too late.

Of course, the fault does not lie entirely with political scientists, most of whom have been indifferent to the problems involved. Psychiatrists too have paid little attention to the research designs that Lasswell has been putting forward for same years. Many of them have been unable or unwilling to engage in that intensive study of patients, including their social and political setting, that Lasswell has repeatedly urged, and on the whole we still know very little about how private illnesses impinge upon public policies and vice versa. Neither the healthy nor the sick, in or out of political life, have been studied by all available methods; indeed, in psychiatry even elementary note-taking on cases leaves much to be desired. While it is hopeful that psychiatry in its current mood is becoming more interested in the social sciences, in terms of both findings and methods, productive collaboration remains to be accomplished.

Another dimension of Lasswell's achievement, and one largely missed by his readers and commentators, is its radical and even revolutionary commitment to democratic goals. Because Lasswell has always used a special vocabulary that most of his political science colleagues have never bothered to understand, and because, further, this vocabulary is notably free of emotive, polemical, and ideological expressions, Lasswell has been frequently misperceived to be an antidemocratic elitist and a reactionary who would do for and to society what B. F. Skinner has done for and to the pigeons. But there is no such thing as the "Lasswell box" in which people would be totally conditioned to respond in a certain fashion to cues and signals provided by a governing elite.

The Lasswellian conception of democracy has always stressed the widest possible shaping and sharing of those values that promote or exemplify human dignity. These values, in versions that he began to articulate in 1930, were safety, income, and deference, but this value triad was gradually broadened and redefined to include power, respect, affection, rectitude, well-being, wealth, enlightenment, and skill. A democratic commonwealth, in Lasswell's view, is characterized by a broad distribution of these values among the population, and not at all by a hoarding of them in accordance with class, color, or heredity. Leadership or access to power, for example, is to depend on merit with leadership opportunities open to all, but even the best (or healthiest) of leaders is, almost by definition, obligated to share power with others rather than monopolize it.

It is his conception of these key values and their role in society that makes Lasswell a radical social thinker. All revolutionary democrats, not merely Rousseau and Marx, have advocated the sharing of wealth and power, but practically none has argued for the democratization of such values as affection (the right to give and receive love, including sexual love), respect (the right to be treated with decency and dignity), and rectitude (the right not to be cheated or "conned," and the obligation not to cheat or "con" one's fellows), among other values. To be sure, Lasswell has not identified the particular institutional transformations that would promote such values, but neither did Rousseau indicate the political system required for the operation of the "general will," nor Marx produce a blueprint for the political economy that would follow the revolution. The fact is, we are so habituated to sloganizing about political and social change that we fail to recognize advocacy of such change unless it is accompanied by a certain barricade rhetoric. Hence the full import has been generally missed of what Lasswell means by political psychiatry and integrative politics.

There is evidence, however, that the essential Lasswell is beginning to be understood. In political science and the other social sciences, in psychiatry and related behavioral areas, the main thrust of Lasswell's thought has begun to take hold, with the result that there is an expanding interest in the relations between personality and politics, and in psychobiography and the psychodynamics of leadership. While it is still too early to regard political psychiatry and integrative politics as discrete research and teaching fields, there can be no mistaking a trend in that direction, one characteristic of which is an increasing collaboration between political scientists and psychiatrists. It is even possible, largely owing to Lasswell's inspiration, that political science, in the years that are left to it in the twentieth century, will become more rather than less relevant to the problems of the age.

REFERENCES

1. Chicago, University of Chicago Press.
2. New York: McGraw-Hill, 1936.
3. New York: W. W. Norton, 1948.
4. Arnold A. Rogow and H. D. Lasswell, *Power, Corruption, and Rectitude* (Englewood Cliffs, N.J.: Prentice-Hall, 1963); Robert Rubenstein and H. D. Lasswell, *The Sharing of Power in a Psychiatric Hospital* (New Haven: Yale University Press, 1966).
5. *American Political Science Review*, 19 (1925):707–17.
6. Compare the beginning of Lasswell's *Politics:* "The study of politics is the study of influence and the influential. The science of politics states conditions; the philosophy of politics justifies preferences. This book, restricted to political analysis, declares no preferences. It states conditions."
7. In E. W. Burgess, ed., *Personality and the Group* (Chicago: University of Chicago Press, 1929), pp. 151–62.
8. In T. V. Smith and L. D. White, eds., *Chicago: An Experiment in Social Change Research* (Chicago: University of Chicago Press, 1929), pp. 177–93.
9. "The Problem of Adequate Personality Records," *American Journal of Psychiatry*, 8 (1929):1057–66.
10. "The Study of the Ill as a Method of Research into Political Personalities," *American Political Science Review*, 23 (1929):996–1001.
11. See "The Policy Orientation," in Daniel Lerner and Harold D. Lasswell, eds., *The Policy Sciences* (Stanford, Calif.: Stanford University Press, 1951). There *developmental constructs* are defined as "speculative models of the principal social changes in our eopch. . . . They specify the institutional pattern *from* which we are moving and the pattern *toward* which we are going" (p. 11). It is in this sense that the developmental construct is predictive, although Lasswell does not argue that prediction is one of its principal utilities. In the 1935 *World Politics and Personal Insecurity* the developmental construct appears in the guise of "developmental analysis"; perhaps

the best example of the developmental construct as an analytic tool is Lasswell's "The Garrison State," *American Journal of Sociology*, 46 (1941):455–68; reprinted in *The Analysis of Political Behavior: An Empirical Approach* (London: Routledge and Kegan Paul, 1948). Current terms close in meaning to the developmental construct are *scenario*, as used by Herman Kahn and his associates, and *conjecture*, as defined and applied by Bertrand de Jouvenel and his *Futuribles* colleagues. See the latter's *The Art of Conjecture* (New York: Basic Books, 1967).

12. "The Triple-Appeal Principle: A Contribution of Psychoanalysis to Political and Social Science," *American Journal of Sociology*, 37 (1932):523–38.

13. "Psychoanalyse und Sozioanalyse," *Imago*, 19 (1933):377–83.

14. "The Psychology of Hitlerism," *Political Quarterly*, 4 (1933):373–84.

15. H. D. Lasswell and G. A. Almond, "Aggressive Behavior by Clients towards Public Relief Administrators," *American Political Science Review*, 28 (1934):643–55.

16. "Verbal References and Physiological Changes during the Psychoanalytic Interview: A Preliminary Communication," *Psychoanalytic Review*, 22 (1935):10–24; "Certain Prognostic Changes during Trial (Psychoanalytic) Interviews," *Psychoanalytic Review*, 23 (1936):241–47.

17. The RADIR (Revolution and the Development of International Relations) Project was conducted by the Hoover Institute of Stanford University during the early 1950s under a grant from the Carnegie Corporation. Daniel Lerner was director of research.

18. H. D. Lasswell and Renzo Sereno, "Governmental and Party Leaders in Fascist Italy," *American Political Science Review*, 31 (1937):914–29.

19. In 1938–39 Lasswell was a colleague at the Washington School of Psychiatry, one of whose faculty members was Harry Stack Sullivan. Sullivan founded *Psychiatry* in 1938.

20. "What Psychiatrists and Political Scientists Can Learn from One Another," *Psychiatry*, 1 (1938):33–39.

21. In Forest Ray Moulton and Paul O. Komora, eds., *Mental Health Publication of the American Association for the Advancement of Science*, no. 9 (Lancaster, Pa.: The Science Press, 1939), pp. 269–75.

22. "Psychology Looks at Morals and Politics," *Ethics*, 51 (1941): 325–36.

23. *Psychoanalysis and the Psychoanalytic Review*, 46 (1959): 3–18. See also "Approaches to Human Personality: William James and Sigmund Freud," *ibid.*, 47 (1960):52–68; and "Political Systems, Styles and Personality," in Lewis Edinger, ed., *Political Leadership and Industrial Societies: Studies in Comparative Analysis* (New York: Wiley and Sons, 1967), p. 316–47.

6

The Study of Political Processes in Psychiatric Illness and Treatment

ROBERT RUBENSTEIN

We're modern enlightened and we don't agree
with locking up patients We prefer therapy
through education and especially art
so that our hospital may play its part
faithfully following according to our lights
the Declaration of Human Rights[1]

IT was not until some thirty years after his pioneering studies in the psychology of politics, for which he interviewed and analyzed the records of participants in the political process who had been hospitalized, that Harold D. Lasswell was once again involved in research in a psychiatric hospital.

Largely under the influence of Maxwell Jones's *Therapeutic Community,*[2] the treatment of hospitalized psychiatric patients was changing drastically at that time. For example, beginning in 1956 at the Yale Psychiatric Institute, individual and small-group psychotherapeutic work was augmented by regularly held patient-staff meetings, forums in which all members of the hospital community participated, including patients, doctors, nurses, social workers, and other staff personnel. These meetings were viewed as therapeutic largely on the basis of elements they had in common with group psychotherapy: they provided an opportunity for self-exploration and the expression of affect; patients who found individual psychotherapeutic work too threatening or demanding could use such meetings for the vicarious expression of their concerns; transferences developed within the group which could be identified and explored. These forums, however, also had something of the character of a town meeting and of a Quaker business meeting: in addition to psychological exploration they were concerned with discussing and making decisions about immediate issues of importance to all members of the hospital community. Because of this recognition of the political character of patient-staff meetings, Lasswell was informed of these developments at the Yale Psychiatric Institute and was invited to join in observing and studying them; the research which resulted was reported in *The Sharing of Power in a Psychiatric Hospital*.[3] Lasswell's work had gone full circle from the application of psychoanalytic technique and the study of records of psychiatric hospital treatment for the elucidation of politics to the use of the psychiatric hospital as a laboratory in which political behavior and processes, the political aspects of forums which were now part of the treatment process, could be examined.

Lasswell was interested in the psychiatric hospital as an island of exemption from democratic practice, one of that group of organizations and institutions which also includes prisons, the armed forces, and most schools. These organizations are by and large not expected to protect the conventional citizenship rights of their participants or in other ways to reflect the prevailing ideology in their operation. Whether such an evasion of democratic practice was justified in the treatment of the psychologically ill was investigated, along with an examination of the grounds for this departure, in terms of its impact on the patient and his treatment, and possible wider implications. Of significance here was the hospital psychiatrist's traditional view of his responsibilities as including the paternalistic direction and control of his patients. He experienced this task as necessary to the fulfillment of his obligations as expert agent of the larger society which worried about and feared the psychologically ill as dangerous to themselves and to others, and as incapable of handling their own affairs or of participating responsibly in the decision process of the community. The emergence of the idea of a therapeutic community with Maxwell Jones' reports of the beneficial effects of patients' active participation in the hospital treatment program undermined this view of the psychiatrist's task. Being the passive recipient of the ministrations of others did not prepare the patient to assume the responsibilities demanded of him beyond the hospital as an active, effective participant in family, school, work, and the larger community. The feasibility of extending to all the hospitalized patient's experience the dignity, respect, responsibility, autonomy, and self-determination long acknowledged as central to psychoanalytic treatment was demonstrated. The psychiatrist was now confronted with evidence that his objectives as healer were in conflict with the authoritarian posture he had assumed toward his patients.

Lasswell's studies of the efforts of elites committed to democratic government to introduce and strengthen power-sharing practices in their newly developing countries enriched his perception of the efforts of psychiatrists and other staff members to involve patients in the hospital decision process. He studied this undertaking in the psychiatric hospital community as a prototype which might inform the devolution of power in larger contexts.[4] Lasswell recognized the changing psychiatric hospital as a setting in which social processes of wide significance could be meaningfully studied in microcosm.

In the federal antipoverty program, for example, which is directed at countering the effects of economic deprivation suffered by a large group of citizens, including many Negroes, efforts to encourage initiatives from these people for the improvement of their own lot have proved frustratingly difficult. This problem has occurred because the impoverished are not only economically disadvantaged but suffer from severe chronic deprivation in other value areas as well, including skill, enlightenment, respect, affection, rectitude, well-being, and power. They have minimal opportunities for education and vocational training, inadequate housing and nutrition, and minimal health services; they are ineffective politically, deprived of dignity, and are too often accepting of a derogatory self-image which reflects their having been discarded by the larger community as inferior and somehow bad. In any of these interrelated areas the obstacles they must struggle against, both within themselves and in society, are much the same, and the comprehensive character of the multiple deprivations they suffer realistically engenders feelings of hopelessness and powerlessness about being able to change their overwhelming, defeating experience in any way.

In the civil rights movement, a different but similarly destructive problem has blocked the fulfillment of objectives: initiatives taken at long last by Negroes themselves are too often violent in character and in other ways undermine the support required from other factions in our pluralistic society. Beyond being politically inept, riots and the cry "black power" reflect the impact of the chronic, comprehensive deprivations, especially in power, which have rendered Negroes unprepared for effecting constructive political participation.

These difficulties are further compounded by the tragic unavailability of responsible, competent, indigenous leadership: as soon as an individual finds the strength to appraise his predicament realistically, to seek out plausible alternatives, to mobilize his energies thoughtfully in quest of what he wants, he is no longer viewed, by himself or by others, as a member of the disadvantaged group.

The study of the hospitalized psychologically ill is relevant to these problems because in many ways they share the same disabilities: a position of inferiority and comprehensive deprivation; training by experience to accept being excluded, victimized, and exploited; lack of skill in, and no emotional preparation for using, the strategies and techniques of effective participation in family, school, work, and the larger communities of which they sought unsuccessfully to be a part; lack of leadership because an individual who begins to find his way is regarded as mentally healthy and leaves or is discharged. The deprivation of well-being, by which the emotionally ill person is identified, is compounded by related deprivations in other areas which are sustained in his treatment in the traditional psychiatric hospital. Frightening thoughts and feelings preoccupy and estrange him.

He is severely deprived in affection, convinced that those important to him do not care; he is unable to accept concern and tenderness, unable to feel or express love for anyone. Fears and longings consume him. He is deprived in power, enlightenment, skill, and wealth; assertive, definitive action has become impossible; attention to the external world, the turning away from inner demands, cannot be sustained; work is disrupted. Being psychiatrically ill is viewed as undermining of his status in the community and conveys ethical implications which reflect against the patient and all who are close to him. He is "put in the care of" experts, deprived of his autonomy and rights as a responsible citizen, subordinated to the direction and surveillance of the hospital staff.

In studying changes in the Yale Psychiatric Institute, the perspectives and predispositions of participants were characterized before and after the introduction of patient-staff conferences and Lasswell's value-institution and decision process techniques of analysis were applied to verbatim transcripts of these meetings. Interviews, questionnaires, and extensive participant-observation were used in gathering information from patients, members of the administrative medical staff, resident physicians, social workers, nurses, and attendants. The impact of these meetings on all members of the hospital community and on the treatment process was scrutinized and the participation of patients in the decision process was evaluated.

The study revealed that power was both authoritatively and effectively shared in the post-innovation hospital, that the innovations did involve patients in the joint consideration of issues individually and collectively important to them, especially in the information-sharing and appraisal phases of the hospital decision process. Nevertheless, its basically authoritarian character remained substantially unchanged despite the modifications introduced. Without consulting or obtaining the consent of the governed, senior physicians were still able to make decisions arbitrarily, to veto decisions made individually or collectively by other staff members or patients, and to act unilaterally without utilizing the institutions which had been established in part to prevent this. Although the new forums provided opportunities for the open, direct examination and criticism of such authoritarian behavior, the effective power of the hospital director and other senior doctors either did not decrease or was limited only enough to permit an appearance of democracy. The limits of democratic process were not openly acknowledged, explicated, or challenged, and as a consequence the burden imposed on the hospital community by the fact that effective power was retained by the senior doctors was compounded by the new, largely implicit, demand that all were now to pretend that the hospital was democratic. Aware of the importance of this fact for students of democracy concerned with the translation of doctrines of freedom into practice, Lasswell was especially interested in just why patients and staff members did not press harder to curb the director's power and make this hospital revolution more revolutionary. A detailed examination of the strivings and concerns of each of the components of the staff revealed that they were preoccupied with maximizing values other than power. Resident physicians, for example, emphasized skill and enlightenment, and sought affection and respect rather than power.

As to the senior doctors, the conflicts of conscience which they experienced when confronted with the significance of the idea of a therapeutic community were assuaged by the limited steps toward power sharing that were taken; giving up more power, which might jeopardize their ability to meet demands made by those in the larger community to whom they were responsible, was therefore not necessary to expiate feelings of guilt.

The use by senior physicians in patient-staff conferences of strategies which maintained their power was documented in the value-institution analyses of meeting transcripts. This was achieved most effectively through their control of the focus of community attention and by their vigorous, persistent application of the therapeutic ideology in moralistic terms.

The critical factor, however, was the ambivalence of patients about further power sharing. They settled for less than necessary under the circumstances and did not press for more. Their past experience as losers, victims, and sufferers contributed to low expectations regarding their capabilities and to relatively modest demands. They were ready to be passive, dominated, and victimized; to have others assume responsibility, take care of them, and direct them; to accept the usurping of their power by others as justified and necessary; and to expect defeat and deprivation. Indeed, when confronted with the opportunity, they were afraid to assume, and had a positive wish to have others assume, difficult and demanding responsibilities, and resisted giving up the role of the deprived and the defeated.

These observations demanded a reexamination of the nature of psychological illness and its treatment which underscored the etiological importance of deprivation and defeat, especially within the family, and questioned the adequacy of the medical model for its treatment. Lasswell appreciated the crucial importance in psychological illness of finding a way to work with others to build and sustain objectives that one cares about and believes in and the necessity of both mastering the strategies and skills of effective participation and struggling with intrapsychic obstacles to using them. He viewed the emergence of the therapeutic community and the vision of power sharing in the psychiatric hospital as an expression of the importance of political change in psychiatric treatment and as a microcosm of the vast social transformation of our time in which the ideology of democracy is transposed from a profession of faith to a way of life.

REFERENCES

1. Coulmier, director of the Clinic of Charenton, welcomes us in the prologue to Peter Weiss's *The Persecution and Assassination of Jean-Paul Marat as Performed by the Inmates of the Asylum of Charenton under the Direction of the Marquis de Sade* (New York: Atheneum, 1965).

2. Maxwell Jones, *The Therapeutic Community: A New Testament Method in Psychiatry* (New York: Basic Books, 1953).

3. Robert Rubenstein and Harold D. Lasswell, *The Sharing of*

Power in a Psychiatric Hospital (New Haven: Yale University Press, 1966).

4. For discussions of prototype research see Harold D. Lasswell, *The Future of Political Science* (New York: Atherton Press, 1963) and *Sharing of Power in a Psychiatric Hospital.*

7

Content Analysis and the Study of the "Symbolic Environment"

MORRIS JANOWITZ

I

IN 1935 Harold Lasswell set forth in *World Politics and Personal Insecurity* the main intellectual ingredients of a continuing world-attention survey based on quantitative content analysis which would be an integral part of the study of international relations.[1] For more than a decade, he had already used content analysis to quantify political communication and to objectify the psychoanalytic interview. In the next two decades, Lasswell and his associates were to be engaged in developing the methodology of content analysis and in applying it to a variety of subject matters.

One of the most ingenious efforts was direct observation of the aggressive behavior of welfare clients toward public relief administrators. Lasswell was making a pioneer contribution to what was later to develop into the social psychology of small group research.[2]

Perhaps the most penetrating example was *World Revolutionary Propaganda,* prepared in collaboration with Dorothy Blumenstock, which he labeled a "big town study of world revolutionary propaganda" since it dealt with communist propaganda during the Great Depression.[3] No doubt the most ambitious enterprise was the War Time Communications project, sponsored by the Library of Congress at the eve of World War II. It sought to put into operation the notions set forth in *World Politics and Personal Insecurity* and to present a worldwide audit of mass communications during the period leading to the outbreak of international hostilities. *Language of Politics: Studies in Quantitative Semantics* presented a sample of these research studies.[4] This project was probably the most comprehensive content analysis study ever undertaken with scholarly objectives. By standards of large-scale social science of the 1960s, this Library of Congress project was a modest undertaking, but the study has never been duplicated and at the time it represented Lasswell's major commitment to explore the potentialities of content analysis. The radio broadcast monitoring services of the United States and Great Britain during and after World War II have been involved in extensive content analysis, although the bulk of these efforts has been for purposes of day-to-day reporting.

In 1963 Harold Lasswell published a study entitled *The Future of Political Science* in which he delimited the theoretical perspectives, the methodology, and the tasks of political research from his policy science standpoint.[5] It is striking to note that there is not a single reference to content analysis in the index, and this basic interest of his is not woven into the architectonics of political research. For Lasswell himself, as well as for interested social scientists and sympathetic critics, quantitative content analysis failed to achieve its expected potentialities although political science, sociology, and social psychology have been enriched by particular penetrating monographs and specific research studies. Content analysis has failed to emerge as a device for describing the essence of mass communications on a long-term trend and social change basis.

In evaluating Lasswell's monumental intellectual contributions it is necessary to explore the reasons for this failure, which involve both inherent limitations in quantitative content analysis as well as the strategic problems that have been encountered in its practical application. The failure to confront these limitations has impoverished the development of social research and strengthened a pervasive reductionism which underemphasizes the role of the symbolic, ideological, and cultural values in fashioning social and political change.

Lasswell's contributions to the social sciences are manifold: the naturalistic analysis of political power, the study of elites, the application of psychoanalytic principles to political behavior, and the study of the social role of the man of knowledge. But within the broad range of problematic issues to which he turned his attention, Lasswell had as a central substantive concern the analysis of the "symbolic environment" and its consequences for human behavior and social morality. More than once he has referred to himself as the son of a preacher who continued his father's interest in preaching in a secular context.

The study of symbolic behavior represents a clear-cut case in which the advocates of the qualitative approach still command the lead over the practitioners of quantitative procedures. It is not very productive to follow Bernard Berelson's reasoning and to argue that there is no fundamental difference between them except in degree because qualitative approaches imply quantification in terms of zero or one. It is true that the practitioners of qualitative analysis recognize that they are searching for the presence or absence of specific traits and for objectivity and reliability between analysts. But the evaluation of content analysis procedures does permit a meaningful discussion of the limits and potentialities of quantification. The basic questions include deciding what the appropriate molecular units of analysis are and how much refinement of frequencies is rewarding. Three sets of barriers to the development of content analysis as a quantitative technique come to mind: (*a*) organizational and administrative, (*b*) substantive, (*c*) methodological and theoretical.

These elements can be thought of as being listed in ascending order of importance. The administrative and organizational components, however, are threshold factors which have not as yet been satisfactorily solved, so that there does not exist an adequate format for the generation and retrieval of essential content analysis data. From a substantive point of view, if content analysis is to yield its potential, it is essential that data be gathered covering a long historical period for a particular source or a particular media. If one examines the substantive literature derived from content analysis research procedures it is clear that quantitative studies, all other things being equal, have a value which is directly proportional to the time span covered. For example, despite the simple categories involved, the study by Hornell Hart of the transformation of social values in the United States as measured by content analysis of magazine articles is highly rewarding because it covers a period of more than a century.[6] Likewise, Leo Lowenthal's analysis of the shift in popular heroes from idols of production to idols of consumption represents not only an interesting set of categories but also the fact that the comparison was made over a relatively long time period.[7] Yet these researches hardly exhaust the capacity of content analysis to deal with historical change. Moreover, neither individual effort nor organized enterprise has emerged which would carry on content analysis in a broad enough and deep enough perspective to relate it to secular long-term change. There exists no formal or informal clearinghouse or content analysis data bank for original data collected by content analysts which would make possible subsequent extension of samples, replications, or comparative analysis.

Social science is in part a cumulative process which is accelerated both by the value of its analytic findings and by the pragmatic implications that are derived from its methodologies. Thus, provocative qualitative studies such as the Wolfenstein and Leites cross-national comparison of movie content have commanded wide intellectual interest but they have not served as a stimulus to replication or amplification by more precise and quantitative studies.[8] In good measure this must be seen as the failure of content analysis to bridge the gap between "theory" and "empirical data." But in part it is also the result of the fact that any social science enterprise is both an intellectual and a professional undertaking which develops in terms of the presumed applications to public policy and its implied social utility. One has only to compare the support generated for the public opinion polls in contrast to the absence of a comparable response for quantitative content analysis. There can be no doubt that Lasswell hoped that content analysis would develop in a way similar to public opinion studies. For better or worse, political groups do not seem to see the intelligence value of the findings of content analysis, nor do employers' associations have the same interest in the contents of labor publications, which were at one time analyzed by commercial agencies, as they do in the attitudes of labor toward specific legislative and economic proposals.[9]

The vastly greater support for opinion surveys does not mean that public opinion surveys have been fully successful in accumulating essential data for describing trends in public attitudes. University-based research tends to be concerned with the formal properties of attitude configurations. Among research scholars there is an emphasis on the modification of research instruments, which interferes with the accumulation of standardized materials through time. Paradoxically, commercially sponsored research or research undertaken for voluntary associations interested in social policy is often based on a more primitive methodology but tends to emphasize long-term trends. Thus, for example, in the area of attitudes toward minority groups there are less than five questions which have been asked in a standardized format since the 1930s, and these are the results, in good measure, of interests of voluntary associations with specific policy objectives. If one looks for basic trends in attitudes toward the Soviet Union, conceptions of the size of the ideal family, or participation in religious institutions over a long period of time, one is more likely to find information in the files of organizations such as Gallup rather than in university research institutes, although there is a growing emphasis on social change in these academic research groups.

In contrast to the present state of opinion surveys, there is no indication that the collection and processing of content analysis data is or will mature as a result of individual effort, cooperative arrangements, or centralized agencies so as to parallel the extensive developments in the study of public opinion research. There is not even the primitive beginnings of library and archival facilities. In fact, there is a kind of intellectual stagnation in the field. The standard methodological treatise on content analysis prepared by Bernard Berelson went out of print ten years after its original publication. It has not been revised nor are there signs of important new efforts in this direction.[10] While it is difficult to estimate the actual volume of content analysis studies, quantitative and qualitative, there has been no expansion during the last decade to parallel the growth of social research generally. The actual number of studies produced has probably not declined, but in proportion to other types of methodological approaches there has been a decline.

Collective and cooperative research undertakings tend to be organized along specialized lines either by methodology or by particular subject matter. In this division of labor, content analysis has suffered because it needs to be fused with other approaches. There seems to be a deemphasis on the fusion of content analysis with other methodologies such as attitude research, and especially audience research. Thus, the format used in *The Community Press in an Urban Setting,* in which the analysis of contents of Chicago community newspapers was integrated into a study of audience response and impact, has not become a standard research strategy.[11] In part this is due to the overinstitutionalization of survey research into separate institutes where it has become detached from the main body of social research.

It should not be overlooked that the methodological emphasis in social research in the United States has meant that there is a body of studies dealing with various technical aspects of content analysis. Research has been carried out on questions of the reliability of coding procedures and on issues of sampling, both questions being of great importance for mass data collection efforts. There have been important efforts to extend statistical procedures for handling content analysis findings; the work of Janis and Fadner, dealing with coefficients of imbalance, is particularly noteworthy since content analysis is concerned with the reporting and detection of distortion in representation.[12] In recent years there has been work on the application of computer technology for the rapid collection and assessment of diverse types of content.[13]

Nevertheless, the basic questions of methodology, as opposed to technical questions of data handling, may be viewed as being relatively unexplored. In this regard, quantitative content analysis is more similar to than different from sample survey research. While there has been progress in specific technical matters, in the case of both content analysis and sample surveys there has been a deemphasis and even a declining concern with essential questions of validity and methodological bias. Both survey research and content analysis have rapidly become highly institutionalized at the expense of continuing scrutiny of the logic of the methodology itself. In the case of the interview, in the last few years there has been a reawakening of interest in interview bias which raises fundamental questions of the validity and relevance of the sample survey. There is a growing effort to see the sample survey and its interviewing technique as an interpersonal and social transaction which is deeply influenced by the expectations of the researcher.

The absence of concern with questions of validity has been even more pervasive in the case of content analysis. On the one hand problems of validity involve a clearer recognition of systematic sources of bias, so as to standardize the procedure and understand better the nature of the data generated. On the other hand problems of validity also require a continuous scrutiny of the theoretical purposes for which the data are being applied.

Content analysis is a diffuse concept which has been transformed into a term of rather specific scope. In one sense, most social scientists are concerned with the analysis of content. Examples include historians who study original documents, legal scholars engaged in the analysis of the development of case law, political scientists evaluating the proceedings of congressional hearings, and anthropologists recording and classifying folk tales. Wherever symbolic behavior is being scrutinized, the analysis of content is involved.

Lasswell sought to bring order into such endeavors by imposing general categories and by developing quantitative indicators. In principle, content analysis implies the standard procedures of scientific investigation: the formulation of explicit propositions, the development of categories of analysis, and the collection of standardized bits of information needed to assess the adequacy of the initial formulations. But content analysis in application involves wide differences in operational procedures. Bernard Berelson (a second-generation student of Lasswell, having been a student of Douglas Waples, one of Lasswell's associates) has limited the operational dimensions of content analysis to the furthest extreme. For him, content analysis deals only with manifest content, a term which remains highly ambiguous despite its wide usage. Lasswell recognized that meaning depends upon the superimposition of some frame of reference, and his conception of content analysis is much broader in that it includes both manifest and latent content. Latent content involves tacit meanings and associations as well as more readily verbalized expressions. Content analysis has to involve the application of historical, cultural, psychological, and legal frames of reference to various levels of meaning, subtleties, and efforts at explication of ambiguities. In the broadest sense content analysis is a system for objectifying the process of inference, for the meaning of the symbolic environment can only be derived by a process of inference.

Therefore, the methodological and theoretical problems in content analysis focus on an explication of the process of reasoning by which inferences are made. In the study of the contents of the mass media, for example, the validity of content analysis depends upon a simple paradox. At any given moment in time, the contents of the mass media are indicators of two very different and even opposing social phenomena. The contents of the mass media are a reflection of the social organization and value system of the society or group interest involved. Simultaneously, the contents of the mass media are purposive elements of social change, agents for modifying the goals and values of social groups. The same formulation holds true in personality terms if one is discussing the interplay of communications and human personalities. The analytic and substantive relevance of any piece of content analysis depends upon an explication of the elements involved in this paradox. The bulk of content analysis research does not, however, explicitly direct itself to these issues, although Lasswell was fully aware of the logical problems involved.

Thus, content analysis as an analytic tool depends upon the recognition of two different sets of inferences. First, content analysis can be used for making inferences from content back to the communicator, in which case the analyst is concerned with understanding the intentions, strategy, and goals of the communicator. (He is also concerned with the impact of content on the communicator himself.) Second, content analysis can be used to make inferences from the content to the audience, in which case the analyst is concerned with audience response and reaction.

It should also be pointed out that content analysis can be purely descriptive, descriptive in the sense that it is engaged in comparing one type of content with another type of content. Such research is legitimate, and it can be of a humanistic or social scientific variety. For example, content analysis can be used to describe the natural history and process of diffusion of a symbol or key idea. Likewise, systematic content analysis which compares one form of content with another can be useful in the detection of distortion and propaganda technique or in assessing mass media content against some desired standard of performance.

II

EVEN though the machinery for quantitative content analysis has been only partly perfected, Harold Lasswell's intellectual aspirations for the study of communication have had a powerful impact. He was a systems analyst long before the term came into vogue. From his very first writings, he stands in contradistinction to those theorists who, no matter how refined their analyses, perceive the mainsprings of change in some single element, whether technological, ecological, economic, or even normative. Lasswell never offered his emphasis on symbolism and the communications process as an alternative reductionism, but as an element in a broader "configurative analysis."

It was of course the intellectual setting of the University of Chicago which nurtured Lasswell's concern with the symbolic processes. He bears the imprint of the Chicago empirical school, which was grounded in the writings of John Dewey and subsequently of George Herbert Mead and W. I. Thomas, the forerunners of symbolic interactional interpretations. Like so many of the social scientists trained in that setting, he developed a sympathetic and creative interest in psychoanalysis, furthered, in his case, by his acquaintance with Harry Stack Sullivan. No less important was his exposure to the work of the anthropologist Edward Sapir in language and symbols.

Early in his career at the University of Chicago he was exposed to economics, while he was studying politics. He came to see his intellectual tasks as the exploration of the possibility of "whether students of politics could work out quantitative ways of describing the data of importance to us. Obviously, some of the important information must come from studies of the content of communications, not price records."[14]

But for Lasswell the technique and approach of content analysis, with its concern for the molecular dissection of communications content, came, as do many advances in the methodology of science, by accident, from the "outside" and in a wholly unanticipated fashion. During World War I, members of the department of English at the University of Chicago, including a distinguished specialist in Chaucer, made important contributions to research in cryptography. Lasswell recalls being exposed to various informal discussions of how these students of original texts applied their techniques of analysis to the deciphering problems of war. This intellectual exercise stimulated his thinking and provided the background for his application of content analysis to political communications.[15]

While still a graduate student he had his first opportunity to try his hand in work on Charles Merriam's project on comparative civic education. A fragment of this effort was published under the title "Prussian Schoolbooks and International Amity."[16] However, Lasswell did not pursue the methodology of content analysis as the basis of his doctoral dissertation. Undoubtedly, the reason lies partly in the then-primitive state of the technique and in his full awareness that this approach was too "risky" for a doctoral thesis. But even more important, Lasswell was not to be limited in his work by the constraints of methodology. His goal was to write a relevant study of World War I propaganda and he would not be limited by methodological issues. This was the pattern Lasswell was to follow repeatedly throughout his career. Despite his vast expenditure of effort on content analysis and his concern with quantification, he would not hesitate to step back and write in the grand theoretical style of political science, although he was to incorporate new categories from sociology and psychoanalysis.

Thus, at the age of twenty-five, he wrote a brilliant doctoral dissertation entitled *Propaganda Technique in the World War.* His search for objectivity, the scope of the archival materials covered, and the richness of the analysis is indeed phenomenal. It is a classic because it deals with the central issue of the social context of propaganda and with the persistent organizational struggle between the foreign office, the military, and the political leadership for the control of the conduct of international propaganda.

In this volume Lasswell already presents his naturalistic definitions, which are to become so influential. For example, there is the core definition of propaganda, which is still operative:

> It refers solely to the control of opinion by significant symbols, or to speak more concretely and less accurately, by stories, rumors, reports, pictures, and other forms of social communication. Propaganda is concerned with the management of opinions and attitudes by the direct manipulation of social suggestion rather than by altering other conditions in the environment or in the organism.[17]

While the conceptual formulation was relatively undifferentiated, the volume contains the basic elements of the orientation which Lasswell was to develop into his theoretical analysis of politics.

In this thesis he presents his basic categories of income, safety and deference, which were to figure centrally in his later reformulation. By means of these categories he incorporated the study of "the management of violence" into the body of political science.

In this thesis, he foreshadows a career in which he is committed to the creative destruction of academic formalism. Although the doctoral thesis was a ritualized form even in 1926, Lasswell's document was amazingly fresh and direct. He foregoes the usual ritualistic acknowledgment of departmental faculty members, nor does he indulge in the mechanical and incomplete review of the literature which is so universal. With a powerful sense of self-assurance and a matter-of-factness which reflects his iconoclasm, he raised academic eyebrows but gained an appointment at Chicago under the sponsorship of Charles E. Merriam. The capacity for strategic innovation in an academic career is displayed very early.[18]

Although this volume has come to be neglected except by careful students of communications and politico-military history, for many years it served to stimulate successive generations of graduate students and scholars. In 1937 I first read *Propaganda Technique in the World War* in the library of the Washington Square College of New York University, only a plate glass removed from the demonstrations and counter-demonstrations of student groups who frequented the Square. While my work has been deeply influenced by Lasswell's categories and definitions, this volume was very powerful in propelling me toward empirical investigation of propaganda and mass persuasion.

In *Propaganda Technique in the World War,* Lasswell wrote about a very concrete problem in the study of communications. Because he viewed society as a system which saw cultural values and communication as "action systems," his approach to the study of propaganda and mass communications was not that of an exposer or of a debunker. Propaganda, especially as conceptualized in his subsequent article in the *Encyclopedia of the Social Sciences,* is not seen as some foreign matter, some intrusion into the body politic, but rather as a generic aspect of the political system. He was fully aware of the ideological connotations of the word, and he recognized that a relabeling of the term would not solve theoretical or policy issues. The process of persuasion is a generic aspect of social control.

His writing and his interest in content analysis moved him toward (a) a more systematic conceptualization of the symbolic environment and the institutions for creating, disseminating, and utilizing symbol systems, and (b) toward establishing standards of performance for judging and evaluating the content and practices of "symbol manipulators" in terms of the requirements of social change and democratic processes.

Lasswell is a prolific writer and one who is prepared to revise and elaborate earlier formulations and categories. Commendable as these virtues are, the reader is led at times into a diversion if he becomes overly concerned with details of these revisions. Nevertheless, there is a powerful continuity in focus in Lasswell's theoretical writings. His style of theorizing emphasizes the substantive goals of social and political institutions. His approach stands in contrast to the central concern with formal categories for describing the social processes in terms of modes of action (universalistic-particularistic, for example) which have dominated the theories generated by contemporary sociologists. Lasswell's background in political science and his concern with policy issues, as well as his substantive concern with the impact of culture, ideology, and communications, underlie his theoretical format.

Each of his major writings, and I would say that there are three, is a redefinition of basic categories rather than an alteration of his fundamental system of analysis. *Politics: Who Gets What, When, and How* is probably his most influential treatise because of its naturalistic language and the broad scope he gives to the subject matter of politics.[19] It serves as the model of the interplay between theory and data from which the "behaviorial school" of political science emerged. *World Politics and Personal Insecurity* is clearly his most intellectually inspiring book because it goes furthest in fusing his interest in psychoanalysis with the study of symbolic behavior in politics. In *Power and Society* he labored hard, with the assistance of Abraham Kaplan, to formalize his definitions for handling the symbolic environment.[20]

III

Lasswell did not distinguish sharply between basic and applied research in the social sciences. Through his writings, and especially in his concern with content analysis, he is constantly raising the general question of "knowledge for what?" Because he studied elites, and especially communications elites, he has been naïvely accused of being an elitist. It is true that he saw an elite as a "requisite" of any social and political order, but he sought to fashion social science as an intellectual process relevant for democratic, pluralistic values. Quantitative content analysis was central, a social invention for helping to establish explicit standards of performance for the communications profession in the form of self-enforcing guidelines. This "end product" never came into being. Instead, along with his research writings, there is a flow of writing in political philosophy in which he seeks to formulate the basic issues concerning the positive role of the mass media in effective political change. Among the noteworthy writings in this vein are *Democracy through Public Opinion* (1941) and the volumes published after his work on the Commission on the Freedom of the Press, *A Free and Responsible Press* (1947) and *National Security and Individual Freedom* (1950). These works have been incorporated into the professional writings and ideologies of an important segment of the specialists in the mass media and teachers in schools of journalism with some, one would hope, growing beneficial consequence. If the level of professional performance in the mass media leaves much to be desired in the United States, it is not mainly because of the absence of social science perspectives. Much more than the rudiments of such a perspective has been set forth in the body of Lasswell's writings on content analysis and the symbolic environment.

REFERENCES

1. Harold D. Lasswell, *World Politics and Personal Insecurity* (New York: McGraw-Hill, 1935).
2. Harold D. Lasswell and Gabriel Almond, "Aggressive Behavior by Clients toward Public Relief Administrators," *American Political Science Review*, 28 (1934):643–55.
3. Harold D. Lasswell and Dorothy Blumenstock, *World Revolutionary Propaganda: A Chicago Study* (New York: Alfred A. Knopf, 1939).
4. Harold D. Lasswell, Nathan Leites, *et al.*, *Language of Politics: Studies in Quantitative Semantics* (New York: George W. Steward, 1949).
5. Harold D. Lasswell, *The Future of Political Science* (New York: Atherton Press, 1964).
6. H. Hornell Hart, "Changing Social Attitudes and Interests," in *Recent Social Trends in the United States* (New York: McGraw-Hill, 1934), pp. 382–443.
7. Leo Lowenthal, "Biographies in Popular Magazines," in *Radio Research, 1942–43* (Fairlawn, N.J.: Essential Books, 1943).
8. Martha Wolfenstein and Nathan Leites, *Movies: A Psychological Study* (Glencoe, Ill.: Free Press, 1950).
9. A careful evaluation of the practicality of qualitative content analysis is presented by Alexander George, a student of Harold Lasswell, and Nathan Leites in their study, *Propaganda Analysis: A Study of Interferences Made from Nazi Propaganda in World War II* (Evanston, Ill.: Row, Peterson and Co., 1959)."The fact that 81 per cent of the FCC (Federal Communications Commission) inferences that could be scored proved to be accurate cannot be taken as a conclusive demonstration of the utility of propaganda analysis for a number of reasons, which are discussed at some length. . . . Nonetheless, the FCC analysts made correct inferences on a wide variety of questions on interest to policy makers at the time, and they were also able to give, over a period of months, a continually reliable analysis on a given intelligence problem (for example, the private expectations of Nazi leaders regarding a possible attempt by the Allies to establish a second front). This strongly suggests that the propaganda analysis method is capable of more than isolated hit or miss successes."
10. Bernard Berelson, *Content Analysis in Communication Research* (Glencoe, Ill.: Free Press, 1952).

11. Morris Janowitz, *The Community Press in an Urban Setting*, 2d ed. (Chicago: University of Chicago Press, 1967).

12. Irving L. Janis and Raymond Fadner, "The Coefficient of Imbalance," in *Language of Politics*, pp. 153–72.

13. Philip Stone, *The General Inquirer* (Cambridge, Mass.: Massachusetts Institute of Technology Press, 1966).

14. Private communication, October 5, 1966. "As a beginning student of politics, I recall my dissatisfaction on realizing that, while economists were plentifully equipped with data about goods and prices, for instance, political scientists were poorly supplied with comparable data showing trends and correlations in political events" (Harold D. Lasswell, "The Qualitative and the Quantitative in Political and Legal Analysis," in David Lerner, ed., *Quantity and Quality* [New York: Free Press, 1961], p. 104).

15. Private communication, October 5, 1966.

16. Harold D. Lasswell, "Prussian Schoolbooks and International Amity," *Journal of Social Forces*, 3 (1925):718–22.

17. *Propaganda Technique in the World War* (New York: A. A. Knopf; London: Kegan Paul, 1927), p. 9.

18. Particularly noteworthy is the fact that his dissertation was published exactly as it was presented, without the laborious translation of "rewriting the dissertation for publication."

19. Harold D. Lasswell, *Politics: Who Gets What, When, and How* (New York: McGraw-Hill, 1935).

20. Harold D. Lasswell and Abraham Kaplan, *Power and Society: A Framework for Inquiry* (New Haven: Yale University Press, 1950).

8

Managing Communication for Modernization: A Developmental Construct

DANIEL LERNER

THE management of communication is an ancient craft and a somewhat less ancient profession. One can readily recast the court astrologers and priestly seers of antiquity in the role of communication managers. The management of symbols in war and crisis, we are told, is no newer than the "rumors whispered about Hannibal."[1]

With due respect for Joshua's trumpets, Trojan horses, and Roman *evocatio*—(the calling out or evocation of protective gods from the walled cities of their adversaries), we shall not delve into the prehistory of our topic.[2] We shall focus, rather, on the conditions of communication management in modern society and particularly in the diverse societies that are seeking to modernize under these conditions. We shall follow the Lasswellian injunction that description of conditions should lead to an analysis of trends and a projection of policy alternatives for the future. The configurative analysis of conditions, trends, and projections yields a "developmental construct," which is the core of policy-science thinking as conceived by Lasswell.

Among the conditions of modern society are three which have fundamentally transformed all processes of public communication everywhere. These are: (1) *technology*, the growth of the mass media; (2) *participation*, the rise of public opinion and spread of media consumption; (3) *globalism*, the political activation of "the opinions of mankind."

We shall turn to closer scrutiny of these modern conditions in a moment. In so doing we shall follow some of the leads given by

Lasswell, who first alerted the intellectual community to the saliency and significance of these new, conditions. Indeed, his studies in communication subsume the whole set of modern conditions. So, too, his essays on the "policy sciences" reveal the primacy of politics as controller of the distribution of public values and as manager of the symbols that represent their private meanings. The interaction and accumulation of values in any "society," from a pair of lovers to a community of nations, is the central business of the social sciences, which Lasswell has referred to as comparative history with a policy purpose.

Since this essay is derived from Lasswell's thinking on these matters, it may be appropriate to say a few prefatory words about my intellectual relationship to the scholar honored by this volume. The first word is personal: Lasswell has never encouraged acolytes and has effectively discouraged the formation of individuals or institutions in his own image. The second word is professional: Lasswell has proposed ideas the testing of which would take a century or more of work by all the social scientists in the world. The third word is conceptual: the application of a theoretical system of policy science such as Lasswell's, which is comprehensive in its space-time dimensions, to the diagnosis and therapy of social processes at particular times and places is a challenging and hazardous enterprise. So far as I am aware, only Lasswell has successfully derived an important "developmental construct" from his own theoretical system.

At the cost of embarrassing Lasswell, who does not suffer fools any more gladly than acolytes, this point is worth stressing as a reminder of the large, unfinished Lasswellian business that awaits social scientists oriented toward public policy. Who but Lasswell himself has articulated a construction of the probable future as powerful—for scientific and for policy thinking—as the prevision of a "garrison-prison" state? Who but Lasswell forecast thirty years ago the probable linkage of "symbol management" with "military necessity" in a global Cold War arena? Who but Lasswell foresaw, a quarter century ago, that the United States would now be spending three-fourths of its national budget—

over seventy billion dollars—under military auspices? So far as I know, only Lasswell did.

In "Sino-Japanese Crisis: The Garrison State versus the Civilian State" (1937), written while Lasswell was in Asia, he foresaw that political acceptance of rising military demands upon national resuorces would transform the political management of national symbols.[3] Four years later, back in the United States, Lasswell predicted the generalization of this process in his famous essay: "The Garrison State and Specialists on Violence" (1941).[4] Alerted to the spreading linkage between "military necessity" and "communication," Lasswell then forecast the shape of the post-World War II arena in his belatedly published and inadequately noticed booklet entitled *World Politics Faces Economics* (1945). The subtitle was "With Special Reference to the Future Relations of the United States and Russia." The embarrassed writer of the Foreword, research director of the Committee for Economic Development, wrote: "Had his manuscript been published when it was first drafted, his reputation as a prophet would be assured."[5] These were the works of the seasoned Lasswell (1937–45). Already behind him were the penetrating theoretical works of his precocious youth such as *Psychopathology and Politics* (1930) and *World Politics and Personal Insecurity* (1935). Before him were the new worlds of intellectual discovery and scientific appraisal in such works as *Power and Personality* (1948) and *Power and Society* (1950)—as well as his brilliant intellectual generalship of the Stanford studies of elites and symbols in the "world revolution of our time" (1950–52).[6] Of his later exploits—such as the reconception of law and policy in *Law and Public Order in Space* (1963) and the policy-scientific projection of our own disciplines in *The Future of Political Science* (1963) —I shall say nothing here. Other, wiser men will speak of these matters in the present volume.

Here I refer to the seasoned Lasswell of the middle years— the Lasswell who had lived through World War I as a youngster and then thought through its historic meaning in his pioneering first book, *Propaganda Technique in the World War* (1927).

It was this analysis of past trends and conditions that enabled Lasswell to project the symbolic buildup, conduct, and aftermath of World War II, which remains the most brilliant example of policy-science thinking about "symbol management" in our time. Before I turn to the substantive topic of this essay—the management of symbols for modernization—a final prefatory word might be said about the "seasoning" of Lasswell. Seasoning, like most words that matter, is ambiguous. It may mean adding spices; it may also mean adding the long experience of changing seasons. Since Lasswell biography and psychography have been presented elsewhere in this volume, I refer only to the value of Lasswell's seasoning as guidance, in personal terms, for future policy scientists. My guess is that most social scientists will not be seasoned for policy thinking until they have tested their theoretical views against comparative situations in the real world of diverse empirical conditions and normative values. This is a point of considerable importance for social scientists. Among mathematicians and physicists, it is now commonly believed that one's major "work" is done by the time one is thirty years old—a widespread conviction that may or may not be true as usually formulated. It is important for social scientists to understand, particularly since they often adopt the lore of physical scientists uncritically, that this particular tenet would itself be improved with more "seasoning" (*cum grano salis* as well as tested experience).

It is to the credit of Lasswell that he has exemplified the point in his own career as well as in his own theory. Lasswell's conception of the policy sciences has always stressed science as a major component of policy thinking. A person must have acquired competence *qua* scientist before he can expect to function effectively *qua* policy scientist. He must learn, in Lasswell's lingo, to describe "trends" and analyze "conditions" before he can project "alternatives" and prescribe "decisions." He must learn also (an especially hard lesson for youth) to take cognizance of his own values as a step toward the normative analysis of all values as data for policy thinking.

These reflections are especially applicable to consideration of the management of symbols because they highlight, in proper perspective, the "science" that one acquires in youth and the "policy" sense that comes with seasoning experience. Let us recall that the management of symbols is, along with the management of resources, the main business of politics largely construed. Resources are what politicians have to work with; symbols are what they justify their work by. Symbol management often determines how politicians are judged by their polities. We begin, therefore, by considering briefly the conditions which have transformed symbol management in modern times.

CONDITIONS

THE three conditions we have specified are: (1) technology, (2) participation, (3) professionalism. To these we now turn.

Communication Technology: The Mass Media

Modern communication technology had its significant origin, along with the technology of global exploration, in the fifteenth century. Shortly before Columbus sailed to the New World, Gutenberg activated his first printing press. The coincidence is noteworthy, for both technologies opened to mankind new worlds of experience hitherto unexplored. Maritime technology was to bring the full range of the earth's surface within man's ken. Media technology was to bring man the even larger universe of vicarious experience—the empathic understanding of persons and places one had never seen, of roles and situations one had never lived through. Small wonder that the times which produced these new technologies have gone into our history books as the "age of exploration."

Over the next five centuries the nations of the world, as they were shaped in their modern mold, sought to advance and apply these technologies as instruments of their nationhood. Every schoolboy knows that Britain's decisive advance toward world supremacy was her defeat of the Spanish Armada in 1588. Thereafter, Britain "ruled the waves" and colonized much of the world.

The decisive defeat of Napoleon at Waterloo some two centuries later was a mopping-up operation necessary to bring Europe and its global hinterland under the rule of the Pax Britannica. Britain remained the supreme maritime power until World War II.

Less often noticed, in this connection, is that Britain emerged during these centuries as the supreme master of communication technology as well. This aspect of British history has been inadequately documented and interpreted by professional historians. We may nevertheless venture the opinion that Britain won supremacy over media technology—as over maritime technology—by promoting innovative as well as adaptive policies simultaneously. Britain innovated the "penny press" just as Britain adapted the English language to the dissemination of cheap public communication to a large national audience. Britain was able to do this because it had foreseen the value of public communication in a mass-participation society (an unarticulated "developmental construct") and had shaped its policies to produce the world's first critical mass (an undocumented trend-statement) of literate citizens.

We stress the emergence of Britain as the world's Number One power for two reasons: (1) it occurred over *five centuries* of effort and achievement; (2) it involved the innovative and adaptive use of both maritime and media technologies to achieve the purposes of national policy. Both of these are critical as we face, in today's transformed world arena, the problems of American policy toward the developing countries of the world.

For, in the contemporary context, five centuries of communication technology have been collapsed into five decades—with results that are more ponderous than pondered. It is less than fifty years since broadcast radio and moving pictures became readily available technologies. Modernized societies of the West, and particularly the United States, showed considerable skill in rapid innovation and adaptation of these "audio-visual" technologies to their national purposes as construed from year to year. They have been less apt, and again particularly the United States as the Number One power of today's world, in foreseeing the impact of new technology upon their relations with the rest of the world. In the twentieth century, as in the fifteenth, we are embarked on an age of exploration. As the fifteenth century explored the oceans by maritime technology, our century is exploring the galaxies by space technology; as a media technology then spread printed words, so our century broadcasts spoken words and pictures. As then, the two technologies are closely linked: already our "space age" includes "communication satellites." The era of astronautical and electronic communication is upon us. Whatever its consequences for the inner man (*pace* Marshall McLuhan), it is rapidly transforming contemporary societies, the developed as well as the underdeveloped. We look next at those modernized societies that engineered communication technology and built institutions adaptive to communication management.

Participation: Public Opinion and Mass Media

In a notable essay on the rise of modern public opinion, Hans Speier traces the historical context back to the *ancien régime* of eighteenth century France.[7] Beset by new demands from sectors of the French population that traditionally had been quiescent, the regime responded in the routine manner of autocracy—by repression and coercion. Our history books, seeking the causes of the French Revolution, recount the heavy burdens of *taille* and *tithe*, *corvée* and *gabelle* upon the French people. These taxes on labor, income, salt became unbearable—so goes the account—and the king's subjects revolted. Under their new Republic, taxes and other deprivations would be decided by citizens or their duly constituted representatives.

The story line is similiar to that told of the American Revolution. Beset by new demands from his colonial subjects, George III tried coercion. But the colonists would have none of this and revolted. They dumped his tea into Boston Harbor and rejected his stamp tax. Under the slogan "no taxation without representation," they declared their independence from the throne and constituted a representative government that would be responsive to the demands of the citizenry.

Our interest in these familiar bits of history is mainly with their lessons for communication sociology. Popular demands, long unfulfilled, cause frustration. Frustration, long unrequitted, leads to revolution. Coercion cannot forever repress frustration and prevent revolution. Only persuasion—the effective management of communication—can shape public opinion in such manner as to reduce popular frustration and prevent political upheaval. This is the great benefit taught by communication sociology, but associated with the benefit is a cost.

The cost-benefit relationship is nicely illustrated in the historical account of prerevolutionary France given by Speier. Since the coercive methods of taxation failed to yield the revenues needed by his regime, the king designated as his finance minister the inventive and innovative Jacques Necker and charged him with finding new and effective solutions to the fiscal problems of the monarchy. Necker turned from the routine methods of coercion to a new mode of persuasion. He proposed, in fine, that the national budget be *made public.*

Necker's reasoning was plain. A public budget would show the people of France what their money was needed for. As these purposes were presumably shared by the people because they were directed to their own best interests—protection of their produce and promotion of their prosperity—communication would make clear what now was confused. The effective management of communication, according to Necker, would reduce popular frustration and increase popular participation. The social costs of conflict thus would be replaced by the social benefits of consensus.

But the achievement of consensus through persuasive communication entails certain political costs, particularly to the regime in power. Commenting on Necker's daring proposal to enlist public opinion in the service of fiscal policy, Count Vergennes wrote a confidential memorandum to warn the king of its subversive potential: "Your Majesty would have to be prepared to see those lead who otherwise obey and those obey who otherwise lead."

The king was not prepared to face the situation foreseen, and pay the costs forecast, by the perspicacious Vergennes. Necker's pregnant idea of public opinion was aborted. The idea survived and bore fruit shortly thereafter in France as well as other modernizing countries of the West as they discovered that modernization required popular participation and that such participation could operate efficiently only on the basis of consensus, not coercion. Consensus, in turn, could only be attained and sustained by the democratic management of communication in a participant social context.

In this way, the policy goal of economic growth (increasing shares of wealth) entailed political participation (increasing shares of power). As the policy goal was amplified to "self-sustaining growth," participant institutions multiplied and diversified to include all social values. During the nineteenth century, the idea of the general welfare was broadened to include public responsibility for such previously private matters as health, respect (interracial and interfaith relations), and enlightenment.

Enlightenment became a participant value of key importance, for the citizen of the modern republic was expected to know more —and to have more opinions—about public issues than had ever before been regarded as appropriate for the subject of any monarchy. The instrument of enlightenment is, of course, communication. This is why we speak of the "communication nexus" in the highly participant and pluralist social systems of modernized nations. Public communication not only disseminated the value consensus indispensable for stability in a participant polity but also multiplied the skilled human resources needed for growth in a participant economy.

The great early victories of popular enlightenment were won by, and for, public education. That fundamental education in the three R's should be freely available to all was a giant step forward in the building of participant institutions. As the benefits of such institutions to the society as well as the individual were increasingly understood, free public education became compulsory and the school-leaving age has been continuously raised. For the citizenry of modern societies, the widening and deepening distribution of enlightenment has passed beyond the realm of individual prerogative into that of civic responsibility.

It is clear that communication management among the stable democracies of the modern West has developed the participant polity based on popular consensus to a degree hitherto unknown in human history. It is equally clear that these Western polities operate the participant economy of self-sustaining growth with a level of skilled human resources that cannot be matched elsewhere in the world. What, then, of the rest of the contemporary world? What about our third condition of "globalism"?

Globalism: The Opinions of Mankind

Relations between the West and the rest of the world have undergone a profound transformation in the postwar years. It is now widely assumed, perhaps for the first time in history on this scale, that all the world's peoples seek to be, and as of right ought to be, about equal. Popular treatises by such scholars as Gunnar Myrdal and Barbara Ward, contrasting rich lands and poor lands, even postulate that it is to the interest of the rich (beyond the obvious interest of the poor) that the gap between them should be obviated or greatly narrowed. This is a new way of talking in the world about the world; that is, it constitutes a new set of symbols. Like all such subtle and barely perceptible shifts in tone of voice, it conveys a myriad of meanings. Salient among them is the new global concern with the opinions of mankind.

History crossed the threshold of this new communication concept of globalism when the American founding fathers justified their Declaration of Independence in terms of "a decent respect to the opinons of mankind." Though echoed elsewhere, and even doubled in spades by the French Universal Declaration of Human Rights, the promise remained inoperative until the modern societies of the West developed a technology competent to produce it and a society competent to absorb it. Technological progress and absorptive capacity grew steadily together through the nineteenth century. The spread of the "penny press" was the significant institutional expression of the communication nexus for these manifold growth processes in the modernizing societies—growth of high-speed printing presses to produce large-circulation daily newspapers, growth of literate populations to consume them, growth of per capita income distribution to make the relationship a paying proposition for all parties involved.

The communication nexus continued to operate through the accelerating "media explosion" of the twentieth century. As print was amplified by radio and film, modern society developed an effective absorptive capacity to deal with the rapid transformation of lifeways wrought by picture magazines and comic books (specialized media aimed mainly at women and children) as well as radio, cinema, and television. Via the communication nexus newspaper readers became also radio listeners and film viewers; furthermore, the highly media-exposed citizens also became the cash customers and opinion holders and, ultimately, the electoral voters. In this way communication became the warp and woof of the web of modern lifeways.

If the modernized Western countries were able to absorb new technology and adapt new sociology to it so effectively, why have the underdeveloped areas found it so hard to shape an operational communication nexus in their drive for modernization? Why, to pose the critical question of globalism in communicaton terms, has it proved so difficult to convey a usable image of the Western model of a modern society?

One factor that accounts for failure in the international communication of contemporary globalism is *tempo*. What the West achieved over centuries of slow, often painful, social change the rest of the world now seeks to accomplish in a few years. But the peoples of the underdeveloped areas are not so plastic, nor are their institutions so absorptive, as to operate efficiently on so drastically foreshortened a time scale. A related factor of great consequence is *balance*. To sustain equilibrium among the many and varied components of a dynamic system is no easy matter. What the rest of the world has not yet fully grasped is that the Western model depicts just such a multivalue and multivariate (pluralist) social system.

The failure of international communication to satisfy demands generated by the new globalism can readily be understood in terms of the recency and complexity of the task thrust upon it. International communication, along with international exploration and colonization, began five centuries ago as the instrument of imperialist expansion by the more developed nations of Europe. Imperial tutelage of a select few among the indigenous elites was a far different problem and process than the international development of mass populations which animates contemporary globalism. The long era of imperialism (subordination) is recently ended; the campaign for international development (equalization) has just begun. In the new process, international communication operates in behalf of different policy purposes under different socioeconomic conditions by different psychopolitical means.

Indeed, in the transition from imperialism to international development, there has been a fundamental change in the role of communication. Under the new conditions of globalism, it has largely replaced the coercive means by which colonial territories were seized and held. The transition from coercion to communication was foreshadowed, even under imperialism, as the empires undertook the developmental tasks of colonization—when indigenous peoples had to be brought from political prostration to economic productivity. Then began the application to natural resources in the colonies of technological and sociological innovations from the metropole, along with communication management that sought to produce rising output per head among the colonials.

Karl Marx, astute observer of the rudimentary international-development undertakings just becoming visible in the nineteenth century, clarified the communication nexus of this process. International development, he perceived, required persuasion by the more developed people and enlightenment among the less developed people. The persuasive transmission of enlightenment is the modern paradigm of international communication. It is greatly to his credit that Marx accorded to this paradigm a place in the later prefaces to his greatest book. In the preface to the fourth edition of *Das Kapital,* Marx wrote: "The more developed society presents to the less developed society *a picture of its own future."*[8]

The phrase "a picture of its own future" captures in a few vivid words three principal components of the role communication plays in the process of international development: (1) there is a "picture"—a depiction, portrayal, image, a "visualization" of the type transmitted, par excellence, by movies, TV, and picture magazines; (2) this picture represents "the future"—it visualizes alternatives to one's present lifeways and preferred situations and shows how things might become and be in a more desirable world; (3) the picture of the future so vividly represented is "one's own"—what *I and mine* might become and be in that more desirable world revealed to us by the magic lanterns from abroad.

Unfortunately, for Marx and for the poorer areas of the world, he never persisted in the exploration of his own insight. Had he done so, he might be known today as the "father of international communication," surely a more constructive role than "father of international communism" with its predictions of international war and prescriptions of global class-conflict. Had he done so, the poorer areas of the world might have embarked a century earlier on the difficult—but more promising—route of international development.

But these are "ifs" which did not happen. It is useful to recall these "ifs" only when they help us understand what did happen. The failure of Karl Marx to amplify his own insight did, in fact, contribute to the perpetuation of European imperialism a full century beyond its time. When the French pretension to European hegemony under Napoleon was defeated, and his conquerors gathered at Vienna in 1815 to write a new concord for Europe, the development of Africa and much of Asia could well have been on the agenda. It wasn't. Neither did Karl Marx put it there over the next generation. The result was that Europeans, then masters of the world, made a "concord" which obligated them not to fight each other in Europe (what we know as the "Pax Britannica"). Instead, they fought a brutal series of wars in their respective colonies—and wound up, finally, by fighting World War I against each other. Nothing deliberate happened to international development during this century except the transmission from the European metropoles to their colonies of provocative "pictures of their own futures."

At the end of World War II three new things happened: (1) Europe was no longer in charge of the future—*decolonization* was the new rule of the game all Europeans played (with most difficulty by the French and Portuguese); (2) the United States took charge of much of the world, with challenges offered only by the Soviet Union and China (and their affiliated communist parties); (3) the poorer countries of the world determined to get richer—as well as independent.

They got independent fast, but they didn't get richer nearly as fast. That is when globalism ran into its unsolved problem: how to make the poorer part of the world richer faster, or, failing that, how to make the poorer part understand why they were getting richer slower and what they could do to accelerate their own development. This was the charge globalism laid upon communication management in the postwar years. How has it been discharged?

TRENDS

PERHAPS the most important single characteristic of postwar trends in the developing countries has been *disequilibrium*. A vivid illustration is the series of "explosions" that have kept the development boat rocking and disrupted the course of economic growth. The most notorious is the "population explosion," which signifies an overproduction of consumers in terms of available goods for consumption. Indeed, this disequilibration of a viable man:land ratio is a master link in the chain of explosions—including the urbanization and communication explosions which are the present subjects of discussion. For these are the principal channels through which underdeveloped peoples have received more developed "pictures of their own future."

The Explosions

The urban explosion was directly entailed by population increase; when there are more men than the land can support the surplus people must go elsewhere. Over the postwar years they have flocked to the cities—a rural jetsam brusquely converted into an urban flotsam. The societal disequilibrium thus created is evident from the *ranchos* of Caracas and the *favellas* of Rio to the *bidonvilles* of Cairo, the *gëçekondü* of Ankara, and the "tin-can cities" that crowd the urban centers of every developing country from Tehran to Jakarta. This is urbanization only in the statistical sense that ever greater numbers of rural rejects are flooding the ever increasing urban agglomerations. It bears no discernible relationship to the historical pattern of Western urbanization, which was linked to industrialization and thereby to the Western cycle of self-sustaining growth. The transfer of population to urban centers in the underdeveloped areas has not been linked to increasing production, as in the West, but rather to increasing consumption. In consequence, this "urbanization" has not contributed to a growth cycle of prosperity but rather has displaced the vicious circle of poverty from its traditional rural setting to an urban environment.

Among the development disequilibria of the postwar period, pseudourbanization (in terms of the Western model) has played a leading role. It has given the semblance of mobility without the substance of participation. The transposed "urban villagers" of the underdeveloped areas are psychic displaced persons rather than productive participants in a development process. In this critical sense their urbanization is a far different matter than it was historically for Western migrants, who gained from their physical mobility (urbanism) significant rewards of social mobility (upward) and psychic mobility (empathy). Thus, mobility became, for Western peoples, the highway to prosperity and participation. By contrast, pseudourbanization today has led the underdeveloped peoples down the path of maimed mobility to deprivation and degradation. Their urbanization has made them neither prosperous nor participant; rather, it has left them pained and petulant.

Carrying the diagnosis a step further, the population and urbanization explosions have been linked to a mass media explosion —sometimes called a "communication revolution." Mediated communication has compounded the disequilibria of development by conveying a "picture of their own future" to people who were ready to consume more good things but not at all prepared to produce them. This is the basic failure of globalist policy, which seeks equalization via international development, in the postwar period. The attempt to *substitute* communication management for policy planning, rather than *supplement* policy by communication, has boomeranged. It has led transitional peoples to expect events that cannot happen, to want things they cannot get. These are the trends on which we focus attention—the revolution of rising expectations and the want : get ratio.

THE REVOLUTION OF RISING EXPECTATIONS

This phrase was popularized early in the postwar period, when expectations of global equalization ran high among the newly liberated peoples of the underdeveloped world—and also among those, mainly Americans, who conceived global equalization as their "mission" in the world. The central expectation was that political independence would lead to economic prosperity, with societal stability taken for granted.

Experience soon proved that societal stability could not be taken for granted; nor did political independence lead to economic prosperity. As the leaders of the new nations perceived that the passing of imperialism did not automatically produce an increase of prosperity, they began to improvise. Because their countries were unready for self-sustaining growth, these leaders displaced their societies' incapacity to absorb onto the gimmicks of communication technology. There emerged from the newly independent and highly expectant peoples of the excolonial world a generation of charismatic leaders—from Nkrumah to Sukarno. Their charisma rested upon their skill in communication management. They told their expectant peoples what they wanted to hear—and they acted *as if* what they had said was done.

The "Number One Voice," as James Reston has styled political leadership, is potent in all countries. So, the charismatic leaders of the emerging nations—using the new mass-media technology available to them—promised much to their peoples. With these promises they created, or nurtured, a revolution of rising expectations. This "revolution" was abortive and its charismatic midwives, from Nkrumah to Sukarno, died with it. But the expectations they heightened, through their management of the mass media, remain high. The mass media that diffused these rising expectations have spread to the most remote areas of the world, with consequences that are only now becoming apparent to students of modernization. A cursory review of postwar development efforts will serve to remind us of what has been happening over the past two decades.

The 1950s: Rising Expectations

It is not unduly parochial to date the massive effort to induce development from the postwar policy initiatives of the United States. These initiatives were the Marshall Plan (1948) and Point IV (1949). The former was an economic aid program designed to achieve European "recovery"—that is, restoration of previous levels of well-being on a war-ravaged but wealthy continent. The latter was a technical assistance program designed to help the impoverished areas of the world attain "modernization" —that is, achievement of new self-sustaining levels of well-being beyond anything these lands had previously known.

This "bold new program" of global modernization suited the postwar feeling that a new deal was needed in the world, a program using constructive means to achieve positive ends. The

American Congress certified this postwar mood by authorizing, despite opposition under both Democratic and Republican administrations, the expenditure of billions of dollars for global modernization during the 1950s. The American intellectual community seconded the motion by framing its studies in an optimistic perspective symbolized, from the very start of the decade, by the phrase "the revolution of rising expectations."[9]

Everywhere the underdeveloped world of traditional societies was on the move. The old imperialisms were disappearing; new nations were emerging. The heady bouquet of independence filled the political atmosphere of the world arena. Everywhere there was new hope that the world would rapidly be made a better place to live for most of its people. Independence would deliver the backward lands from the quartet of traditional evils—impoverishment, illness, illiteracy, immobility. Foreign aid would provide the tools needed to do the job.

Two decades later the job is not done. Nor, it is clear now, is the job likely to be done—in any sense approximating "completion"—during the decades immediately ahead. A major casualty of the 1950s was our pervasive sense of optimism about global modernization. We are now, in the 1960s, rather more concerned about a potential "revolution of rising frustrations" that may be growing out of the record of failures—failures at least in the sense that achievements over the past decade have not merely measured up to aspirations. If it is now argued that expectations generated in the 1950s were excessive, then it must be admitted that excessive expectations have led to excessive disappointments. These failures are now judged even more severely than, by some "objective" criterion, they might deserve.

The 1960s: Rising Frustrations?

These considerations arise from reflection on the course of the developing areas over the past decade. It has not been a smooth course or a consistent one. It has falsified the predictions and belied the assumptions of those who foresaw the rapid coming of the good society to the backward areas. Among its casualties has been the assumption that if some particular input was made—

investment capital, industrial plants, agricultural methods, entre-
preneurial training, or any other "key factor" preferred by the
analyst—then a modernization process would be generated more
or less spontaneously. This is a serious casualty. As L. W. Pye has
aptly written: "Faith in spontaneity died soon after the first excolonial people began to experience frustrations and disappointment at becoming a modern nation."[10]

This bitter experience is relatively new and requires careful
evaluation—particularly by those among us who want the defeats
of the past decades to help prepare the modest victories that may
still be hoped for in the next. The decade of the 1950s witnessed
the spread of economic development projects around much of the
world. People throughout the backward and impoverished areas
suddenly acquired the sense that a better life was available to
them. New leaders arose who encouraged their people to believe
in the imminence of progress and the fulfillment of their new,
often millenial, hopes. A great forward surge of expectancy and
aspiration, of desire and demand, was awakened during the past
decade among peoples who for centuries had remained hopeless
and inert. This forward feeling was shared by those of us whose
unchanging task is to understand.

A significantly different mood characterizes our thinking
about the years before us. There is a new concern that the 1960s
may witness a radical counterformation: *a revolution of rising
frustrations*. Observers have had to temper hope with prudence,
for the limits on rapid growth have become more clearly visible
through our recent experience. There is a seasoned concern with
maintenance of equilibrium in societies undergoing rapid change.
Responsible persons now tend to look for guidance to theory more
than to ideology, to data more than to dogma.

PROJECTIONS

Structural Regularity: The Want:Get Ratio

The spread of frustration in areas developing less rapidly than
their people wish can be seen as the outcome of a deep imbalance
between achievement and aspiration. In simple terms, this situa-

tion arises when many people in a society want far more than they can hope to get. This disparity in the want:get ratio has been studied intensively in the social science literature. Over several decades, psychologists have devised tests and measurements for levels of aspiration and levels of achievement. Lasswell, summarizing this literature and much else besides, early proposed that these levels be conceived as a ratio relationship—what he called the I:D (Indulgence to Deprivation) ratio. This conception was expressed even earlier in an ingenious formula of William James:[11]

$$\text{Satisfaction} = \frac{\text{Achievement}}{\text{Aspiration}}.$$

This formula alerts us to the proposition that an individual's level of satisfaction is always, at any moment of his life, a ratio between what he wants and what he gets, that is, between his aspirations and his achievements. A person with low achievement may be satisfied if his aspirations are equally low. A person with high achievement may still be dissatisfied if his aspirations far exceed his accomplishments. *Relative* deprivation, as has been shown, is the effective measure of satisfaction among individuals and groups.

A serious imbalance in this ratio characterizes areas beset by rising frustrations. Typically, in these situations, the denominator increases faster than the numerator; that is, aspiration outruns achievement to such a degree that many people, even if they are making some progress toward their goal, are dissatisfied because they get much less than they want. Indeed, in some developing countries aspirations have risen high enough to annul significant achievements in the society as a whole.

We call this a regularity because it recurs, one way or another, in virtually all societies seeking development. The regularity is structural in the sense that it is built into any situation where communication *leads* development. This is because communication, especially via the mass media, accelerates rising expectations and multiplies consumer wants. Where communication leads in the formation of modernizing attitudes, as it now does everywhere, expectations are bound to outrun satisfactions and wants are bound to exceed gets. The communication nexus thus tends regularly to disequilibrate development by producing highly imbalanced want:get ratios that result in widening, ultimately disruptive and even revolutionary, frustration.

A Developmental Construct: Revolutionary Frustration

While a little frustration may be a useful stimulant to effort, massive doses of frustration are always counterproductive. The reaction-formations to unrelieved frustrations are either regression or aggression. Neither aids development; both disrupt development.

The regressive reaction was characterized many years ago by William James: "To give up pretensions is just as blessed a relief as to get them gratified, and where disappointment is incessant and the struggle unending, this is what men will always do."[12]

A poignant illustration of the regressive reaction is what polite commentators recently have taken to calling "dysfunctional literacy." What this euphemism refers to is the widespread waste of scarce human resources and downright degradation of precious human motivations that has accompanied literacy campaigns throughout the underdeveloped areas. That their intention is often laudable does not alter the fact that their outcome is often deplorable.

Consider the literacy campaign undertaken some years ago by the Turkish army. At very considerable effort and expense, recruits were to be taught reading as part of their military training. Special teachers were engaged and special materials were prepared; print, film, radio (and even comic books) were enlisted in this campaign to raise literacy. Yet, within a few years, the villages of Anatolia were full of lapsed literates. Once discharged from the army and returned to their villages, these boys found their literacy dysfunctional. First of all, in most villages there was little or nothing to read. Second, those who persisted in efforts to maintain their literacy were derided by their illiterate peers and upbraided by their pious (and purposefully illiterate) elders. Under such conditions their tenuous literacy weakened and died.

Why is such a sequence counterproductive to development? Initially, because it wastes human and technical resources that are indispensable and very scarce. More deeply, because it degrades aspirations that, once fallen, are unlikely ever to rise again. The lapsed literate who has undergone this bitter experience of failure with shame will be less readily motivated to try again than if he had not had his aspirations for literacy raised and crushed once before. His regressive reaction includes a return to traditional quietism and the narcosis of resignation. The modernizers in his society, who need to "mobilize the periphery" by rewarding activism and participation among villagers, can no longer count upon the lapsed literate.

While the regressive reaction is painfully wasteful, the aggressive reaction to extreme frustration is politically disruptive. Among its major manifestations have been the military takeover and the student revolt—phenomena that have spread throughout the developing areas in the postwar period. Their usual effect has been to subvert political stability and disrupt economic development, thereby impairing the dynamic equilibrium that is indispensable to self-sustaining growth.

The developmental construct that the modernizing lands are headed into a revolution of rising frustrations is based in large part upon the increasing incidence of such politically disruptive phenomena. Their incidence is increasing in both frequency and amplitude—the number of occurrences and the number of people involved. At such universities as Damascus and Caracas, it has become normal for students to spend more time in political agitation than in academic learning. There have been years in which these universities functioned educationally only thirty instead of nearly three hundred days. Indeed, in Venezuela, the organization of students for political agitation is already well developed in the secondary schools and is moving out of the urban centers into the primary schools throughout the country.

As student organizations for political subversion grow more numerous and violent, they forge links with other counterformations in the society. Venezuelan student groups have already manifested their capacity to mobilize the frustrated urban villagers of the *ranchos* for political action and to coordinate their political activities with frustrated aspirants of the officers' corps. By such coalitions, dedicated to subversion and seasoned in action, will the approaching "revolutions of rising frustrations" be made.

Some Policy Considerations

The drift toward a state of revolutionary frustration can be attributed largely to the subordination of policy to communication in the developing countries. The impact of the mass media upon the new nations has been dramatic in tempo and pervasive in scope; within a few years, under their lead, the emergent peoples have become the "expectant peoples."[13] Once diffused abroad on the wondrous new airwaves, rising expectations became an integral component of the great transformation of individuals and institutions that we call development. Expectation became the motor of modernization.

We have seen that expectations accelerated too fast too soon, that a structural disequilibrium was produced in the Want:Get ratio. We have seen that such disequilibria have been systematically interactive with personal frustration and political disruption. We have seen, further, that this vicious circle has wasted scarce resources and crippled movement toward self-sustaining growth. How is it, one must ask, that policy makers of the developing countries have permitted communication to lead policy in this irresponsible fashion? Why, in short, have they allowed the mass media to lead them by the nose?

An answer is suggested by Gamal Abdul Nasser, one of the most conspicuous leaders of the developing world in the postwar period—and, thanks to his flair for political tactics, one of the most durable. Shortly after his accession to power in Egypt, Nasser declared:

> It is true that most of our people are still illiterate. But politically that counts far less than it did twenty years ago. . . . Radio has changed everything. . . . Today people in the most remote villages hear of what is happening everywhere and form their opinions. Leaders cannot govern as they once did. We live in a new world.[14]

Nasser's easy dismissal of literacy and ready espousal of the electronic mass media, which operate among illiterate "people in the most remote villages," explains why policy was seduced by communication. Unable to mobilize the skills and resources needed for the harder tasks of real development (rising output and income per head of population), the charismatic leaders took the cheaper and easier way of supplying symbols of modernization via the mass media.

But the glamour of self-serving publicity rarely coincided with the needs of self-sustaining growth. During most of Nasser's fifteen years at the helm, the Egyptian ship of state has been bailing out rather than sailing on. Nasser's most conspicuous achievement via radio is his "Voice of the Arabs," which has been more effective in stimulating disruption abroad than development at home. But Nasser's agitational successes among the Palestinian DP's in Gaza and the streets of Amman have put no more bread in the mouths of Egyptian *fellaheen* nor taught their children to read.

Radio stardom as a substitute for policy leadership has, in fact, carried high long-term costs. These costs, which we have reviewed briefly as the explosions and frustrations that now beset the developing countries, cannot continue long unchecked without producing the revolutionary situation foreseen by our developmental construct. The purpose of those concerned with development policy in the world must be, as a matter of top priority, to check these trends and to reshape the conditions under which they occur. What is wanted, as an indispensable guide to development policy, is a new conception of what modernization requires in terms of institutional and individual behavior.

At the root of such a new conception must be the association of reward with effort. The satisfaction of individual aspirations is a function of individual achievements. The want:get ratio includes a give:get factor. The attainment of self-sustaining growth in a social system is the outcome of its attainment among the people who operate that system.

It is not enough to glory in one's newly found political independence—which, in many of the new nations, is rather an ascribed than an achieved status. Indeed, the image of national grandeur is often counterproductive when it leads to ethnocentrism and xenophobia.[15] No increase of well-being accrued to Iranians when Mossadegh "nationalized" their oil resources, nor was the distribution of values among the *fellaheen* enhanced when Nasser "Egyptianized" the enterprises of long-established non-Muslim minorities. The punitive racism of Indonesians against their Chinese minority or of East Africans against their Indian minority is just as costly to the human condition condition as similar occurrences at Little Rock or Notting Hill Gate. Such outrageous self-indulgence deprives its perpetrators of their humanity without real benefit to their well-being.

The concept of a world commonwealth of human dignity is as essential for the developing areas as it has proved to be for the developed nations. In such a commonwealth, nobody gains durably by depriving others but rather by improving himself—by entering upon that never ending cycle of self-sustaining growth which, when diffused among enough individuals, becomes societal. Once such a clear and comprehensive "picture of their own future" animates policy thinking among developing peoples, an appropriate communication nexus for their internal transformations and global relations can be evolved. Only then will their deep frustrations and fearful disequilibria be reduced to manageable levels and a new course mapped which leads to improvement in the quality of life.

REFERENCES

1. Daniel Lerner, *SYKEWAR: Psychological Warfare against Germany*, Foreword by R. A. McClure (New York: G. W. Stewart, 1948); paperback edition (Cambridge, Mass.: Massachusetts Institute of Technology Press, in press), p. xv.

2. V. Basanoff, *Evocatio, Etude d'un rituel militaire romain* (Paris: Presses Universitaires, 1947).

3. *China Quarterly*, 2 (1937):643–49.

4. *American Journal of Sociology*, 46 (1941):455–68; reprinted in *The Analysis of Political Behaviour* (1948).

5. Preface to *World Politics Faces Economics* (1945), p. vii.

6. These studies were done for the RADIR Project in the Hoover Institution at Stanford. See H. D. Lasswell and D. Lerner, eds., *World Revolutionary Elites* (1965); also the forthcoming Massachusetts Institute of Technology republication of the RADIR "symbol studies" by I. Pool.

7. Hans Speier, *Social Order and the Risks of War*, 2 vols. (Cambridge, Mass.: Massachusetts Institute of Technology Press, 1967).

8. My italics and translation. I believe this rendering is closer to what Marx means to us than the standard, and often stilted, translations of his heavy prose.

9. E. W. Staley, *The Future of Underdeveloped Countries: Political Implications and Economic Development* (New York: Harper & Row, 1951).

10. L. W. Pye, ed., *Communications and Political Development* (Princeton, N.J. University Press, 1963).

11. William James, *Psychology: Briefer Course* (New York: Holt, 1923), p. 187.

12. *Ibid.*

13. Kalman H. Silvert, ed., *Expectant Peoples: Nationalism and Development* (New York: Random House, 1963).

14. Quoted in Daniel Lerner, *The Passing of Traditional Society* (New York: Free Press, 1958), p. 214.

15. See my article "The Ethnocentric Predicament and the Western Model," in *Communication and Change in the Developing Countries*, ed. D. Lerner and W. Schramm (Honolulu: East-West Center Press, 1967).

9

Content Analysis and the Intelligence Function

ITHIEL DE SOLA POOL

To his colleagues, the work of Harold Lasswell symbolizes the movement of the study of man toward science. But as with many of the makers of modern social science, a closer look reveals profound moral concerns that guided his professional career.[1] (It has often been noted that many leading social scientists are sons of ministers.) The study of man has been for Harold Lasswell not a matter of idle curiosity but a tool for promoting the dignity of man.

Content analysis was promoted by Lasswell not because of fascination with numbers but for its "contribution . . . to the special objectives of humane politics."[2]

In its contribution to man's life in society, content analysis is at one with all the social sciences. In general it may be said that the social sciences are the humanities of our era. In previous times scholars considered it part of their role to be teachers of princes. They saw themselves as taming the violence of man's untutored nature by instilling in their young charges the quality of reason and the humane heritage of the liberal arts.

Today the social sciences are our best tools for understanding each others human passions, motives, and plans. They are our most effective instrument for handling man's greatest problem, organized violence. It is the social sciences that give us the most reliable information about where riots will breed, how criminals can be controlled, whether insurgents will maintain rule of a university or a village, and how nuclear war can be avoided. It is the social sciences that best help us understand the conditions by which a group may achieve consensus, the basis of psychopathological disturbances, the needs of minorities for respect. It is the social sciences that are now the best agency for civilizing statesmen.

The education of statesmen is but the latest of a series of functions that the humanities have abandoned to scientific disciplines. Philosophers used to observe and interpret nature, but since the seventeenth century they have abandoned that exercise to men of empirical science. They used to help men in their daily problems of disease, love, war, and farming by knowledge of stars, omens, magic, and potions, but these pretensions they abandoned at about the same time.

Even more recently the humanists have left the field of policy. But now the seer has been replaced as the prince's counselor by the operations analyst. Only the expressive, aesthetic function remains as the undisputed domain of the humanist. Today it has fallen to the policy scientist, as Harold Lasswell has called him, to moderate the action of the specialists in violence. It is the policy scientist who by the practice of intelligence tames the exercise of naked force in the practices of government and preserves respect for the humanity of man.

The importance of instruments of conciliation and moderation is increasingly great in our time, for since 1914 we have lived in an era of unprecedented violence. Our era opened on a note of confidence in democracy. Tocqueville eighty years before World War I, Marx seventy years before it, Ostrogorski a decade before it, and numerous other writers on modern civilization saw equality and democracy as the onrushing wave of the future. Mass organizations were being formed.[3] Mass participation in politics was growing. Social distinctions of status and right were being leveled.

After World War I, however, most social theorists, including Weber and Lasswell, became preoccupied with a new set of problems that grew out of their concern that democratic society might destroy itself. Led by demagogues who manipulated ideology, the mass movements that were the expression of democracy were imposing straitjackets of dogma on society. In Weber's formulation charismatic leaders create machines led by professionals which threaten to bring a dark night of rule by an absolute ethic that does not count costs. In Lasswell's formulation agitators and other political leaders who project complex private motives onto public objects may manipulate symbols of identification, demand, and expectation so as to establish garrison states that deny shared respect to their people. To these theorists democracy seemed far from a sure thing, and the conditions for its achievement and preservation were a major question for the social sciences to tackle. Much of Lasswell's writing in the 1930s and 1940s concerned the "developing science of democracy."

In 1942 Harold Lasswell wrote a piece with that title in a *Festschrift* for his mentor, Charles E. Merriam:

> The developing science of democracy is an arsenal of implements for the achievement of democratic ideals. We know enough to know that democracies do not know how to live; they perish through ignorance. . . . Without knowledge, democracy will surely fail.[4]

Furthermore, as he wrote elsewhere in the same year:

> Modern procedures do make it possible for the first time in the history of large scale social organization to realize some of the aims of democracy. Social and psychological sciences have developed procedures that are capable of reporting the facts about the thoughts and feelings of our fellow men.[5]

Content analysis is one of these procedures:

> We can actually study the thoughts and feelings of each of the major divisions of modern social structure and perfect means of making them fraternally intelligible to one another. . . . By examining the channels of public communication, we may determine the degree to which even the opportunity exists of taking the other fellow into proper account.[6]

Thus, content analysis could, in Lasswell's view, contribute to the objective of humane politics:

The aim of humane politics is a commonwealth in which the dignity of man is accepted in theory and fact. Whatever improves our understanding of attitudes is a potential instrument of humane politics. Up to the present, physical science has not provided us with means of penetrating the skull of a human being and directly reading off his experiences. Hence, we are compelled to rely upon indirect means of piercing the wall that separates us from him. Words provide us with clues.[7]

Content analysis is a systematic and rigorous way of doing what humanistic students of ideas and behavior have always done, namely, to look at what symbols are used in a body of text. Such observations of the flow of symbols become content analysis or social science if some attention is paid to the procedures of observation. Content analysis is only a portion of the intelligence function that makes democratic and rational decision-making possible.

Of seven functions which Lasswell distinguishes as taking place in the process of decision—intelligence, recommendation, prescription, innovation, application, appraisal, and termination[8] —it is the intelligence function that offers the content analyst or other man of learning the opportunity to humanize the exercise of power. The intelligence function is the bringing of knowledge of the conditions and consequences of his action to the consciousness of the decision maker. It includes the devices of interviewing, experimentation, espionage, participant observation, analysis, model building, introspection, computation, the census—everything that if done with rigor and objectivity deserves to be called broadly scientific.

The social scientist, including the content analyst, brings a new and more effective method of observation to bear on the perennial subject of human behavior. There are many ways of studying human behavior. There is the rationalistic approach used by the economist and moral philosopher of the nineteenth century. There is the developmental approach of the historian. There is the quantitative scientific approach of the empirical sociologist. There is the documentary institutional approach of the traditional political scientist. There is the individual psychodynamic approach of the psychologist.

Content analysis, as a rigorous, usually quantitative way of describing that part of human behavior which consists of symbol flows, belongs among the more empirical, positivistic ways of producing intelligence about men's attitudes, expectations, and values. It has been a particularly controversial manifestation of the scientific spirit because its object of study, symbol flows, comes so close to the heart of the humanists' own domain of study. The pretensions of the social scientists in encroaching upon the humanists' expertise in interpreting ideologies, doctrines, and value systems seemed particularly intolerable and philistine to those who disapproved of the social scientists' arrogation to themselves of a dominant role in the intelligence function. Content analysts have been repeatedly attacked on several grounds. Their critics have asserted that intellectual processes are too complex to be treated quantitatively, that in counting manifest symbols the content analyst disregards the nuances of meaning which can only be ascertained from the context, that content analysts naïvely count each symbol as having equal significance.

Perhaps in reaction to these attacks on their legitimacy, practitioners of content analysis have often gone to great lengths to prove how truly scientific they are. They have modeled their work on a prevailing ideal of what science should be.

The dominant image of science in the period since 1935, in which content analysis has been developed, is that of classical mechanics. This is not, however, the only image of science available to social scientists. Earlier social scientists often viewed their role as similar to that of naturalists; they wished to classify and document the variety of human societies and institutions. Other nineteenth century social scientists had an evolutionary image of what science was all about. They sought to formulate laws of history or trace the stages of the origins of institutions. But the dominant image today is certainly that of Galilean physics.

In this image of science, the scientist first formulates some universal proposition stating that the more (or less) of X there is, the more (or less) of Y there will be. He then performs some critical observation to prove the proposition. Needless to say, very little of social science, or for that matter natural science, fits that model. The scientist who describes in detail the steps in an adolescent's initiation into a society or the reproductive organs of a platypus is not behaving that way. Nor does the explorer, whether he is an anthropologist or ornithologist, follow that pattern. The formulator of a theoretical model, whether its elements are called ego, id, and superego, or electron, proton, and neutron, works outside the Galilean model, as does the inventor of a projective test or a laser. The world of science is a full one; it comprises many arts and devices. Nonetheless, most of the students of Lasswell, though not Lasswell himself, have valued content analysis mainly as a means to somehow approximate some externally derived image of science in their study of textual flows. For example, Richard Merritt, who has made some of the most interesting uses of content analysis in recent years, makes this methodological preference explicit:

> Ideally, the analyst formulates his hypotheses (as well as their alternatives) for testing at the onset of his project. Content analysis is useful only when the researcher has questions of a quantitative nature—how often? how much? how many? with what covariance? . . . The task of the analyst is to frame his questions so that quantitative data can answer them clearly, directly, and simply.[9]

A similar methodological preference is expressed by Robert North and his colleagues:

> The attempt to construct and rigorously to test hypotheses in the field of political science . . . has led many investigators on an intensive search for relevant and adequate data. . . .
>
> The following tentative hypothesis might be considered strictly for illustrative purposes:
>
> "If the incoming volume of messages for State A increases sharply over a brief time span, then the key decision-makers of A, as the recipients of this volume of messages, will perceive a sharp rise in hostility."[10]

Certainly, one thing that makes content analysis interesting is its usefulness in the testing of scientific hypotheses. Content analysis, because it does generate quantitative measures that are reasonably independent of the idiosyncratic subjectivity of the observer, is a convenient observational tool for experiments designed to test hypotheses. An observational device, however, is not itself science. It may be useful for science, but an observational device that is useful in science may also be used in many other ways. 'Telescopes are used for recreation, for navigation, and for education, as well as for science. Content analysis also has many possible uses, including the scoring of psychological tests (e.g., for need achievement), the prediction of political behavior (e.g., in wartime intelligence), the comparison of propaganda from different sources, etc.

In some of Harold Lasswell's writings a number of different ways of thinking are distinguished for which content analysis may be relevant, but only one is, strictly speaking, scientific. Among these nonscientific modes of thought are goal (or normative) thinking, trend thinking, and projective thinking.[11]

> Many students of politics, confronted by the ambiguity of existing language, grow pessimistic about the possibility of science. Perhaps, therefore, it is worth emphasizing the point that exact methods of observation yield certain advantages now, quite apart from the contribution they may ultimately make to a highly systematic science of democracy.[12]

Among these other applications of content analysis, Lasswell, as we have already noted, rates the normative ones highly.

> The democratic ideal includes a decent regard for the opinions and sensibilities of our fellows. The moralists who have championed this ideal in the past have made no progress toward the discovery of methods appropriate to the understanding of the thoughts and feelings of others. The instrumentation of morals has had to await reliable methods of observation. . . . This much is clear: Whether or not the methods of scientific observation contribute to the eventual completion of a systematic science of

democracy, they are certain to contribute here and now, to the practice of democratic morals.[13]

Documentation of trends by content analysis may also be useful in letting us know where we stand, but trend thinking by itself has limitations.

> While trend information is indispensable, it is not sufficient to enable us to mould the future. Trends have a way of changing direction; and often we can contribute to these changes. . . . A trend is not a cause of social change; it is a register of the relative strength of the variables that produce it.[14]

That is why scientific knowledge, if we can achieve it, is more interesting and powerful.

> The laws and propositions of science state invariant interrelations. We do not have scientific knowledge when we know, for example, that there was a trend toward world war in 1939; it is only when we can, by comparing war periods, relate war to conditioning factors that we have science. When we look toward the future our aim is not a draw of fatalistic series of trend curves. . . . To extrapolate in this way is necessary, but it is a prelude to the use of creative imagination and of available scientific knowledge in deciding how to influence the future.[15]

But for those interested in policy, like Harold Lasswell, scientific knowledge too has limitations as well as advantages. It is, for one thing, ahistorical. Scientific knowledge is a better instrument for understanding than the merely empirical reporting of trends, but it too is only an input to actions designed to change the course of history.

Lasswell's perspective is intensely historical. Time and discontinuities over time play a central role in his thinking, as they must in that of anyone concerned with policy.

> It is not enough to project scientific generalizations into the future. Scientific propositions avoid time; they treat time where it enters as a factor whose routine of interaction with other variables (at a specified magnitude) is *invariant*. . . .
>
> The mystic and the scientist share a curious ultimate bias against time.[16]

If one introduces time into one's mode of thinking along with goals, trends, and scientific uniformities, one is engaged in what Lasswell calls a "developmental construct."

> Trend and factor (scientific) thinking are requisite to projective thinking, which is concerned with future events. The question is, if we assume that no policy changes will be introduced, how will things turn out? Projective thinking is carried on by the use of developmental constructs, which we characterize as theoretical models of significant cross sections of past and future. Goals . . . are . . . points of departure for these constructs.[17]

Lasswell illustrated the notion of a developmental construct most fully in a gloomy article entitled "The Garrison State and Specialists on Violence" (1941).[18] Lasswell saw around him the collapse of the democracy which had been the focus of his value system. War, communism, and fascism were on the march. Depression seemed endemic to the democratic nations and there were fewer of them every year. The article is a strange one, for it breathes defeat on every page. For once in his life Lasswell was writing not about how to achieve the dignity of man, but rather how to adapt oneself to a society that denied it. While he starts without a commitment to a prophecy of doom, he soon admits to believing that it is the most probable course.[19]

What is this garrison state that Lasswell thought would probably overwhelm us? It is a state in which "specialists on violence are the most powerful group in society":

> The trend of our time is away from dominance of the business man, and toward the supremacy of the soldier.

This trend of growing violence and growing oppression cast such a pall in 1941 that at the conclusion of his essay Lasswell did not ask how the garrison state could be prevented, but how the defeated democrats could live with it.

> It is clear that the friend of democracy views the emergence of the garrison state with repugnance and apprehension. He will do whatever is within his power to defer it. Should the garrison state become unavoidable, however, the friend of democracy will seek

to conserve as many values as possible within the general framework of the new society.[20]

From the perspective of twenty-five years later this air of
pessimism seems at least premature. Yet it would be hard to argue
that Lasswell's construct was wrong. Whether the world is moving toward garrison states seems just as much a matter of both
possibility and doubt today as it did twenty-five years ago. A quarter century has neither put the nightmare to rest nor has it
confirmed it. It is certainly turning out to be true that military dictatorships are a normal mode of rule in the Third World of developing nations. There the military turn out to be the only
well-organized social grouping. Even there, however, military
rule seems to be a passing phase. Military dictatorships are fragile.
They are ambivalent about retaining power. They are often committed to development, and as development does occur, businessmen once more come to the fore. Japan and Mexico are star
examples.

In the communist world 700 million people have fallen under
the veterans of the Long March and the businessmen have disappeared. But in the West the shadow of fascism has passed and the
ideal of democracy is a norm more unquestioned than ever. Few
indeed are the nations that are not a little ashamed of their departures from democracy. They try to deny them in their propaganda even if they do not change.

In Western democracies, however, arms budgets grow ever
larger, though not as a steadily growing percentage of the gross
national product. That varies. Nuclear weapons, hardly dreamed
of in 1941, are with us. Defense plays an unprecedented part in
our politics. Yet a businessman from a motor company has defeated the military establishment of the world's greatest military
power, which is also the world's greatest democracy, and has
made the military carry on their planning in a strictly business-
like style.

It is hard indeed to judge Lasswell's article on the garrison
state even with our advantage of a quarter century of hindsight.

For our purpose here, however, it is not necessary to judge it. We cite it as the clearest example of what Lasswell means by a developmental construct.

It was that time-related historical concept that lay behind both of Lasswell's largest efforts in content analysis: the Library of Congress studies during World War II and the RADIR studies, Both programs made more than a passing effort to contribute to generalizing science, but they were also efforts to contribute to policy by recording and exposing developmental trends in values and ideology in the modern world.[21]

The Library of Congress effort was what Harold Lasswell called a "World Attention Survey."[22] It attempted to plot what changes were taking place in the press of the major nations in their awareness of and attitudes toward other nations and major political symbols. The most basic categories were favorable (plus) and unfavorable (minus) treatment of self and other. These are as fundamental a set of political categories as exist. They can be, and were, elaborated further, but there is a lot to be learned simply from documenting who is becoming more (or less) plus or minus toward whom around the world. These are facts that every diplomat, journalist, and politician intuitively keeps track of. There is much to be gained by compiling systematic, verified knowledge of them.

The Library of Congress study was in substantial part an intelligence effort. It was designed to improve our understanding of the political dynamics of various countries around the world, including the German enemy, third countries, and also ourselves. As an intelligence operation it was not particularly successful. It was operating beyond the state of the art, and as a result it contributed far more to content analysis methodology than to substantive understanding of the enemy at that time. In a parallel effort going on at the same time in the Foreign Broadcast Intelligence Service more intuitive methods of content analysis were being used, with considerable success, to anticipate German actions. These were complementary rather than competing efforts and we have learned a lot from both. The lessons of the FBIS effort have been thoroughly analyzed and evaluated by Alexander George in his book on propaganda analysis for intelligence purposes.[23] George demonstrates that at that time the efforts of the FBIS to use formal quantitative methods were unfruitful. The technology available did not permit flexibility in considering propaganda strategy and in evaluating the varied importance of statements in different contexts if much quantification was to be done. Quantification required rather mechanical simplifications that defeated the intelligence objectives.

It should be added that in 1969 this is no longer necessarily true. The possibility of keypunching text into computer-readable form and of retrieving and regrouping material in an interactive mode might lead to very different conclusions if an effort were made today similar to the 1940s one that George evaluated. The value of the Library of Congress experiment in advancing our understanding of the fundamental problems of statistical analysis of meanings would then be apparent.

The RADIR project (Revolution and the Development of International Relations) undertaken at the Hoover Institution from 1948 to 1953 was also a world attention survey, but this time for a sixty-year period, 1890–1950. The purpose was to document a developmental construct labeled "The World Revolution of Our Time." Newspaper editorials from prestige papers in five countries were examined to ascertain the rise and fall of major political concepts, particularly those pertaining to democracy and authoritarianism, violence and peace, and self and other (i.e., identity).

This time a good deal did emerge that clarified the development of the ideologies of our times. In the democratic powers, the vanishing of the conservative symbols of order and authority was documented and dated. The decline of symbols of Marxist ideology in favor of an ordinary plebeian nationalist symbolism in the Soviet Union continued through the various zigs and zags of the Communist Party line. Everywhere democracy was less often interpreted in terms of rights and freedoms and more often interpreted in terms of mass participation. In America the focus on violence increased. For historians, if they learned to use the new, more precise methods of observation that modern social science permits, the data was rich.

In another of its aspirations, however, the RADIR project did not succeed. The results never became relevant to policy. The designers of the project certainly thought that they were clarifying the central issues of our time, around which the great battles of national policy were being fought. It was no accident that one of the by-products of the RADIR project was a volume called *The Policy Sciences*.[24] It is also no accident that while the volume contained much excellent social science, there was little about policy in it.

As one of those chiefly involved in the RADIR project, I think I may fairly say that however much we were committed to policy relevance, we did not, at that time, understand what that would demand of the research. The policy maker is not satisfied with being told that the total focus of society on violence is increasing, though he might find the fact (if it is a fact) interesting and disturbing. He certainly wants to know things like how to control riots in specific neighborhoods of thirteen cities during three months of the year. Even if we had understood how far our work fell short of policy relevance, however, there was nothing we could have done about it. The technology then available to us precluded anything but a highly generalized, broad-sweep approach to a sixty-year content analysis. This was not obvious at first because the RADIR project generated much data about specific issues, times, and places. We recorded 105,000 instances of occurrence of 416 symbols in some 20,000 editorials from five countries over a sixty-year period. The data were there for very pinpointed analyses. What we lacked was the computational power to make more than a very few analyses of all that data. The data were recorded on manual cards. Nor would it have solved the problem if they had been on IBM cards, for at that time the cards would have had to be analyzed by unit-record equipment. As the RADIR reports pointed out, the structure of language does not lend itself to unit-record file organization. Language is above all relational. The important thing about a symbol is the context of other symbols in which it occurs—which symbols precede it and which follow it.

The point may be illustrated by one of the more interesting results of the RADIR studies concerning the symbol "democracy." There is a widespread view that the word has been a fad. Politicians, regardless of their true ideology, so it is said, label their convictions democratic. But in fact we found that, in general, the use of the symbol "democracy" increased as a function of the total set of symbols representing its subject matter. It was not a fad of the word but a genuine shift of attention to the subject matter of democracy that was taking place in the world revolution of our time.

The introduction to the report of the RADIR symbol studies by Lasswell and associates stated the hope that the evolution of the computer, then just appearing on the horizon, would provide the key to the solution of the problem of quantitative analysis of language, and indeed it has done that.[25] Until that happened, after the end of the RADIR project, there was about a ten-year hiatus in the further development of content analysis for the intelligence function. Content analysis continued to be pursued for limited purposes, usually for the testing of well-defined hypotheses. David McClelland's development of a system for scoring need achievement in stories is an example. But the use of content analysis as a broad social indicator had to await the development of the computer.

The situation is now ripe for a revival of the insight that Harold Lasswell had a quarter of a century ago. In the first place, there is a renewed search for social indicators. Raymond Bauer's book on the subject, an outgrowth of a project of the American Academy of Arts and Sciences, illustrates that widening interest.[26] The growth of programs to accomplish stated national social goals, such as the poverty program and the civil rights program, have made us aware of how meager are our tools for observing the state of society and of changes in it (outside the fields of economics and demography, where published series of indicators have been with us for some time). Similar series are needed to tell us where we stand with regard to other social and political values, such as respect and enlightenment. For years Lasswell has been calling for the development of observational devices to provide intelligence about social and political trends. His plea is now being widely taken up. Thus, a receptive audience exists for a revival of attention surveys.

A second emerging condition for the success of such efforts is the development of structural linguistics. Counting the presence or absence of symbols was always recognized as too simple a method of content analysis to tap trends in meaning. Computational requirements, however, led to severe limitations on the recording of context. From the very beginning of his work on content analysis Lasswell insisted on at least coding each symbol with a pro or contra attitudinal indicator.[27] Much more complicated tagging of symbols to take account of the structures that determine their significance is possible with modern computational equipment, once one understands what options are provided by the structure of language. In recent years, the linguists, particularly the psycholinguists, have had to cope with many of the same problems as content analysts. The progress that the linguists have made permits the conduct of much more meaningful content analyses than in the past.[28]

The third and most critical condition for the revival of content analysis for intelligence purposes has been the development of the computer. There are already numerous computer applications for processing text. Computers are used for making concordances and indexes, for example. They are also used extensively in linguistic research. The main technological requirements are (1) that the computer have a large, readily accessible bulk memory in which to store considerable bodies of text, (2) that the analyst have available a list or string language in which to work so that he can readily process the complex relational data of language, and (3) that the system be interactive and on-line so that the analyst can explore the stored text intelligently, step by step, instead of being swamped by data.

The first major program to take advantage of the potential of the computer for content analysis is reported in Philip Stone's *General Inquirer*.[29] In his preface to the recent volume in which Stone describes this program and the work done with it to date, Lasswell notes that the tedium of hand content analysis had driven most practitioners from the field after a try or two. The General Inquirer has brought creative scholars back into the field. Almost all the significant work in content analysis in the past five years, such as the work of Robert North and his colleagues at Stanford, has used the General Inquirer. As it exists today, this instrument is not yet what is needed for a world attention survey or other intelligence application requiring the rapid processing of very large bodies of text. The General Inquirer was designed for use with moderate-sized bodies of text. It takes a fair amount of processing of the natural language text, and it is not optimized for rapid search over very large memories. It was designed for other purposes such as the efficient creation of dictionaries of key symbols and the close analysis of rich textual material. But whatever else it does, or does not do, the General Inquirer points out the path and demonstrates the feasibility of computerized content analysis.

What is feasible, however, is not necessarily useful. The standard answer of mountain climbers when asked why they climb high peaks is "because they are there." This is not a good enough reason for engaging in content analysis. The fact that propaganda, editorials, speeches, and political material of all sorts is poured out in the public media does not per se make it useful to subject these materials to quantitative measurement of what is in them and how that changes.

Yet it would be useful. One of the greatest problems facing policy makers is the vast flow of unprocessed information that pours past them. Every day the State Department receives about 2,000 cables from abroad. Every day the Foreign Broadcast Intelligence Service records and transcribes the news and public affairs programs broadcast by hundreds of radio stations around the world. Every day politicians, intelligence analysts, and pub-

lic servants comb newspaper columns and editorials from places
of interest looking for clues to reactions to events by various
wings and parties of opinion.

No doubt computerized processing and analysis of this flood
of material is no panacea. Trivial and irrelevant material can be
analyzed to no avail. Clumsy and irrelevant systems can easily be
produced. Indeed, at this early stage of development of information-processing techniques, numerous examples of poorly designed systems can be found. Yet the future expansion of computerized text-processing systems is certain, for there is so much
potential in them for doing what is useful.

Consider, for example, the present techniques of Kremlinol-
ogists and others who attempt to decipher Aesopian communication. Normally, they draw their conclusions from spotting sudden
anomalies in the flow of statements. How much better off they
would be if they had some way of verifying the impression that
the formula spotted is new, or, if it is not new, if they had some
way of knowing where it had occurred before. Or consider the
intelligence analyst trying to assess attitudes in some other country toward the United States. How much better off he would be
if he could mechanically scan and summarize all sources on any
given topic at several points in time in a matter of minutes rather
than being confined to hunches prompted by a dramatic example
or two.

The standard book on content analysis for intelligence purposes tends to deny this apparently obvious conclusion. Alexander
George examined the wartime analyses of German radio propaganda to ascertain what clues and methods yielded valid inferences about German intentions. His judgment was that systematic
quantitative content analysis yielded little. Sensitive human analysts, who looked for little anomalies which they could not have
defined in advance and which depended heavily on context,
yielded a lot.

However, George was pitting a clumsy and now outmoded
content analysis technique against the intuitive skill of the analyst.[30] Note that content analysis as George evaluated it required

that the system of analysis and its categories be fixed in advance and carried on uniformly, regardless of the question put by the analyst. It was this lack of flexible adaptability to the needs of a complex inference structure that George identified as the weakness of quantitative content analysis in World War II intelligence. A modern, computerized retrieval and analysis system would, however, have all the texts in bulk memory and would produce rapid scanning and analysis of them *after* the analyst had come up with a question generated by his intuitive processes. The question and the mode of analysis would be specific and pinpointed to the particular phenomenon that had attracted the analyst's attention. For example, if a World War II analyst noted that a highly prestigious newscaster minimized territorial gain one evening, the analyst might conclude that this man, being close to men of power, was reflecting a policy decision not to press for further expensive advances along the front. But to defend this hunch the analyst would first want to validate his impression that this was a new theme for this newscaster and for newscasters in general, and he would want to do so the same day. Full-time analysts who immerse themselves in a particular subject matter are pretty good at such scanning. Aided by a computerized retrieval and analysis system they could be better.

Whether the initial clue is provided by an anomaly in a systematic time series of a social indicator or by the subtle insight of an experienced observer, George is undoubtedly right in saying that the evaluation of this hunch requires subtle inference processes that are too varied and complex to be preplanned. What has changed, however, is that quantitative content analysis no longer needs to have a rigid, preplanned character.

Thus, the future of content analysis lies, as Lasswell realized from the beginning, in very broad uses in the intelligence function, not just in its occasional use by social scientists for testing general propositions.

In a number of articles Lasswell has described the intelligence function.

The term "intelligence" refers to the stream of fact and comment upon which choices are based. . . . (The term has dropped out of use in recent decades; save in military circles. We revive the word in order to characterize the communications important to policy.)[31]

When we examine the decision process of any body politic . . . it is usually possible to describe the structures specialized to a function. At the Federal level we think at once of the Central Intelligence Agency, the Bureau of the Census, and the like, when we consider the intelligence function.[32]

In closing, let us examine the intelligence function for public policy as it is organized today to determine where content analysis is relevant to it.

There are three main professions which specialize in enlightening the decision maker so that he can act with humanity and judgment. These professions are social scientist, journalist, and government intelligence operative. While mutual recriminations and institutional jealousies may make their allied activities seem remote from each other, these groups actually blend imperceptibly with one another and would gain from bridging their barriers.

What distinguishes social scientists from the other two groups is their interest in the general. Both the reporter and the CIA agent are devoted to the idea that names, dates, and places make news, while the social scientist typically suppresses all such information as raw data. But it is only necessary to state such an ideal-type distinction to recognize how frequently it departs from reality. Political scientists publish case studies. Clearly, these are also journalism. The kind of social scientist who writes for organs like *Foreign Affairs* is very much concerned with names, dates, and places, as is the historical scholar. On the other hand, occasional journalists such as Walter Lippmann, Harold Isaacs, or Douglas Cater write studies which are outstanding contributions to social science. Walter Lippmann's *Public Opinion,* published in 1922, has yet to be supplanted in the social science literature.

Governmental intelligence operatives are different from the

other two groups in that they give their analyses directly to the policy maker rather than publishing them. This too, however, is only an ideal-type distinction, not one which fits reality. The Foreign Broadcast Intelligence Service publishes hundreds of pages a day of transcriptions of political broadcasts from around the world. For the serious student of public affairs these constitute one of the main worldwide sources of public information. On the other hand, social scientists are increasingly employed in staff roles in both business and government, where their analyses and recommendations serve the decision maker directly. Contract research organizations are increasingly commissioned to provide scientific inputs for enlightened decision making in such fields as market research, city planning, strategy, etc.

There is, of course, an elementary moral issue. The respondent or informant should be told the truth about whether his individual inputs will be identified and published. He is aggrieved if information he gave as confidential appears in the public press, and he is equally aggrieved if information he gave on the assumption that it would be published for the scientific community as a whole ends up in a private report for one party. So long as social scientists adhere to the simple standard of candor with their informants, no useful purpose is served by taboos that attempt to confine artificially, within three highly artificial ideal types, the many ways of putting information to use on behalf of human welfare.

On the contrary, the natural and desirable trend is toward the increasing use of social science in both journalism and governmental intelligence. The great human triumph of our age is science. The power of scientific method has made its impact felt with revolutionary consequences in field after field. The consequences in warfare are horrifying because this great folly of the human species has been made so satanically effective. But the revolution wrought by the application of science has been just as great in more desirable human activities. The healing of the sick has become an art completely dominated by science. Communication has been revolutionized by science. So has construction. Field after field of practical activities that used to be pursued by independent craftsmen can now be pursued only with the guidance of scientifically educated professionals.

The same take-over by science is only beginning in the social field, but it will happen. Consider the trend in journalism. Increasingly, the town-crier function of rapid dissemination of spot news is being taken over from the press by electronic media. More and more the newspaper becomes a reference resource that offers the opportunity of exploring specialized interests in greater depth than the electronic media permit. Three sections of the paper have already become highly technical, namely, the business page, the weather report, and the sports' page. These contain large quantities of sophisticated statistics. In the political news, the newspaper reporting of public opinion polls is the first evidence of the likely trend. Social science and psychological research is increasingly used and misused as news. Sooner or later, as social science explanations become more powerful, the regular reporting of significant social indicators may be expected. Content analysis, for example, may provide summary statistics on trends in publicly expressed attitudes and beliefs around the world. Newspapers might report on themselves. Even now some newspapers do run world press roundups which give short quotations from various other newspapers expressing different views. A quantitative summary analysis of the content of the world press based on a representative sample might be a more significant piece of news. Such technical reporting will come, however, only as social science proves its explanatory power. That will happen, but not quickly.

In the same way, the governmental intelligence function is likely to be increasingly infused with social science. Up to now "the intelligence community," as it calls itself, has tended to be negative toward the social sciences other than economics. Collecting economic statistics and making economic projections for foreign countries are part of the standard work of the intelligence agency of any major power. But social research in other fields has never become a recognized portion of the program of intelligence agencies such as the CIA and is relatively trivial in quantity. Intelligence is still the domain of historians whose focus on names and dates and particulars is congenial to the intelligence community. If it could be done, an elite analysis of the CIA might, I suspect, confirm the continued reliance on historians and very minimal use of behavioral scientists. One can hope, however, that this is a passing phase. The growing power of the behavioral sciences will force the intelligence community to modify its archaic image of itself as "old area hands" and to accept behavioral scientists, as it has now accepted economists and electronic engineers.

A central problem for government intelligence agencies is the vast mass of material which they have to process. In addition to the State Department's 2,000 cables a day, the world press runs to thousands of pages. Radio-monitoring reports add to that flow. Systems for retrieval and analysis of this large mass of content can clearly serve to enable the decision maker to act with the judgment and knowledge that this large collection of information makes potentially possible.

There are those in the academic social science community who would like to deny that their activity has anything to do with the process of providing enlightenment to public policy makers. It is hard to understand why any scholar would be unsympathetic to processes of disseminating enlightenment, but scholars too are part of society and are subject to its pressures and hysterias. At the moment of writing the United States is going through one of those periodic waves of anti-intellectual hysteria which plague our society. In each of these waves certain patterns of political behavior recur. One of these is that intellectuals who have purported to be defenders of high moral values are "exposed" by demagogues as really part of a secret conspiracy with satanic forces of evil. The wave of exposure spreads guilt by association to ever larger circles, and the wickedness of the original secret plotters becomes axiomatic. Displaced onto public objects, this fantasy seems to tap very deep feelings in the American man on the street. It relieves his guilt about people who have been urging undesired moral imperatives upon him. It helps him deny his own involvements with movements and organizations that have proved less than perfect. It cuts down the intellectuals to whom he feels inferior. Whether the attacks are directed at anarcho-syndicalists as in the 1920s, or communists as in the 1950s, or the CIA as in the 1960s, they provide agitators like Joseph McCarthy and *Ramparts* with a wide and expandable list of targets. It is not surprising that many honest but fearful scholars seek immunity by protesting that they have no contact with or resemblance to the supposed secret conspirators.

Fortunately, these mass neuroses are passing waves, though each leaves its residue of damage behind. There is no reason to doubt that in the long run the process of providing accurate and complete information to government policy makers will be recognized as an honorable role which contributes to peace and the humanity of governance. There is no reason to doubt that social scientists will proudly recognize that one of their great contributions to society is the improvement of the governmental intelligence process.

It is certain that arms races and wars grow out of situations where incomplete knowledge about the plans and preparations of potential opponents cause exaggerated fears and excessive defensive reactions. Secrecy in the modern world is generally a destabilizing factor. Nothing contributes more to peace and stability than those activities of electronic and photographic eavesdropping, of content analysis and textual interpretation, that have at great cost and effort opened up those nations to realistic assessment who for misguided considerations of short-run advantages have tried to place a curtain of secrecy around themselves.

Once it has been conceded that enlightenment of rulers is a good thing, and that excellent intelligence is likely to make governance more humane, the dilemma of privacy presents itself. This is not particularly a problem stemming from international research and intelligence, for there is little justification in a democratic world for protecting the privacy of rulers. The acute dilemma for social scientists is choosing between the social value of disseminating knowledge widely and the personal value of individual privacy. This dilemma appears in much of Lasswell's writing about the intelligence function. In an essay written in 1943 entitled "Legal Education and Public Policy" he wrote:

> The realism of the decisions made by the officers or members of any organization depend in no small measure on the quality of the intelligence that reaches them. . . . One requirement for an adequate stream of intelligence is disclosure of source. . . . Besides the disclosure of source, positive means of obtaining access to the media of communication are essential. . . . Still a third aspect of the intelligence function is access to facts that interested parties try to conceal.[33]

In 1957, after the phenomenon of McCarthy, Lasswell qualified this view in another essay, "The Normative Impact of the Behavioral Sciences": "By this time, however, I think we have accumulated enough experience to recognize that it is wiser to forego some kinds of knowledge, and to bear the resulting cost, than to break down the barriers to privacy under some circumstances."[34]

On the whole, the lesson of the social sciences seems to be that we must all learn to live with a much higher degree of exposure than earlier, less knowledge-oriented societies tolerated. Psychological and psychoanalytic techniques are modes of revealing the innermost recesses of ourselves. Sociological research, political research, the press, personnel systems, are all ways of making us individually and collectively more conscious of each other. Yet there are and must be limits. This is not the place to explore the question of the limitations we must impose on ourselves as scientists out of respect for the humanity of our subjects. They are clearly many and complex. Yet even more important in the long run, in a world in which science is making knowledge increasingly available, is to learn to live with knowledge.

If social science has exposed us all to the glare of new kinds of observation, it has also given us a new appreciation of the foibles of the human condition. If psychology has exposed us all, it has also perhaps made it possible for us to be more tolerant and appreciative of what is exposed. Perhaps much of the answer to the dilemma of privacy posed by the social sciences is the capacity for greater tolerance that the social sciences also teach. These sciences help us live with each other as we really are.

Content analysis poses the dilemma of privacy less acutely than do most social science techniques of observation. One of its advantages is that it is not intrusive. The analysis of texts that are already parts of an established record is less disturbing to the persons who are the sources than those techniques that require face-to-face disclosures. The social sciences will be increasingly asked to provide social indicators that measure unintrusively the normal flow of human behavior. Content analysis is one of the techniques for doing this.

REFERENCES

1. Note such typical titles in the bibliography of Lasswell's writings as: "The Normative Impact of the Behavioral Sciences," "Clarifying Value Judgments: Principals of Content and Procedure," and "The Developing Science of Democracy: How to Integrate Science, Morals, and Politics."

2. *The Language of Politics* (originally published in 1949), (Cambridge, Mass.: Massachusetts Institute of Technology, 1963), p. 51.

3. Ostrogorski traces the modern pressure group to the Wilkes riots and petitions in 1768. The prevalent view at that time, stated by Horace Walpole, was that the formation of committees that arrogate "a right of considering and deciding on questions pending in Parliament and of censuring or approving the part taken by particular members" was a challenge to the authority of the Parliament, the institution set up precisely for the purpose of discussing what public policy ought to be. Voluntary associations were thought to be unconstitutional and to constitute a "dual power," as Lenin accurately designated them. M. Ostrogorski, *Democracy and the Organization of Political Parties* (New York: Macmillan, 1902), pp. 121–22.

4. L. D. White, ed., *The Future of Government in the United States: Essays in Honor of Charles E. Merriam* (Chicago: University

of Chicago Press, 1942); reprinted in H. D. Lasswell, *The Analysis of Political Behavior* (New York: Oxford University Press, 1947), p. 1.

5. "The Relation of Ideological Intelligence to Public Policy," *Ethics*, 53 (1942):27; reprinted in Lasswell, *Analysis of Political Behavior* (New York: Oxford University Press, 1947), p. 122.

6. *Ibid.*

7. Lasswell, *Language of Politics*, p. 51.

8. Harold D. Lasswell, *The Decision Process: Seven Categories of Functional Analysis* (College Park, Md.: University of Maryland Press, 1956).

9. Richard L. Merritt, "The Representational Model in Gross-National Content Analysis," in *Mathematical Applications in Political Science II*, ed. Joseph L. Bernd (Dallas: Southern Methodist University Press, 1966), p. 46.

10. Robert C. North, Ole R. Holsti, M. George Zaninovich, and Dina A. Zinnes, *Content Analysis* (Evanston, Ill.: Northwestern University Press, 1963), p. 28.

11. Harold D. Lasswell, "Clarifying Value Judgment: Principles of Content and Procedure," *Inquiry*, 1 (1958):94–95.

12. Lasswell, "Developing Science of Democracy," p. 11.

13. *Ibid.*, pp. 11–12.

14. *Ibid.*, p. 32.

15. *Ibid.*, pp. 32–33.

16. Lasswell, "Clarifying Value Judgment," p. 95.

17. *Ibid.*

18. *American Journal of Sociology*, 46 (1941):455–68.

19. He starts out by saying only that the purpose of his article is to consider the possibility that we are moving toward a world of "garrison states," but he then goes on to say: "The picture of the garrison state that is offered here is not a dogmatic forecast. Rather it is a picture of the probable."

20. Lasswell, *Analysis of Political Behavior*, p. 155.

21. There is a passing point to be made of some psychological interest. Timeless generalizing science is a young man's game. (Vide the power of the young in physics and mathematics.) Understanding time and development takes a more mature kind of wisdom. In his forties, Lasswell had development concepts very much in mind as he framed the design of both the Library of Congress project and the RADIR project. As a young man associated peripherally with the one and centrally with the other, I found real excitement only in the scientific generalizing aspects of these studies and bent my own contribu-

tions in that direction, looking for essentially timeless models of symbol interaction (see my quantitative model of communist reaction to defeats in *Language of Politics* and my model of verbal reactions of nations to each other in *Symbols of Internationalism* [Stanford, Calif.: Stanford University Press, 1951]). Now, a decade and a half later, Lasswell's strategy has become far more understandable and congenial to me.

22. Harold D. Lasswell, "World Attention Survey," *Public Opinion Quarterly*, 5 (1941):456–62.

23. Alexander L. George, *Propaganda Analysis* (Evanston, Ill.: Row Peterson and Co., 1959).

24. Harold Lasswell and Daniel Lerner, eds., *The Policy Sciences* (Stanford, Calif.: Stanford University Press, 1951).

25. H. D. Lasswell, D. Lerner, and I. Pool, *The Comparative Study of Symbols: An Introduction* (Stanford, Calif.: Stanford University Press, 1952), p. 63.

26. Raymond A. Bauer, *Social Indicators* (Cambridge, Mass.: Massachusetts Institute of Technology Press, 1966).

27. "A Provisional Classification of Symbol Data," *Psychiatry*, 1 (1938):197—204.

28. The recognition of the possibility of fruitful interaction between content analysis and linguistics stems from the Social Science Research Council's Committee on Psycholinguistics. The results of these deliberations are reported in I. Pool, ed., *Trends in Content Analysis* (Urbana, Ill.: University of Illinois Press, 1959).

29. Philip Stone, *General Inquirer* (Cambridge, Mass.: Massachusetts Institute of Technology Press, 1966).

30. George, *Propaganda Analysis.*

31. "Stabilization Technique and Patterns of Expectation," in *Income Stabilization for a Developing Democracy*, ed. M. F. Millikan (New Haven, Conn.: Yale University Press, 1953), p. 633.

32. Lasswell, *The Decision Process.*

33. In *Analysis of Political Behavior*, p. 78.

34. *Ethics*, 67 (1957):35.

10

Scientific Heroism from a Standpoint within Social Psychology

ARTHUR J. BRODBECK

> To experience, all identification must cease. To experiment, there must be no fear. Fear prevents experience. It is fear that makes for identification. . . . Identification is a refuge. A refuge needs protection, and that which is protected is soon destroyed. Identification brings destruction upon itself, and hence the constant conflict between various identifications.
>
> J. KRISHNAMURTI

SELF-CONGRATULATIONS about how well we are doing is often a way we escape from considering how much more we have to do. Perfection always resides in the future, if only because perfection is an infinite process of achievement. Indeed, the better we become, the more we see to do by way of improvement. Professor Lasswell has stressed this outlook to all of us who have been associated with him without sparing any ego in the process. It seems only to partake of the same spirit he has diffused among us to turn it now back upon him and his work. How are the work and deeds of Professor Lasswell less than perfect? It is possible to raise and answer this question quite without blame or censure or smallness of mind, but, on the contrary, with a sound core of appreciation for his achievements in social science. No tone of self-assertiveness, wherein closed ego confronts closed ego in hostile fashion, is generally compatible with open questioning that searches for truth. However, it is not always easy to adopt this openness toward Professor Lasswell and his work, since his system is often represented as closed and finished, rather than in the process of vigorous growth. Yet, quite without the self-aggrand-izement of anyone, the thrust of this discussion is to ask us all to take another look, precisely because we all share one fundamental goal in common—i.e., that of human dignity, and of human free-dom which is part of such dignity. In my own mind, I am not satisfied as a social psychologist that the system is anywhere near such perfection that it can afford to represent itself as finished and final, even though it is now being used to operationalize World Public Order.

The standpoint from which one looks at issues shapes what one sees about them. My own standpoint is that of a social psy-chologist. Social psychology, in general, takes the interaction between group and individual as a field for study. It attempts to place the individual in social context and, hence, widens the sig-nificance of each individual attribute by seeing the whole mean-ing of it for the common good. On the other hand, it goes deeper than the sciences of group organization, seeing more intensively how groups penetrate the functioning of individuals and what appear to be small details of changes in individuals may have sweeping organization effects once they are stabilized in the per-sonalities of participants. Social psychology thus counteracts both separatism and superficiality in social science. Socialization—the study of the intended and unintended (unconscious) education of pre-adults for adult participation on an aggregate basis—is, above all, the cornerstone of social psychology. Without constant refer-ence to socialization, social psychology fails to correct separatism and superficiality, but merely perpetuates it in some new and often more subtle form.

When I was asked to make a contribution to this volume honoring Professor Lasswell, as part of that task I reviewed the origin and development of social psychology in America, where it took earliest and firmest hold in social science. My original con-tribution[1] became too unwieldy to include in this volume, but it is possible to give the gist of it. I advanced the view that the social psychologist had as his *distinctive* aim, revealed in the very first classics in the field, a burning interest in discovering *how to im-prove and perfect consciousness.* Consciousness became the mechanism through which the highest and best meanings (value) are both discovered in and achieved for the self and for the common good. The deepened control of consciousness, thus, is the control of meaning and value in our living patterns. The maximal use of consciousness (with as much economy as we can command) is, still more, the means toward a promised perfection of valuing. The synthesis of each act of consciousness within and between personalities and groups is, furthermore, the way in which transitory excellence may be sloughed off for excellence that has lasting significance. The work of the social psychologist has always been cut out for him if he can find one single way in which the instrument of valuing can be made still more sensitive and refined, one single way in which it can become more comprehensive of the space-time context in which it works, one single way in which it can be synthesized to function within itself and with others so as to further more mutual refinement and inclusivity of valuing. Indeed, because of this distinctive thrust, social psychologists have tended to shy way from finished systematics, as Jerome Bruner has pointed out on various occasions. The perfection sought is so unending an adventure of inquiry in principle that closure is nowhere in sight.

A view of this sort usually opens further streams of thought, which form a new configuration that one can explore with mounting enthusiasm and growing clarity. What we call heroes are actually those individuals who perform this function of exemplifying a more perfected use of consciousness than has hitherto been achieved. Heroes touch human consciousness in such a way that it is permanently and lastingly improved after being exposed to the heroic figure. A hero strains and stretches to be a prototype of a more perfected consciousness that is potential in man. In the processes of education, children respond eagerly and quickly to legends of heroes, and to all the living heroes that appear in their own lives.[2] Such forms of education are where the conscious and unconscious processes meet in union rather than in conflict. It is a way of *living* life that is heroic, a way of redeeming human self-doubt, laziness, despair, self-pity, meanness and so many other qualities that depress consciousness potential in mankind. Hence, the heroic reference is always to a social context and not merely an individual. In a sense, a hero is someone who *conditions* himself to rise above conditioning and, by so doing, becomes himself a novel condition for others, providing them with a whole new set of possibilities than would otherwise not exist if he had not existed.

From this point of view the appearance of many diverse types of heroes may be regarded as a cultural index of the growth of consciousness. Every culture shows a rhythm that moves back and forth in cycles between growing disorder and chaos and progressive clarity and illumination. A central index that charts this cyclical rise and fall is the emergence of heroism in many areas of the cultural life and the later dwindling of such heroism to a near-zero level. By this index, the present times verge closer to chaos than to clarity. We are dominated, in both our literature and life, by the new cult of "anti-heroes" who play it safe in terms of existing conditions. These are people who are neither very bad nor very good, very right nor very wrong, very happy nor very sad (and never, never, *never* outright villains). Rather, they are self-indulgent and self-serving persons not characterized by any straining toward a great perfection or improvement in self and society. To make reference to a recent popular film depicting one of the breed, they are the "Alfies" of this world, rather lukewarm and drab gray, sunk in unthinking habit, when not downright passive and indifferent toward any ideal. Probably each culture gets the heroes and anti-heroes (like "Alfie") it collectively deserves.[3]

It is my impression that heroes appear in relationship to past imperfect aggregate units. A community or group which cannot bring out the consciousness potential in each individual and the individual who cannot feel himself, while developing his consciousness potential, as contributing to a renewed sense of community both suffer strain that moves them away from the perfection of human life.[4] Heroes arise to right the imbalance between individual and aggregate (group) units. While heroes seldom destroy entirely the types of units already formed, except when such units have utterly exhausted their utility, they do tend to efface the dividing lines between individual and group, as well as between smaller and larger groups while modifying relations sufficiently to allow a larger unity. In Lasswellian terminology, the relations between ego and self are newly identified and the various components of the self are redefined for better harmony and synthesis. All of this is done, however, by *experiencing* the new identity, as if the new social arrangements were already embodied in life as existing conditions. The perfection of consciousness characteristic of a hero tends seldom to be a self-consciousness of the magnitude of what he is doing and has done. Rather, it seems a natural unfolding of one's individuality in a way that allows a true sense of community to replace a phony one. By and large, the cry of "alienation" heard so frequently from youth these days, and the painful signs of "boredom" that accompany it, is part of the pressure building up for the reemergence of heroes in our culture who will rearrange social units in more felicitous ways.

All of this provides us with a background in terms of which we can question where Professor Lasswell might move still further in his own efforts to achieve a perfection of consciousness, stretching beyond the achievements he has already actualized and which have been duly honored. Such suggestions act, too, to challenge those of us who follow after him (in a generation-to-generation flow of consciousness that composes culture) to build upon his work and carry it still further than he has. It is an American tradition to expect that the young will take what we have done and idealize still further than we have. The realism of this attitude came originally from immigrants moving into a new world, handicapped by the past cultures they often brought to the new and unexplored. There is another and newer ground for realism in maintaining this American attitude. Each generation in a fast-moving twentieth century is handicapped by having built up habits under conditions that have since expired and no matter how earnestly we divest ourselves of the old, youth can more easily respond in an uncontaminated way to the new conditions that appear every decade in American life than can their seniors carrying the "past culture" around with them. Even better, in order to ensure the carrying forward of the very best (and, hence, most eternal truths) from the past into the future, the collaboration of senior and junior in ways that remove the necessity for considering these "conditionings" in an interflow of consciousness is, it is hoped, where many of the suggestions raised here can best be used for further perfection of consciousness. The ongoing collaboration of law and socialization that Professor Lasswell and I have long been concerned with could be one such case of "deconditioning." Hence, it is useful to make reference to it in what follows.

In order to place my remarks in interpersonal context, it should be understood that I first discovered Professor Lasswell after America was well into a wave of "anti-heroism." Science and social science were not exempted from this tendency in our general culture. Yet, the setting of the Center for Advanced Study in the Behavioral Sciences during its first year of operations was of exactly the sort, when we met there, to counteract the deterioration of heroism. My own professional training had already imposed the anti-heroic styles in social science that followed from rapidly proliferating the study of man into specialties that divide minds and hearts from one another. The imposition of such divisiveness had been painful and had left my own creative thinking largely dormant, unsatisfied and only mildly self-expressed. For me, Professor Lasswell soon stood as a figure in social science who symbolized the perpetuation of the heroic, once one had gotten by his "elegant" style of respectability. It was his dedication to synthesizing all bodies of knowledge in the study of man by a new method of thought that gave promise of the heroic style. He called for unifying the activities of specialist and beckoned to a natural brotherhood and community ahead of scientific minds. Such an attractive program, no matter what sacrifices it entailed, was what I had been waiting for. It was lastingness Lasswell hoped to achieve, and I wanted to assist. The specialists, acting as the "anti-heroes" of science playing it safe, serve to narrow, constrict, fragment vision and meaning—and, as a result, they keep "changing their mind" about truths in social science as cultural fashions around them change, often swinging wildly from one falsehood and exaggeration to another.[5] Lasswell stood for seeing life steadily and seeing it whole (configurationally). Looking back to those days, it is clearly no accident that a socialization expert should search for and find a social science collaborator, and that collaborator, for me, was Harold D. Lasswell. The content of social psychology, once we see the distinctive aim of the profession as a concern with perfecting consciousness, was really about persons like him. In the process of being "socialized" into his promising system of thought, my hope was to add to my field in a double sense—by first-hand experience as well as by the intellectual application of his system to socialization study.

What has happened, instead, is that the hero ideal I hung around Professor Lasswell's neck, with his initial enthusiastic assistance, has led to a crisis in my own hero-worship. The questioning that characterizes the crisis has, thus, a bearing upon social psychology, capable of being extricated from any specific interpersonal context and, yet, originating within the specific experience of such a context. The questioning revolves around whether Professor Lasswell as person and as thinker has not exempted himself too much in his work and life from the requirements of heroic living and achievement. If so, how can he go beyond "self-congratulations" toward making good on these requirements he may have bypassed? I use "may" quite deliberately, since the aim is to question, not to judge.

The prejudices among the specialists in social science toward Professor Lasswell are so strong that one must speak out against alliance with any such unjust separatism at the start. "If you haven't tried it, don't knock it!" is a blunt American saying that is meant to scotch such prejudice, even among scientists themselves. The configurationalism for which Professor Lasswell stands is in need of all of our support. As I see it, the refinement of thought —and deepened control of consciousness—that social psychologists pursue is to be found in Professor Lasswell's concern with value analysis. The use of his set of eight comprehensive value categories does much to heighten our awareness of the "qualities" of events in our lives and allows "subtle" differences to appear with more empirical sharpness than otherwise would be possible. Our traditional modes of "drive" and "motivational" analysis, characterized by one abstract concept summoned at a time rather than in unison, obscures these subtleties and flattens the qualities discoverable in human experience. By using all eight in unison, we become more deeply aware of how we are making qualitative choices and decisions in every act that composes our lives. When we come to the interest in expanding consciousness that the social psychologist pursues, the categories about forms of thinking (trend, goal, condition, projection, alternative modes) allow us to see problems in larger space-time configurations in which causes are interlinked with causes in mutual reinforcement chains. Thought is thus expanded in the configuration considered, where the pattern is viewed as undergoing change toward and away from what we most cherish in the movement toward the future. Lastly, the concern among social psychologists in synthesizing consciousness is greatly enhanced by the "decision seminar." It becomes possible for people to rise above all the conditions with which they enter the social process of decision (differences in personality, class, interest group, culture, crisis, etc.) to experience a new unity. If real brotherhood is ever to exist within social science, it will certainly come out of getting people from different life-history backgrounds to speak and commune with one another more effortlessly across such social and biological conditionings. The Lasswellian categories to handle the decision process (intelligence, recommendation, prescription, etc.) can help us to understand where conditionings weaken or strengthen the decisions of a scientific brotherhood—or any brotherhood for that matter that creates culture and community through communion rather than mere technics of communication. The social psychologist who ignores or avoids the exploration of these abstract set of categories devised by Professor Lasswell to perfect human consciousness is shirking the responsibility he undertakes in entering the field, quite apart from whether he decides to adopt such systematics himself or not. Every set of categories is an attempt to promote interdisciplinary thinking by refining, expanding, and synthesizing consciousness that otherwise might be fragmented by specialists.

There are at least two sources of tradition that stand in the way of the social psychologist fully exploring these Lasswellian intellectual achievements. First, within social science, there are hidden "postulates" operating in our thought processes that do not allow us to raise certain questions or look at certain matters by first-hand observation, since the "postulates" operate as dogmatic prejudices that create arbitrary boundaries outside of which questioning cannot go. It is one of the characteristics of Professor Lasswell's system that he has sniffed and snuffed out a good many of these prejudicial aromas in our social science thinking and refused to infuse them into his own architecture of ideas. Whatever can be reduced to empirical inquiry is taken out of the logic by which inquiry is conducted. Hence, they cannot act dogmatically in inquiry by logically placing them as "given." In performing this function, Professor Lasswell was bent on purifying social science thought from outworn tradition, and by this process of purification he was simply engaged in building new cultures of thought, the anthropology of the future. Yet, when people explore his system, it seems to them to act as a kind of "intellectual LSD." For many social scientists, it is like communicating in a new foreign tongue in which some of one's most cherished, latent rules of thinking are suspended. Precisely because they are latent, the feeling of confusion—even dizziness—emerges as to what is wrong, and the decision is usually made against Lasswell's new system of thought rather than surrendering one's older thought pattern, without seeing how conservatively one is acting in the process. We are all carrying around with us mul tiple dogmas in the name of "science" that we could easily divest ourselves of to unearth the self-limitations they impose upon us.

Among the many examples of this I discovered in my application of his system to socialization and social psychology, let me choose but one. In terms of value analysis, most learning theorists assume without question that "well-being" is the key value around which all human acts are organized from the beginning of life onward, so that all other values are taken as "secondary" in a learning sequence. In this way, learning takes the "well-being" value as central to everything in individual life much as Marx made the wealth value central to everything in group life. Yet, precisely those learning theorists who most forcibly reject the Marxian pan-wealth orientation have no hesitation or reluctance themselves to engage in a similar mono-valued perspective upon life. When one looks at learning theory after "surrendering" this traditional approach that acts as a prejudice in educational processes, one sees what shaky grounds most of it rests upon, and how it sidesteps a host of empirical observations. The learning theory that explains such empirical facts of life is still to be formulated —and will probably be close to a social psychology of heroism. One can show endless flaws in theory and research study through the systematic use of categories that dogmatize what should have been empirical. It is possible to show, for instance, that the work on achievement motive never allows for achievement with regard to affection (popularity) and rectitude (good character)—values which are likely to be emphasized as achievement avenues more strongly for women than men in our society—and, hence, all the results of studies on achievement motive demean certain forms of achievement unwittingly by unexamined postulates built into the testing.

A second source of difficulty that prevents social psychologists from mastering the Lasswellian system also relates to the "intellectual LSD" properties that use of the system brings to one's experience. Operationalism in America has been heavily influenced by Bridgman, where a concept takes on a more sensationalistic, thing-like sense, since one concept is considered at a time, or few concepts not designed to be as comprehensive as possible are introduced at best. Social science is accustomed to this kind of operationality, so that facts appear to be more "substantial" than they are, since they are "bound" to particular operations. Lasswell keeps reminding us that operations are only part of the job describing human practices and, until we have unearthed the perspectives from which operations issue, we have mere detail that is still not deserving of the name "data." Hence, the sets of systematic concepts that compose his system help us to scan operations to find exactly the background from which operations issue. Where the whole set of concepts is applied in unison in such systematic operationalism (originally advocated by the Vienna school of logical positivism), meaning never appears to be "in" operations and, hence, all one's prior tendencies to see one operation as everywhere and under all circumstances meaning only one concept are undermined. Clearly, social psychology has always stood behind a contextual theory of meaning, so that the same operation is shown never to have the same meaning in all contexts and the same meaning is shown as capable of being expressed by many diverse operations. Yet, Lasswell's systematic sets of categories push this principle way beyond what is now customary in social science. As a result, many experience "anxiety" about the intangibility of facts that systematic analysis induces, as if they were "on a trip" that they wanted to control before it got out of hand.

Everyone now remarks how little contemporary physics depends upon thick masses of fact but can go with ease from but a small amount of observation about significant detail to sweeping visions about the total often unseen whole into which a few key facts must fit. This has, of course, made it difficult for the layman, as Susanne Langer has remarked, to understand physics easily, since the systematics is even more demandingly mathematical than that of Lasswell. The stretching of thought encouraged by the configurational method of Lasswell allows one, in any event, often to sense large configurations into which a few significant details that one systematically analyzes must undoubtedly fit. It promotes a vivid sense of the wider unseen whole which a handful of "facts" calls into being and which revises drastically the ordinary meaning of such facts as viewed without this straining toward the utmost contextuality. The social psychologist is likely to back away uncomfortably before such growing contextualism in the interests of what he has been told is "science." One needs to invoke the model given to us by Einstein, where a fresh, immensely useful, sweeping vision of the universe came out of a tiny assembly of facts systematically and mathematically analyzed—and not very precisely at that, as A. N. Whitehead was to demonstrate to us. Unfortunately, too many of us in social science are today so attached to what we call "the facts" that we cannot get away from them to place them in the wider context in which their true significance emerges. Configurationalism of this sort, furthermore, often invokes a more "spiritual" vision of the universe, since one is unwittingly dealing with the "unseen" by giving concrete facts less "substantial" character through fuller conceptualizing talent.

In terms of socialization study, one example of this sweeping vision is the way in which the emergence of distinct periods in pre-adult life, such as the recognition of an "adolescent" period, is associated with sweeping changes in all social units of organization. Each time we recognize some distinctive stage in pre-adult life histories, there is likely to be bound up with this some shake-up throughout all social institutions. Changes of social class—the emergence of the middle classes, for example—were part and parcel of the recognition of an "adolescent" period. Both emerged together as if part of some larger unity. It has been my hunch that, whenever social scientists turn toward emphasis on infancy, producing some new and significant knowledge, there goes hand in hand with this a greater harmony among adult institutions in society and a greater sense of the common good. The introduction of value thinking into the study of the infant, if my "vision" is correct, should have widespread impact upon the networks of ideas in the social process that promote a sense of the common good.[6] In this latter case, we do not deal with a new recognition of a pre-adult period, but of new knowledge of a period already recognized that deepens our identification with it. I think we will discover more consciousness in the infancy period than we have ever surmised existed. The technics and ideas that allow this unrecognized consciousness to become apparent to us will also be the technics and ideas that are likely to promote wider harmony among groups in society. It is my feeling that the social psychology of music (and of rhythm and sound) will give rise to this technics and to the new harmony-promoting ideas.

Up to now, we have been dealing with understandable but undeserved resistance to Lasswell's systematics. Not all resistance need be pathic, however. The sources of pathic resistance prevent social psychologists from experiencing the adventures of consciousness Lasswell has provided for them in their scientific work. Are there sources of resistance, however, which are more reasonable and, if so, what are they? I suspect that "rational" resistance toward any system ultimately arises from discovery of another system that does more and can handle more with less untoward effects than the one being resisted, even though the initial resistance may not clearly be able to spell out all the contours of the alternative one being invoked. There is a Far Eastern saying: "Do not demolish the temple of another if you cannot forthwith erect a new temple upon the same site, for the site of the temple must never be vacant." It acts to curtail criticism for criticism's sake, that unhappy encouragement of "critical thinking" as an end in itself and as a substitute for appreciative thinking. The territory covered by Professor Lasswell's ideas requires so vast an architecture that it is difficult to construct an alternative that acts as an equal, better, or more "heavenly" substitute for his, without writing at least half what he already has written. Yet my own questioning of his system, often with the very tools he has provided for such questioning, has led me to believe there is such an alternative and to wish to bring it to full expression over time, hopefully in collaboration with him, since a scientific brotherhood demands, for the realization of human dignity and freedom, an absence of any dogged attachment to existing intellectual tools.

In a prior publication,[7] I reported a discovery that continues to hold up and prove central. First, in surveying all theories of socialization, the neglect of investigating mood and feeling in any meaningful way was apparent to me. It is as if a collective repression operated among all socialization theorists. These last few years I have made an effort to develop a social psychology of mood and feeling and to see what modifications it might demand in all of our social science thinking. While only a sketch is provided here, it is the "seed" from which a trunk and many branches and blossoms will grow, I hope, and provides a way of questioning the adequacy of the consciousness systematics Professor Lasswell has developed.

To begin with, it has long been clear that "anxiety" is a very strange emotion both physiologically (see the two volumes on *Emotion and Personality* written by Magda Arnold) as well as psychologically (Freud kept changing his mind about anxiety almost is if his thoughts about anxiety were themselves exemplifications of the state being considered). What is most interesting about the emotion is that it blurs, blocks out, and otherwise distorts the environment, so that "intellectual" mastery of what one is living through is severely handicapped. There is, furthermore, always a sense of something "missing." O. H. Mowrer long ago brought all of this forcibly to our collective attention. Yet, most thinking about anxiety has emphasized the negative well-being component of it; somatic aspects, not always "sexual" in nature but usually with that "instinctual" press, are highlighted. It is necessary to emphasize that what is not being sufficiently highlighted and elaborated is the central (and probably decisive) importance the emotion has for the enlightenment process, which need not be an egoistic matter at all, since a non-narcissistic agreement about "reality" is at issue and at work.

At the same time, it is possible to discover an emotion whose significance for the enlightenment process is completely positive. It is the emotion of "joy." For some, too, it is an egoistic (narcissistic) emotion, a celebration of one's own happy well-being state. We do not need to challenge that either. The serious thing, however, is that the emotion is too frequently experienced under conditions of hardship, where the security, safety, and self-esteem of the person is severely challenged. Cases of this sort where "joy" is "unaccountably" experienced and has "success" value are just too frequent now to be dismissed, and cases where "anxiety" erupts in the midst of material self-indulgence and luxury are equally easy to discover. Indeed, when "joy" appears, it is as if it opens the eyes and ears (dare I say "the heart"?) to the environment so that the enlightenment process goes forward with amazing success under the most stressful conditions. Furthermore, the eruption of anxiety promotes failure where the whole context provides easy success. Under the experience of "joy," the ego feels at one with everything in the environment, as if one could "fit into" and "meet" any demands being made on one and even welcome them as a challenge, although nothing quite "feels" like a demand, even as one recognizes and meets it. In anxiety, a feeling of "unnaturalness" is characteristic, both of self and environment and the fit between them, and even the smallest request is a heavy burden. The ego is estranged from the environment, burdened down by it, and uncertain how to respond to it for a natural fit. "Joy" is, furthermore, a state in which one can say much simply and only say what is needed, whereas anxiety is a state in which one can say little and can say that only prolixly because everything seems overcomplicated, leading to an endless stream of words. In "joy," there is an easy flow into the consciousness of others and a way of finding the right words and gestures by which they can flow into one's own consciousness. In anxiety, the person is more brittle and one has to break past his defense system in order to get into his consciousness, ultimately relating to him only by a cold empathy, rather than the warm sympathy that a joyous person permits. The anxious person's own words often stand in the way of his return show of sympathy and permit only the coldest and most indifferent empathy in which experience is not really shared. In short, these features of the two states place them on opposite ends of a continuum that bears upon enlightenment, with "joy" part of a positive non-defensive extreme and anxiety part of a negative highly defensive extreme. Even more, they differ in promoting and inhibiting the perfection of consciousness in a social context.

When I turned to look at existing theories of socialization with this discovery in mind, what greeted me was quite staggering. None—but *none!*—of our existing, respectable theories of socialization is capable of inspiring "joy"! Nor were any other theories in social science that now claim wide attention. Think of this for a moment. Where is our cherished intellect taking us? How can social science, provided with this mood climate, promote anything but "anti-heroes" given such a perspective?

Moving this strain of thought further along, an outlook upon ourselves and our environment that is *problem-solving* induces joy, no matter what the hardships of the context, so that one sees the road ahead into which one "naturally" and "successfully" and "meaningfully" fits together with others. Furthermore, the heightening of ability to look at our environment in such a way that a problem-solving perspective emerges readily, and even sometimes instantaneously, is itself an offshoot of the emotion of "joy." Anxiety leads us to "defend" ourselves from what is taken to be an environment into which we cannot find a way to fit. Yet, there is a backwash so that what we "repressed" through the blurring that all anxiety is known to instigate still "kicks back" in the process of "the return of the repressed." Verbal prolixity and intellectual word games from this viewpoint often look like an uphill and losing battle in delaying tactics until the backwash can crash through the defenses and overthrow still another anxiety-ridden theory.

As this became more evident, I began to see why so many of my colleagues believed (and said in one form or another) : "The more we *learn*, the less we *know!*" What we are learning is how to produce bigger and better anxiety attacks and less and less enlightenment. What a sterile enterprise we have made of social science, if indeed this is the case! As empirical observations of students, patients, myself, and my friends and colleagues grew, furthermore, it seemed that "joy" and anxiety were the larger emotional "pay-off" for a host of lesser feelings we chose to experience or not to experience in our everyday living. Out of the search for the smaller units of feelings that, cultivated or not cultivated, promote the larger emotions of joy and anxiety as stable states or as "life-savers" and "set-backs," there has developed a social psychology of living ethics.[8] The intellectual tools provided by Professor Lasswell can sometimes be made relevant to this new ongoing social science system but, as far as I can yet see, they are not decisive for it.

With the emergence of this discovery, it became more apparent to me, too, why a climate of what Richard Hofstadter[9] has called (somewhat mistakenly I would say) "anti-intellectualism" has taken hold of our American culture since the last war. The intellectuals may have produced a love of anxiety in place of the wisdom they gave promise of assembling and diffusing. There is disaffection among the mass of men not from intellectuality per se but the uses that have unheroically been made of it to diffuse anxiety rather than any perspective that releases "joy."

One can go a good way further in this suggestive reference to ideas now developing in greater detail about a living ethics for social science. In America, the family stabilized very early in our cultural growth, while Spanish influence was still strong. Hence, the romantic impulse was strongly implanted in the American family. Whiting and Child tell us, for instance, that we are among the most extremely permissive of all cultures with regard to the socialization of aggression in the family. Our educational system stabilized much, much later and, by that time, British influence was strong. Hence, our educational system from stem to stern is governed by the classical impulse. The tension between the two institutions has, at last, broken out around racial integration in the schools, but it has always been there, and the current problems in education envelop all students in protest against an academic system that kills the seed of the romantic impulse implanted by the American family. The tension was once possible to bear, when education was essential to a good job, increased income, and other non-enlightenment assets. It was simply like

learning good etiquette or table manners. Now that enlightenment and education are taken more seriously in an age of affluence, a tension that goes back into our history at least as long as
inequality of the Negro has been greatly inflamed and seeks to
modify the inhibitions the classical tradition in education has
placed upon the creativity of the American mind.

Fanning out still further, we can see, in the eighteenth and
nineteenth centuries, the romantic impulse as something distinctively modern in the Western world. If we follow that impulse as
it seeks expression in Western experience, we witness, so I am
led to believe, the slow, painful emergence of a world culture,
since it is the expression, within the traditions of the West, of
Eastern forms of relating to nature, including human nature. The
trust in one's own experience is pushed so far that individuality
is brought to the utmost expression, against all stabilized and
classical forms, social and intellectual, that prevent the process
from reaching completion. The logic of the romantic impulse is
that a true sense of community can come only from the fullest
expression of each person's individuality. Otherwise, only a false
and "phony" sense of community is possible to promote by way
of political force. Indeed, the romantic impulse would see the
Garrison State as a natural outcome of the logic of classicism,
which seeks to diffuse, in the name of "culture," a predetermined
intellectual pattern and a closed system upon all. The way of
opening up society for the pressures that move toward the evolution of a world culture naturally is by the encouragement of the
romantic sense of individuality in which the trust in one's own
experience leads to find a true and meaningful community. The
time to close into a stable system is nowhere felt, among those
sharing the romantic impulse, to be in this period of rapid growth
where new "elements" in experience are likely to be uncovered.
The cultivation of a feeling climate that promotes a character capable of sustaining "joy" rather than the love of anxiety is seen
to be the antidote to a Garrison State and to give a more rapid
advance of creativity than can unearth new elements in experience.

The concern of our discussion, however, is not with any self-aggrandizement with regard to the need for a social psychology of ethics. That outcome will take care of itself. Rather, the exiguous sketch we have just provided of an alternative architecture of ideas allows us to turn back to Professor Lasswell's system in a spirit of questioning. Such a spirit leaves open how much his own system already incorporates or can be made to incorporate the many concerns arising from a social psychology of living ethics. Rather, it points to places in his own system where, at present, more work is probably needed to take account of the considerations arising from this developing alternative, work that will unify his own classical attitude with the romantic revolution that characterizes so much of modern Western life. For ease of discussion, it is possible to take these as separate points even though they flow many times one into the other. At the conclusion, it is possible to draw them together in a more generalized contour.

THE PROGRAM OF QUESTIONING

1. *The Lasswell of Method and Lasswell of Content*

It will be noticed that I have called attention, when discussing the perfection of consciousness, much more to the intellectual method for reducing divisiveness and dogma that Professor Lasswell has produced than I have to what he says about the social process itself. It is my impression that these two sides of Professor Lasswell are not yet perfectly integrated. Without trying to produce "proof," since proof seldom convinces those who are not predisposed to consider a statement dispassionately anyway, my feeling is that most of the content statements of Lasswell do not explicitly flow from his own use of his own method of systematic categories. The application of psychoanalysis to politics has, of course, been the key content achievement of Lasswell. In a recent *Psychology Today*,[10] he speaks at great length in this area without once bringing in explicitly any of the sets of categories for refinement, expansion, and synthesis of consciousness he has devised, nor is there reason to think they implicitly operate. Indeed, whenever these categories are brought to bear upon any content issue, the discussion tends to become programmatic rather than take on factual character. The factual contours tend only to "illustrate" the systematics, rather than the systematics to "illumine" the factual contour. Many times, Professor Lasswell is himself highly critical of the very ideas of social science and psychoanalysis. Yet, he seems never to be eager to publish any systematic examination of these ideas from his own perspective so as to unearth their inadequacies and, even more, creatively to shape a whole new theory. Furthermore, his own presentation of his systematic categories often takes on a mechanical rote quality, leading many to refer to his system as a "laundry list" of abstract intellectual terms. The way they can be used to "illuminate" living experience is often bypassed for the mere interest in a cognitive game that remains empty of empirical content and, hence, often meaningless and absurd to those who might otherwise be touched by it. In short, I am uncertain, given the lack of application of his systematic categories to his content ideas, whether the latter would be validated when contextualized against the categories of method. In many cases, I do not think unqualified validation would ensue and some of these I will indicate as we go along.

2. The Logic of Outcome and Logic of Discovery

Generally, Professor Lasswell's method of contextualization through sets of categories composes a quite elegant and simple logic. The complexity comes through application of the sets to specific events. Yet, it is possible that the complexity is also to be found in the process of composing the finalized sets of categories. Nowhere does Professor Lasswell provide us with any picture of how he came to these particular sets and what alternatives he considered. Generally, we know that discovery in science and in intellectual matters is more rich in aesthetic and mood factors than we ordinarily like to think. It is as though he were not asking us to look too closely at how the elegant logic of categories came to be what it is and deprived us of experiencing even vicariously the shifts of moods and feelings and the aesthetic concerns that went into the whole enterprise. We never get to see, for instance, what alternatives he considered, nor what empirical problems constrained him to adopt one course rather than another, nor how his own values in the form of mood and feeling led him toward and away from naming his concepts as he has. Keeping the creative process out of sight this way is to deprive the resulting forms of the meaning they might otherwise have through the sympathy experienced toward the flow of consciousness going into them, rather than the cold empathy they now require of us. In short, we never see how these abstractions grew out of his own creative experience. Often, they appear to some to be the result of the intellect "culling" ideas from all other minds engaged in solving problems of substance without Professor Lasswell having the benefit of *experiencing* that process. Hence, many take the result to be mere "intellectuality" in science, and even worse, to be an arbitrary sort of comprehensiveness that some other intellectual culling might with equal justification oppose.

Hence, the resulting set of abstract terms does not strike us as authoritatively binding for science. Since it is possible to smuggle in hidden postulates by the way one chooses categories to form a set, the matter is especially crucial to the anthropology of the future that is dear to Professor Lasswell's heart and to the hearts of us all. Many feel, for instance, that it is wrong to see legal institutions as more highly governed by "power" than by "rectitude," or to see art as more highly governed by "skill" than by "enlightenment" (bypassing as this does the whole history of the idea of beauty in human affairs), or to see religion as more governed by "rectitude" than it is by a sense of love that clearly does not fit into any one of the categories, certainly not the category of "affection" as formulated. Still further, the categories of thought for problem-solving once included metaphysical (derivational) thought which was then gradually excluded, along with a related process of metaphorical thinking. Yet, Owen Barfield's *Speaker's Meaning*[11] suggests that we cannot even begin to understand language and, hence, culture without giving poetic discourse a major place in our theory of language in history. There is every reason to believe that the conditions that operated upon Professor Lasswell during his formative period of growth toward counteracting or facilitating certain cultural formations shaped his ultimate conceptual sets—even his indifference to intellectual developments around him have played a role. The heroic element in Lasswell's contribution, because his creative experience is hidden behind the carefully polished end product of thought, is kept out of sight as "inspiration" to those who wish to follow him.

3. The Intellect in Science

The prior point has made clear how Lasswell has played up the intellectual dimension in science, submerging the aesthetic and poetic and mood-dominated process of creative discovery. He has driven home the point repeatedly that "naming" is crucial to "noticing." Hence, the implication is that, without intellectual elaboration, the life of consciousness becomes cruder, narrower, and more isolated. Yet, the opposite argument is seldom explicitly considered. More and more, youngsters are convinced that intellectuality prevents one from experiencing. A word calls attention to a memory, a past experience, and helps reinstate that past experience in the present. In so doing, it constricts experiencing having anything new within it that is not a repetition of a past pattern. Growth is thereby thought to be prevented and the stranglehold the past has upon one is maximized. One is then imprisoned in a classical impulse composed of repetitive word games and intellectuality. The romantic impulse, working through the poetic uses of language allows for subtle breaking with the past's grip on experiencing and allows for freeing the self for a creative discovery in experience by a looser use of language in aesthetic ways. It seems more and more probable, for instance, that a scientific discovery, coming as it does so frequently through dreams or sudden flashes of association or chance occurrences, when finally clarified could be more simply and more beautifully communicated by a poem, a play, a novel, rather than some ugly jargon that often obscures, through overtechnicalization, how little is really being said.

One cannot help feeling that Professor Lasswell's attitude toward the arts springs from some of his more dogmatic views about politics and the role the arts may play in shaping politics. He has, for instance, strongly expressed himself to me that art always follows the path taken by political power rather than presages and shapes political forms. There is, of course, always an interaction, but the presumption is that influence is to be more heavily weighted on the side of politics than art. During a recent visit last year to the University of Michigan to lecture on mood and feeling, I was informed of a whole conference of artists who had just met there, armed with thick folders of evidence, to demonstrate how in history political forms had been subtly shaped by the variety of emerging new art forms in latent and unnoticed ways. My own work in the social psychology of music[12] supplies mounting evidence that music, in which the role of rhythm is paramount, is the most unconscious form of value influence on people. Music then touches other art forms in which values appear successively closer to consciousness, culminating in sculpture and architecture. As this process unfolds, social and intellectual forms (political and civic) are subtly modified by the cultural impact being produced and diffused. In short, the new "elements" in experience are more likely to be first uncovered in the arts and in those arts in which language as we like to recognize it is least apparent but still insistently at work. The role of mood in composition is great among musicians and less honored by the theory of music or by the history of music than is warranted. New climates of mood are more easily established by music than by the other arts and provide a cultural shift in which social and intellectual forms give way. The relation of heroism to music deserves special study; yet, the point to be made here is that the good respectable classical form preferred by Lasswell may diminish some of his own opportunities to be more heroic with regard to the young.

4. *Shortchanging the Disciplines*

The prior point leads to a further generalization. Lasswell has generously emphasized that all systems of ideas are "equivalent," if each one is extended to deal with the same set of problems and empirical details. His own system is set up in a hierarchy of such systems as a prototype of what all the others must do in order to become equivalent to his own. Alternative systems need not be just like Lasswell's; yet, they must become equivalent in general purpose to his own. His neglect of the aesthetic dimension both in putting forward his own system by way of informing us how he arrived at it (and in terms of the content ideas he advocates) would suggest that closure is premature. Indeed, a similar reservation might be made with regard to spiritual experience, which is not always to be found embedded within conventional religious institutions. His own theory of communication, for instance, was forged under conditions of crisis and with regard to crisis events, conditions under which propaganda and self-defensiveness are high (the studies of war and therapeutic "head-shrinking"). Spiritual communication, and some forms of aesthetic communication, are more pacific in nature. Indeed, it is easy today to study theories of communication in which the whole notion of "communion" appears to have evaporated from sight as part of human potential in interpersonal relations. Instead, technicalized targets and agents engage in manipulative struggles for word victories witnessed by statistical "content analyses" in which the human impulse for cooperation and unity gets little upgrading. Such studies of communication dehumanize the noblest instrument available to man and leave their impress upon the brutalization of language in our time. In any event, the experience that composes aesthetic and spiritual striving when most successfully expressed is lost to political science and to the social science culture Lasswell wishes to promote.

If areas of institutional experience get shortchanged in the Lasswell systematics by way of neglect, more serious are two areas within science itself that get shortchanged within the systematics. They are biology and mathematics, the "extremes" of the material and symbolic aspects of human life, toward which Lasswell seems reluctant to fully journey. He has never clarified whether values have a biological base in physical constitution (as contrasted with political constitution), and he often oscillates between two positions. One is that values are to be considered wholly conscious experiences that physical energies do or do not support, a position that he is most likely to take when speaking programmatically. However, he frequently lapses into a view that values may be held unconsciously in inconsistent ways with conscious intentions, a position he more frequently takes when psychoanalyzing political case histories. Mathematicians and logicians have told me, after studying his system, that it is ambiguous as to which issues in his system are merely definitional or formal in nature and which are to be considered empirical, as though his own sharp intellectuality floundered at the most symbolic extremes. Many mathematicians see his system as only providing raw materials (classifications) for other systems that could be ultimately put into mathematical form. Nor do his discussions of why we should be quantitative do much to remove this ambiguity about what is definition and what is empirical concern. In short, this relative neglect, keeping in mind the sizable thrust his system of ideas does represent, makes me feel it is premature to take it as closed and final as it now stands.

5. *Inner and Outer Public Order*

Professor Lasswell and his many brilliant colleagues at the Yale Law School wish to perfect a system of law that would more fully promote an outcome of human dignity within America and across the globe. The many volumes that have grown out of this nobility of purpose, however, constitute only one aspect of law. Unless authoritative and effective law dovetail into one unity, the former degenerates into pretended power and the latter degenerates into naked power. True law comes only when both coincide. Out of this concern, my own work on socialization at the Yale Law School took root.[13] Socialization study was a key instrument to bring into existence the true law that transpires when conditions producing education are effective in forming the character that supports the political constitution.

In my studies of socialization, the central role mood and feeling occupy in the pursuit of enlightenment and in shaping character became clear to me. Interestingly enough, almost every religious denomination had given detailed attention to such matters and, when one went beyond divisive creed and ritual to the roots from which each religion had sprung, one found agreement about how mood and feeling should be managed. Often the terms might shift, but the basic concepts reappeared with amazing regularity. Out of this has come a concept of character that is both related to enlightenment (and hence science) and to character (and hence law and power). It is almost as if, to dramatize the matter, there is such a discipline as "God's law," found in the most diverse religious creeds and embodied within the living experiences of the spiritual heroes around which each religion has formed, that could be tested within science by all those who wish to consider it without prejudice. In every case, there is strong distrust of mere intellect and words, stronger surely than what now is characteristic of legal institutions. Instead, the emphasis is upon *being*, rather than upon intellectual formulation and expression about being. Freedom is to be found in each case through internal exemplification of character and not through any formalized social organization that speaks with word support for such character. Needless to say, religious organizations often honor the root impulse from which they have grown more in the breach than in the performance. I have asked myself, Are legal institutions likely to do much better? Sociologists have long told us that fear and anxiety is what holds society together in organizational modes. Yet, fearlessness is a state condoned by the root impulse of every religion I have surveyed. Without it, there is no internal freedom. Only love makes fearlessness possible, furthermore, and a true sense of community is felt only when it springs from such fearlessness emerging out of love.

Within the character portrait that develops across the agreements between all religions and around the psychology of mood and feeling, the recognition of human dignity and human indignity—of movement toward and away from freedom—is clear. Lasswell emphasizes that, in order for true law to exist, the inner order of the subjective events must correspond with the outer order of public events. Public order is, thus, true law only when subjective (private) order and objective order dovetail. It is my view that delinquency can be shown historically and in our time to arise out of a sensitive and intelligent awareness of the hypocrisy in human affairs that ensues when these two orders are at variance with one another. Nothing has yet convinced me that the Lasswell system has within it a method for reducing unwitting as well as deliberate hypocrisy in living patterns, however much the wish is that the system would infallibly discipline a common human failing. More and more, in short, I am led to believe that the law which will bring effective and authoritative powers to bear conjointly upon human behavior so that human dignity and freedom will result is to be found within each individual and not within some complicated legal intellectual machinery.

Be that as it may, my point is that the Lasswellian movement toward the defense of world public order has grown up without due consideration of this more romantic trust in individual experience as supplying both authority and effective control. The Lasswellian movement has not sufficiently considered that unwittingly, and often quite deliberately, scientific men may, despite all the precision of intellectual formulations, do little more than past religious institutions have done to perfect human consciousness in ways we all desire. The power of the intellect may always have an aura of pretense about it, until it is disciplined by the language of the heart composed of mood and feeling. If we most change the world by being what we advocate at the most intimate level of being, why then place any of our faith in externalized arrangements of collective coercion that so far have failed to reinforce good character by intellectual precision and organized penalties?

6. *The Units of Value Analysis*

This last point leads into a still more general one regarding Lasswell's value-institution method of analysis. The highest unit of goal analysis is taken to be that of institutions. But institutions as they have and do exist may not deserve the life they have, since none is yet known that can save culture from the "doomed" portrait given to us by Toynbee. The sharing of power within and between institutions may be more "intellectual" than "experiential" (a phony rather than the true sense of community that comes out of individual experience) and, hence, much less intelligent and creative than we like to believe. It seems possible to take heroes of both sexes as units in terms of which one constructs the highest value categories for contextual analysis. If that were done, there is less chance that existing realized structures, taken as a norm, would damage further human growth toward perfection of consciousness and character. For it seems to me that the more structure we have, the less freedom we have, and that this is especially true of "intellectualized" structures that bypass significant human experience embodied in the heroic (and joyous) figures of human life. If Professor Lasswell were to do this, and I suspect he has contemplated it, his value categories might change drastically. Most certainly, social psychology would be restored to a more prominent place in his work, while the abstract categories, culled from scattered scientists, would get a more subservient position. Furthermore, if this were done, socialization study would take on a new life, too. We become what we study. Socializers, and the pre-adults they educate, would take heroism for a norm that suffuses the mind of the experts. All would strive to embody such a norm within the educational experience, whether that of the self-education of the experts or of the diffused education emanating from them to socializers and pre-adults. The rebellion against the conditions of hypocrisy would receive a meaningful corrective. But the study of institutional life as a norm is not where the corrective is to be found. It lies rather in bringing to the fore of our attention the evolution of ever more effective heroes, under conditions where heroism gets harder and harder to improve upon, and more use of consciousness, than has characterized the past. The study of the improvement and perfection of human consciousness that is so distinctively the goal of social psychologists would then get a new lease on life in the scientific mind as a whole, a mind that often appears so overintellectualized that it allows word games to overcomplicate human effort, while losing sight of the living experiences that realistically call out "joy," "joy" in an age too long riddled with unnecessary anxiety. The Garrison State image cannot do that. The Free Man's Commonwealth appears to many of the young, as it does to me, as a kind of comic valentine to psychoanalysis, and at best a minor science-fiction, comic-book story. Only the transitional processes highlighted by the Respect Revolution allow some glimmer of hope to come through to us, precisely because it suggests the heroic element in human potential. The heroic thrusts of thought that would capture the hearts and minds of the next generation now coming up and searching for scientific torchbearers is badly needed. Unfortunately, the thick complicated volumes on law do not speak to the romantic impulse now pressing for expression among the young everywhere as they seek for the relevance of their lives to some significant future.[14]

7. *The Sharing of Power*

For a long time, I believed along with Lasswell, that the more power one shares, the more power one has. Such a philosophy promotes the impulse to compromise with too much eagerness. If one shares power with those whose character is less developed than one's own, whether they be individuals or groups, one's own character undergoes a change and it is *less* frequently for the *better*, even given the strongest wish to maintain a liberal democratic outlook. It is better to lose than to compromise an ideal. For in a sense, the true way to win in situations of conflict is to lose. The loser has given pleasure to the winner and, in that sense, has performed a priceless service. The victor has in some sense to restore damages to the loser and what that takes in terms of that priceless commodity, time, not to mention the gradual restoration of friendship and other values difficult to reinstate, is indeed expensive. Most of all, the ideal remains intact. The loser thus has both given pleasure and has a large bank account of further values coming to him in order to reinstate pre-conflict relations. Clearly, competition is a waste of human energy. The only way to truly win is to win together and that requires integration. It is always possible to find a supergoal that unites in integration conflicting parties, sometimes possible even to go to the roots from which a conflict springs and to find unity therein by recognizing the common source of nourishment. The result of sharing power indiscriminately through compromise may be to lower the character of everyone to the same mean scale, so that one can no longer recognize a good deed in a naughty world but see it only as disguised form of self-service.

Professor Lasswell's writings contain a strain of thought about power that has never been completely developed into a political policy, although it contains a "new politics" of heroism within it. The test of character that can produce a really revolutionary kind of enlightenment is one that maintains "joy" in the face of increasing hardship. All of us are characterized by up-and-down rhythms in positive and negative feelings states. There are those who have steadier states than others, however, reducing the amplitude of the waves moving in either direction. These steadier states are often stabilized on the joyous side—and by people who are frequently exposed to continual, severe hardship. On the other hand, those with steady depressive tendencies are often highly indulged by their environments. How can one stabilize "joy" under continual hardship, without sacrificing one's ideal? While there is an answer to this problem coming out of the way one cultivates day-to-day feelings, one can also discover as a concomitant of this process that one is entertaining "hidden" postulates about reality inside oneself without much self-awareness of doing so. These postulates prevent one from fully stretching one's thought to go from the details of hardship to the "unseen" configuration into which they fit in a larger space-time map. When such larger configurations are sensed, they permit us to see how much of hardship indulges us and how much of indulgence often limits our being able to see life plain and whole. Indeed, more and more I believe this kind of process of experiencing "joy" under hardship is what learning theory should be centrally investigating. Out of it, no doubt, will come a new politics of experience that is now hinted at in the work of R.D. Laing.[15] The inner freedom—and, hence, autogenically released power—lies in a perfect merger of instinct and learning in a way that moves individuality forward to the deepest sense of community possible to experience. One need not wait until life provides tests for developing this internal power, and the enlightenment it demands in terms of discovering and surrendering unnecessary "hidden postulates" we carry around while being amply indulged, but through a deliberate policy of self-sacrifice the tests may be self-administered. Is this not the politics of heroism? Only competition, greed, addiction to creature comforts, and a long list of other ugly traits which are commonly supposed to be "intrinsic" to political life prevent us from making such a new conception of power a reality. The science of politics still has not harnessed the energies in such steady states of "joy" and, hence, some of the mysteries of power remain unexplored by science. During a period of politics that has fallen upon such bad times as the Nixon-Humphrey-Wallace election and the Vietnam demoralization, it is surely time for scientists of politics to explore some new directions, rather than continue to reinforce the old paths by passively observing and explaining them in terms of power as more conventionally understood. If it cannot be by political scientists living the new conception, and hence, teaching through being, let it be at least by conceiving what such a new politics might feel like from the inside and by adding a new game to the battery of intellectual games already instituted among us.

TOWARD AN OVERVIEW

As I see it, Professor Lasswell has taken us all, within a classical tradition, several giant steps further toward enlarging upon human experience by the intellectual tools he has devised and, hence, toward satisfying the distinctive aim of social psychologists of perfecting consciousness. My own feeling is that his work is the wave of the immediate future, staving off much discontent among those in whom the romantic impulse stirs without outlet, thus creating increasing boredom and violence. But my questioning leaves me with a sense that ultimately something still better is required. The features of this "still better" outcome are contained implicitly in my question and in the brief reference to the work I have begun on the social psychology of living ethics. The excesses to which the romantic impulse has gone in the modern world are evident to us all. And, yet, I believe that the logic of romanticism which finds no conflict between the experiencing of the fullest individuality of each person and the deepest sense of community experienced by all constitutes the logic of the far future toward which we are headed. Classicism at present can only delay the date.

The brain, we are now given to understand by those engaged in the new study of brain functioning, is only about 40 percent used. Our own greatest resource, within the existing traditions wherein classical impulses capture culture, lies largely untapped and unused. I cannot help believing that the anxious images of human nature that dominate our scientific literature reflect man existing within such deadening classical impositions, both as scientific inquirer and as subject of inquiry. The collective repression of the study of the life of mood and feeling, furthermore, suggests that, by turning to the long-neglected spiritual roots of all religion, we may find new ways to make man's brain potential more accessible to him within cultures that admit the romantic impulse so new to the West, and the inspirational thinking that characterizes it. Along with it, there will likely come a variety of adventuresome uses of artistic modes of functioning within science, both for discovery and for the diffusion of discovery. The feasible efforts toward intuitionism in mathematics[16] and the still faint beginnings of psychosomatic control to replace dependent psychoanalytic modes of therapy[17] will begin really to blossom and flower in that stabilized far future. It is to that future my questions are aimed—and all "self-congratulations," however deserved, seem somewhat premature as we face the prospect of that exciting era ahead, which our own further development of heroism now could draw closer to us in time, much sooner than a classical outlook permits. The rhythm of the romantic impulse leaps where the classical impulse lags behind.

REFERENCES

1. The original paper was called "Social Psychology: The Science of the Adventures of Consciousness in Value Shaping and Sharing." Copies of it are available upon request.

2. I was first visibly struck by this process when doing a large-scale study of the impact of the assassination of President Kennedy upon the youth of America and Europe. See my "A Public Event as a Socializing Agency: The Impact of the Presidential Assassination upon the Pre-Adult World," a paper read at the conference on children's reactions to the presidential assassination held by the Albert E. Einstein Medical School's Department of Psychiatry in 1964.

3. Written within the Chicago school of social science that Professor Lasswell himself was once intimately associated with, a little volume called *Heroes, Villains, and Fools* by Orrin E. Klapp (Englewood Cliffs, N.J.: Prentice-Hall, 1962) masterfully depicts the deterioration of the American hero in recent times and explains some of the features of the decline. In his description of the corrupted hero, he says "too good to be a villain, too bad to be a hero, too serious to be a clown, too interesting to forget." In *The Absurd Hero* (Austin: University of Texas Press, 1966), David D. Galloway explores recent works of fiction by way of explaining why heroism has become not easier but more difficult in our time. In this book, the works of Updike, Styron, Bellow, and Salinger are considered. The humanistic and nihilistic expressions of the romantic impulse are compared and contrasted, giving both the victorious and defeatist relation to despair.

4. Sri Aurobindo's *The Ideal of Human Unity* (New York: E. P. Dutton & Co., 1950) gives a detailed discussion of the significance of the equilibrium processes as measured by changing group units and relations among and between them.

5. I undertook a study to uncover the sequence in which fashions in academic research around different types of motives crystallized and, then, placed these against the most salient policy problems unfolding in the domestic and international scene. It became clear that at unconscious levels all "pure" research was responding to cultural shifts in "applied" crucial issues of policy, however unwittingly the view of science under which this occurred opposed any such orientation. Details of this study are noted in other articles cited below.

6. See my paper "Opening Up the Field of Infant Study to Value-Institution Analysis" prepared for the yearly conference on infancy at the Merrill-Palmer School in Detroit during 1966.

7. "Language Consciousness and Character Education: A Sketch of a Social Science Conflict plus Some Resolutions," in Clarence H. Faust and Jessica Feingold, *Approaches to Education for Character: Strategies for Change in Higher Education* (New York: Columbia University Press, 1969).

8. See my papers "Toward a 'Living' Social Psychology," and, "Toward a University of Living Ethics," copies available upon request. Both are unpublished manuscripts. Additionally, see my "Dare We Take Love Seriously?" in a forthcoming issue of *Family Circle* magazine.

9. *Anti-Intellectualism in American Life* (New York: Alfred Knopf, 1966). His discussion of the "clerisy" and "avant-garde" intellectual is particularly stimulating, since the two bear different relations to the "hidden postulates" of their society.

10. See Mary Harrington Hall's "A Conversation with Harold Lasswell: The Psychology of Politics" in the October 1968 issue of *Psychology Today*. The author, incidentally, is masterful in presenting the ideas of those she interviews in the most attractive way possible for the general reader and practices journalism at a high level of excellence.

11. Middletown, Conn.: Wesleyan University Press, 1967. The lexical or dictionary meaning of words is distinguished from the speaker's inner meaning given to words and the tension between the two meanings is made a focus of new discoveries about language.

12. A forthcoming book is devoted to summarizing the results of an empirical investigation carried on with Tristran Campbell, Jr., and using the results as a basis for more comprehensive treatment of the

subject. *Music, Value and Mood: The Most Unconscious Basis of Communication* is the working title. Some preliminary statements about ideas influencing the work on music are to be found in my *Human Values in Education* (Dubuque, Iowa: William C. Brown Co., 1969), written with Ray Rucker and V. Clyde Arnspiger.

13. The volume written with Professor Lasswell is titled *Constitution and Character* and remains, after going through several versions, still incomplete.

14. A poignant depiction of the growing "generation gap" is given by Rudolph Steiner in his *The Younger Generation* (New York: Anthroposophic Press, 1967).

15. *The Politics of Experience* (New York: Ballantine Books, 1967). This work continues a strain of thought begun many years back by such writers as Lawrence K. Frank who consider society the patient rather than the individual.

16. A clear idea about the place of intuitionism in mathematics in relation to the rest is given in Max Black's *The Nature of Mathematics* (London: Routledge and Kegan Paul, 1933).

17. As one example of the psychosomatic control method of psychotherapy see Johannes H. Schultz and Wolfgang Luthe, *Autogenic Training* (New York: Grune and Stratton, 1959). The work of the late Nina Bull had begun to push psychosomatic control to new frontiers of consciousness, only some of which saw print. It is hoped that her ideas can be brought to posthumous publication by several of us. She had pushed her attitude theory of emotion to the most exacting and intensive observations yet recorded. The work of the distinguished endocrinologist, William Wolf, in promoting these new therapies on the New York scene is particularly noteworthy for brilliance and soundness. He has enabled me to get a more profound and balanced grasp of the romantic tradition than any other single person.

Author's Note: It seems only fair to point out that the demands of the production schedule were such that my article, as revised by the volume editor, went to press without incorporating a substantial number of changes and emendations I would have made and that, for reasons of space and in the time allowed, only a minimum number of corrections and amplifications could be inserted in the proofs. For example, I should like to have retitled my article "The Social Psychology of Heroes of Science: Professor Lasswell's Work as Case Study."

11

Dynamic Functionalism

ALLAN R. HOLMBERG

INTRODUCTORY NOTE, *by Arnold A. Rogow*

AT THE TIME of his death in 1966 the late Professor Allan
Holmberg, professor of anthropology at Cornell University,
was preparing a chapter on Lasswell's contribution to anthropology. It was not concerned with exploratory exercises such as
the articles published by Professor Lasswell on one aspect of the
ethnology of Taos Pueblo in New Mexico (bibliography, 1935).
Rather, Professor Holmberg was concerned with the application
of Lasswell's fundamental approach to the study of societies commonly regarded as within the domain of anthropology. As Holmberg often said, he found himself remarkably at home with the
"configurative method." It was Holmberg who suggested that
the best way to make the Lasswellian point of view intelligible
to his professional colleagues was to emphasize both its connection with functionalism and its dynamic expansion of the functionalist system. Hence, Holmberg wrote a work-paper entitled
"Dynamic Functionalism," which he distributed (from 1958
on) to his seminar students of anthropology at Cornell. It has
been decided to publish this work-paper here, with the kind
consent of Mrs. Laura Holmberg, in place of the missing chapter
by Professor Holmberg.

The Holmberg-Lasswell collaboration dates from 1954–55,
when they were fellows at the Center for Advanced Study in the
Behavioral Sciences at Stanford. During this year Holmberg's
aim was to rethink the Vicos Project, which he had initiated in the
early fifties. The Quetchua Indians of the Vicos Hacienda in the
Peruvian Andes had traditionally been dominated by a *patrón*

who took advantage of their labor obligation to enrich himself. The point of the Cornell-Peru experiment (prototype) was that an anthropologist took the place of the *patrón* and undertook to guide the community toward modernization and effective decision making. It was a remarkable example of the policy sciences approach, and, more technically, of the dynamic functionalist viewpoint. For information on Vicos see bibliography (1965).

The last article jointly prepared by Professors Holmberg and Lasswell was published in 1966 (see bibliography). Holmberg planned to prepare a long section utilizing Vicos data, but was prevented by illness from doing so.

A. THE FRAMEWORK OF DYNAMIC FUNCTIONALISM

We are examining the Minka* as an exercise in the application of a framework of analysis that we call dynamic functionalism. The framework bears this name as an acknowledgment of our indebtedness to the past of social theory at the same time that we innovate. We believe that no responsible student of the development of the social and behavioral sciences can fail to detect the widely ramifying impact of the functionalist movement in anthropological theory. The triumph of Malinowski, Radcliffe-Brown, and their colleagues has been so overwhelming that anthropologists at least have almost forgotten the state of affairs against which they were rebelling. Today no critical scholar would assume that a valid comparison of two culture patterns has been made if the analysis goes no further than the enumeration of a few points of likeness and difference. Our approach to the Minka is strictly in harmony with this point of view. It would never occur to us to suppose that a significant contribution had been made if we reported no more than that a cooperative work pattern had been identified in certain Andean villages. It would

---

* In this article the descriptive sections dealing with the Minka are omitted to save space. The Minka is an obligation to exchange labor.

not be enough to describe the local peculiarities of the Minka. The challenging problem is to show how the Minka enters into the everyday lives of the members of a given society and how it is interconnected with the entire configuration of local institutions. One is only true to the functionalist approach when the net is flung wide and when inner lives are probed to discover how human beings experience a pattern of culture. Functionalists set no limits in advance upon the potential repercussions of one detail upon another or upon the context as a whole.

The functionalist movement gave a great impetus to field work during the very epoch when the expansion of European civilization had sealed the doom of any culture incapable of commanding advanced sources of energy. Presumably Europeans felt secure enough, at least in some localities, to allow themselves to empathize with the vanishing "savage" and to endure the shock of admitting him to the status of a "folk." No doubt signs of rejuvenation on the part of ancient civilizations played a part in the new tolerance of the non-Christian world.

The questions we shall raise about the Minka are not uniquely our own. On the contrary, they are representative of the issues raised by all modern students of cross-cultural or cross-personal processes. We ask why anyone sponsors a Minka in the first place? Who are the sponsors (in terms of the local structure of society)? Who comes to a Minka and plays the part of a worker whether obligated to do so or not? What are the standard features of the occasion itself? In general, what causes and consequences link the Minka to the total social context in which it is found and with which it perpetually interacts?

To recognize the contribution of anthropology to comparative studies in recent decades is not to deny the concurrent influence of other forms of contextualism. The innovations of Freud could not fail to reveal subtle connections well beyond any conventional range of expectation. Structural psychologists, working mainly in the field of perception, devised experiments which strikingly displayed the links between the details of a setting and the whole design. Physics supplied a new impetus to innovation when radioactivity appeared and upset the complacent assumption that Newton's system was to be regarded as a final chart of nature showing where each stomic billiard ball bounced trimly through its appointed course.

The functionalist movement established the point that while all scientific propositions refer to and depend upon comparison, the crucial question is how to identify valid frames of reference for the purpose; in fact, a valid comparison emerges as an exceedingly complex achievement. This gain of functionalism we intend to keep.

Uncertain Findings

The field studies published by the adherents of the new movement were incalculably more persuasive and exciting as human documents than their predecessors' had been. For years anthropology had something of the status of a cabinet of curiosities which confirmed the prejudice of Europeans about the backward plight of the non-Christian world. The functionalist outlook brought new insight and respect into writings having to do with alien peoples. The effect was intellectually intoxicating since the investigator was liberated to penetrate beneath superficial likenesses and differences and to expend the effort necessary to discern the functional ties that relate each culture trait to its causal setting and total consequences. The resuling exuberance of "funcional" interpretation produced, among others, the fascinating monographs of Malinowski.

But there were disadvantages, and with passing years the limitations of functionalism have become progressively more apparent. A key difficulty arises whenever attempts are made to compare reports of work in the field. For instance, when we examine an account of the Minka in the life of a community the data are often exceedingly full on such points as the significance of the Minka as a means of sustaining family solidarity. But nothing may be said about the Minka in connection with the diffusion of new skills in the construction of houses or in potato raising or other activities. Were there no such functions or is the explanation that the investigator failed to look? Similarly, we may read of the Minka as a contributor to factionalism in one village. But there may be no mention whatever of factionalism anywhere else. Can we assume that because factionalism was mentioned in one case it was looked for in all the others?

The inference is irresistible that we cannot be sure that field observers consistently apply a comprehensive classification of potential functions. Hence, it is inadmissible to rely upon the validity of comparisons made upon the basis of such research reports. At best the interpretation of a field report is a risky business since the process of publication constrains an author to condense his findings to a degree that does some damage to his primary observations. Our present point is that an unnecessary dimension of uncertainty is added when the categories of analysis are not explicit and comprehensive.

Neglect of Process

A further difficulty has made its appearance in the work of modern investigators who follow in the tradition of functionalism. A curious disjunction exists between their free-wheeling accent upon "function" and the relatively rigid preoccupation that they exhibit over matters of "structure." The two modes of analysis do not always fuse. Somehow structures are more fixed and functions more labile than seems convincing.

Part of the trouble comes from a gap that separates the words used to talk about individual "needs" (or "drives" and the like) from the terms ordinarily employed to assess the causes and consequences of a given institution. Every scientist takes it for granted that the impact of the cultural environment molds the direction of discharge of the predispositions of the rising generation of any given society. It is also assumed that a fundamental if unspecified connection exists between the "needs" of original nature and the forms of a particular society. What is the nature of this interplay? How are "structures" and "functions" subordinated to these needs?

Apparently, a more consistently applied conception of "process" is essential if we are to put structural and functional patterns in proper relation to one another. The notion of process emphasizes the sequential phasing of human interactions with another and with the natural environment. It recognizes the place of conscious and unconscious choices in the flow of events. Conscious choice is a "subjective" event (or event sequence); it occupies a discernible position before and after some "movement" events and is concurrent with others. Preconscious events include stimuli originating from the environment and also the "impulses" arising within the psychobiological system of the organism. Some preconscious events are "unconscious," and hence capable of passing into a conscious phase under appropriate circumstances.

Subjective events at the conscious phase are concurrent with neuromuscular activities and other "expressive" events. For some purposes we find it convenient to think of the event-sequence constituting an act as originating in "impulse," and passing through phases of "subjectivity" and "expression" (which may be largely concurrent). But these terms do not bring out an important feature of an act since they do not characterize its component phases as they bear on gratification. Therefore, we speak of the "outcome" phase of an act sequence and distinguish the "pre" and "post" phases from one another. It is obvious, of course, that an act may be stopped short of completion at any phase.

The significance of emphasizing outcomes is that we thereby call attention to a clue that may be helpful in explaining the conduct of an individual throughout his entire career, and especially his acceptance or rejection of specific culture traits or even of a total culture. We accept the postulate that men seek to gratify their wants. They pursue preferred events. They try to maximize gratifying over nongratifying outcomes. For terminological convenience, we designate any preferred event as a "value." Hence, the maximization postulate asserts that men are striving to achieve the most favorable net-value position open to them.

As regards the Minka, for example, the problem is to explain what is done or not done in connection with it by demonstrating that all responses, insofar as they are manifestations of choice (rather than constraint), are the result of expected net-value advantage. Presumably the Minka will rise or fall accordingly, and its structure will change on the same basis.

If the task is conceived in these terms, it is evident why anthropologists must take full account of "process." We pay attention to the occurrence of Minkas through time and have several points in mind: What minimum traits must be found before we identify a given situation as constituting an "occurrence" of a Minka? What frequency of patterning must be observed before we identify a change as "structural"? To what extent can the participation of individuals or the failure to participate be explained by hypotheses inspired by the maximization postulate? Or by factors of constraint (factors limiting choice)? To what extent can the aggregate fate of the institution during any period in a given society be accounted for by similar factors?

Value Outcomes

The two criticisms that we have made of traditional functionalism are closely related to one another. They relate to problems that arise when comparative studies are undertaken. For valid comparisons a fixed list of categories is required, and explanations call for hypotheses within a social process framework.

We now come to a more affirmative discussion. For convenience we characterize any social process briefly as man pursuing values through institutions using resources. We have defined values as "preferred events" (outcomes). An "institution" is composed of the patterns which are relatively specialized to the shaping and sharing of any broad value category.

The first question that occurs to an anthropologist is why distinguish between values and institutions in this way? We do this in order to provide a counterpoint between the requirements of selectivity and of faithful attention to detail. A brief list of key terms (the value categories) is serviceable to the cause of selectivity. For descriptive refinement we operate with an open-ended list which can be extended to enumerate every conceivable pattern of any conceivable society.

The selective intent of the value list may be made clearer if we remind ourselves of the overwhelming diversity among men on matters of detail. At any cross-section of time, at any locus, the social process appears to be a "seamless web" drifting or blowing, but in any case moving, toward the future. As observers, we find it utterly impossible to make comparisons unless we discover "seams" in the web. We must look for culminating occurrences in the flow of events. The specific outcomes of human activity are so varied that it is impractical to operate with the number of words necessary to name each article of food or clothing, each turn of skill, each item of culture that is desired by someone. If we are to find our way through the labyrinth we must classify the specifics into a small number of workable categories.

The present study of the Minka shows how a short list of key terms can serve the purposes of anthropology. We rely upon continuing reference to the list on the part of the field worker to increase the comparability of field results. Hence, when we analyze the deliberate intentions of those who sponsor a Minka we challenge ourselves continually by asking to what extent each potential value outcome in our list enters into the calculations of a sponsor. Presumably the most obvious intentions will often be directed toward economic outcomes. Presumably, too, the intentions of a sponsor will often refer to affectional ties since enough is known of the Minka in a general way to indicate that it is an occasion for bringing members of a family together. It may also be rewarding to think of possible skill objectives, since the sponsor may see that he is in need of competent help. Perhaps prestige (respect) is the principal end in view, or well-being, in the sense that unless their houses are repaired promptly the safety, health, and comfort of the residents will be impaired. Another aim may be to get right with the transempirical forces (God) and to get a reputation for righteousness (rectitude). Perhaps a Minka is sponsored to further political purposes, or to obtain enlightenment by providing a forum for returning travelers. Our procedure is to think of all possible objectives by systematically stimulating our imagination and recall by using the list of eight values which have just been mentioned.

Besides examining the deliberate intentions (C^1) of Minka sponsors we also look for marginally conscious (C^2) or unconscious (C^3) aims. The scientific field worker may conclude that some sponsors are not fully aware of their motives. This may be inferred by discovering that although A is jealous of B and tries to get ahead of him in all prestigeful activities, A may say nothing about this in describing his motives in sponsoring a Minka.

Having considered the sponsors, we turn to the workers. By making sure that the value list is fully utilized we increase the chances that profiles of sponsor and worker intentions will be comparable. We also make another separation for purposes of data reporting, distinguishing between all who participate directly and those who consider the possibility but refrain from doing so. The latter are called "indirect participants" since they have interacted to some extent with an ongoing activity.

By scrutinizing the intentions of all participants we may obtain a comparable image of the degree to which everyone believes that he has freedom of choice or is under constraint. A harvest may almost certainly be ruined unless a labor force gets promptly on the job; thus, the Minka may be the only available means of saving a crop. If an individual does not accept an invitation to work it may be obvious to him that he will himself eventually lose a crop by reason of informal boycott. Is it also possible that as outside observers we will find that strong elements of constraint are present which are not consciously perceived by the participants?

The value categories give guidance when we undertake to relate participants to the social structure of a society. It is possible to develop a description of the social structure at any given time by taking note of the degree of individual control over each value. The general question is: Who occupies an upper, middle, or lower position in terms of wealth, affection, skill, prestige, well-being, rectitude, power, and enlightenment?

As we turn from analyzing who participates in the Minka to study the occasion itself, the value list continues to be of assistance. The first step, however, is to sketch the sequence of institutional practices constituting a Minka. What does a sponsor do to initiate such an occasion? How does one avoid or accept participation? Besides inviting workers, what preparations are called for? How is the affair conducted? How do people handle themselves when it is over?

Once the successive phases of a Minka are identified, it is possible to subject the entire situation to microscopic study in value terms. Each interaction is analyzable according to the degree to which each participant indulges or deprives himself or others in terms of each value. Consider the issuing of an invitation. In typical situations, does the issuer think of himself as indulging or depriving the other person? If the invitation is turned down or avoided does the issuer regard himself as suffering deprivation to a degree that warrants his taking informal or even formal sanctions? What measures does he actually initiate? How does he justify his claim if mediation, conciliation, or some other form of action occurs? How does the target of these operations cope with the threat to his position? How are value positions ultimately affected in fact?

The preparations for Minka, and the management of the occasion itself, can be usefully regarded as a set of "strategies" by which base values can be exploited to maximize the net value position of the sponsor. The base-value inventory is made as we locate the place of each participant in the social structure.

If an institution is to be understood, it is essential to go into the detailed investigation of actual outcomes. Therefore, we devote special sections to the problems that arise. Individual outcomes are considered first; aggregate outcomes later. The value list is a guide to both parts of the study.

When the analyses mentioned in the preceding paragraphs have been concluded, they make it possible to confront "intended" outcomes with "realized" outcomes. It will also be feasible to sum up the factors of choice and constraint that keep the Minka alive as a social institution and bring about adaptations of structure and function.

Science and Policy

By this time it may be reasonably clear why we think that dynamic functionalism is a more satisfactory tool of scientific research than traditional approaches. It is also valuable for other purposes.

The social anthropologist has learned that more is expected of him than the formulation of scientific generalizations. It is taken for granted that his researches will contribute to some extent to our knowledge of the early history of man. Obviously the anthropologist does become acquainted with trends through time and in space. At Vicos, for example, the culture of the Andean Indian, though profoundly influenced by Spanish civilization, has remained in many particulars pre-Columbian. To learn something about the present inhabitants of these spectacular uplands is at the same moment to send a small beam of light toward the past.

The anthropologist is also expected to turn his face from time to time toward the future. It is taken for granted that he will have a judgment worthy of respect concerning he probable course of future events. For example, he may be asked whether the Minka will continue to operate in Vicos during the next few years with more or less vitality. A question of that kind is both "academic" and "practical." It is academic in the sense that it challenges the scholar to consider whether he has asked the right questions of the data. It is practical since all policy decisions step into the future. Rational policy making demands that all assumptions about the future be critically evaluated. It is reasonable to turn to the scholar on these matters and it is appropriate for him to give his best reply.

This brings us to another intellectual challenge confronting the anthropologist: the clarification of goal values. The scholar may decide to postulate his own values and to do what he can to give them definiteness. For instance, we share with most of our colleagues, in this country at least, a personal commitment to the overriding ideal of human dignity (not indignity). We construe the rich though ambiguous expression "human dignity" to mean that desirable institutions share social values rather widely in society instead of holding them as tightly as possible in a few hands.

It is not necessary, however, for the scholar to limit himself to the clarification of his own system of value goals. The scientist as a specialized role player may legitimately aid in clarifying the value goals of others, such as leaders of national policy at home or abroad or influential figures in the folk society with whom he is well acquainted. In any case, it is evident that goal thinking calls for two operations: the postulation or grounding of values and the choice of institutional practices to serve as operational indices of the preferred pattern of value distribution.

Finally, anthropologists are becoming accustomed to requests to propose or to evaluate alternative lines of action contemplated by governments, business organizations, folk societies, or the spokesmen of many other groups. We can refer to Vicos again in this connection since the advice of those involved in the Vicos study has been sought by a wide assortment of policy makers.

The foregoing paragraphs have summed up the five principal dimensions of intellectual tasks in the policy field:

> Description of trend
> Confirmation of scientific generalizations
> Projection of future developments
> Clarification of goal values
> Invention and evaluation of alternatives

We interpret dynamic functionalism to encompass this comprehensive way of orientating the mind of the scholar and scientist toward problem solving in society.

In view of the reluctance displayed by many social scientists to let their minds entertain the policy implications of what they do, it may be pertinent to emphasize the importance that we attach to a theoretical frame of reference in which the traditional specializations of scholarship and science are candidly related to the decision process as a whole.

The integrity of the traditional forms of intellectual activity need not be impaired by perceiving their contextual significance. In our view the deliberate use of each of the five modes of thought can contribute to the strengthening of all. With further experience we should be able to improve the less commonly considered dimensions of the functional approach.

For instance, we believe that projective thinking can be pursued by more disciplined methods. Three bodies of data are available for use in evaluating a "developmental construct," which is our term for a theoretical model devised to characterize the past-future. First, specific time series can be extrapolated. A frequent result of this is often that a clash is foreseen between contradictory projections. Thus two militant empires may be expanding directly toward one another. In estimating whether future conflicts will be avoided or resolved the scholar must turn to the accessible supply of scientifically established generalizations. Suppose that the scientific findings indicate that the empire with the largest population and the most advanced science is likely to come out ahead. Such generalizations help to refine the scholar's image of coming things. This cannot be entirely satisfactory, however, since systematic knowledge is in all probability relatively meager as it relates to the specific factors involved. It is legitimate to use semisystematic information as supplementary evidence of present predispositions. In any case, we are now making the point that developmental constructs need not be arbitrary or capricious. They can be put in the critical fire of judgments that are based upon interconnected kinds of knowledge.

It is of no little significance, as we see it, that the five intellectual tasks of policy thinking can be fruitfully applied to the strategical problems of research management. The Vicos research itself is a case in point. The goal values of key individuals at Cornell had something to do with launching the entire enterprise. The traumatic impact of World War II had been a reminder of how little we understood or controlled modern trends of industrialization and modernization. An overriding objective of the Cornell group was to contribute, however modestly, to the realization of a world community more fit for human habitation. Certainly, the projections relating to the future situation of the world were not sanguine. It was believed that the spreading techno-scientific revolution would probably create such chronic crises of insecurity that our goal values would be in danger of perpetual frustration. We found no reason for satisfaction in the meager supply of pertinent and scientifically established generalizations about the interrelations of civilizations and folk societies. Strictly scientific considerations indicated the desirability of introducing experimental methods at the earliest moment. Fortunately our historical knowledge of the Andean peoples was such that we estimated that certain trends would work in our favor. Among the policy alternatives to which we gave high priority were plans to bring about closer scientific association between North American anthropologists and ambitious and gifted members of the comparatively new profession in South America.

We can accurately report that the Vicos project has already realized to a certain extent the various objectives originally entertained by its initiators. The experience that we have had has strengthened our confidence in the approach which is here named dynamic functionalism. Our conception of its potential importance has been greatly extended and clarified along lines that will be discussed in more detail after the Minka material has been presented.

B. THE POTENTIAL USE OF DYNAMIC FUNCTIONALISM IN FIELD RESEARCH AND COMPARATIVE ANALYSIS

IN this section we give special consideration to problems that arise in the field or in the execution of comparative analyses in harmony with the principles of dynamic functionalism.

It may be helpful to comment upon some of the calculations that led to the specific conceptual tools that we are recommending. We refer particularly to the eight value categories. Before moving in this direction, however, it may be opportune to reiterate our most general methodological point. It is crucially important to have a comprehensive, brief list of categories to apply to all contexts to be compared. Selectivity and refinement call for the technique of opposing such a list to an open-ended enumeration of institutional forms. We are not "selling" eight conceptual tools—neither the number eight in general nor the specific eight in our list. When a brief list is kept constant, it is translatable into any other comprehensive set of categories, and the requirements of method are met.

In choosing the present set of terms we took into consideration the existing division of labor among scholars in the university world of this country and Western Europe. Phenomena relating to power and government engage political scientists, jurists, and specialists on diplomacy. Wealth and economic institutions are the province of economists and students of economic history. Respect and social class structures are in the forefront of inquiry among those sociologists, anthropologists, and jurists who concern themselves with caste and other discriminatory phenomena. Affection and institutions of intimacy, congeniality, and loyalty are within the scope of historians and social scientists, of family and friendship groups, and of large psychosocial formations like nations with whose symbols many individuals become emotionally identified. The well-being value and institutions of safety, comfort, and health are the field of those who specialize in public and private health—more broadly, the social biologists. The skill value and institutions which set and apply performance standards engage historians and practitioners of pedagogy, sociologists of craft, occupations, and professions, and the not inconsiderable body of scholars who specialize in style. The rectitude value and institutions that set, justify, and apply standards of responsible conduct are described and analyzed by historians and scientists of morality and religion. The enlightenment value and institutions that gather and disseminate information about the context of decision attract researchers who study media of communication and the rise and fall of comprehensive conceptions of man and nature.

These specialties are pursued by scholars under various names. Among them are some individuals who concentrate upon comprehensive systems of analysis. They are often described as philosophers of history, theoretical anthropologists, or systematic sociologists.

The study of social process calls for the investigation of "man" and "resources" in addition to "value" goals and "institutions." Specialized fields include comparative psychology, physiology, and morphology, which deal especially with the place of man's psychophysical system in Nature. Possibly the most general picture of "resources" is provided by the emerging synthesis called "human ecology."

We now consider the problems that arise in applying our approach to the concrete challenge of field work. Four steps of successive intensity of inquiry are involved.

Step One: Preliminary Classification of Institutions

For the man who is going to the field or who is beginning a comparative examination of data, the first procedural step is to employ the categories in preparing a preliminary classification of the institutions of the society (or societies) in question. Field work is usually done today in communities about which some authentic information is at hand. Nevertheless, since the present method (or a strictly comparable one) is not likely to have been employed by earlier investigators, most detailed studies will need to be deferred until they can be done on the spot.

The aim of the preliminary operation is to provide a sketch of the known outlines of the total context and to permit files to be started and strategic lines of attack to be chosen. It may be helpful to show how we would set about classifying our own civilization, or civilizations close to it. We shall make frequent reference, of course, to problems that arise in connection with researches directed toward folk societies rather than complex civilizations.

It is essential to be prepared for the fact that the initial assignment of cultural patterns may bear little relation to the final classification at the end of field work. At the beginning we cannot hope to apply fundamental terms with functional depth. Rather, in the interest of initial intelligibility, it is preferable to stay close to conventional meanings. A conventional meaning is the understanding of a word that prevails among those familiar with local usages. Functional meanings, on the other hand, are part of the intellectual equipment of the anthropologist or social scientist. Scholars and scientists engage in a perpetual struggle for precise definitions that aid valid comparisons. A step in this direction is the choice of a handful of key symbols capable of being applied as we used our list in the present report. Since functional definitions are deliberately made to serve the specialized ends of scientific work, any overlapping between them and popular usage is coincidental. It is to be taken for granted that overlapping will occur as long as the words are recognizable in standard English. When translated they are unavoidably turned into the recognized vocabulary of non-English languages.

If we were making a preliminary assignment of American institutions to power there would be no hesitation in recognizing the following: governmental (national government, state governments, local governments, the United Nations, and other intergovernmental institutions in which the United States participates), political parties, pressure groups. Problems come up in connection with the appropriate definitions to be given to the terms "political party" and "pressure group." In some marginal cases an organization which is regarded as belonging to an external conspirative system is not regarded as a political party even though it applies the term to itself. Political scientists sometimes speak of a political order when referring to organizations that call themselves political parties but do not permit freedom of electoral competition at home (National Socialists in Hitler's Germany, for example).

Political scientists sometimes distinguish political parties from pressure groups by two criteria: parties offer candidates in their own name and propose comprehensive programs of government policy. The latter distinction is not conventional in the United States, although it serves the purposes of comparative political science and presumably, therefore, of comparative anthropology. If the distinction just mentioned is accepted, the so-called Prohibition Party would not be regarded as a political party in the functional sense. Although its name may appear on the ballot, it has no comprehensive policy platform. Actually, no distinction is sufficiently recognized to establish a sure legal definition of a pressure group (or "interest association"). Political scientists think of pressure organizations as specialized to the influencing of public officials; other interest associations of a private character are classified according to the dominant value pursued. This raises the question of whether the scientist relies upon public declarations of purpose, upon an "insider's" specification of purpose, or only upon researches that discover the perspectives of top management (professional and lay) and the rank and file.

Just as political parties are distinguishable from political orders, it is also useful to separate the pressure group, whose methods are primarily persuasive, from influencing associations that pursue narrow objectives and rely upon coercion. We call the latter "gangs."

Turning from power to wealth in America, experts have no difficulty in identifying as economic institutions all corporations, partnerships, and independent proprietors expressly engaged in the pursuit of profit. But what of "foundations"? These are formally set up as "nonprofit" institutions. If we listen to some informants from the world of law and politics, we are told that the conventional label does not always correspond to the facts revealed by appropriate investigation. It appears that members of a donor's family (and dependents) may be put in charge of voting shares, which enables them to control business assets and to affect decisions with profit considerations in mind even though the foundation does not distribute what it calls profits. Since this is a controversial matter in a preliminary survey of American institutions, we cannot do more than put such institutions in a file with the uncertainty clearly recognized.

In this rapid reconnaissance we turn to respect and promptly note that the conventional labeling system of the community, which was so useful in enabling us to classify many political and economic organizations, is not helpful. No complete system of legally designated status positions, such as once prevailed in Western European society, is to be found in the United States. We do, however, benefit from many private researches that have been conducted to discover perceived status differences in various sections of the United States. A research newcomer to a folk society must usually depend upon himself to ascertain the social pecking order. In some societies, however, even fragmentary information will reveal the existence of a system of caste in which the respect attributable to a person is in large part settled for life by the position of the family into which he is born. Families themselves may be explicitly ranked. So modifiable are the lives of modern peoples, however, that we may learn at once that the situation is unsettled. Even "half caste" elements may no longer be viewed askance and denied intermarriage.

When we consider medical facilities and classify them as well-being, the problem is not difficult. A borderline question is whether to attribute the armed forces and the police to safety institutions (well-being) or to power. Because of the conventional association of these services with the political position of the body politics as a whole, we adopt the latter alternative (at least at the start). Another question is whether to allocate playing fields and recreational facilities in general to well-being or to regard them as opportunities for the acquisition and exercise of skill. Since the first is presumably the familiar way of thinking, we adopt it provisionally. Another marginal issue is whether to regard physical sexuality as well-being or affection. We also go along with conventional ways of thinking in this country and initially regard sex as part of the context of affection.

One is in little doubt about classifying educational institutions whose role is the cultivation of identifiable skills. Nor is it problematical where to file associations that set performance standards and conduct examinations for craft, occupational, and professional groups. In our civilization we also have critics who devote themselves to formulating, evaluating, and applying performance criteria in many fields of human effort. The true critic in our sense relies upon "intrinsic" standards in making his evaluations. Patterns are therefore judged according to the arrangement of elements that compose a medium of expression. Such an arrangement is "style," and style in this definition carries many of the connotations that we are assigning to the term skill. Thus, musical skill is properly appraised in terms of musical forms and skill in oratory is appropriately assessed in terms of the techniques of gesture and speech, not audience popularity. The latter brings in extraneous criteria of respect or affection.

It is usual to think of churches in the United States as specialized to the articulation of standards of morality, to their justification (especially in terms of alleged transempirical sponsors), and the application of these standards to specific cases. An ethical culture society, whether regarded as a religious organization or not, unquestionably belongs among the rectitude institutions.

In the United States we commonly think of the family as an appropriate stronghold of affection, together with friendship circles and social fraternities. Where exclusivity is the principal feature of a group we call it a respect institution.

Since we rely upon the mass media for so much information, it is not necessary to hesitate before classifying them among enlightenment institutions. Civic education belongs with enlightenment since we conceive of it as concerned with some of the larger outlines of man's place in society. General science education comes in the same category, since the development and dissemination of theories of nature are enlightenment activities.

Step Two: Outcome, Preoutcome, and Postoutcome Situations

We turn now to the second major step to be taken for field or comparative purposes. This consists in making a provisional classification of the outcome, preoutcome, and postoutcome situations found in all the institutional patterns of a society. Where it has been practicable to make a preliminary assignment of social institutions to the eight value categories, these are now reanalyzed to emphasize the culminating events that occur in the social process as carried on within the society. As indicated before, it sometimes happens that little or no helpful information is available about the society which is to be investigated. Under such conditions it is impossible to make a board classification of social institutions; hence, both the first and the second operations must be done in the field. Once in the field the investigator is able to employ the categories as a reminder of major lines of inquiry. Because of the notorious importance of kinship in folk societies, the investigator will be well advised to try as early as possible to find out about family relationships. Having in mind also the comparative importance of the most inclusive unit with a territorial basis, the investigator will inquire at once for community-wide decision-making institutions.

The brief outline of "outcomes" given above is a point of departure for the operations called for at the present stage. To proceed more securely in classifying institutional situations, we shall refine the central categories somewhat. The starting point is again the distinction between conventional and functional meanings.

In the United States, it is part of conventional usage to speak of county officials, for example, as members of "government." And it is true that these officials are authorized to act in the name of the whole county and that their tax decisions are as a rule enforceable against those who do not pay. Detailed knowledge of a county, however, may show that the county commissioners take orders from a handful of people who discuss the tax rate privately but who have no official standing. From our point of view, those who make effective decisions are the power holders of the county on tax questions; in the functional sense they *are* the government. One objective of comparative anthropology and other social scientific disciplines is the discovery of "who makes what decisions."

Although part of the data of any research includes the conventional usages in a society regarding "law, government, and politics," our eventual aim is to pierce the veil of conventionality and to discover the functional power holders.

Functionally speaking, we understand by power those community-wide outcomes which involve severe deprivations. To speak of severe deprivations as "involved" is to refer to two possible states of affairs. In the former the community-wide outcome is being actively imposed, as in military campaigns or police actions. In the other the prevailing expectation is that severe deprivations will be imposed under appropriate contingencies, as when taxes are not paid. A deprivation, of course, is a loss of values or a blocked gain. (An indulgence is a gain or a blocked loss.) Presumably, deprivations can be classified according to their degree of mildness or severity, and one operational definition that must be made explicit by the scientific worker in a given context is the "cut off" point along this hypothetical continuum.

It is useful to introduce subclassifications in identifying decision outcomes. We recommend for this purpose the recognition of prescriptions, applications, and terminations.* A prescription decision formulates a general rule of conduct that, if challenged, is expected to be enforced by the threat or use of severe deprivation. An application is a decision that deals with a concrete situation. Terminations put an end to an enforceable relationship.

In some societies it is easy to identify structures that are relatively specialized to the prescribing function. In the United States, a constitutional convention and a legislature are such structures. As usual, it is essential to probe behind the label affixed by conventional usage to the organ of government. Some "statutes" passed at a given legislative session may not be expected to be enforced; hence, they are not regarded by the scientific analyst as "laws" in the functional meaning of the word. They are formal, though not effective, prescriptions. Our allusion to the county

---

* These categories can be multiplied when comparisons are to be more refined (e.g., intelligence, promotion, invocation, appraisal).

commissioners made the point that investigation may disclose the fact that from a functional viewpoint an entire organ is misnamed in local usage.

In a vast body politic such as the United States it is easy to identify structures conventionally charged with the applying function. Included are most executive, administrative, and judicial organs at every level. The point about the need of alertness in identifying legislatures functionally applies no less immediately to structures of application.

In the United States we do not conventionally think of agencies with terminating functions as distinct organic entities. Hence, research workers cannot easily find a governmental structure conveniently labeled to serve as the take-off point. Special research is necessary to identify the staffs and the facilities engaged in treaty and contract termination, for example.

The foregoing outcome situations are "decisions" in the power process which, when located, make it possible to proceed to identify pre- and postoutcome situations. We perceive preoutcome activities by taking note of attempts to influence outcome situations. This is the sense in which candidate elections are among the preoutcome structures of American political life. Similarly, political parties are in general included among such structures. So, too, are pressure groups. Organs of this kind may be further classified as performing a recommending (promotional) function when we look at them in the total context of decision making.

In folk societies, research may show that a council of elders performs every function mentioned in our analysis of the decision process. Of course, the council may or may not look upon itself as prescribing new and general rules of conduct. Nevertheless, it may be demonstrable by research that old rules are in fact drastically revised, although most of the time of a council is presumably taken up with the applying function. One applying activity may be judicial, if by a judicial tribunal we mean a dispute-settling organ in which one party can bring another party into the arena, whereupon the parties are heard and it is possible for severe deprivations to be imposed upon losing parties. The council may also act as an arbitration tribunal if by this we mean a dispute-settling organ in which controversies are dealt with only if both parties agree to submit the issue and to abide by the result. Moreover, the council may function as a conciliator or mediator, words indicating a more permissive role in relation to the parties than adjudication or arbitration. Besides dispute-settling functions, the council may act as an administrative body directing a host of activities in the name of the community. Some of these activities may involve corresponding decision makers in nearby villages or in larger territorial units (counties, regions, nations, international bodies).

When the investigator has identified decision and predecision situations he is free to concentrate upon the details of each. Key questions become: who (with what qualifications, selected how, with what perspectives), with what base values, employing what strategies, influences the outcomes in what manner and with what immediate and later effects upon individual and aggregate value positions and practices?

In answering these questions it is necessary to refine the distinction between authority and control. Authority is a term that refers to expectations about the established manner of doing things; control has to do with how things are actually done. The informants whom we consult concerning the village council may tell us that only old people of certain distinguished families are proper members. But they may admit that this qualification is often disregarded. And when we analyze the affiliations of councilmen we may find that several relatively young men of "unknown" families are in it. Informants may say that the proper way to choose a council is for new members to be co-opted. Our inquiries may show that a system of nomination and election has grown up. Perhaps our informants will describe the ideal image of how council members are supposed to go about their duties, presumably devoting themselves to settling quarrels and to cultivating the economic advantage of all. On direct study of the councilmen we may also modify this picture; we may find that the government is faction-ridden and full of contenders for the control of land that is expected to fall from communal into private hands. When we get acquainted with the individuals concerned we may see that they are strongly identified with the interests of "narrow," not "extended," families, and that they are anxious to reach out beyond the village and take a hand in national reconstruction. It should be noted that any study of the demands, expectations, and identifications of the participants in the council situation must go beyond the officials themselves to include all who have contacts with them on official matters.

As we pointed out in connection with the Minka, we describe the base values at the disposal of individuals or groups when we locate them in the context of the whole community in reference to each value. During the early phases of field work it is probable that little will be known of the general distribution of values. This information will find its way into the notes as the research proceeds.

In connection with the study of power as a base, it is worth pointing out that authority may be comprehensively phrased and that in many circumstances language may be matched by effective control. Legitimacy is well understood to be a formal matter that may carry with it a huge amount of effective power. We define the formal "jurisdiction" of a decision maker to include all matters about which he is authorized to decide, and this may in fact be accepted throughout a community. As a rule, formal authority also includes an enumeration of the base values which are supposed to be at the disposal of a decision maker (such as tax resources). Authoritative rules may specify the strategies by which base values can legitimately be used (for proper purposes). Formal language may also define the patterns by which, at the outcome phase, a decision is registered (secret ballot, voice ballot, and so on).

At the decision phase, one of the principal questions in the mind of an investigator is how much influence individuals have had upon outcomes. This is more complex than answering a simple question about how the various participants lined up (as winners, losers, noncommitted). A coalition or an individual participant possessing little weight in the final alignment may be shown to have had a pivotal role in the sense that during the preoutcome stage a final result crystallized rapidly after his commitment had been made. Another fact worth examining is who initiates the outcome solution. This may not be the role of a pivotal individual or a faction, nor do the initiators necessarily play a large part in winning coalitions.

We move now to examine some of the questions that come up when the problem is to classify institutions of wealth according to outcome and preoutcome situations. Money outcomes are readily identified when money is offered, accepted, or refused, as in the case of haggling in the produce market; in connection with lending and repayment transactions, or as part of the buying and selling of land or shares of stock referring to assets utilizable in production. We readily recognize transaction outcomes when barter is the mode of exchange. When the members of a household receive subsistence, however, neither barter nor pricing need be involved and making services available to an individual can be merged in a net of relatively undifferentiated interactions which it is often unrewarding to describe in detail.

When we look intensively at wealth activities we note that preoutcome phases are production sequences. Production sequences end in two principal activities. One is consumption; the other is saving and investment. The former, as when food is eaten, is a terminal activity. When there is a prospect of further production we refer to saving and investment. Rather than being used to "enjoy life," individual incomes are devoted to buying more land for crop purposes or to acquiring another fishing boat to increase the disposable catch.

The Minka is an illuminating and varied case. In one perspective we describe it as a "preoutcome" situation in regard to economic affairs. Some occasions were for the final processing of goods to be consumed at once. At other Minkas labor was concentrated upon the preparation of facilities for further production. To a degree, of course, a Minka is an "outcome" situation when food and other commodities are immediately consumed by the participants.

Our study showed the input-output relations of selected Minkas in strictly economic terms, with the result that it was not difficult to see why wage labor is preferred by the more dollar-minded people of Vicos. It is not justifiable to jump immediately to the conclusion that the Minka is a capitalistic institution in disguise because it sometimes operates as a savings and invest-ment device. The complete capitalistic perspective includes profit seeking; it is directly applied by individuals who seek to put themselves in the best possible economic position by getting as much as they can for as little as they can give in return. We re-ported that in a few cases a Minka sponsor might think capital-istically, striving to keep his labor costs down while expanding the surplus of marketable goods and thereby expanding his capi-tal. Perhaps it ought to be emphasized that saving and invest-ment are found in all systems of economy, even when the capital equipment does not go beyond a few simple implements and there is little barter and no money transactions. Chains of mutual aid, however, are always found.

The same questions that arose about power also arise about preoutcome and outcome situations specialized to wealth. Who are the participants, and how are they qualified and selected? What are their perspectives and base values? What strategies do they employ, with what outcomes and effects? In this context our attention is directed toward money claims, if they are present, and technological patterns. By the latter we mean the allocation of resources for production and the processing of output and its disposition (the latter being the detailed transactions constituting the outcome phase). In describing effects the problem is to follow individual outcomes and ultimately to sum up the aggregate flow of production, income, standards of consumption, saving and investment.

Respect outcomes are fused with other social patterns to such an extent that in many societies only a few situations stand out as primarily specialized to the giving or receiving of honorific or of contemptuous modes of address. The typical task of analyzing respect outcomes has been illustrated in the Minka study, where each situation was examined according to the evidence of respect giving, receiving, or withholding.

In the United States we arrange celebrations in honor of such individual heroes as transatlantic flyers, life savers, war veterans, employees who have hung on for fifty years, and the like. Such outcome situations pass through a discernible sequence of preoutcome activities. But in the respect context preoutcome activities can be ignored when nothing more complicated is going on than, for instance, a brief exchange of stereotyped courtesies. In general, of course, the questions that apply to all values are applicable to the shaping and sharing of respect: who (in terms of qualifications, selection, perspective) with what base values employs what strategies to influence respect outcomes and effects?

Our previous discussion has probably made sufficiently clear what is involved in analyzing the remaining six values and institutions.*

The concept of "outcome ratio" suggests an important line of research effort. When goods are bought and sold in a "transaction," money ratios are called prices. Ratios can also be ascertained for barter, and, if the research is quite detailed, for gift chains in which no direct negotiation is allowed. If such intensive inquiries are made, we may discover that the capitalistic calculus is more widespread than is often asserted, or, at least, that it is undermining whatever ambiguities may exist in comparing gifts which are part of the traditional pattern. In the power arena, when they are at hand, votes are among the convenient means of expressing outcome ratios. Otherwise, much ingenuity needs to be expended in finding satisfactory operational indices. Social scientists are not as yet accustomed to thinking as persistently about outcome ratios for other values as for wealth or power. Hence the field worker is on his own to a much greater extent.

* [Tables were included from H. D. Lasswell and A. Kaplan, *Power and Society*, New Haven, Yale University Press, 1950.]

Step Three: Systematic Analysis
of All Interactions by Value and Practice

Some of what we have been saying anticipates the third step in intensifying research. This step consists in the systematic study of all interactions in terms of all values and practices. At this point we assume that research is sufficiently advanced to provide a rather detailed map of the total flow of societal activities during a given time period. The way is clear for more microscopic investigations. The fundamental point we have in mind in connection with our entire approach is that every interaction between two or more persons involves all values in some degree, however slight. The field investigator is never justified in making a "near zero" entry for any context unless he has explicitly considered the possibility that the phenomena are present.

The Minka report shows what is meant. At a certain stage in the study of Vicos it was obvious that Minkas were significant institutional structures. Enough incidental information had been picked up to sketch the institution. It was now decided to focus research attention by attending as many Minka occasions as possible and learning as much as could be found out about the sequence of activties that led up to and followed Minkas. It was also decided to interview on a large scale to obtain an account of Minkas that could not be directly observed. Obviously, it cannot be assumed that every interaction was recorded. Such a goal would be chimerical in any case. But we can safely say that situations were sampled with sufficiently high frequency to warrant a report.

In this connection it may be recorded that data on the Minka were gathered in waves and that the relatively late adoption of the dynamic functionalist approach had a discernible effect. When field work began at the hacienda, no focus was as explicit as this. When the value analysis was adopted, data relating to the Minka were examined in detail. Many gaps appeared. This was not surprising, since what a field worker reports depends largely upon what he is consciously or unconsciously ready to perceive. Additional research in the field provided information omitted during earlier stages. Undoubtedly, the anthropologists who try out dynamic functionalism will find themselves making similar transitions, supplementing and improvising in an effort to plug up the blanks left by missed opportunities.

The third step, to which we are now referring, is taken when the field investigator is able to focus intensively upon the finer structure of a situation. He notes interactions previously left to one side (often in the interest of staying at a uniform introductory level) or overlooked enirely. Now is the time when special effort can be made to catch the subtle byplay that takes place in human relations, to record the less formally organized modalities of interaction, to probe more searchingly toward the inner lives of people.

The entire relationship between the investigator and his society moves along through broadly discernible stages during which the transition from stranger to acquaintance to intimate occurs. There are advance intimations of the deeper depths even as there are dilatory characters who are indifferent, aloof, or hostile. Our expectation is that when a research worker is able to recognize the more delicate phenomena in a social process he is ready for the uniform intensification of most of his work.

As the data from the more intensive phases of field work pile up in the files, it is to be expected that many revisions will be made in the early classification of institutions and situations. Indeed, if this did not happen, the scientific investigator would be both surprised and chagrined. It is clear from every society of which we have knowledge that the surface view offers no one-to-one correspondence with the deeper vistas that eventually open up.

Reclassification may be considered briefly in connection with the transempirical features of a society. As a working rule, it will be recalled that we filed in the general category of rectitude all ceremonies symbolized as controlling or controlled by transempirical forces. By "transempirical" we intend to cover all that is not amenable to empirical vertification. As usual in all field work, this definition must be applied from two standpoints: that of participants in the culture and that of the scientific observers. It is to be found by research whether a given society draws an explicit line between the words that it uses for events which are describable by ordinary psychophysical means and the words for transempirical phenomena which may not be perceived (or, if allegedly perceived, only under circumstances that remain mysterious, that is, fundamentally inexplicable). When we say inexplicable, of course, we are not saying that it is beyond us to explain the factors which account for the subjective event of attributing transempirical significance to a given experience. We can explain the factors that account for the subjective event of experiencing a "luminous glow" without accepting the mystic's explanation that the restrictions of the flesh are transcended and the universal spirit manifests itself.

It will be recalled that at the first step we assigned to rectitude all conventional manifestations of religion, as well as ethical specializations. At the second step the problem was which situations to designate as outcomes and which as preoutcomes. It is convenient in many contexts to take the grand climax of a ceremony as the outcome phase, as when God is said to speak out of the cave and everyone prostrates himself in a prescribed manner before an image and the cave entrance. They key symbols that justify and account for existence may be celebrated here, and all this is part of what we have in mind when we speak of practices specialized to the rectitude value.

Let us imagine that further research presents a more complex picture. As part of the preparation for the great moment (which may be a gesture of acknowledgment and blessing), everyone may bring gifts to the worship area, gifts to be used by the ceremonial officers for their livelihood during the year. Assume that the gifts amount to crop percentages ranging from ten to eight, depending upon the size of the harvest (the richer participants perhaps bringing the most in absolute if not relative terms). What expectations exist concerning the individual who fails to contribute or even attend? Perhaps this is utterly unthinkable and has never happened in the memory of man. Such conduct may be recorded as the equivalent of our "nonhuman" act and assigned to an evil spirit. Plainly, a prescription is at stake whose source is imputed to be transempirical. It belongs unquestionably to the social mores, not to the countermores or expediencies.

Assume, however, that once in a great while someone inadvertently breaks the prescriptive rule, and does in fact languish and die, in effect committing suicide. Unquestionably, this is an extreme deprivation ("self by self"). Shall we classify the prescription in the power rather than the rectitude code? Another question: Assume that on the occasion of each celebration a few individuals offend. They fail to turn over enough property or they are away. What is expected to happen to them? And what does? Suppose they are treated with great severity, perhaps beaten and mutilated, thrown off their land, and reduced to begging. Is this rectitude or power?

Now, in all matters of classification we advise a relatively tentative and approximate approach. The main point is that we should be able to rely upon the integrity of the field worker's reports, not only in the sense that he is an honest and competent observer, but also because he has faithfully reminded himself to think of the total value ramifications that may be present in each interaction. We do not find it necessary in advance to define each term with exactly the same cut-off point (as between power and rectitude, for example). If observations are well reported we can translate the picture into our preferred usages. Since it is well known that folk societies exhibit an abundance of transempirical symbolizations, it is incumbent upon every anthropologist to put each fragment into the contexts where it is thought of or spoken. We take it for granted that features of the local myth may crop up anywhere in the flow of daily, monthly, and annual activities, and will constitute a large part of the bulk of the notes taken on the spot.

For many reasons we find it convenient to define the conception of power as we have, stressing a community-wide context and the severity of the actual or potential deprivation involved.

Our concern for human dignity means that in general we are opposed to the use of coercion in human affairs and desire to enlarge the range of voluntary cooperation. We are sufficiently well informed of the facts of life to cherish no illusions about the rapidity with which progress is likely to be made in this direction on all fronts and in all places. But we are concerned with organizing our knowledge of man in such a way that we can readily see where we are in reference to the overriding goal. Hence, we need to bring into the very heart of research the responsibility for reporting choice and constraint. Severe deprivations are by definition grave limitations upon choice, and we define the conception of power in a way that calls for a summing up of these constraints.

It is evident that we do not assume that all organizations which are locally called "governmental" are entirely devoted to negative sanctions. Our eight value analysis guarantees that any institution will be examined in a framework that reveals the total context of indulgence and deprivation. But a definitional point is significant here; we do not define an institution as performing a political function unless (besides all its other functions) it involves severe deprivations. We believe that our scientific concern for comparisons and our long-range concern for substituting persuasion for the more extreme forms of coercion are served thereby.

We think it likely that in our sense of the term the transempirical institutions found in folk societies are largely political. The degree to which this is so will be brought out in any specific society by the method of successive approximation that we are outlining in this paper.

Our conception of politics may be further exhibited by examining another hypothetical question of reclassification. We referred previously to problems that might arise in identifying the decision outcomes to be attributed to a council of elders. Consider the data that would lead us to make an initial attribution of the council, not to decision making, but to family (affection) institutions. Suppose the conventional outlook in the community is that the council speaks only in the name of a small group of prominent families and has jurisdiction only over the land controlled by these families. Assume that the families are generally known to live interspersed with others rather than contiguously. No doubt our first judgment would incline toward excluding the council from political institutions and adding it to the affection familial file.

Even though the council is not looked upon as an organ whose jurisdiction includes the whole territory, we may eventually list it among the power institutions, not because of the role that it plays for a few families but because of the fact gradually revealed, that its responses must be taken into account throughout the district by the many people who are deeply affected by what it does. For instance, we may learn that adjacent families are expected to pay taxes for the maintenance of roads and certain other facilities in the locality even though they lack formal representation in the council. These families may pay because they expect to undergo severe deprivations if they try to evade payment. Such deprivations may include the cutting off of water or exclusion from highways (which may mean no possibility of marketing crops). It may even be that gangs will be sent to beat up the negligent taxpayers, to set fire to their houses, or to rape their daughters. In our language this is a case of effective political control in an area despite the fact that many of those affected do not concede that taxes are authorized. Less important than classifying the council as "power" or not is the exhibition of the total context of its functional significance in the whole community. Note that our definition of power is such that under some conditions practically the entire network of human relations may be "politicized." A "politicized" society conforms to the Hobbesian image of primitive anarchy in which the hand of every man is raised against every other man. In a psychological sense such a society has been approximated in some modern nations in the form of "prison" or "garrison" regimes. In a setup of this kind not many people are able to select their sex partners, occupations, food, clothes, or other preferred outcomes, and they are explicitly aware of the negative sanctions by which they are hedged in.

This brings us to the problem of classifying situations in which the members of a society, though from our viewpoint possessing little choice, have no consciousness of being put upon or intimidated. This is the "slave who likes it." Here we classify doubly: once from the perspective of the participant and once from our standpoint.

Reference may now be made to a terminological matter. We use the term "power" to designate a relationship in which any value is used for severe sanctioning purposes. What is involved is most obvious, perhaps, in the case of the formal penalties that we ourselves apply in criminal cases. We may confiscate all of a man's wealth, ultimately deprive him of life (well-being), intefere drastically with his freedom of movement (respect), prevent him from seeing his wife and children (affection), cut him off from an accomplishment like playing polo in which he may be a top champion (skill), exclude him from church membership and denounce him vituperatively and continuously as a scandal to God and man (rectitude), prevent him from receiving news (enlightenment), exclude him from citizenship and from all public offices (power). It will be seen that a verbal duplication appears to be involved in speaking of all these as power. But this need not give rise to confusion if it is understood that we add the power reference when severe deprivations are involved, while retaining the other terms. In the same vein we observe that mild deprivations are not, strictly speaking, part of the power process and that a governmental institution in the conventional sense which imposes a mild deprivation is in this instance acting primarily as a respect, wealth, or some other non-power institution.

12

Reflections on Deference

EDWARD SHILS

HAROLD LASSWELL was exceptional in his generation in combining the macrosociological view with a great interest in and familiarity with personality functions and their manifestations. From Marx, Max Weber, and Pareto he elaborated a tough-minded, worldly view of the harsh and constricting life of man in society. From Freud he drew the basic conception of the personality system. To each of these he added what was unequaled in its time and what is still very rare, namely, the alertness and wealth of imagination which permitted him to see the functions of the personality operating in the macrosocial environment—in the presence of power and class conflict, nationalism, war, and revolution.

When I search for a few central variables among the many with which Harold Lasswell has dealt in over forty years of fertile and unremitting inquiry, I think that deference would be one of these. It is not only because on the very first pages of two of his most brilliant books[1] deference was designated, together with income and safety, as one of the three values the distribution of which characterized the main features of any society. It is rather because deference has continued to preoccupy him throughout his long and continuous intellectual evolution.

When he wrote of deference in his early books, he included in it both power and respect, and he did not distinguish them clearly from each other. His psychoanayltic sensitivity disclosed the importance of respect even before he had isolated it in his conceptual schemes. In 1933 he wrote: "Rebuffed by a world which accorded them diminished deference, limited in the opportunities afforded by economic reality, the members of this class (i.e., 'the lower bourgeoisie') needed new objects of devotion and new targets of aggression."[2] In *World Politics and Personal Insecurity* (1935) he wrote: "Denials of deference release tremendous hostility against the environment and the personalities involved remain insecure until they have worked out a positive means of expressing themselves."[3]

It was only during and after the Second World War that he began to distinguish the major components of deference. In 1941 he wrote: "To be deferred to is to be taken into consideration—to be consulted, appreciated and clarified. In a democratic commonwealth there is a relatively general share in power, respect and insight."[4] "Respect" or "appreciation" as objects of human striving and as attitudes accorded to others became more prominent in his thought although, as I have indicated, he had already been very sensitive to their importance. Indeed, one of the reasons he embraced the Hawthorne studies of Mayo, Whitehead, and Rothlisberger so avidly was that they bore testimony to the impact of variations in respect on behavior.

Toward the end of the forties, some changes in terminological usage occurred. Instead of deference including both power and deference, as I shall use it in what follows and as Lasswell sometimes used it in his earliest writings, deference, or in his new terminology, respect, became an independent value. "Respect is the value of status, of honor, of recognition and prestige, the 'glory' or 'reputation' which Hobbes classes with gain and safety as one of the three fundamental human motivations."[5] In the same work, he wrote: "There is in our culture a vast and increasingly intense concern with respect (both from self and others) as a major human value. . . . This concern has however been comparatively inarticulate; certainly social scientists have grossly neglected its value in contrast to the extensive treatment accorded to power and wealth."[6]

Although Harold Lasswell's earliest treatment of deference, in the sense in which I shall be employing the term, had been one major element in his conception of the stratification system of total societies, he did not examine the problems connected with it at any length. In the paper which follows I shall try to explore some of these problems and, in so doing, pay tribute to my much esteemed teacher and friend by extending and elaborating some of the many lines of inquiry which he helped to open up to us three decades ago. It is now almost that long since Herbert Goldhamer and I tried to clarify what Lasswell called deference by breaking it down into power and status.[7] I continue one part of that analysis now.

I

INTO every action of one human toward another there enters an element of appreciation or derogation of the "partner" to whom the action is directed. It enters in varying degrees; some actions contain very little of it and some consist almost entirely of appreciation or derogation. In most actions the appreciative or derogatory elements are mingled with others, such as commanding, coercing, cooperating, purchasing, loving, etc.

Appreciation and derogation—respect and disrespect in Lasswell's usage—are responses to properties of the partner, of the role which he is performing, of the categories into which he is classified, or of the relationships in which he stands to third persons or categories of persons—against the background of the actor's own image of himself with respect to these properties. This element of appreciation or derogation is different from those responses to the past or anticipated actions of the partner which are commands, acts of obedience, the provision of goods or services, the imposition of injuries such as the withholding or withdrawal of goods and services, and acts of love or hatred.

These acts of appreciation or derogation I shall designate as "deference." The term "deference" will refer both to positive or high deference and to negative or low deference or derogation. When I say that one person defers to another, I shall ordinarily mean that he is acknowledging that person's worth or dignity, but when I speak of a person's "deference-position," that might refer to either a high or low deference-position. What I call deference here and what Harold Lasswell calls "respect" is sometimes called "status" by other writers; I myself have called it that in the past. There is nothing wrong with the term "status" except that it has become associated with a conception of the phenomenon which I wish to modify. The term "deference," with its clear intimation of a person who defers, brings out an aspect of the phenomenon which in my view has not been made sufficiently explicit in work on this subject in recent years.

Deference is closely related to such phenomena as prestige, honor, respect (and obscurity, shame, dishonor, and disrespect), fame (and infamy), glory (and ignominy), dignity (and indignity). It will perhaps be worthwhile to make some of the differences in overtones of these words a little more precise, since that might make a little clearer what I mean by deference. Prestige carries with it intimations of centrality; a prestigious person engages the approving attention of many other persons. Deference, on the other hand, involves an entire distribution from high to low. Honor is a consequence of an act of deference objectified by institutions or authorities which are empowered to confer it. (It also has a connotation of an internalized norm of conduct which is thought appropriate to a given deference-position or to a given set of deference-entitlements which are interpreted by their possessor as "conferring" a deference-position on an "objective" scale.) Respect suggests genuineness, not only of the sincerity of the judgment but also of its cognitive correctness in the perception of the attributes of the respected person. Fame is like prestige in that it entails radiation from one or a few to many persons. In contrast to prestige, which implies transience, fame has overtones of relatively long duration. Fame also inheres in particular persons, circles of persons, or corporate bodies; by contrast, deference is granted to anonymous or abstract categories of persons who themselves are not perceived. Dignity is closest to deference; an assessment of deference-position is an attribution or acknowledgment of dignity.

II

Acts of deference are performed in face-to-face relationships and in the relationship of actors who have no direct interactive relationship with each other but who are members of the same society. (It can exist too in the relationships of individual actors or collectivities of different societies, although to the extent that this occurs, the societies in question cease to be totally separate and distinct societies.)

The granting of deference entails an attribution of superiority (or inferiority) but it is not the same as an attribution of goodness or wickedness. It does, however, often have such overtones; occasionally there is a suggestion that the superiority requires goodness for its completeness. It is an attribution of merit (or of defect); it is an assessment which attributes worthiness (or unworthiness) which is quite distinct from an attribution of moral qualities. What this worthiness consists in is an obscure matter.

To be the recipient of deference from another actor is a widespread desire of human beings. Deference may be possessed in several ways: in some tangible or clearly perceivable and discrete form of action from other persons, in an autonomous symbolic form which is regarded as an "objectification of deference" quite apart from the deferential actions of concrete actors, or by believing oneself to be entitled to it through the possession of the qualities which are conventionally accepted as the grounds on which deference is elicited or granted. It might even be said that the desire to be "worthy" is a "need" of human beings in the same way in which affection, erotic gratification, and the satisfaction of organic needs such as nutriment and bodily warmth are "needs."

To grant or accord deference is also a "need" of human beings which is aroused or generated by the process of interaction and by the fact of living in a society which goes beyond the limited radius of face-to-face interaction. Just as they wish to be worthy and to have that worth acknowledged by the deference of other persons, so they also often have a need to live in a social world implanted with worthiness, to acknowledge the embodiments of that worth, and to derogate those who are unworthy.

Deference of the sort which I discuss in this paper is a way of expressing an assessment of the self and of others with respect to macrosocial properties. By macrosocial properties I refer to those characteristics which define the role or position of persons in the larger (usually national) society in which they live. The act or symbolization of deference is an attribution of deference-position or status in the total society. In acts of deference performed within face-to-face relationships or within limited corporate groups, the deference is often but not always accorded primarily with respect to status in the larger society. The extent to which this is so varies; deference can be accorded primarily with respect to roles within a particular relationship or corporate group. The deference accorded to a father as head of a family is not macrosocial deference when it does not make reference to the father's position in the society outside the family. The deference awarded to a superior or colleague within a corporate body is a mixture of deference with respect to intracorporate status and to macrosocial status. The deference accorded to a woman or to women as a category or to a man or to men as a category is at the margin of macrosocial deference. The deference accorded to age or youth is similarly marginal. Both age and sex are significant factors in the determination of the "life chances" of a person and therewith of the likelihood that that person will receive deference. Moreover, they are themselves the objects of deferential judgments. Yet the deference granted to age or to sex seems to be of a different order from that deference which is an appreciation of worthiness or a derogation of unworthiness. I am not sure why this is so.

III

THE disposition to defer and the performance of acts of deference are evoked by the perception, in the person or classes of persons perceived, of certain characteristics or properties of their roles or actions. These characteristics or properties we shall call deference-entitling properties or entitlements. While they do not by themselves automatically arouse judgments of deference, they must be seen or believed to exist for deference to be granted. Deference-entitlements include occupational role and accomplishment, wealth (including type of wealth), income and the mode of its acquisition, style of life, level of educational attainment, political or corporate power, proximity to persons or roles exercising political or corporate power, kinship connections, ethnicity, performance on behalf of the community or society in relation to external communities or societies, and the possession of "objective acknowledgments" of deference such as titles or ranks. Moral qualities such as courage or generosity are also deference-entitlements but they are difficult to perceive except when distinguished by titles, "honors," or other such "objectifications" of deference. But moral qualities require more than the visibility given by "objectification": they are incapable of being the objects of macrosocial deference in a stable and enduring manner unless they are associated with other deference-entitlements. These other entitlements are macrosocial entitlements but, as I wrote above, it is on the basis of the perception of these macrosocial entitlements that individuals and classes or more or less anonymous individuals who are believed to possess some constellation of these entitlements are granted deference; it is on the basis of the possession of these properties that they grant deference to themselves and claim it from others. It is on the basis of simultaneous assessments of their own and of others' deference-entitlements that they regulate their conduct toward others and anticipate the deferential (or derogatory) responses of others.

Why should these properties be singled out as pertinent to macrosocial deference? What is it about them which renders them deference-relevant? Why are they, rather than kindness, amiability, humor, manliness, femininity, and other temperamental qualities which are so much appreciated in life, regarded as relevant to the deference which is granted with regard to position in the whole society—however dimly that is perceived—and which penetrates into sectional, corporate, and even interpersonal deference?

The cognitive maps which human beings form of their world include a map of their society. This map locates the primary or corporate groups of which they are active members and the larger society which includes these groups, but with which they have little active contact. The map which delineates this society entails a sense of membership as such in that society and a sense of the vital character of that membership—as well as an image of one's status in the society. Even though the individual revolts against that society and seeks by denial or departure to give up his membership in his society, it is very seldom that he is able to free himself completely from his sense of membership in it. The society is not just an ecological fact or an environment; it is thought to possess a vitality which is inherent in it and membership in it confers a certain vitality on those who belong to it. It is a significant cosmos from which members derive some of their significance to themselves and to others. This significance is a charismatic significance; that is, it signifies the presence and operation of what is thought to be of ultimate and determinative significance.

If we examine each of the deference-relevant properties with reference to the extent to which, and the way in which, it can have charisma attributed to it, we will see that each obtains its significance as an entitlement to deference primarily by virtue of that attribution.

Occupational role is ordinarily thought of as one of the most significant entitlements to deference. The most esteemed occupations in societies, for which there are survey or impressionistic data, are those which are in their internal structure and in their functions closest to the *centers* of their respective societies. The centers of society are those positions which exercise earthly power and mediate man's relation to the order of existence (spiritual forces, cosmic powers, values and norms) which legitimates or withholds legitimacy from the earthly powers or which dominates earthly existence. The highest "authorities" in society—governors, judges, prime ministers, presidents, and fundamental scientists—are those whose roles enable them to control society or to penetrate into the ultimate laws and forces which are thought to control the world and human life. Occupational roles are ranked in a sequence which appears to correspond approximately with the extent to which each role possesses these properties. The charismatic content of a given occupational role will vary with the centrality of the corporate body or sector in which it is carried on. The most authoritative role in a peripheral corporate body will carry less charisma than the same type of role in a more centrally located corporate body. The roles which exercise no authority and which are thought to have a minimum of contact with transcendent powers call forth least deference.

Of course, occupational roles and their incumbents are also deferred to on account of certain highly correlated deference-entitling properties such as the income which the practice of the occupation provides, the educational level of its practitioners, the ethnic qualities of its incumbents, etc. Conversely, occupational roles which are ill-remunerated and the incumbents of which have little education and are of derogated ethnic stocks receive little deference because of these traits as well as because of the nature and functions of the occupational role itself. Nonetheless, occupational role is an independent entitlement to deference. (These entitlements are linked with each other, and not only statistically; for example, a person of a derogated ethnic stock will, in societies in which ethnicity is believed to contain some vital quality, be thought unfit to exercise occupational roles with an incommensurate quantity of charisma.)

Beyond occupational role, accomplishment within the role is a deference-entitlement both micro- and macrosocially. To be a judge is to be entitled to a high deference-position, but to be an outstanding judge is to be entitled to an even higher one; to be not only a scientist but an outstanding scientist constitutes a further deference-entitlement. This not only because outstanding accomplishment renders its performer more "visible" and therefore more capable of possessing prestige or fame (and more likely to be the recipient of deference), but much more because accomplishment is the realization of the potentiality of creative action. Creativity is a feature of centrality; creative action makes the creator part of the center.

Wealth is deferred to—great wealth is greatly deferred to, and poverty is derogated—because it is powerful. But without association with charismatic occupation or with political power, wealth is not as much deferred to as when it enjoys those associations. Wealth which is manifested only by purchasing power is not as esteemed as wealth which embodies its power in the ownership and management of landed estates or in the directorship of great industrial corporations employing many thousands of persons. In one important aspect wealth is purchasing power, and as such it is like income. But it may also be the power to employ and the power to dismiss from employment. These powers over physiological existence and access to dignity are tremendous, but they are not peculiar to wealth and are quite compatible with the propertylessness of those who exercise these powers. Wealth also calls forth deference when it is associated with a certain style of life, for which it is indeed a condition.

The contempt and hostility toward the *parvenu* (the first generation of wealth) which was noticed in second and third generation plutocratic and grand bourgeois circles at the end of the last century and the early part of the present century was the response of the wealthy who had established their rightful claim to deference by the cultivation of an "appropriate" style of life to those who wished to share their deference-position before they had legitimated themselves by showing that they really knew how to spend their money on consumption, education, charity, etc. To be willing to share a deference position with the *parvenu* would be a denial of their own standards by the established plutocracy; it would entail deferring to those who do not "deserve" it and it would be a derogation of their own worthiness of deference.

Thus, wealth is both a derivative and a conditional entitlement to deference. It is derivative from occupation and from the exercise of power over persons and over the soil; it is conditional to a "style of life."* Alone and in itself it is significant primarily as a potentiality of power. To gain the deference which sociologists often assert is the reward of wealth it must find completion in a wider complex of properties such as the actual exercise of power through an authoritative occupational role, a "validating" style of life, etc.

Income too is regarded as an entitlement to deference as a manifestation of power, although this power is limited and segmental because it is exercised in the specific buyer-seller relationship. Confined as it is to very specific exchange relationships, purchasing power is not a very weighty entitlement to deference. Income alone possesses only potential deference-entitlement.† Nonetheless, a high income, like a large fortune, is regarded as a valid entitlement to deference when it is used to acquire what it can most legitimately be used for, namely, the style of life to which it corresponds, or to acquire other purchasable entitlements like educational opportunity and associational membership. Income is therefore a *conditional* deference-entitlement which ac-

---

* Cf. the anomaly experienced in the assessment of very wealthy persons who do not *use* their wealth in the practice of an appropriate style of life—who exercise no power through its use (employing no one), who exercise no control over the agricultural or industrial properties in which it is invested, and who practice no occupation. All they have is the potentiality which, as is known from the observation of other cases, wealth possesses. They enjoy such deference as they receive—apart from what they might receive by virtue of their family name—because of the potentiality rather than the actuality of their exercise of power. Potentiality calls forth less deference than does actuality. As a result, they are the objects of an ambivalent judgment; deference is granted for the potentiality of power which wealth confers but greater deference is withheld for their failure to complete the potentiality of wealth by manifesting it in the fuller pattern which is incumbent on anyone who is high in any single distribution.

† Although every resource in a particular distributive category contains the potentiality of conversion into a position in another distributive category, resources vary in their degree of specificity. Income can be used to purchase objects at relatively fixed rates (household furnishings, books, education, etc.; education, however, is not equally specific in the response which it is thought to be entitled to call forth. Neither is political authority. In general we can say that the more diffuse a potentiality, the greater is its entitlement to deference.

quires deference primarily when manifested in another category. In itself it possesses such charisma as an immediate and specific potential power confers.

A style of life is a deference-entitlement because it is a pattern of conduct which is a voluntary participation in an order of values. A style of life is value-permeated; it demonstrates a connection with a stratum of being in which true value resides. The conventional and long-standing deference given to the "leisure classes" was not given because idleness was believed to be a virtue or because work or occupation was thought to be a burden, but because leisure was the framework necessary to the cultivation and practice of a value-infused pattern of life. Like an authoritative occupation, it was a value-generating and value-infused existence. More than authoritative occupations, it belongs, despite its material embodiment, to the realm of culture. It includes eating (commensality) "in style," living in the midst of an appropriate decor, in an appropriate quarter (a "good address"),* surrounded by servants who provide ritualized deference as well as labor power.† Much of "style of life" involves association, convivial and commensal, with other persons of established and acknowledged high deference-position. But it is not merely that. The high deference-position itself is a function, the performance of value-infused actions. Such actions manifest "taste," which is discrimination in matters of value, and "style," which is a ritualized embodiment of values. In its highest form, "style of life" was found in courts and palaces, in great country houses and grand bourgeois establishments. Style of life requires income as a condition but it is not an entitlement to deference simply as a direct function of wealth and income or simply as an indicator of wealth and income. It is facilitated by wealth and income but it enhances them and transfigures them. It does so because it par-

---

* A "good address" is one in a quarter where other persons of established and acknowledged high deference-positions reside.

† Of course, "style of life" can be shriveled to hedonistic self-indulgence, "conspicuous consumption," or sheer idleness, all of which are capable of gaining ascendancy within the pattern but which, in doing so, diminish somewhat the amount of deference received.

takes of a charismatic quality which they contain only in their potentiality but not in their sheer and specific actuality.

The level of educational attainment possesses deference-entitling properties partly because it is often conditional to entry into authoritative, creative, and remunerative occupational roles, but even more because it is an assimilation into an ideal realm. It is an assimilation into a pattern of values and beliefs which are part of the center of existence. The "possessor" of a large amount of education is often an incumbent of an authoritative or a creative occupation; as an actual or potential incumbent of such an occupation, he receives deference. Through incumbency in such an occupation, he is likely to receive a higher than average income and an appropriate style of life; for these he receives deference also.* The educated person is one who has received the culture of beliefs and appreciations which are central in the society; he has been initiated into the very center of the central value system. These beliefs may be scientific beliefs about the way the world works, or they may be beliefs about the "essential" nature of the society, its history, its religion, its cultural traditions and objectifications. Education is also the acquisition of skills which prepare for participation in the center of the society through the exercise of authority, technological performance, and the discovery and transmission of vital truths about the universe, man, and society—in short, for *creating* and *ordering*. Education is an autonomous, nonderivative entitlement to deference because it is integral to and testifies to its possessor's participation in the charismatic realm.

The exercise of power, whether in an occupation or through the employment of purchasing power, is determinative of the life chances of the persons over whom it is exercised; therewith it shares in the charisma which is inherent in the control of life. It is difficult to separate power from occupational role because much or even most power is exercised in occupational roles and cor-

* The deference-entitlement of education is also affected by the institutions and countries in which it is acquired. Some schools and universities and university systems are thought to be more central than others. Those educated in them acquire more of a charismatically infused culture.

porate bodies, particularly if we include inherited and entre-preneurially initiated roles and appointed and elected incumbency in roles in the state, church, armies, economic organizations, universities, etc.* Authority exercised through occupational roles becomes more diffuse the higher its position within any corporate hierarchy, whether the hierarchy be religious, political, military, or whatever. Its diffuseness, which is another facet of its creating and ordering responsibility and capacity, is crucial to its deference-entitlement.

There is undoubtedly some power which is not occupational in the locus of its exercise. It might be worthwhile, therefore, to employ a separate category for power as a deference-entitlement for those persons whose charismatic ascendancy is not a function of an occupational role.†

Where all members of a society, or at least all adults, stand in at least one important respect in equal relationship to the exercise of authority in government by virtue of citizenship, deference is dispersed in the direction of equality. The sharing of power and the attendant equalization of deference through citizenship does not abolish the inequality of power or the inequality of deference associated with the unequal distribution of authoritative occupational roles. It does, however, offset it in some situations to a very considerable extent.

Relative proximity to persons in powerful roles is an other deference-entitlement. The proximity may be a fiduciary relation-

---

* Our inherited categories for classifying roles still bear the marks of the nineteenth-century distinctions between the economic and the political spheres. A classification of roles in accordance with the amount of authority they exercise and the creativity they permit would render superfluous the separation of power from occupation as separate entitlements to deference.

† Just as within occupations, there are interindividual differences in creativity or productivity, so it is perfectly conceivable that this creativity can manifest itself avocationally and outside the corporate bodies within which such activities are ordinarily carried on. There are religious prophets who arise from the laity and outside existing religious bodies, revolutionary politicians who are not incorporated into the established political order, and intimates of rulers who have no formal political occupation and whose own occupations are not constitutively endowed with power. All of these are exercisers of power in a way which is independent of their occupational roles.

ship between the incumbent of a very authoritative role and his "personal staff," or it may be a close personal relationship of friendship or affection. It may be little more than the acquaintanceship of frequent encounter, or it may be primordial tie of kinship. In ethnically heterogeneous and hierarchical societies in which ethnicity is an entitlement to deference, ethnic linkage to the dominant ethnic stratum confers deference. Whatever the content of the relationship, the important thing is that the magnitude of its entitlement to deference for a given person is assessed (1) by the deference-position of the person to whom he stands in proximity, and (2) by the degree of proximity. To be the son or cousin or the intimate friend of a person of no significant status adds no status to this in that degree of proximity; indeed, it makes for the insignificant status of those who stand in such proximity. Being a close friend or a frequently met colleague of a person of a high deference-position confers more deference than would a slighter degree of friendship or a less intense collegial intercourse. The deference-position of the person at the end of the chain is determined by the properties already referred to; the relationship is the channel through which a fundamentally charismatic quality is transmitted. Just as the member of a corporate body participates in the charisma of his organization, whether it is a university, a church, or a government, so membership in a personal relationship or in a primordial collectivity (for example, a family) is constituted by or results from a diffusion of the charisma of the central person or role of the collectivity. Those who come from "famous" families and those who keep the company of important persons who move in "important" circles share in the charismatic quality of those whose charisma gives fame to families and importance to circles. The three modes of linkage— primordial, personal, and collegial—are all different from each other and yet each has been regarded as a legitimate channel through which charisma and the consequent entitlement to deference can be shared.

It is relevant to point out that the significance of the kinship link with persons of high deference-position has diminished in modern societies ever since the French Revolution. From the seventeenth century onward critics of the existing social order have stressed the injustice of allocating rewards on the basis of kinship. This indeed, was the basic element in the criticism of aristocracy. It was argued that achievement was a more just entitlement to rewards than kinship. As the center of the economic system passed from agriculture to industry and as the joint stock company restricted the significance of the family firm in industry, kinship connection became less important in the allocation of rewards; it did not by any means become unimportant, but it became less preponderant. The growth of the nuclear family and the attenuation of the sense of identification with lineage (although it has by no means disappeared) have also reduced the importance of kinship as a criterion. Its importance relative to achievement and authority has declined, but it is unlikely to become totally insignificant as long as individuals grow in families and identify themselves with their families.

Ethnicity is very much like the kinship tie—both are primordial, being constituted by the significance attributed to a presumed genetic connection and the primordial unity arising therefrom. Unlike kinship connection as an entitlement to deference, ethnicity does not refer to a genetic link with a particular important person or persons. It is a link with a collectivity in which a vital, charismatic quality is believed to be diffused. It is thought to represent the possession of some quality inherent in the ethnic aggregate and shared by all its members. Indeed, the possession of that "essential" quality, as manifested in certain external features such as color, hair form, physiognomy, and physique, constitutes membership in the aggregate. In societies which are ethnically homogeneous, the ethnic entitlement is neutral; in societies which are ethnically plural, the ethnic entitlement can be neutralized only by an overriding civility or sense of citizenship or by disaggregation in a society to the point where it almost ceases to be a society. It is also conceivable that in an ethnically heterogeneous society, ethnicity might lose its significance as an entitlement to deference. If civility were to become more pronounced within a given society, ethnicity, as well as other entitlements, for example, authority, might diminish in its deference significance to the point of indifference. Likewise, if humanity—simply the possession of human qualities—were to become more pronounced as a deference-entitlement, ethnicity would diminish. It might not disappear under these conditions, but it would not be a major criterion in the allocation of deference even though human beings still continued to identify themselves and others in the light of their ethnic properties. It is also possible that human beings, everywhere or in particular societies, might become ethnically totally indifferent. This might in turn lead to the disappearance of ethnic differences if it were accompanied by randomness in mating. It could, however, only do so if previously there were not a very high correlation between ethnic distribution and the distributions of educational and occupational opportunity. Ethnic differences would also disappear once ethnic identity diminished to the point of indifference if there were far-reaching equality of educational and occupational opportunity.

A real provenience, whether it be rural or urban, regional or local, provincial or metropolitan, can also be a deference-entitlement in a variety of ways. In some respects, it can be derivative from occupational roles and the exercise of authority insofar as particular occupational roles and the exercise of authority tend to be more concentrated—although not necessarily in the same locations—to a greater extent in some areas than in others. It might also be derivative from the greater proximity to authority and eminence which is more likely in some areas than in others. But the soil and the city might be independent entitlements, one gaining ascendancy over the other in accordance with prevailing beliefs concerning the sanctity of the soil or the charisma of urbane existence.

Religious adherence or affiliation is similar to ethnicity in that it is a deference-entitlement referring to membership in a collectivity. In this case, however, the collectivity is constituted by the sharing of beliefs about sacred things and therewith by the sharing of the charisma of the church or sect. Whereas practically all societies are differentiated in occupational roles and in income and power or authority and are bound to be so by their nature as societies, ethnic and religious heterogeneity is not inevitable. Nonetheless, in societies which are religiously heterogeneous, there is likely to be a difference in the deference significance of adherence to the various religions. This might be a function of differences in the concentration of authoritative and creative roles in the various religious communities rather than differences in the intrinsic entitlement to deference attributed to the various religions. (In fact, the existence of religious pluralism, where the religions are taken seriously by their respective adherents, is likely to lead to dissensus regarding the deference-entitlement of the various religious communities.)

Indulgence conferred on the community or on society by protecting it from injury or by enhancing its position—power, wealth, deference—among other communities or societies is regarded as an entitlement to deference for those who confer such indulgence. Successful military men, politicians and statesmen, diplomats, athletes in international competitions, literary men and artists are deferred to within their own societies in proportion to their external deference or their enhancement of the power of their own society vis-à-vis other societies. The enhancement of the deference-position and power of the society enhances the deference-position of its members by virtue of their membership in it. It is the same here as in the case of proximity to importance or membership in primordial collectivities. There is a sense of some shared essential quality with those who "represent" the society.*

A title to deference conferred by the major deference-bearing institutions of the society is an entitlement to deference. Titles, however, are derivative entitlements. They are awarded to those who have achieved something which would in itself, according to the dominant value system, entitle them to deference. They are also awarded to those whose kinship links with persons of

---

* There is a deference-stratification among societies. It includes the deference-stratification of whole societies and an international deference-stratification system of individuals which is, however, extremely fragmentary.

high deference-position would in itself, even without a title, confer deference on them. In a sense, a title confirms and renders more explicit the deference-positions which have been attained through achievement or kinship. Nevertheless, acknowledgment by authority in the form of a title or a distinction has some measure of autonomous value as an entitlement. It operates like proximity since it is the granting of acknowledgment by a person or institution which is itself already established and acknowledged in its deference-position.

Such are the criteria by which deference is allocated in societies. They are not all of equal importance in the formation of deference judgments nor do their relative weights remain constant through time or among societies. Ethnicity, area, and religion might vary considerably in their significance in accordance with the strength of the sense of civility and the extent and intensity of religious belief. Education might become more important when a larger proportion of the population seeks education and possesses different amounts and kinds of education. The more equal the distribution of any given deference-entitlement, the less weight it has in differentiating the deference-positions of the members of a society. This does not mean that it loses its significance in the determination of the allocation of deference; it does mean that it ceases to differentiate the worth of individuals. In fact, while ceasing to differentiate, it might at the same time raise the deference-position of most individuals throughout the society. There is also a possibility that a particular criterion might become irrelevant, or at least diminish in relevance, to deference, losing its influence on the level of deference as it ceases to discriminate among individuals, groups, and strata. We have already discussed the diminution of the significance of kinship connection and ethnicity. The same might be true of the other deference variables. A greater equality of income might diminish the significance of income in differentiating persons and families with respect to deference. (But there is no certainty that it would; small differences might be magnified.) Similarly, if we can imagine a society, the technology of which is so automated that a large part of the gainfully employed population has ceased to be differentiated by occupation, we would be confronted by a situation in which occupations, at least for a large part of the population, would lose their capacity to confer different deference-positions on their practitioners, at least within the stratum in question. Of course, there might develop a very pronounced difference in deference between the minority which performs highly complicated occupations and the rest of the population.

IV

THE phenomena of the stratification system are generally thought of as so massive in their impact on the rest of society that it is only natural that they too should be conceived of as having a substantial existence. Indeed, they are spoken of as if they possessed a continuous, almost physical, tangibility which enables them to be apprehended by relatively gross methods of observation. In fact, many of these properties are very discontinuous or intermittent in their performance. When they are not actual, they fall into a condition of "latency." The different entitlements vary in the continuity and substantiality of their performance or manifestation. And what is true of entitlements to deference applies even more to deference behavior itself.

First of all, however, before considering deference behavior as such, I should like to consider the substantiality and continuity of the entitlements.

For example, occupational roles are performed during one- to two-thirds of the waking life of the human being for most of the days of each week and for most of the weeks of the year over a period of forty to fifty or more years, through youth, adulthood, and old age. A wealthy person usually has his wealth in the form of real property, chattels, or convertible paper, available to him whenever he wishes to call upon it and as long as he owns it. The receipt and expenditure of income is a less continuous property, not only because the amount of income received fluctuates or varies over the course of a decade or a lifetime but also because once expended it ceases to be available and because when not being used it is not visible. Only the results of expended income are visible in the material or tangible components of a style of life. Income is *recurrent;* it can be regularly recurrent as a disposable sum but not *continuously,* and it is not always *substantially* manifested.

The style of life of a person or a family is a pattern heterogeneous in its composition and pervasive in apparel, speech, and domestic arrangements, physical, social, and cultural. Its material apparatus is grossly observable. Among the deference-entitlements it is like occupational role in that it is performed, enacted, or lived in a larger proportion of waking time (and even sleeping time) than the other deference-entitlements. Style of life is, with occupational role, the most substantial and continuous of the various deference-entitlements. It is, with occupation, the most visible.

Level and type of educational attainment is a different kind of thing. It is like kinship in the sense that it is membership in a category which entails no present action. (Indeed, kinship entails no action on the part of the actor in question. It is a *past* biological connection and a *present* genetic composition and classification by self and others.) Level of educational attainment, insofar as it is a past qualification for present incumbency in a role, has ceased to exist except as a mark of a past accomplishment, like a medal awarded for heroism in a long-past battle. Where it is interpreted as an approximate indication of present level of culture, it refers either to very discontinuously performed actions or to a diffuse but more continuous operative state of mind. Insofar as it refers to number of years in which studies were carried on, to the subjects studied and certifications which attest to amounts, etc., it refers to past events which provide a basis for present classification by self and others. The self-designation as a member of a class so characterized is a present action but it does not necessarily entail the diffuse state of mind ("the educated mind") referred to in the preceding sentence. The behavior motivated by awareness of the self as an "educated person" is multiform, diffuse, and difficult to observe. Thus, while to an external analyst, the level of educational atttainment is a stable property of a person, it is not continuously operative in that person's action or interaction with others. It is a fluctuating and intermittent quality, sometimes of high salience, sometimes latent. It need not be so in all societies, in all strata, or in all individuals. In societies or strata which are highly "education-conscious," it will be more continuously salient as a categorial property than in those which are less "education-conscious." Persons of a given level of educational attainment will manifest it more substantially in their speech, thought, and conduct.

Power, which is so closely and often associated with the performance of occupational role, resembles it in this respect too since it is often exercised or performed for significantly continuous periods with sufficiently regular recurrence.

The foregoing observations are intended to render a little more explicit than usual the temporal discontinuity of entitlements, their intermittence and periodicity of performance and visibility. We have done this because these characteristics of entitlement affect their probability of being perceived and therewith of calling forth deference. We have also done it because we wish to call attention to what appear to us to be important, even if not readily evident, features of deference behavior.

The term "status," when it is used to refer to deference-position, ordinarily carries with it, as we suggested earlier, overtones of the stability, continuity, and pervasiveness which are possessed by sex and age. A person who has a given status tends to be thought of as having that status at every moment of his existence as long as that particular status is not replaced by another. One of the reasons we have chosen to use the term "deference-position" in place of "status" is that it makes a little more prominent the fact that status is not a substantial property of the person which arises automatically from the possession of certain entitlements, but is in fact an element in a relationship between the person deferred to and the deferent person. Deference toward another person is an attitude which is manifested in behavior.

Acts of deference judgment are evaluative classifications of self and other. As classifications they transcend in their reference the things classified. A person who is evaluatively classified by an act of deference on the basis of his occupation is in that classification even when he is not performing his occupational role. It is he who is classified and not just his occupation. The classification and the derived deference-judgment are applied to him by himself and by others even when he is not engaged in his occupational role. (For that matter, the classification might not be attached to him in the course of his performance of his occupational role.)

Because it is a generalization, the classificatory deference-judgment attains some measure of independence from the intermittence of entitlements. It has an intermittence of its own which is not necessarily synchronized with that of the entitlements.

Overt, concentrated acts of deference such as greetings and presentations are usually shortlived; that is, they are performed for relatively short periods and then "disappear" until the next appropriate occasion. The appropriate occasions for the performance of concentrated acts of deference might be regular in their recurrence (e.g., annually or weekly or even daily), but except for a few "deference-occupations" they are not performed with the high frequency and density over extended periods in the way in which occupational roles are performed. But does deference consist exclusively of the performance of concentrated deferential actions? Is there a "deference vacuum" when concentrated deferential actions are not being performed? Where does deference go when it is not being expressed in a grossly tangible action?

To answer this question, it is desirable to examine somewhat more closely the character of attenuated deference actions. There are concentrated, exclusively deferential actions which are nothing but deferential actions just as there are exclusively power or style-of-life or occupational actions. Occupational actions are substantial; all effort within a given space and time is devoted to their performance, and they can be seen clearly by actor and observer as occupational actions. The exercise of authority has many of these features, especially when it is exercised in an authoritative occupational role. Expenditures of money are of shorter duration but they too are clearly definable because they too are concentrated. The acts of consumption and conviviality which are comprised in a style of life are of longer duration but they too are clearly defined. On the other hand, level of educational attainment and kinship connection and ethnicity are not actual actions at all; they are classifications in which "objectively" the classified person is continuously present, although once present in the class he might do little or nothing to manifest or affirm it in his actions.

But deference actions—deferring to self and other, receiving deference from self and other—are actions. They result in and are performed with reference to classifications, but they are actions nonetheless. They are not, however, always massive actions of much duration. They occur moreover mainly at the margin of or intertwined with other types of action. Deference actions performed alone are usually very shortlived; they open a sequence of interaction and they close it. Between beginning and fusion with end, deference actions are performed in nondeferential actions. Throughout the process of interaction they are attenuated in the substance of the relationship in which the performance of tasks appropriate to roles in corporate bodies, civil roles, personal relationships, etc., occurs. Deference actions have always been largely components of other actions; they are parts of the pattern of speaking to a colleague, a superior, or an inferior about the "business at hand" in an authoritatively hierarchical corporate body. They are also parts of the pattern of speaking about or to a fellow citizen, of acting toward him over a distance (as in an election). In other words, deference actions seldom appear solely as deference actions, and those which do are not regarded, especially in the United States, as a particularly important part of interaction in most situations. Nonetheless, deference is demanded and is accepted in an attenuated form.

This, then, is the answer to the question of where deference goes when it ceases to be concentrated: it survives in attenuation, in a pervasive, intangible form which enters into all sorts of relationships through tone of speech, demeanor, precedence in speaking, frequency and mode of contradiction, etc.

The deference which is accorded with regard to a particular constellation of entitlements can, however, diminish and be replaced by another deference-judgment. A person who fails to retain his entitlements in the course of time also loses the deference which his entitlements brought him. He might not lose it entirely; ex-prime ministers, professors emeriti, and retired generals continue to receive some of the deference appropriate to their previous roles, although, other things being equal, probably less than they received as active incumbents. Kings in exile and great families fallen on hard times also lose much of their deference, and some who sink into peripheral obscurity cease to be known and their deference becomes entirely local. This, however, is a rather different matter. The question we are concerned with here is whether the deference-position of a person can ever wholly cease to exist. I am not asking here whether a person's deference-position can decline from a very high one to a very low one. That certainly can happen. My question is: can a person ever cease to receive any deference at all? Can the category become entirely "empty"? Or, in other words, can someone respond to him without any component of deference at all? Can we imagine a society in which there are no deference-judgments or deference actions at all, in which deference would not exist as a constituent of other actions? A society constructed entirely on a utilitarian model, in which every person in any relationship, would conform with this model. Such a society is unrealizable, and one of the grounds for its unrealizability lies in the unexpungibility of deference and of the deference system in its various manifestations and sources.

If deference is unexpungible and can nonetheless seldom appear in concentrated, intense forms, it must be capable of large variations in degree of salience.

The salience of deference behavior is closely related to deference-sensitivity. Total and continuous indifference to the receipt of deference is a marginal phenomenon, but individuals, classes, and societies differ in the degree to which they demand deference (whether concentrated or attenuated) and the degree to which they are sensitive to its appropriateness, its presence, or its absence. Snobs are persons whose demands for deference within a hierarchical context is great. Their concern for the deference-position of their associates is their most relevant characteristic. "Democrats" are relatively insensitive to their receipt of hierarchical deference and treat everyone with equal deference, regardless of the extent to which they possess the entitlements with which we have dealt. (The amount of deference they grant might be much or little and it might be granted in concentrated and elaborate forms or in complete fusion with other actions, but the decisive thing is that they grant it equally to whomever they deal with or judge.)

It is one of the features of modern Western societies that they are moving in the direction of deference-indifference, deference-equality, and deference-attenuation. The movement is very uneven among modern societies; the United States, Canada, and Australia are in the lead, with other countries some distance behind, but they too seem to be moving further along than they were a half century ago. The movement is also very uneven within societies, with marked differences between classes and generations and with certain sections of the population being excluded (such as the Negroes in the United States, especially in the South, and the aborigines in Australia).

The equalitarian tendencies of contemporary Western societies are characterized by the attenuation and simplification of deference and its retraction from the forms of concentrated ceremonial deference. Even more important is the partial atrophy of deference between superiors and subordinates, rich and poor, educated and uneducated.

Does it make sense to speak of deference in the relations of equals? Is not equality a point where deference disappears? Concentrated and salient deference behavior was a feature of the relations between the great of the earth and their subordinates. In the past the deference of equals was facilitated by the explicitness and elaborateness of the deference behavior of unequals, which permitted the deference of equals to be constituted by the avoidance of what was appropriate to the relations of unequals. In contrast, the tasks of creating and delineating the deference behavior appropriate to equals are more difficult. There is, to be sure, no elaborate ritual of deference between equals in contemporary Western societies, and particularly in American society, except that which still obtains between heads of states, heads of churches, and heads of universities, etc., on especially ceremonial occasions.

As an equalitarian outlook became more prominent, the rituals of deference fell into the same discredit as distributions of the values they acknowledged. What seems fairly certain is that at present the relationships of equals can and do contain considerable elements of attenuated deference, and, indeed, they cannot dispense with them.

At the same time, concentrated deference actions have by no means disappeared, but they have become less elaborate and with their diminished elaboration they have been abbreviated. They have become less substantial and less separate from other actions. Ceremonial deference and formalized etiquette between unequals and between equals have diminished in magnitude and frequency.

The decline in the power of aristocracies and the diminution of the number of monarchies have been accompanied by a reduction in the amount or proportion of ceremonial deference in societies. Modes of spoken and written address have come to bespeak a more homogeneous deference throughout societies and in doing so they have moved toward simpler, briefer forms. This does not mean that deference has disappeared or that there is "less" deference in society as a whole than there was when the organization of the deference system was more hierarchical. The strata which previously were treated with the minimum of deference, or indeed with negative deference, now receive a greater measure of deference than the peripheral strata used to receive, although they receive it in the simplified and shorter forms of a less ritualized society.

Nonetheless, it would be wrong to fail to acknowledge that

contemporary societies are less oriented toward their centers with respect to deference than were their ancestors of a century ago. This it is not merely because of the decline of aristocracy and monarchy. These are only instances of a more general phenomenon, namely, the diminution of the preponderance of the "ruling class" in the various countries. When elites were smaller, educational opportunity more restricted, and the kinship tie more respected, the various sectors of the center—the political administrative, ecclesiastical, cutural, and military elites (and to some extent the economic elite)—were closer to each other through common origins, common institutional experiences, and shared conviviality and the linkage of kinship than they are now, when the obligations of kinship are less observed in recruitment to the elite, when specialization has gone further, and numbers have greatly increased. One of the consequences of this pluralization of the elites is that their model is less imposing. They evoke less awe. Their authority is less sacred. They are assessed somewhat more functionally than they used to be. The increased importance of the criterion of achievement that helped to break up the image of a unitary ruling class, the reinforcement and enhancement of deference position, are less available to contemporary elites than they once were, and this has produced a decline in the extent of ascendancy of deference-position. As a result, the centers and the peripheries of the deference system are not as remote from each other as they were at one time. Each sector is taken for what it is and, except for the very pinnacle of the head of state and the head of the government, the sense of difference in worth is felt to be less great than it once was.

V

IT has long been characteristic of the study of deference and of the deference-positions (status) which it helps to produce, to ascribe to them a distribution similar in important respects to the distribution of entitlements such as occupational roles, power, income, wealth, styles of life, levels of educational attainment, etc.

The entitlements are all relatively "substantial" things which are not matters of opinion but rather "objective," more or less quantifiable, conditions or attributes; as such, they are capable of being ranged in a univalent and continuous distribution. Every individual has one occupation or another at any given period in time or for a specifiable duration; every individual has—if it could be measured—such and such an average amount of power over a specifiable time period. Every individual has some style of life of which at least certain components are enduring and observable—and he either possesses them or does not possess them. There are, of course, cases of persons who have two very different kinds of occupational roles within the same limited time period ("moonlighting") or who have widely divergent incomes within a given period, but these and other anomalies can quite easily be resolved by specifying procedures for the collection of data and their statistical treatment and presentation.

Present-day sociological notions of deference (status, esteem, prestige, honor, etc.) grew up in association with the "objective" conception of social stratification.* For reasons of convenience in research, and also because common usage practiced a system of classification into "middle," "upper," and "lower" classes,† research workers and theorists attempted to construct a composite index which would amalgamate the positions of each individual in a number of distributions (in particular, the distributions of occupational role and education) into some variant of the three-class distribution. The result was called "social-economic status" (sometimes, "socioeconomic status").

The "subjective" conception of social stratification appreciated the "opinion"-like character of deference, but for reasons of convenience in research procedure and because of the tradi-

---

* The "objective" conception concerned itself with the relatively substantial entitlements; the "subjective" was concerned with the "opinion"-like elements.

† The prevalence of the trichotomous classification and variations on it is probably of Aristotelian origin. There is no obvious reason why reflection on experience and observation alone should have resulted in three classes. This might well be a case where nature has copied art.

tional mode of discourse concerning social stratification, the "subjective factor" itself tended to be "substantialized" and it too was regarded as capable of being ranged in a univalent distribution.* Sometimes, as in the Edwards classification in the United States or in the Registrar-General's classification in the United Kingdom, this "subjective factor," impressionistically assessed by the research worker, was amalgamated with the "objective factors" in arriving at a single indicator of "status." Status was taken to mean a total status which included both deference-position and entitlements and which was constructed by an external observer (not a participant in the system). But this procedure is patently unsatisfactory. Deference-position—or esteem, prestige, or status—belongs to an order of events different from occupational distribution, income and wealth distribution, etc. It belongs to the realm of values; it is the outcome of evaluative judgments regarding positions in the distributions of "objective" characteristics.

The improvement of techniques of field work in community studies and sample surveys has rendered it possible to collect relatively systematic data about these evaluations. It has appeared plausible to assign to each person in a small community or to each occupation on a list a single position in a distribution. Research technique has served to obscure a fundamental conceptual error. As a result, since every person possessed a status (or deference-position), all were ranged in a single distribution. Such a procedure could in fact do justice to reality only under certain conditions. These conditions include: (1) an evaluative consensus throughout the society regarding the criteria in accordance

---

* It is quite possible that this pattern of thought, which emerged in the nineteenth century, was deeply influenced by the conception of social class of the nineteenth-century critics of the *ancien régime* and of the bourgeois social order which succeeded it. In the *ancien régime* the most powerful ranks were designated by legally guaranteed titles which entered into the consciousness of their bearers and those who associated with or considered them. These designations were not "material" or "objective." They did not belong to the "substructure" of society. They were therefore, "subjective" but they were also unambiguous. They could be treated in the same way as "objective" characteristics. By extension, the same procedure could be applied to the other strata.

with which deference is allocated, (2) cognitive consensus throughout the society regarding the characteristics of each position in each distribution and regarding the shape of the distributions of entitlements, (3) consensus throughout the society regarding the weights to be assigned to the various categories of deference- entitling properties,* (4) equal attention to and equal differentiation by each member of the society of strata which are adjacent to his own and those which are remote from it,† (5) equal salience of deference-judgments throughout the society, and (6) univalence of all deference judgments.

Were these conditions to obtain, the distribution of deference-positions in such a society might well have the form which the distributions of "objective" entitlements possess. There are, however, numerous reasons why the distribution of deference-positions or status does not have this form. Some of these reasons are: (1) Some consensus concerning the criteria for the assessment of entitlements might well exist, but like any consensus it is bound to be incomplete both because there are members of the society who do not share in it and because what might appear to be consensus on a general level might turn out to be dissensus when applied to particular instances. Criteria are so ambiguously apprehended that any existent consensus actually covers a wide variety of beliefs about the content of the criteria. (2) Cognitive consensus throughout the society regarding the properties of entitlements and the shape of their distributions is rather unlikely because of the widespread and unequal ignorance of such matters as the occupational roles, incomes, and educational attainments of individuals and strata. (3) The weighting of the various criteria is not only ambiguous, it is likely to vary from stratum to stratum depending on the deference position of the various strata and their positions on the various distributions; it is likely that each

---

* Where these three conditions exist, there would also exist a consensus between the judgment which a person makes of his own deference-position and the judgments which others render about this position. This consensus between judged and judges certainly does not always exist.

† It also presupposes equal knowledge by all members of the society about all other members.

stratum will give a heavier weight to that distribution on which it stands more highly or on which it has a greater chance of improving its position or protecting itself from "invaders." (4) The perceptions of one's own stratum or of adjacent strata are usually much more differentiated and refined and involve more subsidiary criteria than one's perceptions of remote strata; thus, even if the perceptions are compatible with each other there is no identity of the differentiations made by the various strata. (5) Some persons are more sensitive to deference than are others, and this difference in the salience of deference occurs among strata as well. Some persons think frequently in terms of deference position, others think less frequently in those terms. Accordingly, assessments of other human beings and the self may differ markedly, within a given society, among individuals, strata regions and generations with respect to their tendency to respond deferentially rather than affectionately or matter-of-factly or instrumentally. The arrangement of the members of a society into a stratified distribution, as if each of them had a determinate quantity of a homogeneous thing called deference (or status or prestige), does violence to the nature of deference and deference-positions; it further obscures what is in any case a sufficiently opaque reality. The possibility of dissensus in each of the component judgments (cognitive and evaluative) which make up a deference-judgment can, of course, be covered by the construction of measures which hide the dispersion of opinions. If all interindividual disagreements were confined to differences in ranking within a given stratum, the procedure would perhaps be acceptable. But if 80 percent of the members of a population place certain persons in stratum I and 20 percent, place them in stratum II, is it meaningful to say that the persons so judged are in stratum I?

The dissensus which results in interindividually discordant rankings seriously challenges the validity of procedures which construct univalent deference distributions and then disjoin them into strata. This difficulty would exist even if there were agreement about the location of the boundary lines which allegedly separate one deference stratum from another. But there is no certainty that there will be consensus on this matter, and the purpose of realistic understanding is not served by assuming that there is such consensus or by constructing measures which impose the appearance of such a consensus on the data.

The conventional procedure of constructing deference distributions has tended to assume a considerable degree of clarity and differentiation in the perception of the distribution of deference-entitling properties throughout the society. But as a matter of fact, perceptions are vague and undifferentiated. Terminologies and classifications, particularly in relatively "class-unconcious" societies, are not standardized and terms like "poor," "working people," "lower classes," "ordinary people," etc., are used in senses which the user has not reflected upon and which do not have a definite referent. There is no reason—at least until further research has been done—to think that they are interchangeable with each other, although sociologists do treat them as if they are.

If differentiation and specificity are slight in speaking about one's own deference-position and about strata adjacent to one's own, they are even less developed in reference to remoter strata of which the judging person has no direct experience. This does not mean that deference-judgments are not made about these remoter strata; it does mean that such judgments are made with scant knowledge of the extent to which these deference-entitlements actually exist in the persons or strata so judged. The cognitive stratification map becomes more vague with regard to those areas of the society far from the range of experience of the judging person. This too renders cognitive consensus impossible even if evaluative criteria were identical. What one judge looking at his own immediate stratification environment sees as highly differentiated may be seen by another, from a greater distance, as homogeneous. Thus, every sector of the stratification system is highly differentiated but only to those who are living in the midst of that sector.

The question arises therefore whether a distribution of deference positions incorporates the perceptions and categorizations which are applied to remote ones. Whichever alternative is followed, the factitious character of the distribution so constructed is evident.

There is a way out of this which certain writers have followed. They stratify the populations of a society entirely by its own self-rating (e.g., Richard Centers in *The Psychology of Social Classes*). This procedure is perfectly reasonable but it is not a distribution of the population with respect to deference received from others—unless it is shown that deference received from others is identical to deference granted by the self to the self. Ordinarily, when sociologists and historians speak of status or of deference-positions, they do not have in mind self-esteem and self-classification; they usually have in mind something more exterior. The procedure which concentrates on self-classification certainly deals with a real phenomenon and it permits important things to be said, but it deals with only a limited part of the phenomena of status stratification.

If it is unacceptable to draw a deference-distribution map of a society solely on the basis of self-classifications, it is also unacceptable to draw one which makes it appear as if all or even most persons in a society have an equally intense and definite deference-orientation toward every significant sector of their society. The procedure which Professor W. Lloyd Warner used for the study of Newburyport might have been valid for that small city—although I have some reservations about this as well—but it is misleading if applied to an entire society. It goes to the opposite extreme from the procedure used by Professor Centers. It distributes the population in accordance with the allocation of deference to each person (or family) presumed to be made by all other persons in the society. This can never happen in any society above a very small size and it is no solution to the difficulty to assert that the deference-position assigned to each person (and family) is the deference-position which would be assigned to them by everyone else if everyone else were to assess them in accordance with their actually possessed entitlements to deference. Such a construction surely proceeds through the use of fictions, and realistic sociology should have no place for fictitious constructions. Up to this point I have cast doubt on the conventional treatments of the distribution of deference-positions by referring to the diverse sorts of dissensus among individuals, strata, regional cultures, etc. But I wrote as if each of these agents of judgment spoke with a single voice, the voice of an objective mind beyond the subjectivity of individuals. There is some justification for this since there *is* a tendency in many societies and among many persons to regard the deference system as something objective, as *sui generis*, as existing outside the judging persons and independently of their own evaluations and appreciations of persons and strata. This tendency to "objectivize" the distribution of deference is in part a product of the perception of the deference judgments of other persons in one's own society. But it also reperesents a tendency to believe in the "objectivity," the "givenness," of deference stratification, to believe that in addition to our own tastes and dispositions there is a realm of normative being which exists independently of those tastes and values. It does happen, however, that the very persons who speak of an objective deference distribution sometimes say that they think it is wrong, that it is unjust.

Thus, alongside this tendency to believe in an objective order of worthiness there is a widespread alienation from that order. Furthermore, the acceptance and alienation very often exist in the same person. This ambivalence is very difficult to apprehend by present-day techniques of research, and it is even more difficult to deal with systematically—at least for the present. It exists nonetheless and it is apt to become stronger as society becomes more differentiated and as the "ruling class," in the sense of a set of persons who are intimately interrelated through kinship, common institutional experiences, and long personal friendships and who fill most of the positions at the top of the various distributions, gives way before a less unitary and therefore less imposing elite.

There is nothing pathological about this ambivalence. Submission to the ascendancy of the center and to the standards which affirm it is painful because the indignity of inferiority is painful. The ambivalence might be preponderantly affirmative with the alienative tendency manifesting itself only occasionally; alternatively, the alienative tendency might be the stronger. It is not likely that the alienation will exist in a majority of the population for any long period and on a massive scale—it would break the prevailing order if it did—but short of that, it can certainly be rather widespread. At certain points of most modern societies, intensely negative deference toward the center can certainly be found.

The society which focuses on the center imposes such indignity on the periphery. The more highly integrated a society ecologically, the greater will be the strain on the periphery, and the less imposing the elite at the center, the more likely an intensely negative deference toward the center. The implications of this sometimes ambivalent alienation are far-reaching and they cannot be gone into here. Let it suffice to say that the presently prevailing methods of describing deference distributions cannot accommodate these simple facts. Yet without these simple facts of ambivalence and alienation in the stratification system, how can class conflict and movements for reform by the reallocation of deference and its entitlements be dealt with? And what is one to make of the antiauthoritarianism and antinomianism which have been fluctuating through frequent phenomena of modern societies? How do these factors fit into a picture which portrays deference positions as univalently and consensually distributed?

Finally, I should like to conclude these reflections on the problems of deference distribution with some observations on equality. In general, the prevailing techniques for representing deference distributions proceed with a fixed number of strata or by means of scales which rank occupations or persons on a continuum running from 0 to 100. Both procedures assume a constant distance between the extremes and between the intervals or strata. This does not, however, seem to accord with the realities of the movement of modern societies toward a higher degree of equality of deference than was found earlier.

The range of deference distribution probably varies among societies. Some are more equalitarian than others. In what does this equalitarianism consist, apart from increased opportunities or life chances for peripheral strata? Does it not consist in an appreciation of the greater worthiness of the peripheral strata—a judgment shared to some extent throughout society? It entails enhanced self-esteem on the part of the peripheral sections of the society and an enhanced demand on the part of those sections for more deference from the central sectors of the society. In also entails a greater readiness on the part of the central sectors to grant deference to the peripheral sectors. Thus, citizenship and humanity have become more significant entitlements although the other entitlements have by no means lost all their significance. All this is indeed in the sphere of opinion, but the deference system is largely a matter of opinion. I cannot go into the causes of this development.* I wish here only to call attention to its relevance to any realistic description of deference systems.

VI

WHEREAS most of the things valued by men become explicit foci of elaborate institutional systems concerned with their production, acquisition, protection, maintenance, control, and allocation, the same cannot be asserted of deference. Unlike economic or military or political or ecclesiastical institutions, deference institutions are marginal to the valued objects which they seek to affect. There is a College of Heralds, there are chiefs of protocol in departments of foreign affairs, there are *Who's Who's* and *Social Registers,* there are books on deportment and on modes of address, there are advisers to prime ministers and presidents on the awarding of honors, there is an *Almanach de Gotha.* A great many states have a system of honors and many have had systems of titles and orders. Armies award medals and universities award

---

* I have attempted to explain the causes of this movement toward the narrowing of the range of dispersion of deference-positions in "The Theory of Mass Society," *Diogenes,* No. 39 (Fall, 1962).

earned and honorary degrees. Learned societies elect persons to membership and within their membership single out particular persons for further honors. Armies have titles of rank as do universities. Civil services too have ranks and designations which denote differences in authority but which are also titles of deference. Many of those institutions have handbooks which specify orders of precedence. In some societies, duels are fought to rehabilitate affronted honor, and feuds between primordial groups are often intended to reaffirm the honor of the group and to show it worthy of the deference which it demands. All of these institutional arrangements confer or confirm or rehabilitate deference; they seek to express deference, to create and legitimate claims to deference, to specify who should receive it, and to entitle particular persons in a way which objectifies their claims to deference. Only a few of these institutions have sought explicitly to determine a "generalized" deference position, namely, those who sought to control and guarantee memberships in nobilities or aristocracies. Others awarded deference for rather specific qualifications and although in many of these cases the deference was generalized, in others it remained an indicator of a quite specific achievement and thereby attained scarcely any measure of generalization. But at best they have touched only a small part of the societies in which they have functioned, and although they maintain, intensify, and strengthen the deference systems they cannot be said to create or manage it.

The deference system of a society extends throughout the length and breadth of that society. Everybody falls within it, yet very few have their deference-positions determined by the deference-conferring and deference-confirming institutions. The actual, really functioning deference system of a society envelopes the deference institutions and takes them into account, but it is not predominantly determined by them.

Most deference behavior occurs in the face-to-face interaction of individuals, and very few of those who receive some allocation of deference have any titles or medals. The deference which the bearers of titles and honors receive is received from other persons who respond not primarily or exclusively to the titles or honors of which they have heard or emblems which they see on the garments of the persons deferred to, but to the entitling properties which they believe are possessed by the person to whom deference is given. Titles and medals might be taken into account, but even when the title is used in full, the use of the title in addressing the person deferred to is at most only a part of the deference expressed. The title is thought to stand for something more than itself—for substantive entitlements, for kinship connections, for acknowledgment by the sovereign, for occupational role. These too are not ultimate; they are evocative of other characteristics. Snobs, who are so sensitive to deference and so insistent on its explicit forms, are drawn to titles, medals, and honors because these are so unambiguous in their confirmation of deference from its "ultimate" sources.

As I have said earlier, the deference granted is expressed in overtones of speech and action. Very much of deference-in-overtones is expressed in relations of authority because authority is so evocative of deference that deference institutions are unable to contain or control all of the deference so evoked. Although deference appears in the ceremonial arrangements which surround great authority, it also appears with commands and acts of obedience, with the giving of counsel and the taking of counsel, and in the interplay of authorities and subjects or colleagues and neighbors performing the actions called for by authority, collegiality, or neighborliness. Deference-in-overtones is far more subtle and diverse than the prescriptions for the ritual manifestations of deference. Being a duke or a professor or a colonel constitutes only one element—even if a quite considerable element—in the generalized deference which the incumbents of those ranks and the bearers of those titles receive. Those who associate with them and who defer to them respond to other things about them as well as to their ranks and titles. The excellence of their past and current performances, the power which they actually exercise or have exercised, their level of culture and style of life, insofar as these can be perceived or imagined or are already known from previous experiences and from other sources, enter into the determination of the deference granted and expected.

Deference institutions are more important in some types of societies and in some strata than in others. In societies in which there is a sharp disjunction between center and periphery, they will have more influence than in societies in which the periphery has expanded inwardly and overwhelmed the center.

Deference institutions are especially important at or near the center of society although ordinarily it is not the intention of those who manage them to confine their influence to that zone. But because deference is more intense in face-to-face relationships and direct interaction than it is in remote relationships, there is a tendency for deference systems to become dispersed in a particular way. Deference systems tend to become territorially dispersed into local systems which are more differentiated for those who participate in them than is the national system. I do not mean to say that the several systems ranging from local to national are in conflict with each other. Indeed, they can be quite consensual, and the local usually could not be constituted without reference to persons, roles, and symbols of the center. In the various zones and sectors of the periphery, where the center is more remote, the imagery of the center still enters markedly into the deference system, and local differentiations are often simply refined applications of perceptions and evaluations which have the center as their point of reference. Thus, for example, local deference judgments will make more subtle internal distinctions about occupational role and authority, and income and style of life, than would judgments made from a distant point either peripheral or central. Still, the distinctions will refer to distances from some standard which enjoys its highest fulfillment at the center. It seems unlikely that center-blindness can ever be complete in any society.

Nevertheless, the various systems do to some extent have lives of their own. The local deference system is probably more continuously or more frequently in operation than the national system—although as national societies become more integrated and increasingly incorporate with local and regional societies, the national deference system becomes more frequently and more intensely active.

Local and regional territorial deference systems have certain parallels in sectional deference systems. Sectional deference systems are those which are formed with professional communities, communities of belief, or ethnic communities which are sections of a total society and which have in varying degrees their own centers and their own deference systems. Within these sectional systems deference tends to be allocated in accordance with those entitlements which are most germane to the "interests" of the particular section. Thus, within an academic deference system, those persons with the most notable accomplishments in the academic discipline in question will be most esteemed and will receive a generalized deference. The centers of such sectional deference systems tend to become parts of the national deference system; that is, they become recipients of the deference of a national audience outside the academic sector and the deference which they receive has a general character.

In all societies, the deference system is at its most intense and most continuous at the center. The high concentrations of power and wealth and the elaborateness of the style of life all testify to this and call it forth. It is at the center that deference institutions function, and this gives an added focus and stimulus to deference behavior. The center adds the vividness of a local deference system to the massive deference-evoking powers of centrality. Within each local or regional deference system there are some persons who are more sensitive than others to the center and they infuse into the local system some awareness of and sensitivity to the center.

Sometimes individuals whose preoccupations are mainly with the local and sectional deference systems—insofar as they are at all concerned with deference—see themselves on the macrosocial deference map. This self-location (and the perception that others are also locating themselves) is the precondition of a sense of affinity among those who place themselves macrosocially in approximately the same position in the distributions of deference and the entitlements to deference. Of course, the placement of others is made on the basis of fragmentary evidence about occupational role, style of life, or elements of these, and the sense of affinity is alienated and intermittent and the self-location very vague, very inarticulated, and very approximate. Deference class-consciousness is formed in this way. These deference classes or strata have no clear boundaries, and membership can not be certified or specified. It is largely a matter of sensing one's membership and being regarded by others as a member. Those one "knows" are usually members; beyond them, the domain spreads out indefinitely and anonymously in accordance with vague cognitive stratification maps and an inchoate image of the "average man." (Within each stratum, an "average man" possesses the proper combination of positions on the distribution of significant deference-entitlements.)

Thus, the formation of deference strata is a process of the mutual assimilation of local deference systems into a national deference system. It is through class consciousness that deference strata are formed.

In the course of its self-constitution, a deference stratum also defines in a much vaguer way the other deference strata of its society. It draws boundary lines, but except for those it draws about itself, the boundaries are matters of minor significance. Boundary lines are of importance only or mainly to those who are affected by the location of the boundary; that is, those who live close to it on one side or the other. The location of a line of division in the distribution of deference is regarded as important primarily by those who fear that they themselves are in danger of expulsion or who are refused admission to a stratum whose members they regard as equals or to whom they wish to be equal and whose company they regard as more desirable than that to which they would otherwise be confined. The members of any deference stratum are likely to be ignorant of the location of deference stratum boundaries which are remote from them, and if they are not ignorant, they are indifferent.

The various deference strata of local deference systems are in contact with each other through occasional face-to-face contacts. They are present in each other's imaginations and this deferential presence enters into all sorts of nondeferential actions of exchange, conflict, and authority.

The different strata are also in contact with each other within national deference systems, not very much through face-to-face contact but through their presence in each other's imaginations. This presence carries with it the awareness of one's distance from the center and it entails some acceptance of the centrality and greater dignity of the center. It is an implicit belief that the center embodies and enacts standards which are important in the assessment of oneself and one's own stratum.

In some sense, the center is the standard which is derived from the perception, correct or incorrect, of its conduct and bearing. The remote persons and strata which form the center might be deferred to or contemned in speech, and the pattern of their conduct, bearing, outlook, etc., might be emulated or avoided. An "objective existence" is attributed to the rank ordering from centrality to peripherality of the other strata and within this rank ordering one's own stratum. The ontological, nonempirical reality which is attributed to position in the distribution of deference makes it different from "mere" evaluation and sometimes even antithetical to it.

On a much more earthly level, contacts between deference strata occur in many forms—particularly through the division of labor and its coordination through the market, within corporate bodies, and in the struggle for political power. This does not mean that the strata encounter each other in corporately organized forms* or that when there is interstratum contact in the encounter of corporate bodies, these bodies include all or most

---

* Corporate organizations, membership in which is determined by a sense of affinity of deference positions and of positions in other distributions, seldom enlist the active membership of all the members of the stratum or even of all the adult male members of the stratum. Those who are not members of the corporate body are not, however, to be regarded as completely devoid of the sense of affinity with other members of their stratum. "Class consciousness" in this sense is very widespread, but it is a long step from this type of "class consciousness" to the aggressively alienated class consciousness which Marxist doctrine predicted would spread throughout the class of manual workers in industry and Marxist agitation has sought to cultivate.

members of their respective strata. Much of this interstratum contact takes place through intermediaries who act as agents and
who receive a deference which is a response to both their own
deference-entitling properties and those of their principals.
Those who act on behalf of these corporate bodies do so in the
belief that they are "representing" the deference stratum to which
they belong or feel akin.

A society can then have a deference system of relatively self-
distinguishing and self-constituting deference strata, with the
strata being in various kinds of relationship with each other. Such
a situation is entirely compatible with the absence of the type of
objective deference distribution which we rejected in the foregoing section. Each of the deference strata possesses in a vague
form an image of a society-wide deference distribution, but these
images cannot be correct in the sense that they correspond to an
objective deference distribution which might or might not actually exist.

VII

I HAVE emphaszed the importance of the self-constitutive character of the classes which make up a system of deference stratification. I have also emphasized the unreality of the construction
of status distributions on which sociologists have expended so
much effort. At the same time I have also stressed the elements of
integration of the deference strata into a single system focused on
the center of society. Some writers contend that the deference
system and the associated stratification systems of what are called
plural societies are incompatible with this mode of analysis. By a
plural society they mean one in which various ethnic groups are
so segregated from each other that they form societies separate
and distinct from each other. Yet they do not go so far as to say
that the various constituent societies are totally independent of
each other; they acknowledge that they are integrated into a
single economy and that they live under a single political authority. In that sense the constituent societies of a plural society are
parts of a single society.

The problem which this poses for the study of deference systems is well worth consideration. What we find is that the ethnic entitlement is regarded in these societies, particularly by the more powerful, life-chance-controlling section of the dominant ethnic group, as so absolutely crucial that it is made into such a salient criterion of deference that those whose deference-positions are affected by it are included in broad deference strata in comparison with which all other deference-entitlements are of secondary importance. These other deference-entitlements exist and do determine differences in the allocation of deference, but they are capable of generating differences only within each of the major ethnically determined deference strata. Each ethnically determined deference stratum is internally differentiated in accordance with the distribution of deference-entitlements within it. Each approximates a completely self-contained deference system but it does not become completely self-contained. It fails to do so because despite its highly segregated pluralism the society does have a center and this center constitutes a focus of each of the partially separate deference systems. The latter bear some resemblance to the deference systems of whole societies because of the differentiation of occupational roles within each of the ethnic sectors. The occupational structure of each sector is not, however, the complete occupational structure of the total society. That total occupational structure is distributed between the ethnic sectors and there is indeed some overlap between them. It is because of these points of overlap (between the bottom of the superordinate deference stratum and the peak of the subordinate deference stratum) that conflicts arise. These conflicts could only arise because the sectors or strata are parts of a peculiarly integrated, single deference system.

VIII

WHEN it is not treated as an unreal, conceptually constructed amalgam of a number of positions on a variety of distributions, deference has often been treated as an epiphenomenon. It is often considered as having relatively little weight in the determination of conduct—apart from the choice of companions in conviviality or in the motivation of emulatory conduct. Yet it is deference which is responsible for the formation of strata or classes.

Deference is, as a result of its properties as a generalization, the crucial link in the stratification system. Without the intervention of considerations of deference-position, the various very differentiated inequalities in the distribution of any particular facility or reward would not be grouped into a relatively small number of vaguely bounded strata. The very idea of an equivalence among positions in different distributions could not be realized if there were no generalization to cut across them.

By a stratification system, I mean a plurality of strata within a single society with some sense of their internal identity, of the internal similarity, and of their external differences vis-à-vis other strata. The stratification system is constituted by strata which are formed by persons who have approximately similar positions on a variety of separate distributions. This approximate similarity of position is a precondition of the sense of affinity because it strengthens the sense of identity of the self from which the sense of affinity of many selves is formed. If each person were randomly heterogeneous in his cluster of positions, the likelihood of identity and therewith of affinity would be less likely to come into existence.

The sense of identity is a vague perception of self and other which refers to some pervasive qualities of those so identified. These qualities by which strata identify themselves and others are frequently referred to by shorthand terms such as "wealth," "poverty," or "rulers," "people," "workers," or "bosses." These terms refer to positions on particular distributions such as power. Yet for those who use them, these terms have a significance beyond the limited descriptive sense in which they are used. Each term stands for a position on each of a number of distributions and implies that positions in the various distributions are correlated and connected with each other. Those who are "workers" are also "poor," or in any case relatively low in wealth and income distribution. Those who are "bosses" are also "rich," or at least higher in the wealth and income distributions and they usually have more political power. Those who are "well off" have more education and more authority through their occupational roles and through political participation.

The connections between the positions of an individual on the different distributions are of two sorts. One is the connection through "life chances." Life chances are opportunities to enter into a higher position on any distribution from a lower position on that distribution or on several distributions. Life chances are determined by the power of income, by personal, civil, and kinship relationships, and by occupational role and level of education. Any one of these can have a determinative influence on the allocation of life chances, that is, on the opportunity to ascend in that distribution or in others.

A life chance which arises from position on a particular distribution also affects chances for maintaining or acquiring life chances for positions on other distributions. Income permits education to be purchased; the acquisition of education increases the probability of higher deference and higher income; higher education increases the probability of greater political influence; increased political influences increase the likelihood of a greater access to financial resources.

There is a widely experienced aspiration to bring positions on a series of distributions into an appropriate correspondence with each other. Each position provides resources for affecting positions on other distributions. Why should this be so? Why should there be thought to be an "appropriate" relationship among positions, an equilibrium which should be striven for? Why, when a person has much political power, does he not use his political resources exclusively to enhance or maintain his political power instead of expending them on bringing his style of life or the education of his children "into line" with his political position? (Of course, one reply to this question is to say that it is generally believed that improving positions on the nonpolitical distributions is a necessary condition for maintenance or improvement of the position on the political distribution. But is not this very belief in itself evidence of a belief in an appropriate pattern of positions which is thus a precondition for the more "costly" political support necessary for further improvement in political position? Another reply to the question is that most human beings, given the opportunity, will strive to enhance their position in any particular distribution and that being in a better position on one distribution provides resources for betterment on others. But although there is some truth in this assertion it does not confront the fact that there is a sense of an appropriate pattern of positions on different distributions.)

The belief that it is appropriate that the several positions on the various distributions should be consonant or harmonious with each other is attributable to the belief that they each express a common, essential quality. An "inappropriate" pattern of positions bears witness to the absence of the essential quality. There is something "unseemly" or "eccentric" or "perverse" or "unfortunate" about the individual or family whose positions are scattered among a variety of unequal points on the several distributions.

This common or essential quality is the charismatic quality which requires diffuse and pervasive expression in the various distributions. The cognitive element in an act of deference is the perception of the presence of this quality, and its generalization beyond any specific manifestation in action is an acknowledgment of the apparent possession of charismatic quality by the person deferred to. The demand for deference is the demand for a diffuse acknowledgment of the diffuse charisma which is possessed in some measure by the self and which is above all, in its earthly form, resident in the centers of society. Self-respect—deference to the self—is an acknowledgment of one's own charisma and of one's satisfactory proximity to the center in an essential respect.

The cognitive and evaluative map of a stratification system is a differential allocation of deference to a series of aggregates of persons—for the most part anonymous—in accordance with their proximity to the center and thus in accordance with the magnitude of their presumed charisma. The stratification system of a society is the product of imagination working on the hard facts of the unequal allocation of scarce resources and rewards. The charisma is imaginary but it has the effect of being "real" since it is so widely believed in as "real." Deference which is basically a response to charisma is only a matter of opinion, but it is an opinion with profound motivation and represents a response to profound needs in the grantor and the recipient of deference.

REFERENCES

1. *World Politics and Personal Insecurity* (1935) and *Politics: Who Gets What, When, How* (1936).

2. "The Psychology of Hitlerism," in the *Political Quarterly* (1933); reprinted in *The Analysis of Political Behaviour* (1948), p. 236.

3. P. 257.

4. "Psychology Looks at Morals and Politics"; reprinted in *Analysis of Political Behaviour*, p. 18.

5. Lasswell and Kaplan, *Power and Society* (1950), p. 56.

6. *Ibid.*, p. xxiv.

7. Cf. H. Goldhamer and E. Shils, "Types of Power and Status," *American Journal of Sociology*, 1939.

13

Some Quantitative Constraints on
Value Allocation in Society and Politics

KARL W. DEUTSCH

IN a classic study Harold Lasswell and Abraham Kaplan have endeavored to summarize under eight headings all the major substantive values to whose allocation political processes are relevant. The eight values on their list are power, wealth, deference or respect, well-being, affection, skill, enlightenment, and righteousness. Security and liberty (or spontaneity), which are often counted as distinct values, are not so much values in themselves, but rather modes of enjoying any of the values in the eight basic categories. (It is affection, or well-being, or wealth, or power, or all of them together, which we may enjoy securely or freely, not abstract "freedom" or "security" in and by themselves.) A third mode of enjoying values, is "legitimacy." It refers to the possibility of pursuing or enjoying any one or several of the eight basic substantive values without inflicting intolerable damage upon the pursuit or enjoyment of any other of these eight essential values. Thus if we were to pursue physical well-being to the point of ruining our wealth, or pursue wealth to the point of destroying our well-being or our enjoyment of affection, such blind pursuit of a single value would be no longer legitimate. Legitimacy is thus the compatibility of the pursuit of a plurality of values. It is in some way akin to security but it can be conceptually distinguished from it.

Work utilized in this paper was supported by the Carnegie Corporation and by NIH Grant No. MH 08607. I am indebted to J. David Singer and Anatol Rapoport for enlightening comments, but the responsibility for the present formulations remains mine. An earlier draft appeared in *Behavioral Science*, 114 (July, 1966):245–52.

A CLASSIC THEORY
OF VALUE ALLOCATION

ACCORDING to Lasswell and Kaplan, every actor in society can be thought of as controlling by his actions and decisions some amount of each of these values in regard to other people, so that he can increase or decrease by his own actions or decisions the relevant value positions of those other persons.[1] The transferable values thus controlled by each actor are called his base values; the values which one or more other actors can be induced to transfer to him in consideration of, or exchange for, any units of any base values he controls are called the scope values over which this actor has political influence owing to his base value position. Thus, men's actions are seen as controlled by a balance between value increments ("indulgences") and value decrements ("deprivations") somewhat reminiscent of the concept of the "pleasure-pain" calculus of Jeremy Bentham, but the workings of this "indulgence-deprivation" balance are now made susceptible to far more detailed and specific analysis.

It is not the purpose of the present paper to attempt any general critical discussion of this classic scheme.[2] Rather, this paper will indicate more specifically certain quantitative constraints upon the social, economic, and political processes of value allocation described in more general terms by Lasswell and Kaplan, and it will point out a connection between certain aspects of these processes and a major distinction in the theory of games.

If we call the influencer "ego" and each of those to be influenced "alter," then it is helpful to remember that ego's base values are values enjoyed by alter which can be increased or diminished by what ego may decide to do. Conversely, ego's scope values are values enjoyed by ego which can be increased or decreased by alter's actions. Ego thus manipulates some of the values which alter would like to enjoy, and since ego controls them, they are the bases of ego's power over alter. In exchange for the increases in these values which ego permits alter to get, alter in turn increases, through some of his actions or omissions, at least one of the values ego desires to enjoy, that is, one of ego's scope values which lies within the scope of those of ego's own values which ego himself indirectly controls to the extent that he controls the base values the desire for which in turn controls the behavior of alter. The whole process is thus an exchange cycle in which ego changes the flow of some of his base values, which are scope values for alter, so that in the end each actor has manipulated—and usually diminished—his base values and increased one or more of his preferred scope values. Lasswell and Kaplan have tried to give names to the particular exchanges that can result, and these are shown in the appropriate cells of their Table 1.

ALLOCATION THEORIES VS. PRODUCTION THEORIES IN POLITICS AND ECONOMICS

IN its formal aspects, Lasswell and Kaplan's table can be viewed as a trading scheme. Actors give up certain units of the base values they control which are desired by other actors, and they do so in exchange for, or in expectation of, receiving certain increments in scope values which are controlled by those other actors but are desired by themselves.

Values are treated in this scheme as consisting of valued goods or services or, more broadly speaking, as valued "outcomes" or patterns of behavior such as the acts of obedience that enhance another man's power, the acts of deference that increase his respect position in the community, or the health and sport facilities and services that promote his well-being. (Thus usage differs from the second usage of "value" in the sense of "value orientation," such as "beauty," 'honor," or some other general categories of preferences, which then may or may not be met or filled by specific collections of preferred objects or actions. "Value orientation" is to value as a lock is to a key or as a job slot is to a candidate or an incumbent.) Thus, values in Lasswell and Kaplan's sense always imply the actual supply of valued goods or acts of performance. Hence they have costs: their supply,

TABLE I*

FORMS OF INFLUENCE AND POWER

BASE VALUES	SCOPE VALUES							
	Power	Respect	Rectitude	Affection	Well-Being	Wealth	Skill	Enlightenment
Power	Political power	Homage	Inculcation	Fealty	Compulsion	Polinomic power	Directorship	Indoctrination
Respect	Councilorship	Sponsorship	Suasion	Esteem	Charisma	Credit	Guidance	Authoritativeness
Rectitude	Mentorship	Approbation	Moral authority	Devotion	Chastisement	Ethonomic influence	Injunction	Censorship
Affection	Personal influence	Regard	Moral influence	Love	Guardianship	Benefaction	Zeal	Edification
Well-Being	Violence	Terror	Discipline	Rape	Brute force	Brigandage	Forced labor	Inquisition
Wealth	Ecopolitical power	Standing	Simony	Venality	Subsistence power	Economic influence	Employment	Advertising
Skill	Expertness	Admiration	Casuistry	Ingratiation	Prowess	Productivity	Management	Intelligence
Enlightenment	Advisory influence	Fame	Wisdom	Sympathy	Regimen	Economic foresight	Instruction	Education

* Reprinted from Lasswell & Kaplan (1950), p. 87.

procurement, or performance requires time and resources, and they are subject to quantitative limitations.

This scheme carries with it four obvious implications:

1. The actors prize the increments in scope value which they expect to get more highly than the amounts of base values which they give up in order to get them.

2. The scope value of one actor must be the base value of another if an exchange is to be effected.

3. The total amount of each scope value to be obtained by all actors through this allocative process cannot be larger than the total amount of the same value surrendered as a base value by other actors in the same society.

4. The total amount of each value is treated as relatively fixed, at least over the time span relevant to a short-run political process. The result of this implication is that politics are treated less as the use of the coercion-compliance processes of politics, and particularly of the power of the state, for the production of values. Rather, politics are treated predominantly as the process of allocating those values whose existence or production is treated as already given.[3]

This emphasis on allocation is quite legitimate for a certain stage in the analysis of a social process. At a corresponding stage in the development of economics, the volume of goods and services was treated as given in the short run, and this assumption then permitted significant progress to be made in the understanding of many economic processes influencing income distribution, wages and prices, and inflation and monetary stability. Nonetheless, at a later stage, these restrictive assumptions were relaxed. The more recent Keynesian and post-Keynesian economics paid more attention to the fuller utilization of credit and of unemployed manpower and capital, and generally of unused productive capacities, even in the short run. To this, then, has been added a more explicit interest in increasing the productivity of labor, of capital, and of entire national economies in the more recent economic theories of development and growth.

It should be noted that Lasswell and Kaplan's own theoretical

scheme explicitly indicates the possibility of a similar development, and that it already suggests specific analytic steps in this
direction. Thus Lasswell and Kaplan speak of the "shaping" of
each value (as the process which leads to its eventual "enjoyment" by its recipient) in a manner very similar to the way in
which the concept of the "production" of each value is being
used in the present essay; and they have applied the specific term
"production" to the "shaping" of one of their listed basic values,
namely wealth.[4] Nonetheless, most of the readers, research
workers, and theorists who have been influenced by their work
seem to have paid most attention to its implication for the study
of the allocation of values, while leads towards an analysis of
the role of politics in the production of values within and by
society thus far have been relatively neglected.

Political theory, it may be suggested, likewise may also move
eventually beyond a concern with value allocation to include the
broader problem of the role of politics in the processes of value
production and value growth. This is, after all, the classic political problem of the good society: how to use government so as to
make that society and its people more *productive* of the values
which they need and want. A more fully developed theory in
politics, as in economics, would then no longer have to choose
between the rival emphases on allocation and production. Rather,
it would try to trace the entire causal loop or feedback process, in
which value production permits a range of choices in regard to
allocation, and where the results of this allocation process in turn
modify the process of production, in cycle after cycle of cumulative development.

A BASIC DISTINCTION FROM
THE THEORY OF GAMES

As a process of value allocation, politics can be treated as a
game. If the amount of available values is fixed, it is a fixed-sum
or zero-sum game: what one claimant gets, another must forego.
In that case, claimants cannot all get richer, or all more powerful

or more respected; politics is indeed a struggle in which any weakness or diversion of competitive effort leads to loss. If the amount of relevant values can be increased in the short run, however, politics becomes a variable-sum game. Certain strategies may then leave all contestants better off, and it becomes a task for statesmen, as well as for students of politics, to discover these strategies and the possibilities of applying them in specific situations.[5]

Economic analysis shows the different roles of credit in economic situations which resemble either type of game. In zero-sum situations, the anticipatory claims of credit for any one actor must be made to prevail to the detriment of some competitors, while in variable-sum situations credit can be used as an instrument to mobilize unused resources and increase the value of goods and services available for allocation among all.

As should be clear, the considerations of growth and increased productivity, and of using credit as an instrument for their attainment, do not abolish the interest in allocation but supplement it for the purpose of a broader understanding. What individuals will get in the end depends on both allocation and production, and a more adequate theory must concern itself with both processes.

ECONOMIC CREDIT AND POLITICAL PRESTIGE

FROM well-known principles of economic theory it can be shown that credit expansion does not force a rise in prices if unused factors of production can be brought quickly into play, in adequately balanced combinations, as required by current production functions. The volume of variable-sum—or noninflationary—credit is thus limited by the volume of capacities for early additional production. Beyond this point, credit becomes a fixed-sum game: any goods (or services) claimed by one actor from the existing stock, *before* he has produced an equivalent input, must diminish another actor's opportunity to claim the same goods or service in advance of having produced any equivalent in exchange for it. Economists then speak of a credit inflation; students of politics see this situation as likely to lead to an increased power struggle.

Prestige is the claim to deference or respect regardless of affection or righteousness. Operationally, it is the claim to a preferred status in social communication. Messages from a prestigious source are to be accorded priority in attention and transmission, and greater statistical weight in the combinatorial process of decision-making. Prestige is acquired by power, or the memory or expectations of the power of the prestigious actor, in the minds of other actors. In relation to society, prestige, like credit, is a role. In relation to power, prestige is to power as credit is to cash.

The allocation of prestige among several actors is a variable-sum game so long as additional capacities for mutual attention, communication, and responsiveness can be brought into play rapidly, and at an equal or faster rate than the growth of claims upon them. Thus, the volume of variable-sum—or noninflationary—prestige or respect values in a society is limited by its capacities for early increases in attention, communication, and responsiveness.

Beyond this point, increasing communication overload is likely to result. Its effects, in turn, are likely to reveal that there has been an inflation of prestige and of respect values in the society which may eventually have to be reduced, either by voluntary retirement of a sufficient proportion of the inflated prestige claims or by means of an increased power struggle.

OTHER INTERPERSONAL VALUES: POWER AND AFFECTION

IT might be asked to what extent, if any, the same principle might hold for all of Lasswell and Kaplan's eight fundamental values. In addition to wealth and deference, which have just been discussed, these values are power, affection, well-being, skill, enlightenment, and rectitude.

Power over men depends on their capacity to obey in ways that are still meaningful and rewarding to the powerholders, and on the latters' capacity to perceive such acts of obedience as having these functions for themselves. Up to this point, some actors can increase their social or political power without diminishing the power of others. Beyond it, claims to power become inflationary and the allocation of actual power becomes a fixed-sum game.

Something similar holds for the total volume of claims to affection, or promises of affection, in a society. This too is limited by the volume of capacities available to give affection, or to increase it quickly, but it is further limited by two important constraints. (1) Affection is highly specific among individuals, so that the effectiveness of interpersonal substitution in satisfying the needs of any one actor is more highly restricted than in regard to any other value. (2) Much or most of an individual's capacity for communicating affection is directly effective only in increasing the enjoyment of this value by other individuals. It can only indirectly enhance the value position of its producer so far as the experience and enjoyment of affection is concerned.

PARTIALLY AUTONOMOUS VALUES: WELL-BEING, SKILL, AND ENLIGHTENMENT

WELL-BEING, skill, and enlightenment all depend to some extent upon external facilities and the cooperation of other actors for their procurement or preservation. To the extent that this is so, the same rules hold. Claims upon any of these three values are noninflationary, and their allocation among actors is a variable-sum game so long as the volume of claims remains equal to, or smaller than, the volume of quickly mobilizable capacities for their production. Beyond this point, value claims once again become inflationary and value allocation becomes a fixed-sum game.

In the case of these last three values from Lasswell and Kaplan's list, however, these rules hold only to a far more limited extent. For health and well-being, skill, and enlightenment can also be procured in some considerable measure by almost every mature individual for himself and by his own efforts. To the extent that well-being, skill, and enlightenment can be produced autonomously by individuals for themselves—or by small groups for their members—the allocation of these values again becomes a variable-sum game, with the added constraint that a considerable part of the autonomously produced increments in well-being, skill, and enlightenment are less likely to be capable of being transferred impersonally—like commodities—from their producers to other individuals. On the contrary, they are more likely to increase the value position of their originators. It is perhaps not surprising that religions and philosophies of contemplation and asceticism have tended to stress these last three values in particular, for their pursuit permits the believer to adjust to the world by withdrawing from some or most of its pursuits and to gain for himself increases in some or all of these three values by his own endeavors.

THE PARADOX OF RECTITUDE

IF the religion or philosophy in question prescribes a corresponding code of conduct, if the believer has internalized this code, and if he now perceives himself as living up to it, he is also likely to experience a gain in his own feelings of righteousness or, as Lasswell calls it, rectitude. For rectitude—the last of our values from Lasswell and Kaplan's list—consists operationally in the perception of congruence between an individual's strongly internalized code of conduct and his perception of his own behavior, that is, his entire behavior—overt, covert, and in his imagination.

Thus, rectitude represents something of a paradox. At any moment, its experience is to a large extent internal to the individual. It depends upon the code of conduct which has become part of the structure of his personality as well as upon his own behavior, which he can endeavor to make congruent with that code or voice of conscience. To that extent, rectitude or righteousness can be considered autonomous, and its attainment would be something the world could neither give nor take away.

In fact, however, righteousness contains a large and often crucial interpersonal component, as the ancient warnings against "self-righteousness" might have led us to suspect. It is from other persons, particularly from their own families and ultimately from society, that individuals learn the codes of conduct which they then make their own and from which they draw some of their self-respect. Moreover, it is from other persons, from society, and often from politics and government that people receive many of the positive or negative reinforcements which may then influence their retention or changing of their internal codes. Still further, the codes themselves, as taught to individuals, may be more or less congruent with their physical, emotional, and mental needs, and with the experiences they have in life.

Finally, society may be organized in a way that facilitates the reasonable fulfilment of an internalized ethical code without intolerable cross-pressures and conflicts, permitting a feeling of multiple value compatibility and consonance—that is, of legitimacy—to be experienced by most individuals. On the other hand, society can be organized in a way that multiplies the individual's experience of unresolvable contradictions, inescapable guilt, and shattering value conflicts; such experiences may fix the marks of illegitimacy and absurdity upon the individual's image of the world and of himself.

To the extent that the value of rectitude depends upon interpersonal relations, it is subject to processes of social and political allocation, and to the distinction between zero-sum and variable-sum games. Governments can lend support and legitimacy to the learning and acting out of certain moral codes while penalizing and frustrating the observance of others or associating them with intolerable conflicts in relation to the pursuit of other values.

To the extent that society and government can only support, tolerate, or facilitate the observance of a rigidly limited set of codes, politics and ethics become once more a zero-sum game. Any gain for one code, religion, philosophy, view, or morality can only occur to the detriment of others. The more righteous the adherents of the winning creed are permitted to feel, the worse will be the inner conflicts and frustrations of the believers in some other code who must share the same society and polity with them—except to the extent to which the losers in the struggle succeed in withdrawing from the public arena and consolidating their own individual and small-group sources of feelings of righteousness and of psychological support for them.

It is possible, however, for society, government, and the general culture to enhance their capacities to tolerate, and even to nurture and support, a widening range of different codes of conduct, or of ethics or religion, without intolerable conflicts with other believers or with other values. As these capacities for conflict management, value tolerance, and value support increase, the pursuit of righteousness also becomes a variable-sum game. In this case actors can gain not only from diverting away from competing creeds or codes some interpersonal support for the pursuit of their own particular variety of rectitude, but they can also gain even in the short run from an increase in the capacities of society and government to facilitate the pursuit of the actors' own version of rectitude, together with the pursuit of different versions of rectitude by others, within real but perhaps widening limits.

What has just been described is, of course, the ancient vision of the good society and its modern version, the vision of a dynamic, expanding, and self-transforming democracy. What has perhaps been added here is a demonstration that the three hard, pragmatic, and relatively value-free styles of reasoning of Lasswell's politics, of economic analysis, and of the theory of games all are not only mutually relevant and consistent with each other but that through the concepts of value productivity and variable-sum games all three bodies of thought are also consistent with, and relevant to, some of the oldest and most basic aspirations of normative political thought. It is the aspiration—and the tradition—of seeing government not only as an allocator of existing

values among competing claimants but also, and more fundamentally, as an instrumentality to aid men in organizing themselves to produce, maintain and enhance the entire range of values
—in its largest possible diversity and richness—more effectively
and more abundantly.

FROM ASPIRATIONS TO NECESSITIES: THE IMPACT OF ECONOMIC AND POLITICAL DEVELOPMENT

THE actual process of economic development and political modernization in many countries has been transforming the allocation
and the production of values at very different rates. In many countries and societies, a "revolution of rising expectations" has in-
exorably widened the circle of claimants and almost inevitably
inflated the aggregate volume of their claims far beyond current
capacity for value production. Thus, the bitter political mood of
rapidly developing countries has been characterized by cycles of
hope and disappointment and by alternation between "divine discontent" and disillusionment with the "God that failed" or between hopeful images of vast new vistas and bitter images of the
"deadly game"—the zero-sum game of power and greed.

At one stage and in one form this cycle involved the adoption
of ideologies making vast claims and promises of value acquisition, or even promises of greatly enlarged value production in
terms of more wealth, more righteousness, and more brotherhood
or affection. These adoptions were often followed by a stage of
crises and partial or total rejection of the same ideologies in the
stage of emotional deflation and disillusionment.

In another form this cycle involved the projection of increased value claims not on a new ideology or social order but
rather on a new political unit or a new scale of political organization within which, it is hoped, the old social system will work
better and the new value claims can be pressed more rewardingly.
Secessions into smaller nation-states, or mergers into larger em-

pires or federations may become fraught with such hopes, and if these hopes are largely disappointed, such forms of political integration and disintegration may come to form another cycle.[6]

Under different and more favorable conditions, the rapid growth of value claims in developing countries may be matched, if only in part, by an increase in the supply of at least some widely claimed values. In these more fortunate developing countries (such as the United States in the nineteenth century, the imbalance between quickly and widely expanded value claims and more slowly and unevenly expanding value supplies has taken the form of widespread psychic and social tensions, competitiveness, restlessness, and diffuse discontent. Alexis de Tocqueville commented on the air of unhappiness he observed in many Americans; it seemed to him that whatever they were doing, they regretted at the same time missing the opportunity of doing something else.[7] The value aspirations of the people de Tocqueville observed had become so inflated, in the language of the analysis offered here, that for them the opportunity cost of their own time had become larger than the value they could obtain from almost any actual way of spending it. They were in a position similar to that of an owner of some grossly overvalued currency who feels vaguely cheated in any actual purchase because his money is only current at a far more modest value. Some of the psychological sources of the discontent of university students and the crisis of universities in the late 1960s may have come out of a similar process in which rapidly expanding value claims were frustrated by poorly expanding value production, in many dimensions at the same time.

Modesty, contentment, the slowing down of the rate at which value claims of individuals are expanded or of the rate at which new millions enter the circle of effective claimants—all these have been the time honored responses of conservative statesmen and of many humane and honest thinkers.[8]

Almost none of this advice has been effective. The widening value claims have been driven by population growth and by the inevitable demonstration effects of the rising technology, with its spectacular demonstration of human powers. They have been accelerated by the deep changes in personalities and aspiration levels produced by the spread of literacy, mass education, and mass communications; and they have been made irreversible by the cumulative changes in the ecological and technological bases of the lives of ever increasing masses of people, which have turned an increasing proportion of these old values into new necessities. It actually takes more wealth, more skill, more enlightenment, more well-being and energy, more power, more respect, and perhaps more solidarity and affection to survive in an ever more industrialized, urban, and technological society—and even the value of righteousness and self-respect may become of more crucial importance for the individual in such conditions.

THE RECURRENT CRISES OF LEGITIMACY

As society, economics, and politics become more complex, the impact of the pursuit of any one value upon the pursuit of other values becomes more serious. The compatibility of several values, both in their pursuit and in their enjoyment, can even less readily be taken for granted on the contrary, value compatibility must increasingly be thought about and striven for. Legitimate strategies for the pursuit of values—that is, strategies making compatibility more likely—must be discovered and developed, often under great difficulty and with considerable cost.

The processes by which this occurs are likely to be quite uneven. In earlier days and under simpler conditions, strategies of pursuing one value often were quite compatible with the pursuing of other values. People who grew up under these conditions where value compatibility was easier and where legitimacy was less of a problem are likely to have incorporated the corresponding images and preference patterns into the structure of their own habits and personalities. If under the more recent and complex conditions the old patterns of value pursuing behavior may now begin to damage and destroy other values equally important to them, they themselves may be the last to notice it, if ever they do. They may be apt to ignore, deny, or repress all messages or indications that might tell them so. For any doubts about the legitimacy of their own habitual behavior will seem to them a threat to their cognitive consonance, to their self-respect, and to the affection and respect which they expect to enjoy in their own families and in the small groups of persons most relevant to them.

If the objective conditions for legitimate behavior in society change more slowly than the success of generations of people when they become politically socialized in society, legitimacy crises are likely to be absent or mild. If these conditions change at a significantly faster pace, older generations socialized to older patterns of what once was a legitimate behavior may now be acting in ways which involve increasing value conflicts and value damage, and thus are becoming visibly less legitimate, even though they themselves for the most part may be unwilling or unable to perceive this.

But their children will perceive it, since they will be politically socialized in their own adolescence, by their own experiences, under new conditions. They cannot help perceiving not only what their elders think and say, but also what they do. Above all they cannot help seeing the results of these actions including the mounting contradictions and value conflicts which these actions now produce. Some of the things which still seem legitimate to their elders then cannot and will not seem legitimate to the young; and an important part of the value conflict in society will take manifest shape as a conflict among generations.

In time, almost inevitably, the new generation will take over; and many of their own notions of legitimacy—though by no means all of them—are likely to become part of the fabric of beliefs that are now accepted. If during the same period the capacity of society to produce additional amounts of values has increased, the new legitimacy patterns will prove workable for a time and the legitimacy crisis may subside. If change continues at a rapid pace, however, and the value production continues to lag, and if value damages continue to mount and if conflict among value pursuing strategies continues to increase, the legitimacy crisis may continue, or a new crisis of legitimacy may develop very quickly.

If advances in value production and in the discovery of strategies for the legitimate pursuit of values should continue at an uneven pace, as seems most likely, we may expect once again the appearance of the cyclical process. Crises in legitimacy may then alternate with periods of considerable agreement among different social groups and generations as to what is legitimate, and further periods of legitimacy crises and of perceived value consonance may follow.

Therefore, wherever countries develop rapidly, waves of ideological conversions will recur, often aided temporarily by the elevation of charismatic leaders. Such conversions often, though not always, later give way to the deflationary and disillusioning phases of the cycle, until a new wave of rising expectations starts the next cycle.[9]

Underneath this seeming ebb and flow of rising and disappointed value claims, the cumulative forces of the tidal process are at work. Under favorable conditions they may slowly but automatically erode the obstacles to greater value production, to the greater compatibility of values, and hence to greater powers and higher hopes for men. In the long course of history, there are not only examples where such obstacles were removed, as chattel slavery was removed in the nineteenth century and mass unemployment may yet be removed in the twentieth, but there is some evidence to suggest that the value-creating, value-producing, and value-combining capabilities of persons and societies may have increased, albeit partially, uncertainly, and fitfully.

Too often, however, the automatic workings of the cycle may do little or nothing of the kind. The more abundant production of a widening range of values is a matter of increasing motivations and skills—of competence and compassion—on all levels of human life, including those of social and political organization. Such motivations, knowledge, and skills must be discovered, invented, learned, or otherwise created. It is here, in every accelerated stage of this unending process of social transformation, that the politics of value appropriation reveal their limitations most sharply—important as they are within these limits—and that sooner or later the test of the politics of value production, of innovation and of creativity, must be faced.

REFERENCES

1. Harold D. Lasswell and Abraham Kaplan, *Power and Society* (New Haven: Yale University Press, 1950).

2. It could be argued that at this stage it may somewhat underemphasize the elements of combinatorial novelty, spontaneity, and initiative that are observable in history and politics. These three factors have received more attention in the writings of the late Joseph A. Schumpeter and in recent cybernetic and systems theoretic models. See Schumpeter, *Aufsätze zur Soziologie* (Tübingen: Mohr [Siebeck], 1953); Norbert Wiener, *Cybernetics*, 2d ed. (Cambridge, Mass.: Massachusetts Institute of Technology Press, 1962), chap. 1; and K. W. Deutsch, *The Nerves of Government* (New York: Free Press, 1963). For an analysis oriented somewhat more toward systems preservation, see also David Easton, *A Systems Analysis of Political Life* (New York: Wiley, 1965).

3. One of Lasswell's best-known books is called *Politics: Who Gets What, When, How*, rather than "Who Creates or Produces What?" For a similar emphasis on allocation, see David Easton, *The Political System* (New York: Knopf, 1953).

4. Lasswell and Kaplan (note 1, above), pp. 80–82, and p. 72, Table 1.

5. On the distinction between fixed-sum and variable-sum games, see J. Von Neumann and O. Morgenstern, *The Theory of Games and Economic Behavior* (Princeton, N.J.: Princeton University Press, 1944); Anatol Rapoport, *Fights, Games, and Debates* (Ann Arbor, Mich.: University of Michigan Press, 1960), Part II, and *Strategy and Conscience* (New York: Harper & Row, 1964); William H. Riker, *The Theory of Political Coalitions* (New Haven: Yale University Press, 1962).

In the strict sense, zero-sum games are a subclass of fixed-sum games in which the sum of payoffs to all players equals zero. In zero-sum games it is particularly obvious that what one player wins another player must lose, and hence such games have received particular attention in much of the literature. In a wider sense, every fixed-sum game can be viewed as a zero-sum game at the margin: the marginal increment of the aggregate of payoffs to all players equals zero. Differently put, all payoffs in game theory are assumed to be quantified in terms of units of utility. Since utility scales—like the centigrade scale of temperature—are interval scales with an arbitrary zero point, any constant-sum game can be treated as a zero-sum game by an appropriate choice of zero point. In that more general sense, inflation can be called a zero-sum game. I am indebted to Anatol Rapoport for help on this point.

6. For historical examples of this cycle of expectations and disappointments in regard to the size of political units in Central and Eastern Europe, see K. W. Deutsch, "Problems and Prospects of Federation," in C. E. Black, ed., *Challenge in Eastern Europe* (New Brunswick, N.J.: Rutgers University Press, 1954), pp. 219–44.

7. Alexis de Tocqueville, *Democracy in America* (New York: Oxford University Press, 1947), pp. 344–46.

8. For a thoughtful and responsible version of this argument, see Ernst B. Haas, "Toward Controlling International Change: A Personal Plea," *World Politics*, 17 (October, 1964): 1–12.

9. For the charismatic aspects of leadership in the early development of the United States, see Seymour Martin Lipset, *The First New Nation* (New York: Basic Books, 1963), pp. 16–23.

14

Harold D. Lasswell and the Study of World Politics:
Configurative Analysis, Garrison State,
and World Commonwealth

WILLIAM T. R. FOX

IF Thomas Kuhn is correct in stating that advances in modern science come less by small increments than by innovating paradigms, then Harold D. Lasswell's configurative analysis is a revolutionary contribution to the study of world politics.[1] The simple determinisms of Marx and Mahan, normatively ambiguous studies of the formal institutions of international government, political realists preaching about a future that can hardly be altered, encyclopedism that conceals key relations which the study of world politics ought to identify and illuminate, efforts to compress world politics into the formal framework of interstate relations—all these have been challenged by the Lasswellian reformulation of world politics.

Through four decades Harold Lasswell has insisted upon the unity of the world political process. He has reiterated that domestic, comparative, and international politics must be fitted into a common theoretical framework. This recurrent theme has sometimes been expressed in almost deliberately outrageous ways. Thus, Lasswell has come to assert that not even *world* politics provides a broad enough framework for investigation. We are, he suggests, at the dawn of an age of astropolitics when we must people our enlarged political universe with astrobeings and perhaps also with "transhuman" beings who may be the product of either genetic or computer technology.[2] Whether or not Professor Lasswell really means that it is time for his fellow political scientists to take seriously astropolitics, biotechnology, and superintelligent machine-actors may be unimportant. In either case he has effectively put us on warning that the dramatis personae in the world political process are indeed subject to drastic change. In an era of bloc actors, "third world" mini-states, and integration among the rich, Atlantic, and dominantly white countries, who can say which will be the important classes of actors in tomorrow's world politics? The Lasswellian paradigm for the study of world politics is ready to accommodate these new classes of actors; many others are not.

The configurative analysis set forth in the first chapter of *World Politics and Personal Insecurity*, with its twin emphases on equilibrium and trend, seems as serviceable as ever three decades after its initial presentation.[3] The developmental constructs in that pioneering volume have been modified in detail, but they were not meant to be accepted as the final revelation of the master student of world politics. They are far more open-ended than the constructs of the Toynbees, the Spenglers, and similar historical sociologists. An imaginative interplay between the developmental construct and the data collected in accordance with the construct has pointed the way toward a progressive modification of the trends being investigated.[4]

It is rare for system-maintenance and system-transformation theories of world politics to be wholly integrated, and *World Politics and Personal Insecurity* is no exception. Lasswell can properly claim, however, that his configurative analysis gave substantially equal recognition to the need for a theory which accounts for both stability and change. Moreover, in a decade in which "systems theory" is a fashionable term, the record does not show that the systems theorists of the 1960s have been more successful than the Lasswell of the 1930s in integrating trend analysis with equilibrium analysis.

The open-endedness of Lasswell's developmental constructs reflects his belief in the social utility of political analysis, including world political analysis. Such analysis has the function of clarifying choices in public policy. It follows that for Harold Lasswell interesting orientations toward the future all involve contingent predictions. A world of garrison states may be a probability, but it is by no means a certainty.[5] Careful analysis of the garrison-state contingency and its attendant costs in terms of Lasswell's specified cardinal values may help to disconfirm the undesired but contingent prediction. Estimates of the low probability of early achievement of world unity are another matter, and Lasswell wastes no effort prescribing for the impossible. If world unity is highly improbable, potentials for voluntary integration are, in his view, by no means nonexistent. Systematic examination of these potentials and of attendant benefits if they should be realized tends to make the contingent assertion of integrative tendencies self-confirming.[6]

If Harold Lasswell has a profound belief in the power of the intellect to move men of good will toward a future world that is to be preferred to other possible future worlds, in ways that he specifies, he is full of respect for the toughness of the existing world political structure. Even the scientific and technological changes of the atomic age have in his view "been singularly without effect on the fundamental structure of world politics."[7] Until central integrating institutions emerge, the expectation of violence will persist, for war is the residual form of conflict adjustment left to territorially organized competitors when other procedures for settling conflicts fail. Since 1945, the family of great powers has suffered losses, but the great power system persists. Nowhere do vested interests cope voluntarily with urgent problems of change by divesting themselves of their interests, and territorially organized interests are no different from other vested interests. The principle of "least cost elite adjustment" may cause governing elites to see foreign war as a lesser evil than fundamental domestic social change. There is perhaps an echo of the socialist optimism which was confounded by the events of 1914 in Lasswell's suggestion of a "strategy of parallel action at representative places over the globe" by the nonvested alternate elites as an effective way to cope with the selfish vested interest.[8] On the other hand, the proposition that the class struggle is in our era being superseded by a skill struggle does open the way for common action by transnational groups with shared skills.

The world political structure is tough, and the game of world politics goes on, in Lasswell's view, mainly because innovation is always local.[9] The innovation may be ideological or material. It may result from changed patterns in rates of forced saving and of sacrifice in support of foreign policy goals or from an invention being brought into production first in some one part of the world. It may be the consequence of some novel combination of ideological and material stimuli. In all cases its effects are at first uneven and impart dynamism to the equilibrating processes of world politics by changing unequally the competitive positions of the main actors. The recurrent patterns of local innovation, geographic diffusion, and partial incorporation have kept any of the competitors in world politics from achieving total domination. World unity via world conquest is no more probable in the near future than world unity via spontaneous consensus, and Lasswell sheds no tears over the prediction. He evidently wishes to see potentials for involuntary integration minimized as much as he would like to see potentials for voluntary integration maximized.[10]

If there is an implication of an "iron law" or fixed supply of value or of a zero-sum game in the elementary version of Harold Lasswell's definition of politics as the study of "who gets what, when, and how," it is not a necessary implication nor one which an assessment of Lasswell's whole body of political science writing sustains. Political science, "the study of the value patterns of society," is not in his view a purely distributive subject. The values of society, including the values of world society, are subject not only to redistribution but also to reshaping, for they are partly fungible. A little bit of private enlightenment may, for example, produce a great deal of public good. The size of the pie to be cut up may be enlarged, and the value mix may change.

The who-gets-what Lasswellian trademark and the meliorist perspective of its author are in sharp contrast. Increasingly, Harold Lasswell has been explicit as to his preference for a world of shared power, universal human dignity, and the opportunity for every human being to realize his full potential for development. Talent and skill would replace caste, class, and ultimately even the nation-state. Skill groups now serving a divided globe would realize globally integrative potentialities of a world of "meritocracies."

Predictions of an "inevitable" Soviet-American third world war—or Sino-American third world war or any other allegedly inevitable particular man-made catastrophe—fill Lasswell with as much scorn as predictions of inevitable progress. Lasswell is both dispassionate observer and dedicated participant in the world political process. To the prognosticators of any particular unwanted future he responds with a "challenge to impose the human will upon the historical process."[11]

The Latin, Greek, and Hebrew mottoes of American colleges and universities offer many interesting variations on the theme, "the truth shall make you free."[12] If this sentiment has been pure rhetoric for most American scholars, it has been at the heart of Harold Lasswell's faith in the perfectibility of human society. He has acted upon this faith and accepted joyously the challenge to impose the human will upon a historical process which could easily go awry. He has insistently proclaimed the necessity for patient, systematic, and hard work to meet that challenge.

The garden of human creativity is not so naturally fertile that the full flowering of the human mind in its effort to master our Hobbesian world politics will come automatically. Basic data is the soil in which the plant of the intellect must grow. A generation before the computer and the data bank, before exciting new research technologies of information storage and retrieval had developed, Harold Lasswell was calling for bodies of data to be collected for which neither Wall Street nor Washington then saw a need. He wanted more "facts about the thoughts, feelings and conduct of others."[13] He did not want the social scientist to be limited in his analyses by the accidental availability of data collected for the purposes of public administration, diplomacy, military intelligence, and business forecasting.

The political arithmetic of a bureaucracy needed to be expanded, he thought, into a social arithmetic for a society whose intellectual leaders were self-consciously organizing their inquiries

to clarify the future choices of society. In his call for and specification of the terms of a "world attention survey," Lasswell was
indicating the area of greatest deficiency in the then-existing
machinery for systematic data collection.[14] His coauthorship of
The World Handbook of Political and Social Indicators, published a quarter century after the call for a world attention survey, demonstrates the persistence of Lasswell's interest in continuing and systematic inventories.[15] So does his substantial role
in the Yale Political Data Program.[16]

If data is the soil in the garden of creativity, its fertilizer is
imagination. If one cannot predict which apple falling upon
which head will yield an insight into social affairs comparable to
Newton's laws of gravity, one can take steps to make sure that
there is an orchard and to increase the chance that there will be
a Newton. The process of elaborating the full range of future
contingencies for which it is appropriate to predict and to plan is
not entirely hit or miss. Lasswell's developmental constructs afford full scope for scientific and technological change and for
identifying the problems various changes pose and the opportunities they afford. They enable him to speculate even to the
margins of fantasy.[17] After the reader has recovered from the
shock of reading about political problems in a world also popu-
lated by genetically induced superhumans and humanoids, and
of the expansion of the balancing process to the infinitely broadened universe of astropolitics, he will find his own imagination
has been stretched too.[18] He may not yet be quite prepared to
deal with the political problems of transhumanity and thinking
machines, but he will be much more prone to consider highly
unorthodox possible developments in the world political process
as the limiting cases in future policy planning.

Harold Lasswell has abounding confidence in the ultimate
policy payoff of a perfected intelligence function and a more
sophisticated orientation toward the future. He is prepared to
justify a wide variety of investigations into fundamental political processes in the way medical researchers justify using funds
obtained for research on the causes and cure of cancer for funda-

mental biological research.[19] War is for the student of world politics what cancer is for medical research. For the contemporary student of world politics, as for the antimilitaristic civilian liberal of the nineteenth century, "war is the enemy, not the enemy." It is also his bread and butter.

The relation between new knowledge about world politics and public policies which accord with Lasswell's specified cardinal values may not be direct or obvious. Nevertheless, since the future is at most semidetermined, trends may be reversed, goals which violate human dignity modified, and parochial loyalty patterns transcended. If the road we are presently traveling seems to lead to a world of garrison-prison states, there is another road, says Harold Lasswell, which leads to world commonwealth. It is not one Rome or two Carthages which he offers as the main choice, but one Rome or many Spartas. The emerging international culture of transnational skill groups may find ways to deal with both the North-South problem and the East-West problem.[20] The shared interests of transnational skill groups would not be to promote the interests of one of the two superpowers against the other nor to protect the economic interests of the advanced industrial states. In this special kind of functionalist utopia inclusive, not exclusive, interests would flourish.

Harold Lasswell is prudent enough, however, to posit interim goals for an immediate future in which substantial progress toward world unity is not foreseen. Thus, *National Security and Individual Freedom* was deliberately prescriptive for the United States in the menacing period of the Korean War.[21] Accepting the necessity for a high-level defense mobilization with all that protracted high-level defense mobilization implies for the elevation in the skill struggle of those with military skills, Lasswell then asks how the values of dignity, shared power, and widespread opportunity for self-realization can be best promoted on a national basis. He posits adequate external defense arrangements and then prescribes how to deal with the consequent internal threat to the values which the defense effort is supposed to be protecting.

Others, such as Pendleton Herring, had earlier posited a functioning democracy and asked whether democratic society was capable of imposing upon itself the discipline and sacrifice necessary to preserve itself in a hostile world.[22] Herring's affirmative answer seems to have been partly confirmed by the outcome of the two *world* wars of the twentieth century. What, however, about the compatibility of protracted high-level defense mobilization and free society in the era of cold war and limited war?

Both Samuel P. Huntington and David C. Rapoport, in their assessment of trends in civil-military relations, see somewhat different alternative futures than Lasswell. Rapoport observes that the dominance of the military is in almost exactly inverse relation to the degree of political, social, and economic development of the regime concerned.[23] Marx was wrong in expecting the socialist revolution to occur first in an economically advanced country where the clash of the class struggle had been sharpened. Similarly, Lasswell may, if we accept Rapoport's view, be wrong in suggesting that the higher the rate of defense mobilization among developed countries with efficient military machines the more likely its officers are to undermine principles of civilian supremacy. One explanation, and one that accords with Huntington's view, would be that the civilianization of the military effort in advanced industrial societies in the second half of the twentieth century has revealed a "fusionist" alternative to the stark dichotomy of garrison state or world commonwealth.[24]

Most students of American civil-military relations and national security policy in the post-World War II period have assumed both civilian supremacy and, at least until the late 1960s, a sufficient civilian willingness to sacrifice. In keeping with their implied acceptance of the fusionist alternative they have been relatively more concerned than Lasswell with assuring the competence of the civilian decision-makers in a world that called for technically difficult politico-military decisions and that was relatively less concerned with civilian supremacy for its own sake. His concern has in a sense been more old-fashioned and in the Anglo-American tradition since the time of Oliver Cromwell.

In this tradition the problem of civil-military relations has traditionally been seen as a problem of strengthening political institutions and attitudes guaranteed to keep the high brass from taking over. Like his predecessors in the Anglo-American civilian-liberal tradition, Lasswell portrays the military as not just another skill group in society, but a skill group outside civilian society with values and attitudes antithetical to that society.

If the perceived necessity for national defense mobilization in time of peace as well as war has led to a militarization of civilian life, the changed technological basis of war has led to the civilianization of the military effort, about which Lasswell has had much less to say. The whole gamut of the skills of civilian society are drawn upon in the continuing effort to protect the country by the use of force and the threat of force. The defense effort is no longer the preserve of a single skill group, and defense policy is not always dominated by the value preferences and attitudes of that group. To Lasswell's proposition that the new world politics is characterized by the emergence of transnational skill groups one might also add that it is also characterized by "trans-skill" national groups. It is this fusionist alternative which has been explicitly embraced by Huntington and implicitly accepted by most contemporary American students of national security policy. Furthermore, without challenging the premise that a skill group is often overconfident of the all-purpose utility to society of its distinctive skill, one can assert that the soldier of today is far less isolated from the conforming pressures of the society he serves than were fighting men of an earlier generation.

This subordination of the military instrument to the goals of a civilian society Samuel P. Huntington has called "objective control."[25] If the soldiers of democracy are imbued with the values of democracy, if they are a part of and not outside democratic society, their decisions about the organization and use of military means will presumably be in full conformity with the value preferences of their civilian masters and of the electorate which put those civilian masters into office. Until the goal of national security can be replaced by a premise of world security such as Harold Lasswell posits for the integrated world which he envisions,[26] this second kind of civilianization of the military effort may be politically even more significant than the first.

If Harold Lasswell stresses the "perpetual threat of war" as the "common institutional enemy," if he portrays a future of "new caste societies in the form of self-perpetuating soldier-police elites in a world of garrison-prison states" in which the "stress of prolonged war and near-war" leads to a "consolidation of garrison states," he may only be saying that there is grave danger to future prospects for a world of universal human dignity even if the superpowers somehow avoid annihilating each other.[27] Furthermore, the ultimate choice, he sometimes seems to say, may not be quite so stark as that between the garrison state and the world commonwealth. In an article written in the early postwar years, "Prospects of Cooperation in a Bipolar World," the road to Rome seems to lie *through* two Spartas. No more than any other student of world politics in the late 1940s does Lasswell seem to have forecast the stabilizing role of retaliatory countercity striking force in the nuclear age or the great falling out between the Soviet Union and the Chinese Peoples' Republic,[28] but he does identify plainly the contingency of a stable Soviet-Western balance based upon reciprocal deterrence and examines carefully the possibilities for improved Soviet-American relations which that prospect would afford. It is easier to see in 1969 than in the era of American atomic monopoly that nuclear weapons duopoly and nuclear weapons parity are not quite the same thing. It is hardly surprising, therefore, that Lasswell paid relatively little attention to the unique possibilities for modifying the world order open to a nuclear power which had lost its monopoly but retained a quantitative and qualitative leadership.

If Harold Lasswell has been willing to leave to others such parochial tasks as identifying for the American polity ways to exploit its residual nuclear leadership to protect and promote the cardinal values which he repeatedly specifies, his concern with the organization of social knowledge to illuminate the margin of manipulable choice in the pattern of future events remains enormous. One choice which Lasswell examines in detail is the deliberate remolding of Soviet expectations of "capitalist encirclement."[29] No matter how implacable the hostility of the Soviet opponent, Soviet expectations of malevolent American behavior, he believes, can in the long run be falsified and modified by prudent American policies. Ultimately, as Soviet expectations become more realistic, Soviet behavior, he predicted, would change. Furthermore, no matter how strident and unacceptable the demands which a Communist opponent may make on governments of the free world, its bellicose behavior may be modified by fostering demands in the Communist bloc for "more now." Identifications can be changed. New zones of peace in which governments cease to make plans for the contingency of war on each other can emerge. Institutions can be built which reflect these new attitudes.[30] Finally, on the horizon, the possibilities are not absolutely nonexistent for coping with the common institutional enemy, war, by the discovery of an integrating world myth which transcends obsolescing capitalistic-communist differences. Thus, we are brought back to the concluding chapter of *World Politics and Personal Insecurity*, "In Quest of a World Myth."

What are we to say about a social scientist who believes that social science may possibly be able to lever the bad old world off its hinges and thus make way for a good new world? Is Harold Lasswell proposing a social science technocracy in which the technocrats would turn all choices into problems, once they have specified their cardinal values? This is a facile, but I believe incorrect, interpretation.[31] Spelling out methods of attaining the specified goals involves specifying the costs. As unanticipated direct and by-product costs are revealed, some goals may be abandoned because they involve too great costs to higher priority goals. Unanticipated economies and by-product benefits may on the other hand expand the range of choice and lead to a shift in priorities. If social science cannot always (or ever) tell us what is right, it can sometimes tell us that what we had thought was right had unanticipated consequences which now make us think it is wrong. The organization of intelligence for policy-making made possible by the building of "systematic multi-valued models of the social process,"[32] which Lasswell urges, does not make choice obsolete. Rather, by revealing the full and often previously unsuspected range of choice, it points to a more rational relating of plural ends to the available plural means.

Choice is blind when the choosers have exaggerated or wrong expectations. It is denied when forecasts are made in unconditional terms. It is frustrated when choices made with respect to a particular value turn out to have uncalculated and undesired by-product effects on other values. Exaggerated expectations that "victory" will firmly and finally frustrate the implacable opponent, the forecast of invincible hostility by first one and now another of the Communist great powers, and inattention to by-product costs of various means proposed for free world defense—all involve avoidable irrationalities from which Lasswellian world politics would rescue us.

The study of world politics does not have to be policy-oriented to be policy-relevant. It does not have to be purged of policy relevance to be theoretically significant. It does not have to be purged of theoretical significance to be a policy science.[33] If Harold Lasswell has been among the most theoretical of contemporary students of world politics, he has in a larger sense been among the most practical. The study of international relations has in his hands become world politics, one of the political sciences—in Harold Lasswell's preferred terminology, a policy science.

REFERENCES

1. Thomas Kuhn, *The Structure of Scientific Revolutions* (Chicago: University of Chicago Press, 1962). In Lasswell's usage, "world politics" refers to a field of inquiry roughly the same as "international relations." "World politics" suggests stronger linkages between the global system and the national subsystems than does "international relations."

2. An early prominent reference in Harold Lasswell's writings to

the politics of biotechnology is in his presidential address to the American Political Science Association in 1956, "The Political Science of Science," *American Political Science Review* (1956), pp. 961–79. This theme and that of the "thinking machine"-actor are more fully developed in *The Future of Political Science* (New York: Atherton Press, 1962). Astropolitics is discussed in "Men in Space," *Annals of the New York Academy of Sciences,* 72 (1958):180–94. All three "transhumanity" themes are discussed in the new introduction to the paperback edition of *World Politics and Personal Insecurity* (New York: Free Press, 1965).

3. New York: McGraw-Hill, 1935.

4. See the new introduction to *World Politics and Personal Insecurity* referred to in note 3.

5. The garrison-state hypothesis was first outlined in two 1937 Chinese publications, "The Relation of Skill Politics to Class Politics and National Politics," *Chinese Social and Political Science Review,* 21 (1937):298–313; and "Sino-Japanese Crisis: The Garrison State versus the Civilian State," *China Quarterly,* 11 (1937):643–49. It was fully developed in "The Garrison State," *American Journal of Sociology,* 46 (1941):455–68. Lasswell's continuing concern with the garrison-state contingency is manifest in his *National Security and Individual Freedom* (New York: McGraw-Hill, 1950) and in "The Garrison State Hypothesis Today," in *Changing Patterns of Military Politics,* ed. Samuel P. Huntington (New York: Free Press, 1962).

6. "The Problem of World Unity: In Quest of a Myth," *International Journal of Ethics,* 44 (1933):68–93, was the basis for the concluding chapter of *World Politics and Personal Insecurity.*

7. *The Future of Political Science,* p. 9.

8. "Science, Scientists and World Policy," in *Science and the Future of Mankind,* ed. Hugo Boyko (The Hague: W. Junk, 1961), p. 81.

9. This is a central theme in *World Politics and Personal Insecurity.*

10. See, for example, "Toward a Skill Commonwealth: A Workable Goal of World Politics," in *Approaches to Group Understanding,* ed. Lyman Bryson (New York: Harper, 1947), pp. 290–302.

11. "'Inevitable' War," *World Politics,* 2 (1949):3.

12. For example, the motto of the University of Chicago, where Harold Lasswell studied and taught for almost the entire interwar period, is "Crescat scientia vita excolatur."

13. "The Relation of Ideological Intelligence to Public Policy," *Ethics,* 53 (1942):25–34; reprinted as "Policy and the Intelligence

Function," in *The Analysis of Political Behavior* (London: Routledge and Kegan Paul, 1948).

14. "The World Attention Survey," *Public Opinion Quarterly*, 5 (1941):456–62.

15. Bruce M. Russett, Hayward R. Alker, Jr., Karl W. Deutsch, and Harold D. Lasswell, *World Handbook of Political and Social Indicators* (New Haven: Yale University Press, 1964).

16. See Richard L. Merritt and Stein Rokkan, eds., *Comparing Nations: The Use of Quantitative Data in Cross-National Research* (New Haven: Yale University Press, 1966), pp. 81–94.

17. See, for example, his "Men in Space."

18. The initial effect may be paralyzing, as one of my Columbia University colleagues, Warner R. Schilling, has discovered when he has occasionally asked doctoral candidates in their oral examinations to justify the inclusion of a student of "world" politics in the first observational team to be sent to Venus after there had come to be good reason for believing that Venus was inhabited by intelligent beings.

19. *The Future of Political Science*, p. 144.

20. See Lasswell's "Emerging International Culture," in *Science, Technology and Development*, vol. 10, United States Papers Prepared for the United Nations Conference on the Application of Science and Technology for the Benefit of the Less Developed Areas (Washington, D.C., 1963).

21. New York: McGraw-Hill, 1950.

22. Pendleton Herring, *The Impact of War* (New York: Farrar and Rinehart, 1941).

23. "A Comparative Theory of Military and Political Types," in *Changing Patterns of Military Politics*, ed. Samuel P. Huntington (New York: Free Press, 1962), p. 77.

24. See Samuel P. Huntington, *The Soldier and the State* (Cambridge, Mass.: Harvard University Press, 1957), pp. 346–58, for a critique of the garrison-state hypothesis largely in terms of Lasswell's alleged failure to take account of the "fusionist alternative." Huntington gives Lasswell high marks for a "conscious, systematic and sophisticated theory of civil-military relations" even though he rejects the theory. Huntington's criticism of Lasswell's theory (because it implies that "history must come to an end one way or another"—in a world of garrison-prison states or in a world commonwealth)—does not, however, seem to be sustained by the whole body of Lasswell's writing. See particularly "The Prospects of Cooperation in a Bipolar World," *University of Chicago Law Review*, 15 (1948):877–901.

25. "Objective control" is discussed specifically in the context of civil-military relations in *The Soldier and the State*. Carl J. Friedrich had earlier discussed it in more general terms of the control of any expert by the political leadership.

26. The premise of world security is made explicit in *World Politics Faces Economics* (New York: McGraw-Hill, 1945).

27. The quoted phrases, except for the last, are from "The Prospects of Cooperation in a Bipolar World." The last is from "The Relation of Skill Politics to Class Politics and National Politics."

28. Lasswell did not specifically forecast the great Sino-Soviet mutual disenchantment (or any other specific event), but the processes of partial incorporation and geographic differentiation described in *World Politics and Personal Insecurity* are nowhere better illustrated than in Sino-Soviet relations.

29. " 'Inevitable' War."

30. There are in Harold Lasswell's writings many fewer references to patterns of regional integration and the building of regional institutions than references to world integration and world institutions.

31. It is this technocratic interpretation which Bernard Crick puts upon Lasswell's work in *The American Science of Politics* (Berkeley and Los Angeles: University of California Press, 1959). He places Harold Lasswell, and indeed the whole Chicago school, in the "sociocratic" tradition of Lester F. Ward. By somewhat underplaying Lasswell's emphasis on shared power and the emerging competition among skill groups in a commonwealth of merit, Crick makes his characterization of Lasswell's writings seem plausible.

32. "The Quantitative and the Qualitative in Political and Legal Analysis," *Daedalus* (Fall, 1959):642.

33. In "The Scientific Study of International Relations," *The Year Book of World Affairs*, 12 (1958):2–3, Lasswell distinguishes four among "several mutually supporting intellectual tasks": (1) scientific thinking or explanation (which may or may not be policy-relevant); (2) projective thinking, "the task of estimating the future"; (3) goal thinking or normative theory; and (4) policy thinking which "arises because of discrepancies between events that happen and events that are preferred." For a different view of the relation between theoretical and policy analysis, see James N. Rosenau's introduction in Rosenau, ed., *International Politics and Foreign Policy* (New York: Free Press, 1961).

15

*Legal Education for a Free Society:
Our Collective Responsibility*

MYRES S. MCDOUGAL

SOME twenty-five years ago, Professor Harold Lasswell and I
suggested, in our article "Legal Education and Public Policy:
Professional Training in the Public Interest,"[1] that a first indispensable step toward the effective reform of legal education in
our country was the clarification of ultimate aim. The ultimate
aim we urged was that "if legal education in the contemporary
world is adequately to serve the needs of a free and productive
commonwealth, it must be conscious, efficient, and systematic
training for policy making."[2] "The proper function of our law
schools is," we insisted, "to contribute to the training of policy-
makers for the ever more complete achievement of the democratic values that constitute the professed ends of American polity."[3] We found that the principal impediments to the acceptance
and implementation of such a goal by our schools were derived
from several factors: a continuing narrow conception of the role
and nature of law and legal institutions, a shapeless curriculum
largely organized about time-worn and overlapping technical
legal concepts rather than community values, and a pervasive
lack of emphasis upon many relevant skills in thinking, observation, and management. "What is needed now," we concluded, "is

This essay was delivered as the presidential address at the 1966 annual
meeting of the Association of American Law Schools (1966 Proceedings of the
Association of American Law Schools (Washington, D.C., 1967, part II, p.
33). It is not suggested that it offers more than the barest glimpse of the major
outlines of the policy-oriented jurisprudence which is so preeminently Professor Lasswell's creation. To summarize the contributions of Harold Lasswell to
jurisprudence, considered as theory for inquiry about law, would require a
substantial book. Indeed, his contributions are expressed in many books.

to implement ancient insights by reorienting every phase of law school curricula and skill training toward the achievement of clearly defined democratic values in all the areas of social life where lawyers have or can assert responsibility."[4]

It must be conceded, of course, that in the twenty-five years that have elapsed since we first offered this appraisal and recommendation, enormous changes—many for the better—have occurred in American legal education. The important questions, however, are whether these changes, as momentous as they have been, are of the character and magnitude necessary in a national community increasingly aspiring—under increasingly difficult conditions in both the lesser communities which constitute it and the larger communities of which it is a member—toward freedom, security, and abundance, and whether legal scholars are effectively seizing all the opportunities and initiatives open for improving the quality of legal education. In seeking to make a contribution to the general theme of reevaluation, I propose to explore briefly: (1) our present state of clarity about goals in legal education; (2) the broad outlines of the progress we have made toward adequacy in serving such goals; (3) the major contours of continuing inadequacies in achievement; (4) the factors which will affect our future achievement and the present configuration of these factors; and (5) certain alternatives which may be open to us, in the management of such factors, to improve the quality of our performance and achievement.

CLARITY IN GOALS

Happily, it does appear that we are today moving toward a more effective consensus about the major goals of legal education. It is no longer revolutionary to note the inescapable interdeterminations of legal process and social process and to suggest that, while not all policy may be law, all law—when law is appropriately conceived as decision conjoining authority and control—is irretrievably community policy. The recognition is widespread that the kind of constitutive process a community can establish and maintain very vitally affects the freedom, security, and abundance of its public order, and that the quality of public order a community can attain in turn largely conditions the character and economy of its constitutive process. Furthermore, in our contemporary community people have largely ceased to think of law as serving only the rather primitive functions of maintaining minimum order, preserving the peace, and minimizing unauthorized coercion; instead, they have generally come to think of it as a positive instrument for promoting optimum order and securing the greater production and wider distribution of all community values.

It is from this heightened perception of the interdeterminations of legal and social process that we find emerging a more realistic perception of the social function and responsibility of the lawyer. One current and widely accepted conception of a profession is that it is a group which possesses a special skill and has an enlightened view of the goals and aggregate consequences attending the exercise of its skill. From this perspective we can observe that the legal profession, when regarded functionally rather than conventionally, is composed of the members of the community who have a special skill in the management of processes of authoritative decision and whose distinctive social role is to establish and operate such processes in accordance with basic community policies. A representative, and extraordinarily eloquent, statement of this now popular conception of the distinctive role of the lawyer may be taken from Mr. Justice Fortas' dedicatory address at Rutgers:

> A lawyer is not merely a craftsman—or even an artist. He has a special role in our society. He is a professional. He is not merely a practitioner of a difficult, exacting and subtle art form. He is a professional, specially ordained to perform at the crisis time of the life of other people; and almost daily, to make moral judgments of great sensitivity. He is the principal laboratory worker in the mixing of governmental prescriptions. His is an important hand at the wheel of our economy because, as lawyer, he has a profoundly important voice in business transactions. And, of

course, he is the custodian of the flaming sword of individual, justice and personal liberty, as well as of the public order.[5]

It is from this more comprehensive, more realistic, conception of the social role of the lawyer that, as the late Albert J. Harno insisted,[6] our increasing consensus about the major goals of legal education is derived. If it is the distinctive function of the lawyer —as official, advocate, and counselor—to establish and manage processes of authoritative decision, then it must be the overriding goal of legal education to contribute to the enlightenment, and to afford the training in specific skills, necessary to the effective performance of this function. Indeed, there would appear to be widespread agreement today in the active profession and among legal scholars that the principal tasks of contemporary legal education, in implementing this overriding goal, extend to three different, but related, types of activities:

1. Professional training

This may be defined as the transmission from generation to generation of our accumulated knowledge about the management of legal process and training in the specific skills required for high quality professional performance.

The relevant time-span extends from the prospective lawyer's first selection of career through prelegal and law school studies, and transitional and refresher training, to the most intense specialization.

2. Research and inquiry

Fundamental inquiry about the operations of legal process and the interrelations of legal process and social process is designed to contribute to both the quality of professional training and the improvement of legal institutions and process. It is axiomatic that what we teach, and the improvements we recommend, cannot rise above our own knowledge.

3. Improvement of legal institutions and process

Such improvement depends upon anticipating emerging problems, recommending measures for solution, and taking the initiative in the promotion of improved policies, structures, and procedures.

PROGRESS TOWARD GOALS

THE progress that we have made in recent years in putting these major goals of legal education into controlling effect in this country, and the role of our Association in contributing to that progress, are matters of great pride for us all. In the quarter-century under review we have seen great schools created or developed over the entire country, from the deep South to the far West, and the once dominant Eastern schools are now but equals among many. Enough partial successes have been achieved in the performance of the various indispensable professional and intellectual tasks to suggest that, with appropriate financial support and more effective planning on a national scale, still more comprehensive and cumulative successes might be achieved in the future.

The more important advances which potentially affect the quality of professional training in all our schools are easily identifiable. A full itemization would include at least the following: the more frequent organization of curricula and courses in a framework of social-process events or problems rather than in the traditional focus upon complementary and ambiguous legal concepts; the introduction into casebooks, or other teaching instruments, of materials designed to facilitate a more contextual evaluation of problems and proposed solutions; the development of new interdisciplinary courses and seminars which draw upon skills from many fields other than law; a more conscious and systematic effort to afford training in the multiple skills required for the many different professional tasks of the lawyer; and, finally, the development of new and more effective teaching methods which build upon contemporary technologies and techniques and the findings of behavioral science.

Similarly, a considerable number of successful projects in fundamental, policy-oriented research, completed within recent years, offer convincing evidence of the important contributions that scholars might be able to make under more propitious conditions. In a very penetrating report, the Committee on Research offers a partial itemization:

In legal research, the fruits of certain major research undertakings have begun to appear: The University of Chicago jury project, the Columbia Project for Effective Justice, and the American Bar Foundation studies in the administration of criminal justice, and several studies of automobile claims have produced important published results. A number of smaller scale projects which have recently appeared are of equally interesting consequence—for example, the bail studies, Professor Gellhorn's comparative study of the Ombundsman and analagous agencies. Professor Goebel's edition of the Hamilton legal papers, Professor Beutel's study of bad checks, Professor Dunham's study of property transmissions at death, and the recent U.C.L.A. Law Review study of homosexuality and the law, to name only a few.

Finally, the continuing contributions of our law schools to the improvement of legal institutions and processes are written large in the activities of law reform commissions, governmental committees, and other recommending groups, and in an unceasing flow of publication and private promotion.

INADEQUACIES IN ACHIEVEMENT

In our less self-congratulatory moods, however, we all recognize that the progress we are making toward the shared, major goals of legal education is much too glacial. We contiune to be beset by too many conspicuous inadequacies in achievement to enjoy complacency. Despite the spread of great schools across the country, there remain several different levels of legal education in our country. Even within our Association there are "big-budget" schools and "little-budget" schools, and though our Association standards are not high, there are many schools and agencies dispensing legal education which we do not regard as meeting our standards. Most important, the "little-budget" schools and the nonmember schools and agencies are training most of our country's lawyers, and all of us together are not training enough lawyers of any kind, much less with the appropriate skills, to meet our national community needs.

The principal inadequacies in our contemporary professional

training derive both from a poor integration of the law-school and post-law-school experiences made available to prospective and neophyte lawyers and from certain abiding weaknesses in the content provided for these experiences. The total formal education of lawyers remains, unfortunately, divided between two different groups of institutions: the law schools, which assume a responsibility only for the first three or four years of training, and a whole conglomerate group of national and local organizations upon which is imposed responsibility for guiding transition to the profession, refresher training, and specialization. Within our law schools themselves, despite all the movement made toward the functional reorganization of courses, we still have not established comprehensive and homogeneous curricula which can map and guide inquiry and training throughout the whole range of important contemporary community problems. Even with the considerable expansion of interdisciplinary effort, the introduction of social-process materials to facilitate contextual analysis remains largely superficial and fragmentary. Our expanding emphasis upon training in news skills and upon employment of new techniques of instruction is still but a shadowy approximation of what would appear possible and needed. Despite all our high aspirations, our schools continue to be, as Professors Casner and Kaplan summarize, "conspicuously deficient" in "cultivating long perspectives in the minds of their students" and in "giving them a large view of the law" and of "its place and functions in society."[7] Furthermore, all these inadequacies of the law schools would appear to be compounded in most of the agencies engaged in the legal education which follows law school.

The relatively laggard state in our schools of policy-relevant research about law is common knowledge. The essential point was made sharply by Professor Willard Hurst:

> This series of developments—the great modern treatises, the invention of the law review, the uniform laws movement, and the Restatements—share a limiting factor, useful and great as their accomplishments have been. In their main emphasis, these developments have been essentially taxonomic enterprises. They have

been concerned chiefly with doctrinal classification, with developing large frames of ordered concepts, to bring great bodies of otherwise scattered official determination into meaningful relations in terms of values served and rules and procedures to implement values. But all of this went on with relatively little inquiry into the kind of questions which Holmes had raised in *The Common Law*. How does all this official decision making really work and what are the values and accomplishments for which it stands, as measured in its working operations?[8]

In the same vein, the report of the Committee on Research quoted above, after noting the insistent new challenges of our time to legal order, concludes: "Indeed, it does not seem too much to say that unless new research departures are made, the law schools and the legal profession may well become ineffectual and perhaps redundant in regard to the major legal issues of the day and of the future."

Leadership in law improvement, for a final illustration of continuing inadequacy, still too often founders upon the lack of properly tested knowledge, failures in the organization of cooperative effort, and the indifference of an otherwise overburdened academic community.

FACTORS AFFECTING THE FUTURE

WHEN we turn from description of where we now are in legal education to exploration of the factors likely to affect our future, we can, I believe, observe at least some modest bases for optimism. Anthropologically viewed, legal education is a distinctive social process which occurs in a large community context. It is affected by factors both internal to its own specialized processes and having impact upon it from the external context. Comprehensively stated, the factors internal to legal education include: the participants in the process, with all their special characteristics and disinctive perspectives; the structures and organizations established; the resources secured and put into use; and the strategies or techniques of inquiry and instruction employed. The most critical of these factors, however, would appear to be the perspectives of the participants: the demands they make upon themselves for inquiry and teaching, the communities they identify with, and the expectations or understanding they have about law and its potential role in community process. Similarly, the factors external to legal education would include, if comprehensively formulated, all the significant features of the whole "big, blooming, buzzing" earth-space community process. Again, however, the most critical factors would appear capable of economic specification simply in terms of the demands which the members of the relevant external communities make upon legal education and of the resources which they make available for legal education. The resources which community members make available for legal education must, of course, in realistic derivation from the maximization postulate, be a function of the net advantages to public order which they expect to gain from such subsidization.

The factor affording the best hope for future improvement of legal education, and for persuading the general community that such improvement is feasible and imminent, would appear to be that comprised of the changing perspectives of those most directly engaged in legal education. The explicitly policy-oriented nature of the demands which many contemporary legal educators make upon themselves with respect to both inquiry and teaching has already been sufficiently indicated in our description of the increasing consensus about major goals. The more recent activities of this Association, and the generous support accorded by many leaders of the American Bar Association, offer ample documentation of the increasing number of people who can identify themselves, beyond their own particular locality or school or organization, with the larger community interest in the whole of American legal education and, hence, concern themselves with national, and even international, goals and aggregate consequences. Most important, however, is the fact that the perspectives of many contemporary scholars would appear to be converging upon the clarification and employment of a new and more comprehensive theory *about* law—a jurisprudence or philosophy of law—which could greatly facilitate the acquisition and communication of policy-relevant knowledge about the reciprocal impacts of legal process and social process. Heir to many historic developments in jurisprudence and social thought, and formulated by different scholars in many different equivalences of language, this emerging theory about law seeks three ends: the first is to distinguish clearly the observational standpoint of the scholar from that of the more active participant in processes of decision; the second is to achieve a focus of inquiry which comprehensively and economically locates the processes of authoritative decision, to which lawyers are specialized, in the larger community processes in which they occur; the third is to encourage, and specify procedures for, the systematic, disciplined, and contextual performance of the whole range of intellectual tasks indispensable to rational policy choice and implementation.

In its search for a focus of inquiry which can increase the policy relevance of both inquiry and teaching, this emerging, contemporary theory about law projects certain important, interrelated emphases:

1. A balanced emphasis upon perspectives and operations
   Both the traditional overemphasis on perspectives, as expressed in rules, and the behavioristic exclusive concern for operations are rejected. A focus is sought squarely upon *decision*, including both perspectives and operations. In this way the formal, manifest content of perspectives may be pierced for observation of choices in fact made, and perspectives may be realistically studied as important influences upon choice.

2. Clarity in conception of both authority and control
   Authority is defined empirically in terms of the expectations of community members about the requirements of decision; control is defined as participation in the making of effective choices. Law is regarded as decision in which authority and control are conjoned.

   In this conception, both authority and control can be subjected to systematic and disciplined inquiry by employment of all the techniques of modern science.

3. Comprehensiveness in conception of process of authoritative decision

Every community is observed to maintain a continuing, constitutive process of authoritative decision which identifies appropriate decision-makers, clarifies basic community policies, establishes structures of authority, maintains bases of power, authorizes implementing procedures, and projects the many different types of decisions necessary to the making and application of community policy. It is this process which secures and protects the community's public order in the sense that it makes the decisions which affect the shaping and sharing of wealth, enlightenment, respect, health, and all other demanded values.

From this perspective law is not confined to what courts do and the many vacuous distinctions between "legal" and "political" become untenable. Inquiry is appropriately extended to all the features of the process by which law is made and applied and to their consequences for preferred public order.

4. Relation of law to social process

Authoritative decision is not regarded as something which happens spontaneously or autonomously but as a response to events occurring in social process. This response is affected by many different events in social process and has, in turn, consequences for the future distribution of values.

By appropriate employment of "value" and "institutional" concepts, the claims which people make to authoritative decision, and particular types of decisions, may be categorized in ways that facilitate the comparison, through time and across territorial boundaries, of the factors that affect decision and of the public-order consequences of decisions.

5. Relation of law to its larger community context

It is recognized that today social process occurs on a global scale, and that just as we have a global community in science and technology, so also do we have authoritative decision on a comparable scale. The global process of authoritative decision is seen to operate at many different community levels and in many different, interpenetrating patterns of authority and control. It affects, and is affected by, both the social process transcending all particular communities and that internal to the different communities.

From such a perspective, international law and comparative law offer an indispensable center and circumference for inquiry and teaching which would be consequential and which would afford promise of more effective appraisal of contending ideologies and constitutive processes aspiring toward completion on the global scale.

The intellectual tasks which the new, emerging theory about law recommends for performance with respect to the area of inquiry so identified are not confined to the lawyer's traditional skill in logical derivation, or even to modern scientific skills, but—in persistent effort to increase the policy relevance of teaching and inquiry—extend to a variety of distinguishable, but intimately interrelated, specific skills:

1. Clarification of community policies

As recommended, clarification begins with the postulation of a comprehensive set of community goals and then seeks the more detailed specification of these goals, at all levels of abstraction, in empirical terms which make explicit reference to events in social process. In the degree that economy permits, it is urged that every choice be related to its larger community context and to all important community policies. The procedures recommended for such specification demand knowledge of past trends in decision, past conditioning factors, future probabilities, and possible alternatives; hence, these procedures require the simultaneous and systematic performance of all the other relevant intellectual tasks.

2. Description of past trends in decision

Past trends in decision are described, systematically rather than anecdotally, in terms of their approximations to clarified policies. The events which precipitate claims to authoritative decision, the factors affecting decision, and the consequences of decision for social process are all described, as indicated above, in the double reference "value" and "institutional" categories which permit effective comparison of decisions and consequences through time and across community boundaries.

3. Analysis of factors affecting decision

Comprehensive theories which explain decision are formulated and tested by the appropriate procedures of contemporary science. Overwhelming importance is not ascribed to any one factor or category of factors (such as those relating to wealth), and inquiry is made into the interplay of multiple factors. The significance of factors deriving from culture, class, interest, personality, exposure to crisis, and resource environment is explicitly recognized. Rigor is sought in theoretical models, but not by an overemphasis on the importance of measurement or experiment. Many different observational standpoints and both extensive and intensive procedures are employed in data gathering and processing.

4. Projection of future trends in decision

It is sought to make expectations about the future as conscious, realistic, and explicit as possible. The simple linear or chronological extrapolations of conventional legal theory are subjected to the discipline of knowledge about conditioning factors and other pertinent bases of inference. Developmental constructs embodying varying anticipations of the future are deliberately formulated and tested in the light of all available information.

5. Invention and evaluation of policy alternatives

Creativity is encouraged by the demand for the deliberate invention and assessment of new alternatives in policy, institutional structures, and procedures. It is recommended that every phase of the decision process, whether of constitutive process or relating to public order, be examined for opportunities for innovation which may influence decision toward greater conformity with the clarified goal. Assessment of particular alternatives is made in terms of gains and losses with respect to all clarified goals and is disciplined by knowledge of trends, conditioning factors, and future probabilities. Special procedures for encouraging creativity include expansions and contractions of the focus of attention, alter nation of periods of intensive concentration and inattention, free association, and experiment with random combinations.[9]

The comprehensive goal values which most contemporary scholars postulate for clarification and implementation are, of course, the values, which we commonly characterize as those of a free society or of human dignity. These values were first expressed clearly in Western European civilization and are now slowly diffusing about the globe. In their most abstract formulation, these values stipulate the greatest production and the widest possible sharing of all the respresentative values of our culture. Today they infuse both authoritative prescription and private utterance, and are continuously being defined and redefined—by application of the various relevant intellectual tasks—in both decision and scholarship, for relation to particular problems and choices. Fortunately, many of us recognize increasingly that however much we may aspire to be detached or neutral, our inquiries and appraisals must of necessity have value consequences, and, hence, that it is our opportunity and obligation, as specialized intellectuals who are both scholars and members of the legal profession, not merely to relate law to some kind of policy, but rather, and further, to clarify and promote the policies, institutional structures, and procedures best designed to serve the particular kind of public order we cherish.

If we turn from our own internal perspectives to the factors in the external context which will in the future most directly affect the quality of legal education, a factor of critical significance would appear to be, as suggested above, the demands which the various communities of which we are members—international, national, and local—will make upon us for improved performance. These demands can scarcely be expected to be less enormous or less intense than the demands which will be made upon law itself. In our recently emerged nuclear–space age[10]—with its expanding and uniformizing civilization of science and technology, its exploding and increasingly migratory populations, and its ever accelerating rate of change in all features—enormous demands are already being made, and can be expected to intensify, in all our communities for improved, more adequate law with respect to every feature of both constitutive process and public order. In the larger earth-space community these demands are most insistent with respect to such problems as security or minimum order, the minimization of unauthorized violence and coercion; the peaceful change of archaic and inefficient territorial groupings into viable, integrated, regional communities; the establishment and maintenance of a more abundant international economy with a greater production and wider distribution of goods and services; and the more effective promotion and protection of basic human rights both within the different territorial communities and across their boundaries. In our own national community, as in other such communities, comparable demands are no less insistent with respect to such problems as minimizing criminal violence and coercion, controlling civil disobedience, improving the efficiency of constitutive process and securing wider participation in all effective power processes, establishing appropriate community and resource planning and maintaining an abundant internal economy whose fruits are widely shared, facilitating education and encouraging the acquisition and dissemination of new knowledge, increasing the protection of basic human rights and civil liberties, promoting congenial personal relationships and fostering the loyalties necessary to serve public order goals, cultivating and disseminating effective norms of responsible conduct, and so on. If all these demands are to be met by improvement in processes of authoritative decision rather than by assertions of naked power, it should require little argument to establish that the parallel demands from all our communities upon legal education for fundamental research, for the training of more and better lawyers, and for leadership initiatives can only be of a magnitude we have not hitherto known.

The unhappy paradox is, however, that the different communities which have so much at stake in legal education have not, historically, been willing to make available to it resources commensurate with the demands made upon it. It hardly needs documentation that financial support for legal education throughout our country, whether in state-supported schools or private schools, has always been small and remains insubstantial both in relation to need and in comparison to the support made available to the physical sciences and the other social sciences. For all the major goals specified above, our law schools have been and are, when high standards of performance are stipulated, relatively impoverished institutions. A recent study by Dean Robert B. McKay, made under the auspices of the Association of American Law Schools and of the American Bar Association and through the generosity of the Walter E. Meyer Institute of Law, confirms that during the past decade the support made available for the fundamental inquiry indispensable to both effective teaching and rational law improvement continued to be very modest and came mostly from a single source, the Ford Foundation. It would not appear that we have been overly successful in persuading our various communities that the net advantages to public order to be gained from our more extensive subsidization are likely to be in fact what they are in potential.

ALTERNATIVES FOR IMPROVEMENT

IN conclusion, the important question to which we must now come is that of what alternatives, in the management of the factors recounted above, will permit us to improve our performance and increase our contribution to the kind of public order we postulate and demand. For an enterprise embracing as many different activities and affected by as many different variables as "legal education," promising alternatives are of course legion, and different appraisers prescribe many different remedies. As has been remarked about making love to an octopus, the difficulty is in knowing how best to catch hold of the damned thing. From the perspectives sketched above, however, three specialized types of activity, and a proposal for the establishment of a new organization exclusively dedicated to the problems of legal education, would appear to offer greatest promise of immediate, high returns in improvement. What is involved in each of these possible alternatives may be briefly indicated.

First, we might intensify our efforts, as Lasswell and I recommended twenty-five years ago and as our presently preferred theories about law require, to reorient the basic curricula of our schools toward a more comprehensive and systematic coverage of all the more important contemporary problems of our different communities. The consequences of our basic curricula, and of the principles of their organization, for the effectiveness of our work cannot be overestimated: they map our inquiry and affect what we learn; they organize and condition the student's experiences in his most formative years; and they mold the abiding predispositions of the whole profession. One of our most urgent needs is for still more experimentation in the testing of new ways of organizing the different segments of a curriculum, and of relating the various segments to the whole, for two purposes: to bring to bear upon every segment the findings and techniques of modern science and other knowledge, and to facilitate a genuine, contextual analysis of all problems through employment of all the different, relevant intellectual skills.

Second, we might seek to institutionalize, on a national scale, continuous intelligence and planning functions with respect to legal education and related activities. In our present ignorance about the details of what we are doing and of its consequences for public order, it is difficult for us to make rational plans for improvement or to persuade our different communities to make available the resources necessary to support projected improvement. What is badly needed is no "one-shot" study, like the famous Flexner report on medical education or the somewhat less influential Reed report on legal education, but rather the establishment and maintenance of a comprehensive overview, with continuing audit and assessment in terms of national community needs, of total professional performance in relation to legal research and training and the improvement of legal institutions and process. Unfortunately, no existing agency or group has either the capabilities or responsibility for taking on this function.

Third, we might make a much more deliberate and organized effort to secure the additional resources we so urgently require. It is probable that funds of the magnitude necessary for effective pursuit of all our purposes can come only from the federal government, but other sources might be persuaded—in aid of our independence—to make substantial contributions. Both private philanthropy and the federal government appear predisposed to make huge sums available to medicine, the physical sciences, the humanities, and the other social sciences; it can scarcely be conceded that such donees either have or can make a better case for support than we have and can make. Some years ago, when he was president of the American Bar Association, Ross Malone made a suggestion, still not acted upon, for the establishment of a national legal education fund, comparable to the National Fund for Medical Education founded so successful by the doctors, to which members of the legal profession and others could contribute for disbursement on a national scale.[11] During a recent Congress proposals were made for the establishment of a national foundation for the social sciences, which would include law, and there was even some talk about the need of a special national foundation for law. In this context of community predisposition, it would appear that we have only our poverty to lose by taking strong, affirmative action.

The proposal for the establishment of a new, private organization exclusively dedicated to legal education and law improvement has origins in several simultaneous initiatives and has been under discussion in recent years both in the Special Committee on Financial Resources of the Association of American Law Schools and in an informal group of officers and representatives of this Association and of the American Bar Association. The proposal expresses a conscious awareness of past limitations and a deep concern and motivation for future improvement. While all formulations are still most tentative and will require further discussion in various groups before any definitive step can be taken, the alternative which at the moment appears to achieve the highest degree of consensus among the discussants would project a new, independent, private foundation in which all branches of the profession and the public would be represented and which would be charged with the whole variety of functions necessary to the effective pursuit of our contemporary goals in legal education and law improvement. The fact that it may be necessary to have recourse to the federal government to secure funds of the magnitude required to serve all goals is thought merely to enhance the need for private initiative, planning, and participation in control. To emphasize its comprehensiveness in purpose and its national perspectives, it has been suggested that the new foundation should be named the American Law Foundation.

The broad outlines of what this foundation might undertake can perhaps be most economically indicated by a seriatim enumeration of the specific functions contemplated for it. Of course, it would be expected that the foundation would build adequacy block by block, or step-wise, as resources become available to it, but the functions, at present largely unperformed by other agencies, which have been suggested for inclusion in its charter are somewhat formidable in total proportion:

1. Intelligence and planning

The central task of the ALF would be to establish and maintain a comprehensive overview, with continuing audit and assessment in terms of national community needs, of professional performance in relation to all the major purposes of legal education and law improvement.

For example, the ALF might be constituted as a continuing commission of inquiry and recommendation about the quality and conditions of legal education, including both that offered by law schools and that acquired from other agencies and through later experiences.

Most important, the ALF might afford a voluntary forum in which the most experienced and responsible members of all branches of the profession could share views, meet with experts from other disciplines, and increase their awareness of problems and possible solutions.

2. Assembling and managing financial resources

The ALF would assist in the search for, and assembly of, funds adequate to serve all the important purposes for which it is established.

A primary function of the ALF would be to assist the law

schools and other relevant agencies in increasing their own resources.

The ALF would, however, seek resources for its own operations, and it could serve as an economic granting agency in the funding of various types of activities. Thus, the ALF might, as broker for the great multipurpose foundations or the federal government, offer a simple and economic procedure for the processing of applications from individual scholars or others for relatively small, but still important, projects.

Similarly, in an effort to encourage diversity, the ALF might afford occasional support for especially daring individuals and institutions and for projects which do not fit into the generally accepted patterns.

The ALF would make the necessary studies and prepare plans for encouraging the federal government to assist in the provision of the funds necessary for strengthening the legal profession and for improving legal institutions and process.

3. Training of qualified personnel

The ALF would plan for, and undertake to secure the establishment of, programs to increase our resources of personnel qualified for teaching, research, and leadership in law reform.

The ALF would conduct, or stimulate others to conduct, workshops and seminars designed to enable established teachers and scholars to increase their mastery over the new techniques made possible by advancing science and technology.

The ALF would promote the establishment of fellowships and other forms of assistance designed to encourage new recruits for careers in research, teaching, and law improvement.

The ALF would establish, or promote the establishment of, appropriate programs for the training of law librarians and other experts on the storage, retrieval, and dissemination of knowledge.

The ALF would conduct, or stimulate others to conduct, workshops for judges, legislators, and administrative officers from all levels of authority.

4. Promotion of research and law improvement activities

The ALF would encourage the most promising initiatives,

wherever they may be found, in conducting relevant research and undertaking appropriate law improvement activities.

The ALF would encourage individual and group or institutional (including governmental) understakings.

The ALF would maintain a staff with appropriate interdisciplinary skills to assist in the formulation and execution of projects.

The ALF would seek to identify the problems to which interdisciplinary efforts can make needed contributions and to establish appropriate teams for inquiry.

The ALF would especially promote the dissemination of the results of inquiry and the establishment of a better network of information throughout the community of interested parties.

5. Conduct of research

While the primary objective of the ALF would be to encourage research by others, it would itself undertake important projects which could not be expected to interest other agencies or organizations.

Thus, the ALF would conduct such necessary studies as those relating to the role of the profession and its modalities in organization—including admission to practice, the establishment of national standards and procedures, accreditation of schools, the promotion of specialization, and so on—and those relating to the "unauthorized practice" of law or the rendering of professional services by lawyer "equivalents" or "ancillaries."

6. Engaging in law improvement activities

The ALF would undertake operations of an experimental, model, or prototypic character designed to encourage others to emulation.

The ALF would promote increasing awareness among non-lawyers of the intimate interrelations of legal process and social process and of the fruits of inquiry about this interrelation in specific instances.

The ALF would conduct, or stimulate others to conduct, workshops and seminars designed to provide more general education about the role of law in society.

As a distinguished English international lawyer has insisted, the time is always ripe for something that needs to be done. "Time," he wrote, "is a forelock and, after great wars and great upheavals, that forelock hangs out like a bell-rope and needs to be pulled."[12] It is not my suggestion that the alternatives outlined above comprise all the opportunities open to us for increasing our contribution to, and discharging our responsibility for, the clarification and maintenance of a public order of freedom and human dignity. I suggest only that the time is most ripe, in this age of nuclear and space upheavals and of ever increasing demands by all our communities upon law, for us to adopt and make effective, if not these proposals, then some equivalent or comparable alternatives.

REFERENCES

1. *Yale Law Journal*, 52 (1943):203.
2. *Ibid.*, p. 206.
3. *Ibid.*
4. *Ibid.*, p. 207.
5. Abe Fortas, "The Training of the Practitioner," dedicatory address given at Rutgers University School of Law on September 10, 1966. Published in David Haber and Julius Cohen, eds., *The Law School of Tomorrow: The Projection of an Ideal* (1968).
6. Albert James Harno, "American Legal Education," *American Bar Association Journal*, 46 (1960):845, 847; *Legal Education in the United States* (San Francisco: Bancroft-Whitney, 1953).
7. James A. Casner and Benjamin Kaplan, "The Law School's Role in Developing a Lawyer," in *The Law Schools Look Ahead* (Ann Arbor: University of Michigan Law School, 1959), pp. 98, 99.
8. Willard Hurst, "Perspectives upon Research into Legal Order," *Wisconsin Law Review*, 1961, pp. 356, 362.
9. The sketch here has drawn upon M. S. McDougal, "Jurisprudence for a Free Society," *Georgia Law Review*, 1 (1966):1. A more extended statement appears in H. D. Lasswell and M. S. McDougal, "Jurisprudence in Policy-Oriented Perspective," *University of Florida Law Review*, 19 (1967):19.
10. This appellation is employed in a perceptive statement in Glenn T. Seaborg, "Science, the Humanities and the Federal Govern-

ment—Partners in Progress," *American Council of Learned Societies Newsletter,* 17 (May, 1966):1.

11. Ross L. Malone, "Our First Responsibility: The President's Annual Address," *American Bar Association Journal,* 45 (1959): 1023.

12. W. Harvey Moore, "International Law and Rights of the Individual," *Transactions of the Grotius Society,* 31 (1945):106.

Bibliography of Works by Harold D. Lasswell

Compiled by JERRY GASTON

1923

Articles

"Chicago's Old First Ward." *National Municipal Review* 12 (1923): 127–31.
"Political Policies and the International Investment Market." *Journal of Political Economy* 31 (1923): 380–400.

1924

Book

Labor Attitudes and Problems (with Willard Earl Atkins). New York: Prentice-Hall, Inc., 1924.

Article

"Current Public Opinion and the Public Service Commissions" (with C. E. Merriam). In *Public Utility Regulation*, edited by Morris L. Cooke. New York: Ronald Press, 1924. Pp. 276–95.

1925

Articles

"German Pacifists in Wartime." *The Messengers of Peace* (Hamburg), 50 (1925):177–92.
"Prussian Schoolbooks and International Amity." *Journal of Social Forces* 3 (1925):718–22.
"The Status of Research on International Propaganda and Opinion." *American Journal of Sociology* 32 (1925):198–209.
"Two Forgotten Studies in Political Psychology." *American Political Science Review* 19 (1925):707–17.

Reviews

Blanc, Elsie Terry. *Co-operative Movement in Russia. American Journal of Sociology* 31 (1925):108–9.

Bowden, R. D. *The Evolution of the Politician. American Journal of Sociology* 30 (1925):492.

Brooks, Robert C. *Political Parties and Electorate Problems. American Journal of Sociology* 30 (1925):492.

Cooke, Richard J. *Religion in Russian under the Soviets. American Journal of Sociology* 31 (1925):108–9.

Rice, Stuart A. *Farmers and Workers in American Politics. American Journal of Sociology* 31 (1925):108.

Sorokin, Pitirim. *Leaves from a Russian Diary. American Journal of Sociology* 31 (1925):108–9.

1926

Reviews

Bakeless, John. *The Origin of the Next War. American Journal of Sociology* 32 (1926):147–48.

Carroll, E. Malcolm. *Origins of the Whig Party. American Journal of Sociology* 31 (1926):701.

Lippmann, Walter. *The Phantom Public. American Journal of Sociology* 31 (1926):533–35.

Overstreet, H. A. *Influencing Human Behavior. American Journal of Sociology* 32 (1926):141–42.

Stoddard, Lothrop. *Social Classes in Post-War Europe. American Journal of Sociology* 31 (1926):701.

1927

Book

Propaganda Technique in the World War. New York: A. A. Knopf; London: Kegan Paul, 1927. (Ph.D. dissertation.)

Articles

"The Theory of Political Propaganda." *American Political Science Review* 21 (1927):627–31.

"Types of Political Personalities." *Proceedings of the American Sociological Society* 22 (1927):159–69.

Reviews

Albion, Robert G. *Forests and Sea Power. American Journal of Sociology* 33 (1927):138–39.

Angell, Norman. *The Public Mind. American Journal of Sociology* 33 (1927):142–43.

Brown, Ralph M. *Legal Psychology. American Journal of Sociology* 33 (1927):147–48.

Buchholz, H. E. *United States: A Second Study in Democracy. American Journal of Sociology* 32 (1927):673.

Callender, Clarence N. *American Courts: Organization and Procedure. American Journal of Sociology* 33 (1927):314.

Casson, Hebert N. *Tips on Leadership: Life Stories of Twenty-five Leaders. American Journal of Sociology* 33 (1927):154.

Clarke, John H. *America and World Peace. American Journal of Sociology* 32 (1927):673.

Eldridge, Seba. *Political Action. American Journal of Sociology* 32 (1927):1007–8.

Lennes, N. J. *Whither Democracy? American Political Science Review* 21 (1927):654–55.

Pasquet, D. *An Essay on the Origins of the House of Commons. American Journal of Sociology* 32 (1927):658–59.

Pipkin, Charles W. *The Idea of Social Justice. American Political Science Review* 21 (1927):654–55.

Simon, E. D. *A City Council from Within. American Journal of Sociology* 33 (1927):143–44.

Tead, Ordway, and Metcalf, Henry C. *Personnel Administration: Its Principles and Practice* (2d ed., Revised). *American Journal of Sociology* 32 (1927):1017–18.

Wooddy, Carroll Hill. *The Chicago Primary of 1926. American Journal of Sociology* 32 (1927):848–49.

1928

Articles

"Foreign Influences on American Labor." In *American Labor Dynamics*, edited by J. B. S. Hardman. New York: Harcourt, Brace, 1928. Pp. 360–65.

"Function of the Propagandist." *International Journal of Ethics* 38 (1928):258–68.

Reviews

Bruce, Harold R. *American Parties and Politics. American Journal of Sociology* 34 (1928):235–36.

Delaisi, Francis. *Political Myths and Economic Realities. American Journal of Sociology* 34 (1928):234.

Dickinson, John. *Administrative Justice and the Supremacy of Law in the United States. American Journal of Sociology* 33 (1928): 1006–8.

Frankfurter, Felix, and Landis, James M. *The Business of the Supreme Court. American Journal of Sociology* 34 (1928):230.

Lippmann, Walter. *American Inquisitors. American Journal of Sociology* 34 (1928):558–59.

Pollard, A. F. *The Evolution of Parliament. American Journal of Sociology* 32 (1928):658–59.

Ripley, W. Z. *Main Street and Wall Street. American Journal of Sociology* 33 (1928):658–59.

Roberts, Penfield. *An Introduction to American Politics. American Journal of Sociology* 34 (1928):235–36.

Ward, Paul W. *Sovereignty. American Journal of Sociology* 34 (1928):559.

Warnotte, Daniel. *Les Origines sociologiques de l'obligation contractuelle. American Journal of Sociology* 33 (1928):671.

Zimmern, Alfred. *The Third British Empire. American Journal of Sociology* 33 (1928):677.

1929

Articles

"Personality Studies." In *Chicago: An Experiment in Social Science Research,* edited by T. V. Smith and L. D. White. Chicago: University of Chicago Press, 1929. Pp. 177–93.

"Problem of Adequate Personality Records: A Proposal." *American Journal of Psychiatry* 7 (1929):1057–66.

"The Study of the Ill as a Method of Research into Political Personalities." *American Political Science Review* 23 (1929):996–1001.

Reviews

Elliott, W. Y. *The Pragmatic Revolt in Politics: Syndicalism, Fascism, and the Constitutional State. American Journal of Sociology* 35 (1929):134–35.

Florence, P. Sargent. *Economics and Human Behaviour. American Journal of Sociology* 34 (1929):751–52.

de Ruggiero, Guido. *The History of European Liberalism. American Journal of Sociology* 34 (1929):730–31.

Thompson, John Griffin. *Urbanization: Its Effect on Government and Society. American Journal of Sociology* 34 (1929):744.

Reprint

"Types of Political Personalities." In *Personality and Group*, edited by E. W. Burgess. Chicago: University of Chicago Press, 1929. Pp. 151–61.

1930

Book

Psychopathology and Politics. Chicago: University of Chicago Press, 1930.

Articles

"Adams, Brooks." *Encyclopedia of the Social Sciences* 1 (1930): 429–30.

"Agitation." *Encyclopedia of the Social Sciences* 1 (1930):487–88.

"Bribery." *Encyclopedia of the Social Sciences* 2 (1930):690–92.

"Censorship." *Encyclopedia of the Social Sciences* 3 (1930): 290–94.

"Chauvinism." *Encylopedia of the Social Sciences* 3 (1930):361.

"Personality System and Its Substitutive Reactions." *Journal of Abnormal Psychology* 24 (1930):433–40.

"Psychoanalytic Interviews as a Method of Research on Personalities." *Childs Emotions*, February, 1930:136–57.

"The Scientific Study of Human Biography." *Scientific Monthly* 30 (1930):79–80.

"Self-analysis and Judicial Thinking." *International Journal of Ethics* 40 (1930):354–62.

Reviews

Adler, Alfred. *The Science of Living. American Journal of Sociology* 36 (1930):492–93.

Alexander, Franz, and Staub, Hugo. *Der Verbrecher und seine Richter, Ein Psychoanalytischer Einblick in der Welt der Paragraphen. American Journal of Sociology* 35 (1930):653–55.

Bianchi, Leonardo. *Foundations of Mental Health. American Journal of Sociology* 36 (1930):492–93.

Calverton, V. F. *Sex in Civilisation. American Journal of Sociology* 35 (1930):662–63.

Clarke, Edwin Leavitt. *The Art of Straight Thinking. American Political Science Review* 24 (1930):473–76.

Grattan, C. Hartley. *Why We Fought. New Republic* 62 (1930): 104–5.

Gross, Hans. *Archiv für Kriminologie. American Journal of Sociology* 36 (1930):492–93.

House, Floyd N. *The Range of Social Theory. American Political Science Review* 24 (1930):473–76.

Jones, Thomas Jesse. *Essentials of Civilization: A Study of Social Values. American Political Science Review* 24 (1930):473–76.

Murchison, Carl. *Social Psychology: The Psychology of Political Domination. American Political Science Review* 24 (1930):473–76.

Odum, Howard W. *An Introduction to Social Research. American Political Science Review* 24 (1930):473–76.

Petrescu, Nicholas. *The Interpretation of National Differentiations. American Journal of Sociology* 36 (1930):506.

Potter, Pitman B. *This World of Nations. American Journal of Sociology* 36 (1930):506.

Wells, George Ross. *Individuality and Social Restraint. American Political Science Review* 24 (1930):473–76.

1931

Articles

"The Comparative Methods of James Bryce." In *Methods in Social Science: A Case Book*, edited by Stuart A. Rice. Chicago: University of Chicago Press, 1931. Pp. 468–79.

"Compromise." *Encyclopedia of the Social Sciences* 4 (1931):147–49.

"Conflict, Social." *Encyclopedia of the Social Sciences* 4 (1931):194–96.

"Faction." *Encyclopedia of the Social Sciences* 6 (1931):49–51.

"Feuds." *Encyclopedia of the Social Sciences* 6 (1931):220–21.

"Fraternizing." *Encyclopedia of the Social Sciences* 6 (1931): 425–27.

"An Hypothesis Rooted in the Preconceptions of a Single Civilization Tested by Bronislaw Malinowski." In *Methods in Social Science: A Case Book*, edited by Stuart A. Rice. Chicago: University of Chicago Press, 1931. Pp. 480–88.

"The Measurement of Public Opinion." *American Political Science Review* 25 (1931):311–26.

Reviews

Coleman, Emily Holmes. *The Shutter of Snow. American Journal of Sociology* 37 (1931):328–31.

Freud, Sigmund. *Civilization and Its Discontents. American Journal of Sociology* 37 (1931):328–31.

Healy, William, Bronner, Augusta F., and Bowers, Anna Mae. *The Structure and Meaning of Psychoanalysis as Related to Personality and Behaviour. American Journal of Sociology* 36 (1931):652–54.

Hesseltine, William Best. *Civil War Prisons: A Study in War Psychology. American Political Science Review* 25 (1931):234.

Jordan, E. *Theory of Legislation: An Essay on the Dynamics of the Public Mind. American Journal of Sociology* 37 (1931):335–36.

Kolnai, Aurel. *Sexualethik, Sinn und Grundlagen der Geschelechtsmoral. American Journal of Sociology* 37 (1931):328–31.

Mowrer, Edgar Ansel. *Sinon, or the Future of Politics. American Political Science Review* 25 (1931):1070.

Other

"Professor Harold D. Lasswell's Classification." Appendix B in *Methods in Social Science: A Case Book*, edited by Stuart A. Rice. Chicago: University of Chicago Press, 1931. Pp. 740–42.

1932
Articles

"Der amerikanische Prazendenzfall und das Problem der politischen Einigung der Welt." *Amerika-Post* (Hamburg), 4 (1932):21–28.

"Triple-Appeal Principle: A Contribution of Psychoanalysis to Political and Social Science." *American Journal of Sociology* 37 (1932): 523–38.

Reviews

Dodge, Raymond, and Kahn, Eugen. *The Craving for Superiority.* *American Journal of Sociology* 38 (1932):332.

Kahn, Eugen. *Psychopathic Personalities.* *American Journal of Sociology* 38 (1932):143–45.

MacCartney, Clarence Edward. *Lincoln and His Cabinet.* *American Journal of Sociology* 37 (1932):851.

Nomad, Max. *Rebels and Renegades.* *American Journal of Sociology* 38 (1932):466.

Peck, Martin. *The Meaning of Psychoanalysis.* *American Journal of Sociology* 38 (1932):146–48.

Pierce, Frederick. *Dreams and Personality.* *American Journal of Sociology* 38 (1932):143–45.

Rank, Otto. *Modern Education: A Critique of Its Fundamental Ideas.* *American Journal of Sociology* 38 (1932):304–5.

Sherrill, Charles H. *Bismarck and Mussolini.* *American Journal of Sociology* 38 (1932):346.

Thompson, Dow. *A Mind That Was Different.* *American Journal of Sociology* 38 (1932):143–45.

Wittels, Fritz. *Freud and His Time.* *American Journal of Sociology* 38 (1932):146–48.

Worcester, Elwood, and McComb, Samuel. *Body, Mind, and Spirit.* *American Journal of Sociology* 38 (1932):146–48.

1933

Articles

"Morale." *Encyclopedia of the Social Sciences* 10 (1933):640–42.

"Problem of World Unity: In Quest of a Myth." *International Journal of Ethics* 44 (1933):68–93.

"Psychoanalyse and Sozioanalyse." *Imago* (Vienna), 19 (1933): 377–83.

"Psychology of Hitlerism." *Political Quarterly* (London), 4 (1933): 373–84.

"The Strategy of Revolutionary and War Propaganda." In *Public Opinion and World Politics*, edited by Quincy Wright. Chicago: University of Chicago Press, 1933. Pp. 185–221.

Reviews

Jastrow, Joseph. *The House That Freud Built*. American Journal of Sociology 34 (1933):143–44.

Ortega y Gasset, Jose. *The Revolt of the Masses*. American Political Science Review 27 (1933):120.

Thimme, Hans. *Weltkrieg ohne Waffen*. American Political Science Review 27 (1933):485–86.

Webb, Sidney, and Webb, Beatrice. *Methods of Social Study*. American Political Review 27 (1933):845–46.

1934

Articles

"Aggressive Behavior by Clients toward Public Relief Administrators" (with Gabriel Almond). *American Political Science Review* 28 (1934):643–55.

"Propaganda." *Encyclopedia of the Social Sciences* 12 (1934):521–27.

Reviews

Adams, Grace. *Psychology: Science or Superstition?* American Journal of Sociology 40 (1934):253–54.

Allers, Rudolf. *The New Psychologies*. American Journal of Sociology 40 (1934):426.

Childs, Harwood L. *A Reference Guide to the Study of Public Opinion*. American Political Science Review 28 (1934):1139.

Clark, L. Pierce. *Lincoln: A Psycho-biography*. American Journal of Sociology 39 (1934):541–42.

Engelbrecht, H. C., and Hanighen, F. C. *Merchants of Death*. American Political Science Review 28 (1934):1135.

Lumley, Frederick E. *The Propaganda Menace*. American Journal of Sociology 39 (1934):542–43.

Reik, Theodor. *Ritual: Psycho-analytic Studies*. American Journal of Sociology 40 (1934):409–10.

Schmalhausen, Samuel D., ed. *Our Neurotic Age: A Consultation*. American Journal of Sociology 40 (1934):253–54.

1935

Books

Propaganda and Promotional Activities: An Annotated Bibliography (with R. D. Casey and B. L. Smith). Minneapolis: University of Minnesota Press, 1935.

World Politics and Personal Insecurity. New York: McGraw-Hill, 1935.

Articles

"Collective Autism as a Consequence of Culture Contact: Notes on Religious Training and the Peyote Cult at Taos." *Zeitschrift fur Sozialforschung* 4 (1935):232–46.

"The Moral Vocation of the Middle-Income Skill Group." *International Journal of Ethics* 45 (1935):127–37.

"Person: Subject and Object of Propaganda." *Annals of the American Academy of Political and Social Science* 179 (1935):189–93.

"Research on the Distribution of Symbol Specialists." *Journalism Quarterly* 12 (1935):146–56.

"The Study and Practice of Propaganda." In *Propaganda and Promotional Activities: An Annotated Bibliography*, edited by H. D. Lasswell, R. D. Casey, and B. L. Smith. Minneapolis: University of Minnesota Press, 1935. Pp. 3–27.

"Twisting Relief Rules" (with Gabriel Almond). *Personnel Journal* 13 (1935):338–43.

"Verbal References and Physiological Changes during the Psychoanalytic Interview: A Preliminary Communication." *Psychoanalytic Review* 22 (1935):10–24.

Review

Bogardus, Emory S. *Leaders and Leadership. American Journal of Sociology* 41 (1935):377.

1936

Books

National Libraries and Foreign Scholarships (with Douglas Waples). Chicago: University of Chicago Press, 1936.

Politics: Who Gets What, When, How. New York: McGraw-Hill, 1936.

Articles

"Certain Prognostic Changes during Trial (Psychoanalytic) Interviews." *Psychoanalytic Review* 23 (1936):241–47.

"Encyclopedia of the Social Sciences in Review." *International Journal of Ethics* 46 (1936):388–96.

"The Scope of Research on Propaganda and Dictatorship." In *Propaganda and Dictatorship*, edited by Harwood Lawrence Childs. Princeton, N.J.: Princeton University Press, 1936. Pp. 105–21.

Reprint

"Triple-Appeal Principle: A Contribution of Psychoanalysis to Political and Social Science." *Almanach der Psychoanalysis*. Vienna: Internationaler Psychoanalytischer Verlag, 1936.

1937

Articles

"Governmental and Party Leaders in Fascist Italy" (with Renzo Sereno). *American Political Science Review* 31 (1937):914–29.

"The Influence of the Intellectual Exile." *Social Research* 4 (1937): 305–16.

"Making the Foreign Policy Articulate." *American Association of University Women* 31 (1937):33–35.

"A Method of Interlapping Observation in the Study of Personality in Culture." *Journal of Abnormal Psychology* 32 (1937):240–43.

"Propaganda and the Channels of Communication." In *Education against Propaganda*, edited by Elmer Ellis. Seventh Yearbook of the National Council for the Social Studies, 1937. Pp. 14–26.

"Propaganda in a Planned Society." In *Planned Society: Yesterday, Today, Tomorrow*, edited by Findlay Mackenzie. New York: Prentice-Hall, 1937. Pp. 629–40.

"Relation of Skill Politics to Class Politics and National Politics." *Chinese Social and Political Science Review* 21 (1937):298–313.

"Sino-Japanese Crisis: The Garrison State versus the Civilian State." *China Quarterly* 2 (1937):643–49.

"Veranderungen an einer Versuchsperson wahrend einer kurzen Folge von psychoanalytischen Interviews." *Imago* (Vienna), 23 (1937): 375–80.

Reviews

Lengyel, Emil. *Millions of Dictators. American Journal of Sociology* 42 (1937):952.

Simpson, George Eaton. *The Negro in the Philadelphia Slum. American Journal of Sociology* 42 (1937): 602–3.

1938

Articles

"Chinese Resistance to Japanese Invasion: The Predictive Value of Precrisis Symbols." *American Journal of Sociology* 43 (1938):704–16.

"Intensive and Extensive Methods of Observing the Personality-Culture Manifold." *Yenching Journal of Social Studies* (Peking), 1 (1938):72–86.

"Materials for the Study of Propaganda, Number 1." *Psychiatry* 1 (1938):421–47.

"A Provisional Classification of Symbol Data." *Psychiatry* 1 (1938): 197–204.

"The Technique of Slogans in Communistic Propaganda" (with Dorothy Blumenstock Jones). *Psychiatry* 1 (1938):505–20.

"What Psychiatrists and Political Scientists Can Learn from One Another." *Psychiatry* 1 (1938):33–39.

Reviews

Chase, Stuart. *The Tyranny of Words. American Sociological Review* 3 (1938):579–80.

Lasker, Bruno, and Roman, Agnes. *Propaganda from China and Japan. American Journal of Sociology* 44 (1938):307–8.

Other

"Foreword." In *Allied Propaganda and the Collapse of the German Empire in 1918,* by George G. Bruntz. Palo Alto, Calif.: Stanford University Press, 1938. Pp. iv–v.

Reprint

Propaganda Techniques in the World War. New York: Peter Smith, 1938.

1939

Book

World Revolutionary Propaganda: A Chicago Study (with Dorothy Blumenstock Jones). New York: A. A. Knopf, 1939.

Articles

"The Contribution of Freud's Insight Interview to the Social Sciences." *American Journal of Sociology* 45 (1939): 375–90.

"Person, Personality, Group, Culture." *Psychiatry* 2 (1939):533–61.

"Political Psychiatry: The Study and Practice of Integrative Politics." In *Mental Health Publication of the American Association for the Advancement of Science*, Number 9, edited by Forest Ray Moulton and Paul O. Komora. Lancaster, Pa.: Science Press, 1939. Pp. 269–75.

"The Propaganda Technique of Recent Proposals for the Foreign Policy of the U.S.A., Materials for the Study of Propaganda, Number 2." *Psychiatry* 2 (1939):281–87.

"Propagandist Bids for Power." *American Scholar* 8 (1939):350–57.

"The Volume of Communist Propaganda in Chicago" (with Dorothy Blumenstock Jones). *Public Opinion Quarterly* 1 (1939):63–78.

Reviews

Abel, Theodore. *Why Hitler Came into Power: An Answer Based on the Original Life Histories of Six Hundred of His Followers. American Journal of Sociology* 44 (1939):1003–4.

Dollard, John, *et al. Frustration and Aggression. American Political Science Review* 33 (1939):1133.

Salter, J. T., ed. *The American Politician. The American Political Science Review* 33 (1939):696–97.

Other

"Human Nature in Action." Weekly broadcast on National Broadcasting Company, Station WEAF. May 17–July 12.

1940

Article

"American Voices" (with Albert Nathaniel Williams). *Scribner's Commentator* 9 (1940):108–11.

Other

"Human Nature in Action." (Broadcast resumed.) January 12–
December 17.
"Science and Democracy." *Vital Speeches* 7 (1940):85–87.

1941

Book

Democracy through Public Opinion. Menasha, Wis.: George Banta
Publishing Company, 1941.

Articles

"The Achievement Standards of a Democratic Press." In *Freedom of
the Press Today,* compiled by Harold L. Ickes. New York: Van-
guard Press, 1941. Pp. 171–78.
"The Garrison State." *American Journal of Sociology* 46 (1941):
455–68.
"Psychology Looks at Morals and Politics." *Ethics* 51 (1941):325–36.
"Public Opinion and British-American Unity." In *Conference on
North Atlantic Relations.* Princeton, N.J.: American Committee for
International Studies, 1941. Pp. 1–9.
"Radio as an Instrument of Reducing Personal Insecurity." *Studies in
Philosophy and Social Science* 9 (1941):49–64.
"Toward a Science of Democracy." In *Science, Philosophy, and Re-
ligion,* edited by Lyman Bryson and Louis Finkelstein. New York:
Conference on Science, Philosophy, and Religion, 1941. Pp. 238–47.
"World Attention Survey." *Public Opinion Quarterly* 5 (1941):456–
62.

Reviews

Browder, Earl. *Fighting for Peace and the People's Front. American
Journal of Sociology* 46 (1941):761.
Foster, William Z. *From Bryan to Stalin. American Journal of Sociol-
ogy* 46 (1941):761–62.
Gitlow, Benjamin. *I Confess: The Truth about American Commu-
nism. American Journal of Sociology* 46 (1941):762.

Hughes, Helen MacGill. *News and the Human Interest Story. American Journal of Sociology* 47 (1941):122–23.

McFadden, Charles J. *The Philosophy of Communism. American Journal of Sociology* 46 (1941):761.

1942

Articles

"Analyzing the Content of Mass Communication: A Brief Introduction." Library of Congress, Experimental Division for Study of War-Time Communications, Document Number 11. Washington, D.C., 1942.

"The Commonwealth of Science." In *Science and Man*, edited by Ruth Nanda Anshen. New York: Harcourt, Brace, Inc., 1942. Pp. 398–405.

"Communication Research and Politics." In *Print, Radio, and Film in a Democracy*, edited by Douglas Waples. Chicago: University of Chicago Press, 1942. Pp. 101–17.

"The Developing Science of Democracy." In *The Future of Government in the United States*, edited by Leonard D. White. Chicago: University of Chicago Press, 1942. Pp. 25–48.

"An Experimental Comparison of Four Ways of Coding Editorial Content" (with A. Geller and D. Kaplan). *Journalism Quarterly* 19 (1942):362–71.

"The Politically Significant Content of the Press: Coding Procedures." *Journalism Quarterly* 19 (1942):12–23.

"Relation of Ideological Intelligence to Public Policy." *Ethics* 53 (1942):25–34.

Review

Lavine, Harold, and Wechsler, James. *War Propaganda and the United States. American Journal of Sociology* 48 (1942):430.

Other

"Comment on Democracy." In *A Treasury of Democracy*, edited by Norman Cousins. New York: Coward-McCann, 1942. Pp. 225–26.

"Communications Front." *Vital Speeches* 8 (1942):761–65.

1943

Book

Public Opinion in War and Peace (with Howard H. Cummings). Washington: National Education Association, 1943.

Articles

"Legal Education and Public Policy: Professional Training in the Public Interest." *Yale Law Journal* 52 (1943):203–95.

"A Non-Bureaucratic Alternative to Minority Stockholders' Suits." *Columbia Law Review* 43 (1943):1036–48.

"Reliability of a Content Analysis Technique Based on Propaganda Analysis: Method of World Attention Survey" (with I. L. Janis and others). *Public Opinion Quarterly* 7 (1943):293–96.

Reviews

Spier, Leslie, Hallowell, A. Irving, and Newman, Stanley S., eds. *Language, Culture, and Personality: Essays in Memory of Edward Sapir*. *American Journal of Sociology* 48 (1943):618.

University of Pennsylvania Bicentennial Conference. *Studies in Political Science and Sociology*. *American Sociological Review* 8 (1943): 236–37.

1944

Article

"Political Significance of German National Socialism." *Religious Education* 29 (1944):20–24.

1945

Book

World Politics Faces Economics. New York: McGraw-Hill, 1945.

Article

"The Science of Communication and the Function of Libraries." *College and Research Libraries* 6 (1945):387–94.

Review

Hunt, J. McV., ed. *Personality and Behavior Disorders. American Sociological Review* 10 (1945):813–14.

1946

Book

Propaganda, Communication, and Public Opinion: A Comprehensive Reference Guide (edited with Ralph D. Casey and Bruce Lannes Smith). Princeton, N.J.: Princeton University Press, 1946.

Articles

"Describing the Contents of Communications." In *Propaganda, Communication, and Public Opinion: A Comprehensive Reference Guide,* edited by H. D. Lasswell, R. D. Casey, and B. L. Smith. Princeton, N.J.: Princeton University Press, 1946. Pp. 74–79.

"Describing the Effects of Communication." In *Propaganda, Communication, and Public Opinion: A Comprehensive Reference Guide,* edited by H. D. Lasswell, R. D. Casey, and B. L. Smith. Princeton: Princeton University Press, 1946. Pp. 95–117.

"Interrelations of World Organization and Society." *Yale Law Journal* 5 (1946):889–909.

"Orthopsychiatry and World Harmony." *American Journal of Orthopsychiatry* 16 (1946):381–90.

Review

Harper, Paul V., ed. *The Russia I Believe In: The Memoirs of Samuel N. Harper, 1902–1941. American Journal of Sociology* 51 (1946): 580.

Other

"Democracy" (film). Chicago: Encyclopedia Britannica Films, Inc., February, 1946.

"Despotism" (film). Chicago: Encyclopedia Britannica Films, Inc., February, 1946.

"Public Opinion" (film). Chicago: Encyclopedia Britannica Films, Inc., November, 1946.

1947

Book

A Free and Responsible Press (with the Commission of Freedom of the Press). Chicago: University of Chicago Press, 1947.

Articles

"The Data of Psychoanalysis and the Social Sciences." *American Journal of Psychoanalysis* 7 (1947):26–35.
"Public Attention, Opinion and Action" (with Joseph M. Golden). *International Journal of Opinion and Attitude Research* 1 (1947): 3–11.
"Toward a Skill Commonwealth: A Workable Goal of World Politics." In *Approaches to Group Understanding*, edited by Lyman Bryson, Louis Finkleman, and R. M. MacIver. New York: Harper, 1947. Pp. 290–302.

1948

Books

The Analysis of Political Behaviour: An Empirical Approach. London: Routledge and Kegan Paul, Ltd., 1948.
Power and Personality. New York: W. W. Norton, 1948.

Articles

"Attention Structure and Social Structure." In *The Communication of Ideas*, edited by Lyman Bryson. New York: Institute for Religious and Social Studies, 1948. Pp. 243–76.
"Clarifier of Public Discussion." *Quarterly Journal of Speech* 34 (1948):451–54.
"Prospects of Cooperation in a Bipolar World." *University of Chicago Law Review* 15 (1948):877–901.
"Self Observation: Recording the Focus of Attention." In *The Analysis of Political Behaviour: An Empirical Approach.* London: Routledge and Kegan Paul, Ltd., 1948. Pp. 279–86.
"The Structure and Functions of Communication in Society." In *The Communication of Ideas*, edited by Lyman Bryson. New York: Institute for Religious and Social Studies, 1948. Pp. 37–51.
"World Loyalty." In *The World Community*, edited by Quincy Wright. Chicago: University of Chicago Press, 1948. Pp. 200–225.

Review

Oneal, James, and Werner, G. A. *American Communism: A Critical Analysis of Its Origins, Development and Programs. American Journal of Sociology* 54 (1948):270.

Reprints

"The Changing Italian Elite." In *The Analysis of Political Behaviour: An Empirical Approach*. London: Routledge and Kegan Paul, Ltd., 1948. Pp. 158–72.

"The Developing Science of Democracy." In *The Analysis of Political Behaviour: An Empirical Approach*. London: Routledge and Kegan Paul, Ltd., 1948. Pp. 1–12.

"The Garrison State and Specialists on Violence." In *The Analysis of Political Behaviour: An Empirical Approach*. London: Routledge and Kegan Paul, Ltd., 1948. Pp. 146–57.

"General Framework: Person, Personality, Group, Culture." In *The Analysis of Political Behaviour: An Empirical Approach*. London: Routledge and Kegan Paul, Ltd., 1948. Pp. 195–234.

"Legal Education and Public Policy: Professional Training in the Public Interest" (with Myres S. McDougal). In *The Analysis of Political Behaviour: An Empirical Approach*. London: Routledge and Kegan Paul, Ltd., 1948. Pp. 21–119.

"The Participant Observer: A Study of Administrative Rules in Action" (with Gabriel Almond). In *The Analysis of Political Behaviour: An Empirical Approach*. London: Routledge and Kegan Paul, Ltd., 1948. Pp. 261–78.

"Policy and the Intelligence Function: Ideological Intelligence." In *The Analysis of Political Behaviour: An Empirical Approach*. London: Routledge and Kegan Paul, Ltd., 1948. Pp. 120–31.

"The Prolonged Insight Interview of Freud." In *The Analysis of Human Behaviour: An Empirical Approach*. London: Routledge and Kegan Paul, Ltd., 1948. Pp. 287–95.

"Psychology Looks at Morals and Politics." In *The Analysis of Political Behaviour: An Empirical Approach*. London: Routledge and Kegan Paul, Ltd., 1948. Pp. 13–20.

"The Psychology of Hitlerism as a Response of the Lower Middle Classes to Continuing Insecurity." In *The Analysis of Political Behaviour: An Empirical Approach*. London: Routledge and Kegan Paul, Ltd., 1948. Pp. 235–45.

"Radio as an Instrument of Reducing Personal Insecurity." In *Analysis of Human Behaviour: An Empirical Approach*. London: Routledge and Kegan Paul, Ltd., 1948. Pp. 246–60.

"The Rise of the Propagandist." In *The Analysis of Political Behaviour: An Empirical Approach*. London: Routledge and Kegan Paul, Ltd., 1948. Pp. 173–79.

"Skill Politics and Skill Revolution." In *The Analysis of Political Behaviour: An Empirical Approach*. London: Routledge and Kegan Paul, Ltd., 1948. Pp. 133–45.

"The Triple-Appeal Principle." In *The Analysis of Political Behaviour: An Empirical Approach*. London: Routledge and Kegan Paul, Ltd., 1948. Pp. 180–94.

"The World Attention Survey." In *The Analysis of Political Behaviour: An Empirical Approach*. London: Routledge and Kegan Paul, Ltd., 1948. Pp. 296–303.

1949

Book

Language of Politics: Studies in Quantitative Semantics (with Nathan Leites *et al.*). New York: George Stewart, 1949.

Articles

"Detection: Propaganda Detection and the Courts." In *Language of Politics: Studies in Quantitative Semantics*, by H. D. Lasswell, Nathan Leites *et al.* New York: George Stewart, 1949. Pp. 173–232.

" 'Inevitable' War: A Problem in the Control of Long-Range Expectations." *World Politics* 2 (1949):1–40.

"The Language of Power." In *Language of Politics: Studies in Quantitative Semantics*, by H. D. Lasswell, Nathan Leites, *et al.* New York: George Stewart, 1949. Pp. 3–19.

Psychological Aspects of Foreign Aid and Development Programs. Washington, D.C.: Department of State, Foreign Service Institute, 1949. Pp. 1–17.

"Trend: May Day Slogans in Soviet Russia, 1918–1943" (with Sergius Yakobson). In *Language of Politics: Studies in Quantitative Semantics*, by H. D. Lasswell, Nathan Leites, *et al.* New York: George Stewart, 1949. Pp. 233–97.

"The Structure and Function of Communication." In *Mass Communi-*

cations, edited by Wilbur Lang Schramm. Urbana: University of Illinois Press, 1949. Pp. 102–15.

"Style in the Language of Politics." In *Language of Politics: Studies in Quantitative Semantics*, by H. D. Lasswell, Nathan Leites, *et al.* New York: George Stewart, 1949. Pp. 20–39.

"Why Be Quantitative?" In *Language of Politics: Studies in Quantitative Semantics*, by H. D. Lasswell, Nathan Leites, *et al.* New York: George Stewart, 1949. Pp. 40–52.

Review

Laski, Harold J. *The American Democracy. American Sociological Review* 14 (1949):431–32.

Reprint

"Recording and Context Units—Four Ways of Coding Editorial Content" (with Alan Grey and David Kaplan). In *Language of Politics: Studies in Quantitative Semantics*, by H. D. Lasswell, Nathan Leites, *et al.* New York: George Stewart, 1949. Pp. 113–26.

1950

Books

National Security and Individual Freedom. New York: McGraw-Hill, 1950.

Power and Society (with Abraham Kaplan). New Haven, Conn.: Yale University Press, 1950.

A Study of Power (with C. E. Merriam and T. V. Smith). Glencoe, Ill.: Free Press, 1950.

Articles

"Conditions of Security in a Bi-Polarizing World." *American Society of International Law Proceedings*, 1950, pp. 3–8.

"Our Columnists on the A-Bomb" (with Janet Besse). *World Politics* 3 (1950):72–87.

"Propaganda and Mass Insecurity." *Psychiatry* 13 (1950):283–300.

"Psychology and Political Science in the U.S.A." In *Contemporary Political Science: A Survey of Methods, Research, and Teaching.* Paris: UNESCO, 1950. Pp. 526–37.

Other

"Discussion" of "The Semantics of Political Science," by Charner Perry. *American Political Science Review* 44 (1950):422–25.

Reprint

World Politics and Personal Insecurity. In *A Study of Power*, by H. D. Lasswell, C. E. Merriam, and T. V. Smith. Glencoe, Ill.: Free Press, 1950. Pp. 1–307.

1951

Books

The Policy Sciences: Recent Developments in Scope and Method (edited with Daniel Lerner). Stanford, Calif.: Stanford University Press, 1951.

The Political Writings of Harold D. Lasswell. Glencoe, Ill.: Free Press, 1951.

Les "sciences de la politique" aux Etats-Unis: Domaines et techniques (edited with Daniel Lerner). Paris: Librairie Armond Colin, 1951.

The World Revolution of Our Time: A Framework for Basic Policy Research. Hoover Institute Series. Stanford, Calif.: Stanford University Press, 1951.

Articles

"Democratic Character." In *The Political Writings of Harold D. Lasswell*. Glencoe, Ill.: Free Press, 1951. Pp. 465–525.

"Does the Garrison State Threaten Civil Rights?" *Annals of the American Academy of Political and Social Science* 275 (1951):111–16.

"The Immediate Future of Research Policy and Method in Political Science." *American Political Science Review* 45 (1951):133–42.

"The Policy Orientation." In *The Policy Sciences: Recent Developments in Scope and Method,* edited by H. D. Lasswell and Daniel Lerner. Stanford, Calif.: Stanford University Press, 1951. Pp. 3–15.

"Political and Psychological Warfare." In *Propaganda in War and Crisis: Materials for American Policy,* edited by Daniel Lerner. New York: George W. Stewart, 1951. Pp. 261–66.

"The Scientific Study of Bipolar Attitudes." *American Journal of Psychiatry* 107 (1951):644–49.

"Strategy of Soviet Propaganda." *Proceedings of the Academy of Political Science* 24 (1951):214–26.

Review

Rossi, A. *A Communist Party in Action: An Account of the Organization and Operations in France. American Journal of Sociology* 57 (1951):96.

Reprints

Politics: Who Gets What, When, How. In *The Political Writings of Harold D. Lasswell.* Glencoe, Ill.: Free Press, 1951. Pp. 295–461.
"Propaganda and Mass Insecurity." In *Personality and Political Crisis,* edited by A. H. Stanton and S. E. Perry. Glencoe, Ill.: Free Press, 1951. Pp. 15–43.
Psychopathology and Politics. In *The Political Writings of Harold D. Lasswell.* Glencoe, Ill.: Free Press, 1951. Pp. 1–282.
"The Strategy of Soviet Propaganda." In *Psychological Warfare.* Headline Series Number 86. New York: Foreign Policy Association, 1951. Pp. 57–62.
"World Organization and Society." In *The Policy Sciences: Recent Developments in Scope and Method,* edited by H. D. Lasswell and Daniel Lerner. Stanford, Calif.: Stanford University Press, 1951. Pp. 102–17.

1952

Books

The Comparative Study of Elites (with Daniel Lerner and C. Easton Rothwell). Hoover Institute Studies. Stanford, Calif.: Stanford University Press, 1952.
The Comparative Study of Symbols (with Daniel Lerner and Ithiel de Sola Pool). Hoover Institute Studies. Stanford, Calif.: Stanford University Press, 1952.

Articles

"Appraising the Effects of Technology." *International Social Science Bulletin* 4 (1952):328–39.
"Political Factors in the Foundation of Strategy." *Information Service for Officers* (U.S. Naval War College), 4 (1952):49–64.

"Psychological Policy Research and Total Strategy." *Public Opinion Quarterly* 16 (1952):491–500.
"The Threat to Privacy." In *Conflict of Loyalties*, edited by R. M. MacIver. New York: Institute for Religious and Social Studies, 1952. Pp. 121–39.

Other

"Social Process" (film). Chicago: Encyclopedia Britannica Films, Inc., October, 1952.

Reprint

"The Psychology of Hitlerism as a Response of the Lower Middle Classes to Continuing Insecurity." In *Readings in Social Psychology*, revised edition, edited by Guy E. Swanson, Theodore M. Newcomb, and Eugene L. Hartley. New York: Henry Holt and Company, 1952. Pp. 171–77.

1953

Articles

"Legislative Policy, Conformity and Psychiatry." *Proceedings of the American Psychopathological Association* 42 (1953):13–40.
"Commentary." In "Religion and Modernization in the Far East: A Symposium." *Far Eastern Quarterly* 12 (1953):163–72.

Other

"Research in Comparative Politics: Comments on the Seminar Report." *American Political Science Review* 47 (1953):661–63.

1954

Articles

"Key Symbols, Signs, and Icons." In *Symbols and Values: An Initial Study*, edited by L. Bryson, L. Finkelstein, R. M. MacIver, and R. McKeon. Conference on Science, Philosophy and Religion. New York: Harper, 1954. Pp. 201–10.
"Political Factors in the Formulation of National Strategy." *Naval War College* 19 (1954):34–44.
"Selective Effects of Personality on Political Participation." In *Studies*

in the Scope and Method of "The Authoritarian Personality," edited by Richard Christie and Marie Jahoda. Glencoe, Ill.: Free Press, 1954. Pp. 197–225.
"The World Revolutionary Situation." In *Totalitarianism*, edited by Carl J. Friedrich. Cambridge, Mass.: Harvard University Press, 1954. Pp. 360–72.

Review

Deutsch, Karl W. *Nationalism and Social Communication: An Inquiry into the Foundations of Nationality. American Political Science Review* 48 (1954):554–56.

Other

"Defining Democracy" (film). Chicago: Encyclopedia Britannica Films, Inc., March, 1954.

Reprint

"The Strategy of Soviet Propaganda." In *The Process and Effects of Mass Communication*, edited by Wilbur Schramm. Urbana: University of Illinois Press, 1954. Pp. 537–47.

1955

Book

Recent Developments in American Political Science and Jurisprudence (edited with Takeyasu Kimura). Tokyo: Tokyo Daigaku Shuppan Kai, 1955.

Articles

"Current Studies in the Decision Process: Automation versus Creativity." *Western Political Quarterly* 8 (1955):381–85.
"Public Order under Law: The Role of the Advisor-Draftsman in the Formation of Code or Constitution" (with G. H. Dession). *Yale Law Journal* 65 (1955):174–95.

Reprint

"Legislative Policy, Conformity and Psychiatry." In *Psychiatry and the Law*, edited by P. H. Hoch and J. Zubin. New York: Grune and Stratton, 1955. Pp. 13–40.

1956

Book

The Decision Process: Seven Categories of Functional Analysis. College Park: University of Maryland Press, 1956.

Articles

"Impact of Psychoanalytic Thinking on the Social Sciences." In *The State of the Social Sciences*, edited by Leonard D. White. Chicago: University of Chicago Press, 1956. Pp. 84–115.

"The Political Science of Science: An Inquiry into the Possible Reconciliation of Mastery and Freedom." *American Political Science Review* 50 (1956):961–79.

"The Research Frontier." *Saturday Review*, November 3, 1956:50–51.

Review

"Some Reflections on the Study of International Relations." (Quincy Wright, *The Study of International Relations.*) *World Politics* 8 (1956):560–65.

Reprint

"Power and Personality." In *Political Behavior: A Reader in Theory and Research*, edited by Heinz Eulau *et al.* Glencoe, Ill.: Free Press, 1956. Pp. 90–103.

1957

Articles

"Impact of Public Opinion Research on Our Society." *Public Opinion Quarterly* 21 (1957):33–38.

"Language of Politics." In *Language: An Inquiry into Its Meaning and Function*, edited by Ruth Nanda Anshen. New York: Harper and Brothers, 1957. Pp. 270–84.

"The Normative Impact of the Behavioral Sciences." *Ethics* 67 (1957):1–42.

"Political Power and Democratic Values." In *Problems of Power in American Democracy*, edited by Arthur William Kornhauser. Detroit: Wayne State University Press, 1957. Pp. 57–82.

"Socio-Political Situation." *Educational Research Bulletin* 36 (1957): 69–77.

Reprint

"The Political Science of Science: An Inquiry into the Possible Reconciliation of Mastery and Freedom." *The Scientific Monthly,* 84 (1957):34–44.

1958

Articles

"Clarifying Value Judgments: Principles of Content and Procedure." *Inquiry* 1 (1958):87–98.
"Communication as an Emerging Discipline." *Audio-visual Communication Review* 6 (1958):245–54.
"A Cross-Cultural Test of Self-Image" (with J. Kennedy). *Human Organization* 17 (1958):41–43.
"Men in Space." *Annals of the New York Academy of Sciences* 72 (1958):180–94.
"The Scientific Study of International Relations." *The Year Book of World Affairs* 12 (1958):1–28.
"The Value of Analysis of Legal Discourse." *Western Reserve Law Review* 9 (1958): 188–98.

Reviews

Blaisdell, Donald C. *American Democracy Under Pressure. University of Pennsylvania Law Review* 107 (1958):295–96.
Shils, E. A. *The Torment of Secrecy: The Background and Consequences of American Security Policies. American Journal of Sociology* 63 (1958):431–32.
Young, Roland, ed. *Approaches to the Study of Politics. American Sociological Review* 23 (1958):751–52.

Reprint

Politics: Who Gets What, When, How (with a new postscript). New York: World Publishing Company, 1958.

1959

Articles

"The Continuing Debate over Responsibility: An Introduction to Isolating the Condemnation Sanction" (with R. Donnelly). *Yale Law Journal* 68 (1959):869–99.

"The Identifications and Appraisal of Diverse Systems of Public Order" (with Myres S. McDougal). *American Journal of International Law* 53 (1959):1–29.

"The Intelligence Function: Built in Error." *Prod* 3 (1959):3–7.

"The Lawyer of the Future." *New York County Lawyers' Association Bar Bulletin* 16 (1959):144–48.

"Political Constitution and Character." *Psychoanalysis and the Psychoanalytic Review* 46 (1959):3–18.

"The Qualitative and Quantitative in Political and Legal Analysis." *Daedalus: Journal of the American Academy of Arts and Sciences* 88 (1959):633–45.

"The Social Consequences of Automation." *Proceedings of the Western Joint Computer Conference*, 1959, pp. 7–10.

"The Social Setting of Creativity." In *Creativity and Its Cultivation*, edited by H. H. Anderson. New York: Harper and Brothers, 1959. Pp. 203–21.

"Space Agents." *Saturday Review*, April 4, 1959:64–65.

"State of the Nation's Mental Health." *The National Parent-Teacher* 44 (1959):28–36.

"Strategies of Inquiry: The Rational Use of Observation." In *The Human Meaning of Social Sciences*, edited by Daniel Lerner. New York: Meridian Books, 1959. Pp. 89–113.

"Universality in Perspective." *Proceedings of the American Society of International Law* 53 (1959):1–9.

Reviews

"To Verify Universal Values." (Arnold Brecht, *Political Theory: The Foundation of Twentieth-Century Political Thought*) *Saturday Review*, June 20, 1959:14.

Howe, Irving, and Coser, Lewis. *The American Communist Party. American Sociological Review* 24 (1959):720.

1960

Book

Studies in World Public Order (with Myres S. McDougal *et. al*). New Haven, Conn.: Yale University Press, 1960.

Articles

"Approaches to Human Personality: William James and S. Freud." *Psychoanalysis and the Psychoanalytic Review* 47 (1960):52–68.

"The Common Frontiers of Psychiatry and Law" (with L. Z. Freedman). *American Journal of Psychiatry* 117 (1960):490–98.
"Impact of Psychiatry upon Jurisprudence." *Ohio State Law Journal* 21 (1960):17–27.
"Technique of Decision Seminars." *Midwest Journal of Political Science* 4 (1960):213–36.

Reprints

"The Identification and Appraisal of Diverse Systems of Public Order" (with Myres S. McDougal). In *Studies in World Public Order*, by H. D. Lasswell, M. S. McDougal, *et al.* New Haven, Conn.: Yale University Press, 1960. Pp. 3–41.
"Legal Education and Public Policy: Professional Training in the Public Interest" (with Myres S. McDougal). In *Studies in World Public Order*, by H. D. Lasswell, M. S. McDougal *et al.* New Haven, Conn.: Yale University Press, 1960. Pp. 42–154.
Psychopathology and Politics (with Afterthoughts). New York: Viking Press, 1960.

1961

Book

In Defense of Public Order: The Emerging Field of Sanction Law (with Richard Arens). New York: Columbia University Press, 1961.

Articles

"Agenda for the Study of Political Elites." In *Political Decision-Makers*, edited by Dwaine Marvick. New York: Free Press of Glencoe, 1961. Pp. 264–87.
"Communication and the Mind." In *Control of the Mind*, edited by S. M. Farber and R. H. L. Wilson. New York: McGraw-Hill, 1961. Pp. 249–67.
"Cooperation for Research in Psychiatry and Law" (with L. Z. Freedman). *American Journal of Psychiatry* 117 (1961):692–94.
"Interplay of Economic, Political, and Social Criteria in Legal Policy." *Vanderbilt Law Review* 14 (1961):451–71.
"A National Institute of Social and Behavioral Pathology." *American Journal of Psychiatry* 117 (1961):847–48.
"Psychoanalytic Conceptions in Political Science." In *Psychoanalysis*

and *Social Process,* edited by J. H. Masserman. Volume IV of *Science and Psychoanalysis.* New York: Grune and Stratton, 1961. Pp. 60–76.

"The Qualitative and Quantitative in Political and Legal Analysis." In *Quantity and Quality,* edited by Daniel Lerner. Glencoe, Ill.: Free Press, 1961. Pp. 103–16.

"Research in Politics, Government, and Law." In *Trends in Social Science,* edited by D. A. Ray. New York: Philosophical Library, 1961. Pp. 27–59.

"Science, Scientists and World Policy." In *Science and the Future of Mankind,* edited by Hugo Boyko. The Hague: Dr. W. Junk, 1961. Pp. 77–82.

Reviews

Llewellyn, Karl N. *The Common Law Tradition-Deciding Appeals. Columbia Law Review* 61 (1961):931–48.

"World Building." (Adda Bozeman, *Politics and Culture in International History;* and Carlton J. H. Hayes, *Nationalism: A Religion.*) *Saturday Review,* January 14, 1961:31.

Other

"Introduction: Universality versus Parochialism." In *Law and Minimum Public Order: The Legal Regulation of International Coercion,* by M. S. McDougal and F. P. Feliciano. New Haven, Conn. and London: Yale University Press, 1961. Pp. xix–xxvi.

"Foreword." In *Personality in Social Process: Values and Strategies in a Free Society,* by V. Clyde Arnspiger. Chicago: Follett Publishing Company, 1961. Pp. vii–viii.

1962

Books

The Ethic of Power: The Interplay of Religion, Philosophy and Politics (edited with Harlan Cleveland). New York: Harper and Row, 1962.

Ethics and Bigness: Scientific, Academic, Religious, Political, and Military (edited with Harlan Cleveland). New York: Harper and Row, 1962.

Articles

"The Future of Public Affairs Programs." In *Educational Television: The Next Ten Years.* Stanford, Calif.: Institute for Communications Research, 1962. Pp. 92–102.

"The Garrison State Hypothesis Today." In *Changing Patterns of Military Politics,* edited by S. P. Huntington. New York: Free Press of Glencoe, 1962. Pp. 51–70.

"The Impact of Crowd Psychology upon International Law." *Philippine International Law Journal* 1 (1962):293–309.

"Integrating Communities into More Inclusive Systems." *Human Organization* 21 (1962):116–21.

"The Major Trends in World Politics." In *The Ethic of Power: The Interplay of Religion, Philosophy, and Politics,* edited by H. D. Lasswell and H. Cleveland. Conference on Science, Philosophy and Religion. New York: Harper & Brothers, 1962. Pp. 43–55.

"Political Science." In *A New Survey of the Social Sciences,* edited by B. N. Vorma. Bombay: Asia Publishing House, 1962. Pp. 15–20.

"The Public Interest: Proposing Principles of Content and Procedure." In *The Public Interest,* edited by Carl J. Friedrich. New York: Atherton Press, 1962. Pp. 54–79.

Other

"Introduction" (with Harland Cleveland). In *Ethics and Business: Scientific, Academic, Religious, Political, and Military,* edited by H. D. Lasswell and H. Cleveland. New York: Harper and Row, 1962. Pp. xii–xxi.

1963

Books

The Future of Political Science. New York: Atherton Press, 1963.

Law and Public Order in Space (with Myres S. McDougal and Ivan A. Vlasic). New Haven, Conn.: Yale University Press, 1963.

Power, Corruption, and Rectitude (with Arnold A. Rogow). Englewood Cliffs, N.J.: Prentice-Hall, Inc., 1963.

Articles

"Brief Discourse about Method in the Current Madness." *American Society of International Law Proceedings* 57 (1963):72–98.

"Emerging International Culture." In *International Cooperation and Problems of Transfer and Adoption*. Volume X of *Science, Technology, and Development*. Washington, D.C.: Government Printing Office, 1963. Pp. 1–7.

"Enjoyment and Acquisition of Resources in Outer Space" (with Myres S. McDougal *et al.*). *University of Pennsylvania Law Review* 111 (1963):521.

"Propaganda." *Encyclopedia Britannica* 18 (1963):580–83.

"The Yale Political Data Program" (with others). *Yale Papers In Political Science* 4 (1963).

1964

Book

World Handbook of Political and Social Indicators (with Bruce M. Russett, Hayward R. Alker, Jr., and Karl W. Deutsch). New Haven, Conn. and London: Yale University Press, 1964.

Articles

"Asia in the Study of World Politics." In *Approaches to Asian Civilization*, edited by W. T. deBary and A. T. Embree. New York and London: Columbia University Press, 1964. Pp. 122–33.

"Toward a General Theory of Sanctions" (with Richard Arens). *Iowa Law Review* 49 (1964):233–76.

Review

De Grazia, Sebastian. *Of Time, Work, and Leisure*. American Political Science Review 58 (1964):405–6.

Other

"Foreword" (with Myres S. McDougal). In *The Personality of Lawyers: A Comparative Study of Subjective Factors in Law, Based on Interviews with German Lawyers*, by Walter Weyrauch. New Haven, Conn. and London: Yale University Press, 1964. Pp. xi–xv.

"Introduction." In *George Luckacs' Marxism: Alienation, Dialectics, Revolution-Study in Utopia and Ideology*, by Victor Zitta. The Hague: Martinus Nijhhoff, 1964. Pp. ix–x.

"Introduction." In *Political Power*, edited by Charles E. Merriam. New York: Collier Books, 1964. Pp. 7–14.

"Preface." In *Moral Indignation and Middle Class Psychology: A Sociological Study*, by Svend Ranulf. New York: Schocken Books, 1964. Pp. ix–xiii.

1965

Book

World Revolutionary Elites: Studies in Coercive Ideological Movements (edited with Daniel Lerner). Cambridge, Mass.: Massachusetts Institute of Technology Press, 1965.

Articles

"The Emerging Policy Sciences of Development: The Vicos Case." *American Behavioral Scientist* 8 (1965):28–33.

"The Climate of International Action." In *International Behavior: A Social-Psychological Analysis*, edited by H. C. Kelman. New York: Holt, Rinehart and Winston, 1965. Pp. 337–53.

"Freedom and Responsibility." In *The Future of Commercial Television, 1965–1975*, edited by Stanley T. Donner. Stanford Television Seminar. 1965. Pp. 102–15.

"Introduction: The Study of Political Elites." In *World Revolutionary Elites: Studies in Coercive Ideological Movements*, edited by H. D. Lasswell and D. Lerner. Cambridge, Mass.: Massachusetts Institute of Technology Press, 1965. Pp. 3–28.

"The Role of Communication Arts and Sciences in University Life." *Audio-Visual Communication Review* 13 (1965): 361–73.

Reviews

Edelman, Murray. *The Symbolic Uses of Politics. American Journal of Sociology* 70 (1965):735.

"The Policy Science of Development." (Lucian W. Pye, ed., *Communications and Political Development;* Joseph La Palombara, *Bureaucracy and Political Development;* and Robert E. Ward and Dankwart A. Rustow, eds., *Political Modernization in Japan and Turkey*.) *World Politics* 17 (1965):286–309.

Other

"Foreword." In *The Judicial Mind: The Attitudes and Ideologies of Supreme Court Justices, 1946–1963*, by Glendon Schubert. Evanston, Ill.: Northwestern University Press, 1965. Pp. vii–x.

"Introduction" (with Daniel Lerner). In *The Emerging Elite: A Study of Political Leadership in Ceylon*, by Marshall R. Singer. Cambridge, Mass.: Massachusetts Institute of Technology Press, 1965. Pp. ix-xiii.

"Introduction: The Shape of the Future." *American Behavioral Scientist* 8 (1965):3.

Reprints

"The Fascists: The Changing Italian Elite" (with Renzo Sereno). In *World Revolutionary Elites: Studies in Coercive Ideological Movements*, edited by H. D. Lasswell and D. Lerner. Cambridge, Mass.: Massachusetts Institute of Technology Press, 1965. Pp. 179–93.

Language of Politics: Studies in Quantitative Semantics (with Nathan Leites *et al.*) Cambridge, Mass.: Massachusetts Institute of Technology Press, 1965.

World Politics and Personal Insecurity. New York: The Free Press, 1965.

"The World Revolution of Our Time: A Framework for Basic Policy Research." In *World Revolutionary Elites: Studies in Coercive Ideological Movements*, edited by H. D. Lasswell and D. Lerner. Cambridge, Mass.: Massachusetts Institute of Technology Press, 1965. Pp. 29–96.

1966

Book

The Sharing of Power in a Psychiatric Hospital (with Robert Rubenstein). New Haven, Conn.: Yale University Press, 1966.

Articles

"An Application of the Policy Science Orientation: The Sharing of Power in a Psychiatric Hospital" (with Robert Rubenstein). In *Political Science Annual: An International Review*, vol. 1, edited by James A. Robinson. Minneapolis and New York: Bobbs-Merrill Company, 1966. Pp. 191–241.

"The Changing Image of Human Nature." *American Journal of Psychoanalysis* 26 (1966):157–66.

"Conflict and Leadership: The Process of Decision and the Nature of

Authority." In *Ciba Foundation Symposium on Conflict in Sociology*, edited by A. V. S. de Reuck and Julie Knight. London: J. and A. Churchill, Ltd., 1966. Pp. 210–28.

"Decision Seminars: The Contextual Use of Audiovisual Means in Teaching, Research, and Consultation." In *Comparing Nations: The Use of Quantitative Data in Cross-National Research*, edited by R. L. Merrit and Stein Rokkan. New Haven, Conn.: Yale University Press, 1966. Pp. 499–524.

"Policy Problems of a Data-Rich Civilization." Seventh International Documentation Conference. *Wilson Library Bulletin* 41 (1966): 58–65.

"Russia and China in a Modernizing World: A Concluding Note." In *Soviet and Chinese Communism*, edited by Donald W. Treadgold. Seattle: University of Washington Press, 1966. Pp. 429–42.

"Toward a General Theory of Directed Value Accumulation and Institutional Development" (with Allan R. Holmberg). In *Comparative Theories of Social Change*, edited by Hollis W. Peter. Ann Arbor, Mich.: Foundation for Research on Human Behavior, 1966. Pp. 12–50.

"The Yale Political Data Program" (with others). In *Comparing Nations: The Use of Quantitative Data in Cross-National Research*, edited by R. L. Merrit and Stein Rokkan. New Haven, Conn.: Yale University Press, 1966. Pp. 81–94.

Others

"Foreword." In *Toward a Theory of War Prevention*, by Richard A. Falk and Saul H. Mendlovitz. New York: World Law Fund, 1966. Pp. iii–v.

"Foreword." In *The General Inquirer: A Computer Approach to Content Analysis*, by Philip J. Stone *et al.* Cambridge, Mass.: Massachusetts Institute of Technology Press, 1966. Pp. vii–ix.

1967

Books

Formosa, China, and the United Nations: Formosa's Future in the World Community (with Lung-chu Chen). New York: St. Martin's Press, 1967.

The Interpretation of Agreements and World Public Order: Principles of Content and Procedure (with Myres S. McDougal and James C. Miller). New Haven, Conn.: Yale University Press, 1967.

Articles

"Civil Education in the Techno-scientific Age." In *Approaches to Education for Character*, edited by Clarence H. Faust and Jessica Feingold. New York: Harper and Row, 1967.

"Jurisprudence in Policy-Oriented Perspective" (with Myres S. McDougal). *University of Florida Law Review* 19 (1967):486–513.

"Political Systems, Styles and Personality." In *Political Leadership and Industrial Societies: Studies in Comparative Analysis*, edited by Lewis Edinger. New York: John Wiley and Sons, 1967. Pp. 316–47.

"The Role of Sanction in Conflict Resolution" (with Richard Arens). *Journal of Conflict Resolution* 9 (1967):27–39.

"The Social and Economic Framework of War and Peace." In *Aggression and Defense,* edited by Carmine D. Clemente and Donald B. Lindsley. Berkeley and Los Angeles: University of California Press, 1967. Pp. 317–25.

"Toward Continuing Appraisal of the Impact of Law on Society." *Rutgers Law Review* 21 (1967):645–77.

"The World Constitutive Process of Authoritative Decision" (with Myres S. McDougal and W. Michael Reisman). *Journal of Legal Education* 19 (1967):253–300, 403–37.

Reprint

"The Emerging International Culture." In *The Challenge of Development,* edited by Richard J. Ward. Chicago: Aldine Publishing Company, 1967. Pp. 489–95.

1968

Articles

"Comment (on) Ramkrishna Mukherjee, 'Some Observations on the Diachronic and Synchronic Aspects of Social Change,'" *Social Science Information* 7 (1968):54–55.

"The Future of the Comparative Method," *Comparative Politics* 1 (1968):3–18.

"A Note on 'Types' of Political Personality: Nuclear, Co-relational, Developmental," *Journal of Social Issues* 24 (1968):81–91.
"The Psychology of Politics," *Psychology Today*, October, 1968, pp. 56–63.
"Policy Sciences" *International Encyclopedia of the Social Sciences* 12 (1968):181–89.
"Theories about International Law: Prologue to a Configurative Jurisprudence" (with Myres S. McDougal and W. Michael Reisman), *Virginia Journal of International Law* 8 (1968):188–299.
"The Uses of Content Analysis Data in Studying Social Change," *Social Science Information* 7 (1968):57–70.

Other

"Foreword." In *Propaganda and World Public Order*, by B. S. Murty. New Haven, Conn.: Yale University Press, 1968.

Reprint

"The Impact of Crowd Psychology upon International Law," *William and Mary Law Review* 9 (1968):664–81.

1969

Book

Political Communication: The Public Language of the Political Elites in India and the United States (with Satish K. Arora). New York: Holt, Rinehart and Winston, 1969.

To Be Published

Article

"Value Analysis of American Party Platforms" (with J. Zvi Namenwirth).

Contributors

ARTHUR J. BRODBECK is a member of the Department of Psychology and Social Sciences, Pennsylvania State University, Middletown, Pennsylvania.

KARL W. DEUTSCH, Professor of Government, Harvard University, is the author of *Nerves of Government* (1963, 1966) and *The Analysis of International Relations* (1968). He taught at Yale from 1958 to 1967 where, in collaboration with Harold Lasswell, he founded the Yale Political Data Program and was coauthor of the first *World Handbook of Political and Social Indicators* (1964).

HEINZ EULAU is Professor of Political Science at Stanford University. A former fellow of the Center for Advanced Study in the Behavioral Sciences at Stanford, he is the author of *The Behavioral Persuasion in Politics* (1963) and many other publications.

WILLIAM T. R. FOX is James T. Shotwell Professor of International Relations and Director of the Institute of War and Peace Studies at Columbia University.

JERRY GASTON is completing work for the Ph.D. in sociology at Yale University.

ROY R. GRINKER, SR., M.D., is Director of the Institute for Psychosomatic Research and Training of the Michael Reese Hospital and Medical Center, Chicago.

ALLAN R. HOLMBERG was Professor of Anthropology at Cornell University at the time of his death in 1966 (see pp. 261–62).

MORRIS JANOWITZ is a member of the faculty of the University of Chicago.

DANIEL LERNER is Ford Professor of Sociology and International Communication, Department of Political Science, Massachusetts Institute of Technology.

MYRES S. McDOUGAL is Sterling Professor of Law, Yale Law School. He is a member of the United States Panel and the Permanent Court of Arbitration, and the past president of the American Society of International Law and the Association of American Law Schools.

445

Ithiel de Sola Pool received his Ph.D. from the University of Chicago in 1952. He has been affliated with Hobart College, the Hoover Institute at Stanford University, and the Massachusetts Institute of Technology, where he is presently Chairman of the Political Science Department.

Arnold A. Rogow is Graduate Professor of Political Science at the City University of New York.

Leo Rosten is the author of *The Education of H*Y*M*A*N K*A*P*L*A*N, The Washington Correspondents, Hollywood: The Movie Colony, Captain Newman, M.D.*, and *The Joys of Yiddish*. After receiving his Ph.D. from the University of Chicago, he was Deputy Director of the Office of War Information and an early senior staff member at RAND. He has taught at Yale University and was visiting Ford Professor at the University of California (Berkeley). He lives in New York and serves as special editorial adviser to *Look* magazine, for which he writes a regular column entitled "The World of Leo Rosten."

Robert Rubenstein, M.D., a psychoanalyst, is Medical Director of the Yale Psychiatric Institute. He is also Associate Clinical Professor of Psychiatry and Fellow, Ezra Stiles College, Yale University. His research has included studies of altered states of consciousness, dream processes, and attempted suicide. His research with Harold Lasswell on political aspects of psychiatric treatment are reported in *The Sharing of Power in a Psychiatric Hospital* (1966).

Edward Shils is Professor of Sociology and Social Thought at the University of Chicago, Fellow of King's College, Cambridge, and editor of *Minerva*.

Bruce Lannes Smith is Professor of Political Science at Michigan State University. His specialties are international relations and comparative politics. In the early 1930s he was a student of Professor Lasswell, and since then has collaborated with him in research on a number of occasions.

Index

447